Why Texans Fought in the Civil War

Number Twenty:

SAM RAYBURN SERIES ON RURAL LIFE

Sponsored by Texas A&M University–Commerce

M. HUNTER HAYES, *General Editor*

WHY TEXANS FOUGHT IN THE CIVIL WAR

Charles David Grear

TEXAS A&M UNIVERSITY PRESS
College Station

This paper meets the requirements of ANSI/NISO Z39.48-1992 (Permanence of Paper).
Binding materials have been chosen for durability.

Library of Congress Cataloging-in-Publication Data
Grear, Charles D., 1976–
Why Texans fought in the Civil War / Charles David Grear. — 1st ed.
p. cm.— (Sam Rayburn series on rural life ; no. 20)
Includes bibliographical references and index.
ISBN 978-1-60344-172-8 (cloth : alk. paper)
ISBN 978-1-60344-809-3 (paper)
1. Texas—History—Civil War, 1861–1865. 2. United States—History—Civil War, 1861–1865.
3. Soldiers—Texas—Attitudes—History—19th century. 4. Soldiers—Texas—Psychology—
History—19th century. I. Title. II. Series: Sam Rayburn series on rural life ; no. 20.
E580.G74 2010
976.4'05—dc22
2009030317

To my mentors:
Donald S. Frazier,
Alwyn Barr,
David L. Snead,
and
Steven E. Woodworth

I am indebted to these fine historians for all their guidance,
insight, and friendship.

CONTENTS

ILLUSTRATIONS AND MAPS

Illustrations

Maps

ACKNOWLEDGMENTS
AND A NOTE ON EDITORIAL METHOD

It is impossible to express my gratitude for all the people who have supported me in this endeavor. Throughout the process numerous individuals have contributed in many different ways. I owe appreciation to my academic mentors, Donald Frazier, Alwyn Barr, David Snead, and Steven E. Woodworth. Professors Barr and Snead at Texas Tech University set me on the path for this book by influencing me to study Richard M. Gano for my thesis. My research on Gano led me to this work, which actually began in the office of my first mentor, Donald S. Frazier. During one visit to his office at McMurry University we discussed a paper on the Grapevine Volunteers that I was preparing for publication. While discussing the paper, he gave me the idea to answer the simple question, why did Texans want to fight so far from home and for other states?

The person who poked and prodded the idea out of me and allowed this simple idea to bloom is a man whose integrity and passion I hold in highest regard, Steven E. Woodworth at Texas Christian University. Throughout my struggle to write this book, he offered useful advice and inspired me to tackle such a huge project. Another scholar who deserves special recognition is my colleague as a graduate student, collaborator on several projects now, and most important, my friend, Alexander Mendoza. Throughout this project I could discuss my ideas and concepts with him and hear some of his own. Alex also read the entire manuscript several times, through its many stages.

Other noted historians who gave me advice on this project include Dale Baum, Walter Buenger, Charles Brooks, Randolph "Mike" Campbell, Gregg Cantrell, Donald Chipman, Joseph Dawson, Rick Eiserman, Kenneth Howell, Walter Kamphoefner, Todd Kerstetter, Arnold Krammer, Richard Lowe, Richard McCaslin, Robert Pace, Adam Seipp, Susannah Ural, Robert Wettemann, and Ralph Wooster.

Others have helped me in other ways. Topping the list is Peggy Fox at what was then the Texas Confederate Research Center at Hill College, now known as the Texas Heritage Museum. Her dedication to researchers and especially to me is beyond words. There is a reason why so many historians mention her in their acknowledgments. Her successor, Kendall Milton, also provided ample service during the final stages of this publication. Another archivist I am indebted to is Julie Holcomb, who was in charge of the Charles and Peggy Pearce Collection of Civil War Documents at Navarro College. Her courteous manner and the pristine condition of the collection are second to none. Joyce Martindale, Kay Edmondson, and Jill Kendle in the Interlibrary Loan Department at the Mary Couts Burnett Library at Texas Christian University are among the hardest working people I know. They did an outstanding job processing the hundreds of books and microfilm I ordered from around the country. Their contribution to my research is immeasurable. I also thank the staffs at the Center for American History at the University of Texas at Austin, the Texas State Library and Archives, the Brown Special Collections Library at Abilene Christian University, the National Archives, the Center for Twentieth Century Texas Studies at Moody Mansion and Museum in Galveston, the Library at Texas A&M University at Commerce, the Athletic Academic Services Office at TCU, UTSA's Institute of Texan Cultures Library, the Sophienburg New Braunfels Archives and Museum of History, and of course all the staff at the Texas Heritage Museum at Hill College. Finally, I thank the Nesbitt Memorial Library in Columbus, Texas—especially its most prominent librarian and my late friend Bill Stein. His insight and sense of humor will be missed.

Assistance came in other forms. Steve Sherwood at the William L. Adams Center for Writing at TCU proofread my chapters, improved my writing, and gave general support throughout the entire process. Another to whom I am grateful is Mike Stevens, whose financial assistance in every part of my education at TCU through the Heartland Alliance Scholarship and the Mike Stevens Research Grant allowed me to complete my studies and to research the National Archives at Washington, D.C. I also thank the Texas State Historical Association for granting me the Lawrence T. Jones III Research Fellowship in Civil War Texas History. With that fellowship, I was able to travel to the many different archives in Texas to complete my dissertation and consequently this book.

Last, I thank the most important people in my life, my friends and family. These people inspired me on this project because of their influence on my life and, most important, my attachment to them. While writing this book, my mind always drifted to my family: the Grears, Garzas, Koehls, and Blassingames. Many thanks to my mother and father for always supporting me in my decisions and helping me persevere whenever I struggled in life. I am indebted to my brothers, Shawn and Chad. Chad, my special brother and the person I hold dearest in my life, inspired me throughout my life with his love and his ability to achieve what I and the rest of our family thought was impossible. I also thank my friends from every stage in my life. They know who they are; I thank them for their continued support. The last people I wish to thank are my stepdaughter Haley and my wife Edna. Haley helped me with my maps and provided a source of entertainment and welcome distractions when this project began to make me feel overwhelmed. Edna deserves more appreciation than I can show her. With her love, she supported me throughout my trials and tribulations in graduate school and writing this book. She is a major reason for my achievements—both personal and professional.

A Note on Editorial Method

Discovering the motivations of Texas soldiers required reading thousands of letters, diaries, reminiscences, and family histories; passages from many of them are included in this work to demonstrate in their own words the thoughts and emotions these Texans experienced. All quotations in this book, with the exceptions of a noted few, are true to their original text—including misspellings, poor grammar, run-on sentences, lack of punctuation, or any other imaginative writing styles of these nineteenth-century Texans. Leaving intact the words of the participants lets their character, education, and culture show through, providing a more human element to these pieces of paper and ink.

Why Texans Fought in the Civil War

1

INTRODUCTION

Though I will suffer hardships, toil, and pain
For the good time is sure to come
I'll battle long that I may gain
My freedom and my home
I will return, though foes may stand
Disputing every rod [road]
My own dear home my native land
I'll return to you yet by and by.

ANDREW J. FOGLE, 9TH TEXAS INFANTRY

ON July 2, 1863, the cracking of the rifles and the burst of cannons rung loud in the ears of Maj. Gen. John Bell Hood's Texans as they rushed through the Devil's Den toward Little Round Top, near Gettysburg, Pennsylvania. A Texas officer "pointed to 'Little Round Top' in the distance, and said 'Follow the Lone Star Flag to the top of the mountain.'" As the men encroached upon the hill, a Union battery found their range and landed a shot that exploded in their midst, killing and wounding several. One of the men, George A. Branard, a young Texan color bearer of the 1st Texas Infantry, unfurled the Lone Star Flag, swearing to all the men around him that he would brandish it over the cannon that fired the devastating shot or die trying. Bravely he ran in front of his comrades, inspiring them along the way through the murderous showers of lead. As the vulnerable Branard neared the Union lines, he planted the flag in the ground to show his determination. At that moment a Union shell exploded, splintering the flag staff and blinding the Texan in one eye.[1] On that day, 1,300 miles away from the nascent state they called home, dozens of Texans lost their lives in a vain attempt to capture Little Round Top. The Texans failed to take the hill, the army lost the battle, and many of their friends never left Gettysburg. Yet those who survived continued to fight for the South for almost two more years. What motivated these men to risk their lives so far from home?

In New Mexico, the westernmost theater of the American Civil War, Texans also suffered tremendously. Men straggled across the hundred miles of dusty and arid plains of the Jornada del Muerto, Spanish for "dead man's journey." Pvt. Felix Robert Collard labeled the New Mexico desert "Horn Alley" because of "the quantities of buffalo horns and bones scattered over its surface." the Jornada possessed "not a bush, a blade of grass, a lizard, or any living thing, either vegetable or animal nor a drop of water on this extended and arid waste. A jack rabbit to cross it would have to take his vi[c]tuals with him."[2] Men choked on the dry air of New Mexico as their lips cracked and throats swelled. These Texans were nine hundred miles from home with little food, not enough water, no horses, shoddy clothes, and worn shoes, suffering through terrible weather on their way back from a campaign that was a complete failure. And yet those who made it back to the Lone Star State remained in the army and soldiered on for another three years. What motivated these men to fight in New Mexico, so far from the main theater of the Civil War?

If one were to ask a Texan today what motivated men from the Lone Star State to fight in the Civil War, the typical response would be a question: Do Texans ever need an excuse to fight? Texans had a reputation as fighters even before the firing on Fort Sumter. Within a short period of time, 1835 to 1861, Texas experienced a string of prominent conflicts, including the Texas Revolution, three expeditions during the Republic era (Santa Fe, Somervell, and Mier), the Mexican-American War, numerous fights with Native Americans by citizens and the Texas Rangers, and conflicts with Mexican bandits such as Juan Cortina. One could conclude that Texans love a good fight and had already experienced a civil war with the Texas Revolution; in other words, Texas men and society were ready for the war between North and South. With this evidence, it is easy to see why Texans today view their past ancestors in a martial light. But contrary to these popular beliefs, the men truly needed some motivation to leave their families and risk their lives.[3]

For over a century, historians have examined what motivated men to fight in the Civil War. Many of the works examine either one or both sides of the war or a particular state involved. Some of the motivating factors historians have analyzed include slavery, adventure, honor, proof of manhood, religion, and the protection of hearth and home. Though numerous historians have examined the subject, the study of soldier motivation remains one of the most exciting areas of Civil War research. Despite such attention, no one has explored why Texans participated in the conflict.

The first seminal contribution to the study of soldier motivation in the Civil War was by Bell I. Wiley with two works, *The Life of Johnny Reb* and *The Life of Billy Yank.* These books focused on the lives of the enlisted soldiers in the war and presented them as common people, not heroic figures in paintings. In *Johnny Reb,* Wiley concluded that Confederates fought for two main reasons: an opportunity for adventure and as a reaction to the hostility they felt from the North. The war gave Southern men the opportunity to get from behind their plows and defend against the perceived threat to their way of life. In *Billy Yank,* Wiley concluded that Northern soldiers fought for their abolitionist beliefs, to protect democracy, to earn some money, and to fight alongside their lifelong friends. Additionally, Wiley concluded that more Northern men fought to maintain the Union than to advance abolitionism. These two studies had a significant impact on how scholars viewed the common Civil War soldier, dispelling some of the romantic views of the rank and file while clearly explaining why they fought.[4]

Decades later, James I. Robertson's *Soldiers Blue and Gray* followed a similar argument. Written as a supplement to Wiley's two groundbreaking books, Robertson's study presents mostly the same conclusions. Some of the aspects of Civil War soldiers examined by Robertson include states' rights, state pride, and the avoidance of conscription as motivations for Southerners to fight. His work provides a more enriched study of soldier motivation with a concise evaluation.[5]

James M. McPherson contributed further to the study by tracing the importance of slavery to the men fighting in the Civil War through several works, including *Battle Cry of Freedom, Drawn with the Sword,* and *For Cause and Comrades.* In all of these books, the main motivating factor for the men to fight was their idea of freedom and how slavery influenced it. The North wanted freedom for the government to maintain the Union and liberty for slaves, and the South associated white freedom with slavery. By defending slavery, white Southerners believed they were fighting for their own freedom. After examining thousands of letters written by men throughout the North and the South for his book *For Cause and Comrades,* McPherson added more reasons why the men fought, including fighting for the friends they served with and vengeance toward the opposing side.[6]

Honor also provided significant motivation. The definitive work on the culture of honor is Bertram Wyatt-Brown's *Southern Honor: Ethics and Behavior in the Old South,* which argues that the South's code of honor was the cornerstone of its slaveholding ethics. Many matters separated the North and South, but the crucial difference lay in their division over matters of honor. According to Wyatt-Brown, honor was the defining characteristic of Southern life. Honor defined men and gave them status. When the Civil War started, it provided an opportunity for men across the South to earn honor for themselves and to promote themselves within Southern society.[7]

Closely related to the concept of honor was that of manhood. Proof of manhood compelled men to fight in the Civil War, as explored in Reid Mitchell's *The Vacant Chair*. Mitchell examines every aspect, including social and cultural experiences, of the Union soldier during the war, except the military training and fighting in which they participated. He focuses on how soldiers during the Civil War sought manhood and how they achieved it in combat and concludes that nineteenth-century men believed that combat was the surest means to reach manhood. Accordingly, this belief influenced men to leave their homes and families to join the army.[8] In his *To Appomattox and Beyond*, Larry Logue further shifts the perspective on the Civil War and its aftermath from generals and politicians to the ordinary soldier and concludes that both Northern and Southern soldiers enlisted in the armies because they felt that combat proved the men's manhood to themselves and their communities. Manhood was important to men from all classes of society, and they believed that enlisting and fighting improved their status in society.[9]

Although manhood may have been vital in motivating the rank and file, the spiritual world of religion kept the men in the army. A work that examines the religious aspects of the Civil War is Steven E. Woodworth's *While God Is Marching On*. Woodworth explores the religious world of enlisted men in both armies and concludes that Northern soldiers viewed the South as defying God since they disobeyed their government by seceding. Southern soldiers, on the other hand, felt that they were defending their faith since in the decades before the Civil War the church had institutionalized slavery. Religion thus allowed Southern men to justify their defense of slavery. More important, religion allowed men to endure the circumstances surrounding warfare.[10]

Another influence was the soldiers' devotion to their home communities. Woodworth has also suggested that local attachment was a major motivating factor in a book he coauthored with the late Warren Wilkinson, *A Scythe of Fire*. In this book, Woodworth examines the 8th Georgia Infantry from its inception to the end of the war. In regard to soldier motivation, Woodworth suggests that the men fought to keep the Yankees away from their home counties and were more prone to desert if the Yankees threatened or occupied those places.[11]

These scholars have suggested a variety of motivations for Civil War soldiers. None of these works exclusively investigates the inspirations of Texas soldiers to fight. Some major works analyze the state and its men in the war, such as Ralph Wooster's *Texas and Texans in the Civil War* and Ernest Wallace's *Texas in Turmoil, 1849–1875*. Yet neither studies soldier motivation exclusively. Additionally, most of the scholars have concluded that the defense of hearth and home was a primary factor pushing men to the front. None of them, however, have clearly defined or examined the complex nature of this influence. Home and hearth is essentially a collection of attachments that people develop throughout their lifetimes. The attachments the soldiers developed throughout their lives involve issues that concerned them the most, including families—both immediate and extended—and friends; localities, where they were born, their current homestead, and places where they lived for a time or had significant experiences; and a way of life, ranging from occupations and hobbies to slavery and social status. All of these attachments had a direct impact on Southern soldiers' decisions to leave their homes and families while enduring hardships and chancing death for the Confederacy. Attachments affected soldiers from every state, but Texans demonstrate most clearly the complexity and extent of this motivation to drive men to risk their lives in combat, since they came from many places and, unlike any other state, served in all theaters of the war.[12]

Although Texas had many similarities to the rest of the South, there were also differences. A major difference was that Texans had multiple local attachments. Since the majority of Texans were born in other states, they had more than one hometown, usually both the town where they grew up and the town where they lived in Texas at the onset of the war. Essentially, there was more than one location with which they had a significant emotional attachment or sense of loyalty, so men had to decide which place they wanted to protect. When the war began, the Lone Star State was relatively safe, since it was far removed from the bulk of the fighting. With their current homes and families not directly threatened by the war and its destruction, Texans felt a strong desire to return to their former states or regions to defend their hometowns and or family members who still lived there.[13]

Where a Texan came from had a direct impact on why he fought in the Civil War and, more important, where he fought. Multiple local attachments affected more Texans than residents of the rest of the Confederacy because in the mid-nineteenth-century Texas was a migrant state. The population of the state nearly tripled in the decade before the war, from 212,592 in 1850 to 604,215 in 1860, mostly from migration from within the United States. These people brought not only themselves and their knowledge but their cultural "baggage." Since a majority came from the old South, they directly influenced the culture of the state, making it Southern.[14]

At the onset of the war, Texans were heavily influenced by their local connections when they made their decision to fight and their choice of which unit to join. Texans who had recently moved to the state viewed their new home as far removed from the dangers of battles and thus felt no pressing need for the immediate defense of their wives and children in Texas. Because the perceived threat to their homes in Texas was slight, such men wanted to return to their native regions to defend the town where their parents raised them and the extended family they left behind. On the other hand, men born in Texas had little or no connection with any other state in the South. Many of them tended to join units earmarked to stay in Texas since they had no other place to defend.

Several factors helped determine whether a man would feel compelled to defend some locality other than his current residence. Most significant was whether family or friends still lived in the distant location, but a man might decide to fight for his ancestral home or birthplace even if no living persons tied him to that place. This was all the more true if he perceived it to be threatened and his current residence seemed safe. Texans decided to defend their old hometowns early in the war since Texas, located at the extreme west of the Confederacy, was not initially a major priority for the authorities in Washington, D.C. As the war progressed, the threat to the state increased as the Union navy established a stronger blockade and the army moved closer to its borders. When the threat to Texas increased, so did the priority Texans placed on defending their homes, businesses, and families in the state.

In this book I explore the previously unexamined question of why Texans fought, especially the impact of attachments on their decision to fight. Attachments affected soldiers from every state, but Texans demonstrate most clearly the complexity and extent of this motivation to drive men to risk their lives in combat because Texas is unique in several ways. Compared to that in other states, the Texas population in the years leading up to the war remained much more diverse in its origins; Texans, being on the western flank of the Confederacy, had more choices of locations to serve; and most notably the men from the Lone Star State served in all theaters of the war and in more states and territories than any other Confederate or Union soldiers. Essentially, Texans had many more connections to people and places outside of the state than men from any other state in either the Union or the Confederacy.

Though the examination of attachments on Texas soldiers is the focus of this book, chapter 2 provides a broad foundation to support the influences of attachments by focusing on the general motivations of Texans to enlist in the Confederate and Union armies. At the start of the Civil War, the culture of Texas was essentially Southern since the majority of the population originated from the region and brought with them their culture and institutions. Texas, in 1861, contained slaves, a plantation economy, a strict code of duty and honor, Southern churches, and a unionist minority; most significant, Texans, like everyone else, had strong feelings toward their families. These aspects of Texans' motivation to fight mirrored their counterparts throughout the South. On the other hand, Texas differed from the rest of the South in several important ways. The most significant of these was that the Lone Star State contained a large number of migrants who had strong connections to other states but at the same time associated themselves with the strong Texas nationalism developed through the struggle for independence. All of these factors, both similarities and differences, influenced Texans in their decisions to take up arms and fight for the Confederacy.[15]

Chapter 3 examines the men who chose to join units created to defend the trans-Mississippi, who tended to have their strongest connection with Texas. Texans, whose state and homes were far removed from the enemy and not immediately threatened, were free to enlist in units promising to serve in any theater of the war. The choices they made starkly revealed their motivation for fighting. Soldiers from the Lone Star State could fight in the cis-Mississippi (east of the Mississippi River) or the trans-Mississippi (primarily the states just west of the river, Texas itself, the Texas frontier, and New Mexico).[16] Where they decided to fight depended on their attachments to those localities. A majority of these men settled the Lone Star years before the outbreak of the war and established themselves in their community through businesses and families. The length of time and responsibilities in the area created a strong attachment to that location. They had more to lose by enlisting to fight outside of the trans-Mississippi. Some of these men even wanted to fight in specific locations within the state. Those from the coast tended to want to protect their homes from a Union invasion via the Gulf of Mexico; those on the frontier wished to defend their homes from Native American attacks. Men who enlisted to fight in New Mexico wanted to expand Texas' borders to ensure a strong economic future for their state. The highest priority of the Texans who fought in the trans-Mississippi was the defense of Texas.[17]

Chapter 4 examines Texans who had recently moved to Texas and had a strong desire to defend their old hometowns and families back east. Since most of these men's families migrated from states east of the Mississippi River, they enlisted in Texas units that organized to fight in the East. At the beginning of the war, Virginia was the only theater in the East in which these men could fight. As the war progressed, new theaters such as Kentucky emerged, giving the men more choices. Texans whose hometowns were closer to Kentucky than Virginia changed their mind on where they wanted to fight and worked to get transferred to other units fighting in that region. Some Texans went so far as to join regiments from other states—the most famous being Richard M. Gano and Adam Rankin Johnson. Gano raised a Texas squadron that later became the nucleus of the 7th Kentucky Cavalry, and Johnson traveled to the Blue Grass State and formed several Kentucky units. Local attachments east of the Mississippi River influenced these Texans to leave their families in Texas to defend other regions they held dear.[18]

Chapter 5 explores why Texans returned to the trans-Mississippi as the pull of local attachments east of the Mississippi River waned. At the onset of the war, Texas was relatively secure because it was far from the initial theater of the war and there was no major Union presence near the state. As the war progressed, so did the threats to the security of Texas. When the Union army threatened their state, Texas soldiers reconsidered their priorities. Major events such as the battles at Pea Ridge, Galveston, and Vicksburg created the impression that Texas was no longer secure. Texans reacted to these perceived threats by requesting transfers, resigning their commissions, and sometimes deserting so they could join the Confederate army west of the Mississippi. Vicksburg proved to be the most crucial event because the loss of the city, along with the demise of Port Hudson five days later, gave the Union army complete control of the Mississippi. During the first half of the war, the river served as a psychological barrier in the minds of Texans, allaying their fears that the Union army could seriously threaten Texas. Once the Mississippi came under Federal control, Texas troops changed their minds about serving east of the river and a significant number deserted to serve in the trans-Mississippi. The prioritization of local connections was not set from the beginning; it changed as the war unfolded.

Chapter 6 examines the decisions of minorities in Texas. The state contained the second highest number of free minorities of any state in the Union or Confederacy—the two largest groups being Germans and Tejanos. Where they lived within Texas and how long they had lived there usually determined where they fought and for which side. Germans who settled before 1848 and lived between Austin and the coast tended to fight for the Confederacy; the length of time they had lived in Texas acclimated them to Southern culture. Germans who came to Texas after 1848 mainly settled on the frontier and tended to resist joining the Confederate army because they had not developed any true connection to the state. In fact, many Germans immigrated to Texas after 1848 specifically to avoid the revolutions in Europe. They had no desire to fight and just wanted to be left alone. Tejanos tended to distrust Anglo-Texans because of the treatment they had received before the war. In addition, most joined the Union army for pay and clothes. Local attachment was a major factor in the decisions of these two groups of immigrants in Texas to fight for the Confederacy or against.[19]

Local attachment as an influence was not exclusive to Texans. It motivated many other Confederate soldiers. Three fine examples of this motivation influencing Southern men to leave their homes to fight are the 8th Georgia Infantry, the "Red River Company" of the 14th Tennessee Infantry, and William E. Minor of the 6th Kentucky Infantry. The men in the 8th Georgia behaved in the same manner as the Texans when the Union army threatened and then occupied their hometown of Rome, Georgia, late in the war. Desertion rates increased during the time the city fell under the influence of Northern soldiers. The war became essentially meaningless to these men, since they could no longer defend their hometown. Local attachments had a different effect on the men of the 14th Tennessee Infantry. They lost their hometowns to the enemy early in the war with the fall of Fort Donelson. When they reorganized themselves in 1862, the men reexamined their reasons for remaining together as a fighting unit and produced a contract among themselves titled the "Red River Company Agreement." In the document, which all the men in the company signed, they outlined their motivation to remain in the Confederate army. These Tennesseans wanted to continue "to stand together and drive that enemy from our Childhood homes—from the home of our Fathers and Mothers." They welded a strong desire to "remain united and joined as a band of brothers, honorable representatives of the Old Red River Neighborhood" to "make an effort in behalf of our Red River homes." The main motivation of the Red River Company was to take back their hometowns, the only places in the United States they had a connection to. William E. Minor, a private in the 6th Kentucky Infantry, wrote about why he fought to the Louisville *Weekly Courier* early in the war: "The North don't understand our spirit. They mistake for what we are fighting. They had as well try to quench the fire of life—as to try to subjugate those who are satisfied they are fighting for their mothers, fathers, sisters, kindred, and the tender ones of their hearts." All these men sought the defense of their homes and families, demonstrating that the influence of attachments extended to the rest of the country. But this influence was the most pronounced in Texans, since they had more than one home, forcing them to decide which one to defend.[20]

Overall, the influence of local attachments was a determining factor in men's decision to fight in the Civil War and is the most noticeable in Texans. Soldiers from the Lone Star State were a group with roots that stretched far and ran deep in many different directions. When the war came, those roots helped each Texan decide if, and where, he should fight. Though local attachments are not the only reason Texans and others from across the United States fought in the Civil War, they were one of the most important and a factor that no historian has studied thoroughly.

2

INTO THE FRAY

Why Texans Fought in the Civil War

> Our cuntry is threatened on every side—already the clanking of the
> tyrants chain is heard—. . . No, but we will be free, we will be made
> indepenant again. Then let the fires of patriatism be kindled in every heart
> and let every man who can, to arm! and "Strike for the green groves
> of our sires for God and our native land!"
>
> JAMES K. STREET, 9TH TEXAS INFANTRY

> We are fighting for our property and our homes; they [Yankees], for the
> flimsy and abstract idea that a negro is equal to an Anglo American.
>
> H. C. MEDFORD, 11TH TEXAS INFANTRY

B Y 1861, when the Civil War began, Texas had launched a successful revolution and existed as both a republic and a state for a quarter of a century.
Throughout this period, many different people and cultures exerted their
influences on the Lone Star State. In the time before the Texas Revolution, as part of the Mexican state Coahuila y Tejas, it had a significant Hispanic
influence. After independence—in the Republic era and early statehood—the
trend changed, since most people who settled in Texas came from the southern
United States. Southerners brought with them their culture and institutions,
making Texas very similar to the rest of the South in many respects. Texas in
1861 contained slaves, a plantation economy, a strict code of duty and honor,
Southern churches, and a unionist minority; most important, the new Texans
had strong feelings toward their families. On the other hand, Texas differed from
the rest of the South in several important ways. The most significant of these
was that it contained a large number of migrants who had strong connections to
other states. At the same time, these new arrivals associated themselves with the
strong Texas nationalism that developed during the struggle for independence
from Mexico and the nine years of independence. All of these factors, both simi-

larities and differences, influenced Texans in their decisions to take up arms and fight for the Confederacy.[1]

The most noticeable influence of Southern culture on Texas in 1861 and motivation to fight in the Civil War was slavery. The institution of slavery had existed in Texas for more than forty years by time the war started, ever since the first Anglo settlers had brought their slaves into the region during the second decade of the nineteenth century. The slave trade opened in Texas before its independence, but it was not the principal source of bond labor in the region. Some slaves came to Texas through the African trade during the Republic era, but it provided only a small fraction of the total slave population. A majority of Texas slaves moved to the new region with their masters from the old South. This influx of slaveowners and slaves from the old South allowed Southern culture to permeate Texas, and the state developed a dependence on the "Peculiar Institution."[2]

In the decades prior to the Civil War, Texas experienced a major influx of slaves. In the 1840s, the slave population increased at a steady rate as migrants from Southern states brought their slaves with them and others were imported illegally from Africa. Slaves comprised 27 percent of the population in 1840, numbering 38,753 in the 1847 census taken two years after the annexation of Texas. The slave population experienced a dramatic increase during the 1850s, reaching more than 30 percent of the total population of the state, with increased migration after Texas gained U.S. statehood. Though the proportion of the bondsman population appears to have risen only 3 percent during the period, this growth is significant because of the simultaneous white migration into the state from the South and foreign countries. By the eve of the Civil War, the total number of slaves in Texas had grown to 182,566.[3]

During slavery's growth in Texas, residents developed strong feelings about the institution and the role it would play in their future. Texans believed slavery was key to the agricultural economy of the state. The bondsmen's toil had rendered Texas agriculture profitable and made the state self-sufficient in food production, convincing the majority of Texas economic leaders that the Peculiar Institution was a boon to the state. Editor Charles DeMorse expressed his opinion of slavery in the columns of his newspaper, the Clarksville *Northern Standard:* "We want more slaves—we need them. . . . We care nothing for . . . slavery as an abstraction—but we desire the practicality, the increase of our productions; the increase of the comforts and wealth of the populations; and if slavery, or slave labor, or Negro Apprentice labor ministers to this, why that is what we want."[4] Texans associated slavery with economic prosperity for their state, for themselves, and, more important, for their future.

Texans noticed the growth of slavery in their state. Spurred on by the expansion of white settlers across the state, they realized the opportunities slavery provided as the frontier pushed west, especially in the north-central plains where the institution had room to grow. In addition, they noticed that the productivity of the slaves increased in the decade before the Civil War. Their optimism was not limitless, however. Slaveholders realized that the institution could not spread to every section of the state. West of the Cross Timbers, rainfall was judged insufficient to make cotton a profitable crop and Mexico too close to render slave "property" secure, since masters always feared their slaves escaping across the border. Since West Texas was not deemed viable for slavery and the region was relatively unsettled, Texas slaveowners concentrated their bondsmen on the plantations and farms of middle coastal, Central, and East Texas.[5]

Plantations were key to the prosperity of East Texas. The business created by large plantations drove the region's economy, as they bought food from yeomen farmers and lumber from local mills. The best example of East Texas' dependence on the Peculiar Institution was Harrison County during the 1850s. In that decade, Harrison had more slaves than any other county in Texas. Planters and slaveholding farmers owned more than 90 percent of the county's improved acreage and cash value of land, making slavery the lifeblood of the county's economy and agricultural production.[6]

In general, slaveholding families lived in the older regions of Texas and comprised only a fourth of the total population of the state. During the 1850s, the influence of slaveholders increased as the number of Southerners migrating into the state grew. By the end of the decade, 77 percent of households in Texas were Southern born. The migration of Southerners did little to increase the percentage of Texas slaveholders who were from the South, which jumped only from 89 percent in 1850 to 90 percent in 1860. The significance is noticeable, however, in the increase of the total number of slaveholders from 1840 to 1860. In 1840, only 2,203 slaveholders lived in Texas; by 1850 the number had reached 7,747. The greatest increase in the number of slaveholders occurred in the 1850s, with 21,878 slaveowners living in Texas by the end of the decade, a total increase of almost 1,000 percent since 1840.[7]

The majority of the Texas population did not own slaves; those who did owned very few. Within the slaveholding population, the majority owned fewer than five slaves, with a quarter of slaveowners owning only one. A fifth of Lone Star slaveholders owned 96 percent of the slaves. Only sixty Texans owned a hundred or more slaves. With so few large plantation owners, their influence over their community and the state was greater.[8]

Large plantation owners' influence over the state was evident in the percentage of their population in the state compared to the percentage of slaveholders who held political office. By 1860, slaveholders constituted just over a quarter of the household heads but 68 percent of Texas politicians at every level—federal, state, and local. Slaveowners had the influence and leisure needed to gain office, and they had a vested interest in the continuation of slavery and the protection of their property. Slaveholder dominance did not create much discontent among whites in Texas because it mirrored their lives back in the old South—the only exception being North Texas. Foreigners and minorities, on the other hand, did not understand the political dynamics of the South and grew to resent the influence of the planter minority. With the mandate of the majority of Texans, the slaveholders made a strong stand for slavery, even though it was a symbol of difference and conflict with the North.[9]

Politics and government were not the only things slavery influenced in Texas. As the population of slaves increased in Texas, so did racial fears. Austin, from 1840 to 1860, provides a great example. As the number of slaves in the city increased, so did whites anxiety, because of the fear of a slave insurrection. With the increase in the number of bondsmen in Austin, blacks "assumed liberties and displayed an independence that violated the prevailing concept of race relations: white supremacy and black servitude."[10] The everpresent fear of a slave revolt or emancipation was not limited to Austin but haunted white Texans across the state. In Dallas, the city government established strict race laws restricting African Americans and mulattos, both free and slave, to a lower status than the rest of the community, thus dealing with their apprehension of the enslaved population along legal terms. Their anxieties never reached the same level of fear white South Carolinians felt, but Texans realized the potential role of slavery in the future of their state and their lives. Fear of a slave revolt gripped the lives of Texans and forced them to strike hard at any real or imaginary threats to the Peculiar Institution. White Texans reacted in such drastic ways because the thought of armed slaves roaming the countryside made them fear that their families might be slain.[11]

Texans' fear of a slave insurrection reached its peak in the summer of 1860. It was a hot and dry summer plagued by a series of fires around Dallas, dubbed the "Texas Troubles." The first fire started on July 8, 1860, in Dallas and consumed the business section, and two hours later fires began to spring up in Denton, burning down half of the town square and decimating a store in Pilot Point. On the same day buildings and farms in Black Jack Grove, Milford, Pilot Point, Ladonia, Millwood, Jefferson, Waxahachie, and Honey Grove burst into flames. The Texas Troubles created excitement, concern, and fear across the state, as far as Guadalupe County, and throughout the South.[12]

Texans immediately searched for answers for the fires. Though some blamed the fires on a new type of phosphorus match that ignited spontaneously, an occurrence later witnessed by storeowners and shoppers while the matches sat on the shelf, most Texans jumped to the conclusion that the Texas Troubles were a slave insurrection. Texans and other Southerners alike believed that Northern Republicans had organized and orchestrated the fires; Southerners did not think slaves had the mental capacity to arrange such an event. The conspiracy revolved around the idea that abolitionists influenced blacks to set the fires. Vigilante committees formed to discover the abolitionist terrorists and focused their attention on both Northern and Southern whites with sympathy or connections to free states. Texans concluded that "[Parson] Blount and McKinney, friends of abolition preachers who were expelled from the county last year, were the instigators of the plot."[13] Others such as Anthony Bewley, a minister of the Northern Methodist Church just south of Fort Worth, found his life in danger after Texas newspapers published a provocative letter expressing his anti-slavery views. Bewley quickly escaped the state with most of his family and sought sanctuary in Kansas. His flight proved futile, though; Texas vigilantes tracked him down in Cassville, Missouri, and lynched him. The punishment for the fires was death to all those found guilty, even by association. The fires continued through the rest of the summer, and from July to September the hanging of abolitionists and slaves was a daily event. In mid-August a man who "engaged in the laudable undertaking of selling maps, has been hung in Eastern Texas, for tampering with negroes."[14] Less than a month later, "two persons were . . . hung in Robertson county for tampering with negroes."[15]

The Texas Troubles had an impact on Texans. Most noticeable were the financial losses. Approximately a million dollars worth of property burned to ashes, much of it on the frontier. Less tangible effects included an alarmed citizenry and the brewing of secessionist beliefs. According to the Dallas *Herald,* "Before the expulsion of Northern Methodist preachers from Fannin [County] . . . masters and servants lived in harmony; but ever since, certain of the latter have become sullen and disobedient—evidently under some secret influence."[16] After the fires, citizens realized the hazard of abolitionist doctrines and in response increased their vigilance of slave discipline. Sentiments toward breaking away from the Union increased throughout Texas and the rest of the South because of the fires, as news of them spread through the nation. The chaos of the Texas Troubles in 1860 influenced Texans to think about the future of their homes and families.[17]

Before the fires had finished smoldering, Texans asked themselves, what other problems would emerge if a "Black Republican" presided over the country? Viewing the Republican Party as a direct threat to slavery—essentially the foundation of the South's economic and social system—and believing they were in the middle of a race war, Texans preferred secession to prevent economic and racial disorder. Those who had the most to lose by emancipation were the men controlling secession—the slaveowners. Threats to slavery created tension that slaveholders could not ignore. They would lose their livelihood, and that was important enough to motivate them to fight to keep the institution in their state and the South. The controlling influence of the slaveholders contributed to Texas' secession from the Union.[18]

Texans admitted their dependence on the institution in the Ordinance of Secession presented to the people of Texas and in their amnesty appeals after the war. Texas was the only Southern state that allowed a popular referendum to approve secession from the United States. Included in the ordinance was "A Declaration of the Causes Which Impel the State of Texas to Secede from the Federal Union," which outlined all the reasons Texas wanted to leave the United States. Chief among the reasons—consisting of two-thirds of the document—was slavery.[19] After the war James E. Harrison wrote to President Andrew Johnson for amnesty for serving in the Confederate army. In his letter he listed the reasons he fought against the United States. In one section he wrote, "I favored secession from the Federal Union as the only means of according to my judgment, of presenting what I deemed the rights and institutions on which the prosperity and happiness of the Southern States depended."[20] Before and after the war Texas and Texans admitted that they fought the war to maintain the institution of slavery because emancipation would destroy the Southern way of life.

The economic impact of emancipation would indirectly affect all Texans, even those who did not own slaves. Though a significant concern, other matters proved more important. Non-slaveowners believed that if the slaves gained their freedom it would threaten the social order of the South, because poor whites would have to compete with the freedmen socially. These concerns existed from the introduction of slavery into Texas, but the Texas Troubles intensified them. Though most white Texans did not own slaves, the institution defined their lives. White Southerners believed that the only way they could feel free and have liberty was through the existence of slavery. In other words, as long as blacks in the South remained subjugated, white Southerners, no matter how poor or unrefined, would not be the lowest class in society.[21]

Texans believed that the social order established by slavery was best for the future of their state, and, more important, for their hometowns and families. As long as they could maintain the social order, the localities to which they had established attachments would flourish in safety. John Marshall expressed his belief in maintaining the social order in his newspaper, the *State Gazette,* when he wrote, "It is essential to the honor and safety of every poor white man to keep the negro in his present state of subordination and discipline."[22] Even late in the war, soldiers asserted their stance against racial equality. Layfette Orr wrote to his brothers, Henry and Robert, that white Southerners should "never give it up, and bee put on an [equal] footing with the negros."[23] The end of the war and the announcement of emancipation did nothing to stem their beliefs. After the war, William H. Hamman of the 4th Texas Infantry wrote, "The question is not one of dollars and cents, but whether the noblest, the proudest, the most chivalrous, the most moral and christian people will suffer themselves to be dragged down to the level with the negro, and then still lower to keep pace with the negro in his retrogradation in his liberated state, until finally our rich, prosperous, and happy land shall present the condition of Hayti, Mexico and the Central American States."[24]

Contributing to Texans' worries of losing the social order of the South was a fear of Northerners enslaving Southern whites. James K. Street, of the 9th Texas Infantry, warned, "Our cuntry is threatened on every side—already the clanking of the tyrants chain is heard—. . . shall we not sacrifice the endearments of home for a season rather the lie so finely upon our backs and wait till we are all bound hand and foot and the fair daughters of the south reduced to a level with the flat footed thick-liped negro? No, but we will be free, we will be made indepenant again."[25] Perpetuating these thoughts was the publication of captured letters written by Union soldiers, such as one written by James Donley on April 27, 1862, in Hamburg, Tennessee. The Union soldier claimed, "I have my eye on a fine situation, and how happy we will live when we get our Southern home. When we get possession of the land we can make the men raise cotton and corn, and the women can act in the capacity of domestic servants. The women are very ignorant—only a grade above the negro, and we can live like kings."[26] The validity of the letter can certainly be questioned, but a James Donley does appear on muster roles for three Illinois regiments. Whether or not this particular letter is legitimate, Texans and people across the South did indeed expect such motivations from their enemy.[27]

That Texans fought to defend the institution that brought social order to the South becomes further evident in their views about fighting black soldiers. Rufus King Felder of the 5th Texas Infantry wrote, "It is very humiliating to know that we have to fight & expose our lives to this mixed horde of black & white demons."[28] Another Texan, George Washington Littlefield, a member of Terry's Texas Rangers, commented in a letter home about the possibility of fighting black troops, "All of our command determined if we were put into a fight there to kill all we captured."[29] Some Texans did participate in the slaying of captured black troops. Durant Motier Dansby of the 3rd Texas Cavalry claimed that, when he fought in the Battle of Iuka, "at the first opening of the fight the colored soldiers fled in dismay. There was some brutal murders perpetrated by our troops after they surrendered, but the boys were mad to think the Negro would have the gall to shoot a gun at them."[30] Texans participated in the infamous slaying of African American soldiers at Port Hudson. William D. Lawther of the 17th Texas Infantry (Consolidated) wrote to his wife, "We killed a great many of their negro soldiers. They had one Rgt of 700 negros all were killed but 100. We show them no quarters." To the credit of the black soldiers, with some qualifying, Lawther later stated, "the Feds make them drunk before they go into a fight. Some of them have fought like very devils. They made one of the boldest bayonet charges at P[ort] H[udson] that has been made during the war."[31]

The most notorious example of Texans killing black soldiers occurred at Poison Spring, Arkansas, in 1864. At the Battle of Poison Spring, a significant number of African American soldiers received no quarter from the 5th Texas Cavalry Brigade, commonly known as Gano's Brigade. Accounts from both sides confirm that Texans, along with the Confederate Indians fighting with them, killed many soldiers of the 1st Kansas Colored Volunteer Infantry after they had surrendered or while they lay wounded. At Poison Spring, Texas soldiers reacted to the thought of the disruption of the social order and felt justified in punishing those who promoted the idea of emancipation, as Texans had done before the war with the Texas Troubles. Slavery influenced most non-slaveowning Texans to fight in the Civil War not exclusively for the institution itself but for the future of Texas and to preserve the social order. Texas slaveholders fought to keep slavery in order to maintain their influence in their community and their way of life.[32]

Even in the postwar years the reactions of the defeated Texans bear witness to their reliance on and desire for the institution of slavery. John Faulk, the son of a slaveowner in Henderson County and member of the 17th Texas Cavalry, left for the war with Jere, his personal slave. After the surrender of the Confederate army, Faulk returned home. The world as he knew it had transformed, but his father held firm to the only way of life he knew and refused to inform "the negroes that they are free." Soon thereafter the slaves discovered their newly found freedom, and "nineteen left at one time. The next morning after they left (it being our custom to get up before daylight, negroes and all to get out of the farm), we looked down at the negroes' quarters and could see only one or two lights. It looked very dark and lonesome and when we all began to realize that the negroes were free. I think we all shed tears—Father, Mother, children and all. I did I am sure. These were trying times."[33] The Faulks lost almost everything they had gained before the war, especially the reason John fought in the war— their society and way of life.

After the war, Robert S. Gould, colonel of the 6th Texas Cavalry, expressed Texans' desire to defend the institution of slavery and racial beliefs in the state while arguing that he fought to defend states' rights:

I fought in behalf of the right of self-government and not to support the institution of slavery. The negro being in our midst, ignorant, debased and of inferior capacity, I felt that we were justified in keeping him in subjection, as the least of evils. But whether that position were right or wrong, I felt that it was not for northern men to decide the question of us of the south, and force us to submit to their decision. My whole nature was stirred to assert our right to regulate our own domestic institutions, to throw off a government which was being *perverted* to our injury, and to organize another deemed by us better fitted to promote our welfare.[34]

Similarly, S. E. Moseley of the 4th Texas Infantry responded to a letter from Union doctor Alfred Mercer, who asked what Confederates were fighting for. Though Moseley argued that he and others in the Confederate army fought for states' rights, he explained it as the right to maintain the institution of slavery. The Texan did not argue that the U.S. government impeded any of his liberties but rather that the Confederacy protected "our *peculiar* and much abused tenet of States Rights . . . embraced in our [Confederate] Constitution"—slavery. Additionally Moseley stated that the "fanatical and Puritanical abolitionists" in the North essentially nullified the "Fugitive Slave Law." The Texan continued to defend slavery: "The negro in his present condition of bondage is in the state and condition suitable to his capacity and disposition, and is infinitely happier than in any other condition his liberation would likely confer on him." Throughout the lengthy letter and the many reasons Confederates including Texans fought in the Civil War, the topic clearly mentioned the most is slavery.[35]

Slavery represented one of the greatest motivations for Texans to fight in the war. Regardless of their arguments after the war that they did *not* fight for slavery, the Peculiar Institution was ingrained in every facet of Southern society. Without slavery the future prosperity of the state, economic and social, was uncertain for the entire white population.

Related to the institution of slavery was the defense of property and livelihood. Texans, many with memories of the "Runaway Scrape" from the Texas Revolution, saw the war and the potential Northern invasions as a threat to their home and property. As evident in all wars, the combating armies will destroy or consume almost every piece of food, clothing, animals, buildings, and civilian property. From the first campaign, Texas soldiers wrote home describing the devastation they witnessed on the battlefront. Richard Marion Cadell of the 3rd Texas Regiment, Arizona Brigade, recorded the devastation he saw in Aroyelles Parish, Louisiana, in a letter to friend: "The yankees have badly burned this country. They have taken all of the negros and mules and wagons out of it. They have stripped this country entirely an have torn down nearly all of the fences that they could and burned them up. And that they could not burn they would tare down and leave lying there."[36] Similarly, Col. Richard Waterhouse of the 19th Texas Infantry reported to his wife from Arkansas that "many families on the Mississippi River where the Federal army have been have even had their homes burned, negroes and stock destroyed and stolen and had no protection for families who were entirely defenseless."[37] Texans were not ignorant of such consequences when the war started, and they wanted to prevent these scenes of destruction in their native state by enlisting in the Confederate army. With a show of force they hoped to deter the Union army from approaching the Lone Star State.

Other aspects of the South, such as the culture of honor, also influenced Texans to fight. Southerners stressed the importance of maintaining a good outward appearance and keeping their word in all instances. Parents and family members indoctrinated their boys and young men with a strong desire to gain and maintain their honor. The first stage in raising boys with these values was at age four, when they "dropped the slip," the dress toddlers wore, and put on pants. At this point fathers acted with a sterner attitude toward their sons and informally trained them about the importance of valor and the need to repress their feelings of fear and shame.[38]

The second stage of a man's indoctrination into Southern honor started around school age. At this point in his life, the boy learned what Southern society expected of him in terms of manhood. Fathers, if they had the means, would send boys away to a boarding school to gain independence, while poorer whites sent their sons to work in the fields. Also during this time, mothers were no longer as influential, as the boys were torn away from the "apron strings." A young man's education in the finer arts of manhood and honor ended in the third stage, during adolescence. During this time, the young man's entry into manhood took more of a social form, especially at college or when they left home. He would participate in all the activities that tested and increased his honor, such as "fighting, horse racing, gambling, swearing, drinking, and wenching."[39]

An aspect of the lives of young Southern men during this stage was dueling and the desire for combat. The *code duello* between young men was more common than among older, more-established men. Youths looking for a place in society could not risk even the slightest insult to their honor and felt it necessary to defend it at every opportunity. In the South, duels were the most public form of gaining and maintaining honor during peacetime. The most famous duel in Texas occurred during the Republic era and involved Felix Huston and Albert Sidney Johnston. An upset Huston initiated the duel when President Sam Houston appointed Johnston commander of the Texas army. After five to six shots, Huston hit Johnston in the hip; Johnston made a full recovery, and Huston kept his honor intact. Dueling was a form of combat, so when the Civil War broke out excitement spread among the young men to join the ranks. After all, military service was the surest and quickest way to gain and protect their honor. They wanted to been seen in a good light by their peers in order to gain or maintain their reputation. In other words, they did not want to be known as the opposite of an honorable man, a coward.[40]

The Civil War provided a major catalyst in the perception of manhood, because by joining the army men essentially joined a fraternal order. According to Mary Ann Clawson, fraternalism can be identified in four concepts: corporate idiom, ritual, proprietorship, and masculinity. Corporate idiom is a feeling of belonging to something larger than oneself, which in the case of these Texans was the Confederate army. Rituals are another unifying factor because armies are enriched with rituals, such as marching, drilling, and other ceremonies such as flag presentations. The army also provided proprietorship or a code of conduct, something already strong in Southern society. Finally, through association with other men, members could gain an increased sense of masculinity. John Mark Smither, a member of the 5th Texas Infantry, wrote to his sister on his twenty-first birthday in regard to his feelings about joining the army and how joining a fraternity of soldiers influenced his view of himself: "Did you know what day this is? This is your hopeful brothers birthday. Today I cease to be a boy and become a man. I don't know but I think I became a man on the 2nd of August 1861 when I enlisted in the c.s.a."[41]

The army also provided an opportunity for Texans to display their masculinity through fighting. Acts of masculinity—the most coveted and consequently the most dangerous acts being planting flags in enemy positions and taking the enemy's colors—allowed men to demonstrate the amount of courage they possessed. A. B. Peticolas, a soldier in the 4th Texas Mounted Volunteers, who fought in New Mexico, recorded in his journal the influence of courage on him and his unit in the first year of the war: "We are now beginning to experience about the greatest of the manifold hardships of war. Upon the battlefield there was the fierce din of conflict and the danger to face, but we had our courage and our convictions of the importance of winning the day to sustain us."[42] Southern soldiers cherished courage, especially in the first years of the war, because it was a way to gain honor in the eyes of their fellow soldiers.[43]

Duty to one's country and family went hand in hand with honor. Many Texans felt it was their duty to fight in the Civil War. William Moody of the 7th Texas Infantry wrote to a woman named Lizzie about why he enlisted: "You know with what spirit I joined. That it was for neither fame nor gain, but an uncontrollable sense of duty to my country."[44] Moody was not alone in his desire to perform his duty. William Williston Heartsill concurred, writing, "I was prompted to enlist because of a strict sense of duty."[45] Additionally, John M. Holcombe, a soldier in the 17th Texas Infantry, explained to his wife that "it is only a sence of duty that I owe my country that enables me to bear up under being so far from loved ones at home to say nothing of the hardships of a souldiers life."[46]

If Texans and other Southerners ignored their duty, they would face ridicule by society. John Marshall, editor of the *State Gazette*, used shame to encourage young Texans ignoring the call to duty by writing in his newspaper, "Young man, you who stay at home during this war, did you ever think of what your position ten or twenty years from now will be as compared with your comrade who shares in the perils and the glories of the fold."[47] Fear of ridicule or of losing their honor by not joining the war effort affected many men. Billy and Robert Gaston, who fought in Hood's Texas Brigade, expressed their concern of public shame to their father: "For I think that it will be a great deal better for us to toil through a long war or even to die on the battlefield than to stay at home & ever have the finger of scorn pointed at us as those who were afraid to contend for their rights."[48]

Fearing scorn from his community in Texas, Newton Asbury Keen of the 6th Texas Cavalry refused an offer from Union Maj. Gen. Judson Kilpatrick to become a galvanized Yankee soldier and fight American Indians on the frontier to avoid being sent to a prison camp. Keen, a native of Indiana, refused the offer, stating, "I did not feel it was right to do that and that I had taken an oath to be true to the South; and felt like other would not respect me if I broke my oath." Kilpatrick replied "that I would have to stay in prison until the war was over and that I would not be exchanged." Keen simply replied that he prefered to go to prison.[49] Keen refused the easy and potentially healthier alternative to the disease and filth of the prison camp because of his indoctrination into Southern culture and the fear of being scorned by his community when he returned to the Lone Star State. Texans and all Southerners alike would avoid ridicule from their community by simply enlisting, but the stress to maintain a man's honor did not end there.

Concern for honor continued throughout the war, since many of the men enlisted in the same unit with family members and friends from their community. Texans never completely left their community, because part of it traveled with them. As the men entered combat, it was important to them to maintain their honor, because if they showed any sign of cowardice the men from their community would report their actions to those back home. If a letter got home accusing a soldier of cowardice, he and his family would not be able figuratively to hold their heads up in their community again. The most common acts of cowardice involved men pretending to be sick so they could avoid combat. These actions by skulkers forced those men who really suffered from ailments to leave the hospital when combat started because they feared that others would call them cowards. Others with duties behind the lines would make special arrangements to see combat so they too could prove their honor.[50]

Another fear of Southerners, and humans in general, is the feeling of not belonging. If the men did not conform to the needs of their society, people from their community would ostracize them. Bertram Wyatt-Brown, a leading historian of Southern culture, stated it well when he wrote, "The comings and goings of relatives and friends, the thin excuses to go up to the courthouse, the interminable 'friendly' games, and the personal contests of arms and fists attested not only to Southerners' desperate need to conquer *ennui* but also their compulsion to find social place in the midst of gatherings. That was the great charm of the South, the willingness to create good times with others, but behind that trait was fear of being left alone, bored, and depressed."[51] Enlisting in the army allowed the men to stay a part of Southern society and at the same time gave them the opportunity to gain the favor of leading families, especially if they were the recruiters of the unit. By joining the Confederate army, Texans no longer had to fear being left alone. William Randolph Howell of the 4th Texas Infantry reassured himself against his fear of being alone as he recorded his feelings in his journal on August 14, 1861: "The Confederate States soldier goes to battle with the belief that our cause is just and right and that if he lives or dies the God of battles will not suffer him to pass unnoticed or unattended in his dying moments."[52]

Honor not only drove Texans to join the Confederate army but also motivated the men not to desert. Throughout the war many Texans felt the temptation to desert the army, and many acted on the impulses. Lawrence Sullivan Ross felt the desire to leave the army and recorded these feelings in letters to his wife Lizzie. "I must confess that I desire to return," Ross wrote. "Yet I feel that my duty to my Country demands the course I am pursuing, and hence it becomes more tolerable."[53] Later in the war, as he experienced the hardships of warfare, Ross wrote again: "I would resign and return home—but I feel that my duty to you and my Country demands of me, all the service and sacrifice I can render or make—Very many of the old Officers are retiring from the service and returning home I do not feel that I could do so honorably while my Country bleeds at Every pore."[54] Personal honor influenced Ross to ignore his desire to desert and return to the comforts of home.

Men were also reluctant to desert in fear that their community would find out about their actions. Soldiers, when possible, continuously communicated with their family and friends back home, and they were not afraid of exposing the actions of their neighbors who enlisted with them, especially when it involved desertion. Alexander C. Crain of the 16th Texas Cavalry reported to his wife that "you must not say any thing about it but Mr. Frankling is a diserter."[55] If rumors such as this circulated through the community, a man's honor would be tarnished and his neighbors would view him as a coward. This was detrimental to his future back home because people would no longer associate with him, thus restricting employment and business opportunities.

The culture of honor directly influenced the motivations of Texans to fight in the Civil War, but other more divine institutions played similar roles.[56] Religion was essential in motivating Confederate soldiers to keep fighting through the ordeal of war. In Texas, the churches were social centers. Churches provided an opportunity for people to come together to discuss issues of the day, crops, weather, and politics. Though there were many denominations in Texas, the Protestant churches had the strongest influence, since they had the greatest number of churches and parishioners. Additionally, affiliation with the religious denominations strengthened the bonds between kin and the community as a whole.[57]

Though many considered the Civil War armies the most religious in American history, early in the war most soldiers, especially the young men, did not concern themselves with religion, especially in camp. The sights and smells of camp life were new to these young men, as was the freedom from their parents and other familiar moral figures. Consequently, soldiering was too exciting for the men to focus on religion, and vices existed throughout the camps. Men drank when they could procure libations, played cards, rolled dice, and frequented brothels that sprang up around the encampments. Virgil S. Rabb of Walker's Division bragged to his brother back home about "a spree" he and his comrades in the army experienced. Rabb and his friends "got 3 gallons and a half of Whiskey with our $140.00, and had a jolly time of it Christmas eve night. I don't want you to say anything about our *Frollick to any body*."[58]

The effects of these activities had a deep impact on the men. Newton A. Keen of the 6th Texas Cavalry experienced religious indifference like many other Confederates. Keen expressed his feelings when he wrote, "This very much disturbed my mind. for I had by degrees lost my religion, that is was not over wicked, but knew I was not fit for heaven, and consequently not for death."[59] J. Mark Smither was another Texan who experienced the temptation of vice. He expressed his concern in a letter to his mother: "Mother pray to God to make me a better man! I know my own sins and unworthiness but there was so many temptations that beset a person in this Army that I see no chance of becoming any better until I am out of it."[60] Robert Gaston, a man able to stay away from the vices, stated, "I find that if a person will try, they can avoid the violation of their Maker's laws as well in camp as at home."[61] Religious indifference did not last very long as the newness of camp life and the excitement of vice wore off.

Religion in the Civil War provided many answers to fighting soldiers. Some of the mens' concerns included the role God played in their life and the war, whether they could be good Christians and kill the enemy, and when death might take them and what the end of their life would be like. All these issues had a direct influence on why the men continued to fight and were able to bear the stress of being soldiers. Samuel S. Watson of the 1st Texas Infantry explained to a friend how Christianity helped him. "The righteous have many promises of protection left on record for them, I would earnestly recommend to you the Christian religion," Watson wrote. "It will help you bear up under your troubles here in this world, and fit you for everlasting happiness in the world to come."[62] Similarly, A. J. Nelson, a Swedish immigrant fighting in Waul's Texas Legion, wrote to his brother August in their native language, "Do not grieve for me but [ill.] yourselves that the Lord had protected me as long as He has. I trust in the Lord's power that He will continue to save and protect me so I again may see you here in life."[63] Texans, like many other Southerners, turned to religion to find the strength to continue fighting for the Confederacy.

In the mid-nineteenth century, most Americans believed God intervened in daily life to care for his creation. Soldiers and others called God's intercession providence. Through special intervention and general oversight, God preserved soldiers in battle. The idea that God interfered gave the men some hope before they went into battle. As Edward Richardson Crockett of the 4th Texas Infantry wrote in his diary on April 20, 1864, "We are once more on our way to the battle-fields of Virginia. We go to meet Grant and his legions in fine spirits. Through the goodness of God we expect to whip him and bring peace to our country."[64] Even though the Confederacy was frequently losing both battles and territory to the Union army, Crockett believed that God would bring victory to the Southern cause. Similarly, Bryan Marsh of the 17th Texas Cavalry expressed his confidence in God's intervention: "Divine providence has spared us so far & I have faith to believe he will throo the war."[65]

If religion produced optimism in some men, it brought fatalistic thoughts to others. Fatalism, commonly confused with defeatism, is the belief that all the circumstances of one's life, including death, are in no way dependent on one's own actions. A belief in providence could easily shade into fatalism, in the form of a belief that God already has a plan for everyone and nothing can change it, no matter how a pious Christian may act or feel. With this sense of predestination, some soldiers felt that one place or position in combat was as dangerous as the next. In a letter to his wife, William P. Edwards of the 4th Texas Infantry wrote, "I do not feel much alarmed about going into battle for if it is the will of God I will not be hurt and to him alone do I look for help."[66] Fatalism grew out of Christian belief, at the time, that God was present, acted, spoke to humans, and was never idle.[67]

Another negative aspect of providence involved the feelings of defeatism that emerged in Confederate soldiers when they experienced losses in battle. Particularly upsetting were the defeats at Vicksburg, Tullahoma, and Gettysburg. The Southern troops began to think that God was no longer on their side. At the onset of the war, they won almost every battle, allowing Texans and other Confederates to assume that God was on their side. From then on, they attributed every victory and defeat to God's providence, even to the end of the war. Crockett recorded this belief in his diary in mid-May. "Thousands upon thousands of Yankees slain cover the battlefields," he wrote. "We have resisted Grant for eight days with great success, hurrah! Hurrah! For the Southern Confederacy. The Lord is with us and who shall be against us? Bless the Lord O! my soul."[68] When Confederates experienced the opposite, especially by 1863–65, their religious beliefs undermined the Confederacy. After the fall of Vicksburg and the Confederate defeat at Gettysburg, Maurice Kavanaugh Simons of the 2nd Texas Infantry expressed his feelings of defeatism in his journal: "I some times find my self ready to accuse the good Lord of having delt harshly with us. . . . Yet we are apt to think when arvy thing goes rong with us to think the lord had forgotten us. . . . Then we must continualy submit to the will of God. He can [bring] light out of darkness and out of confusion & Peace out of war. God grant that what seams to us a day to be a calamity may soon reveal its self to us as being a blessing sent from God."[69] Other Texans hoped to regain God's graces. Samuel S. Watson of the 1st Texas Infantry wrote of soldiers changing their behavior to please God so they could win the war: "There is quite a religious feeling in the Army. Prayer-meetings are held nightly, and great interest is manifested. One seldom hears an oath, or sees a game of cards. . . . For when the people quit their wickedness God will quit his scourge."[70] Throughout the war, Confederate soldiers sought to discover what role God played in their lives and the war. Their belief in providence inspired some men to continue to fight and led others to lose faith in their cause.

Religion also provided a way for soldiers to deal with breaking the biblical commandment "Thou shalt not kill." Men rationalized the concept of killing another human through religion, by making it a just war for the holy cause of liberty. Religion allowed men to kill each other under certain circumstances such as self-defense and in the heat of combat. It also allowed men to make a distinction between lawful combat and murder, allowing them, in their own minds, to justify killing the enemy. Soldiers struggled with the idea of killing another human, but religion influenced them to rationalize their predicament.[71]

The danger of combat and the prospect of death at any moment were constant concerns of the men. Soldiers in the Civil War wrote about many different aspects of army life and the weather, but another subject they devoted a significant amount of ink and paper to was death. Men turned to religion to seek salvation from death, more for hope than certainty, and recorded these feelings in letters and diaries. Crockett recorded comments common to many soldiers, such as "Death is in the wind" and "I had a singular dream, one of Death, is it an omen?"[72] Others felt that they had cheated death and it was only a matter of time before they died. In a letter to his mother, John Mark Smither recorded his belief that his time had come to an end: "I felt so utterly unworthy after being carried safe through the perils of so many battles when friend after friend was shot down at my side. It maybe that I am destined to be killed in the next fight but if my life is a drop in the bucket towards restoring liberty and peace to our Confederacy I could not devote it to a better cause."[73] Though death was a serious subject to the men, they sometimes employed humor to mask their fears.

E. P. Petty joked about death with his sweetheart back home while displaying his disdain for Arkansas: "I didn't come to Arkansas to die—I think that God would never resurrect me here."[74]

With thoughts of death in soldiers' heads, the men turned to religion for reassurance that their souls would continue in another world. Belief in the afterlife allowed the men to cope with their possible death and the loss of their friends and loved ones, because God would reunite them in heaven. William P. Edwards wrote to his wife that "if I am killed I hope that I will be taken to a land of rest where war, sorrow, and trouble never come. I feel that I can Put my trust in my God, and if he will be pleased to spare me."[75] Wesley M. Barnes of the 31st Texas Cavalry wrote to reassure his wife about the afterlife after the death of his friend, Thomas L. Anderson, of his regiment. In an almost poetic manner Barnes wrote, "We do not die. The soul, the immortal part, and the body, the mortal part, simply separates and the body returns to its mother—Earth and the soul returns to God to whom it belongs. Another happy thought, in heaven there is no war, there is no sickness nor death but all peace and all life. There the wicked cease to trouble and the weary are at rest."[76] Similar to Anderson's letter are some journal entries of Dewitt Clinton Giddings, lieutenant colonel of the 21st Texas Cavalry. Giddings's wife had died at the beginning of the Civil War. Grieving her loss on the year anniversary of her death, he recorded his feelings that "if she cannot come to me I must go to her the Lord knows when but I hope to meet in that better wourld whear parting will be no more."[77] Sometimes soldiers did not direct their reference to meeting loved ones in heaven to a single individual but to groups of people. Samuel S. Watson of the 1st Texas Infantry, a regiment in Hood's Texas Brigade that suffered some of the highest mortality rates in the Confederate army, wrote, "I hope to meet all my friends in that upper and better world."[78] Belief that they would meet their friends and family members in heaven eased the fear of death and allowed the men to cope with the grief of losing a loved one.[79]

Religious activities also allowed soldiers to endure the circumstances surrounding warfare. The Sabbath and prayer provided outlets for the soldiers to reassure themselves before battle, and participation in these activities reminded them of their lives in Texas before the war. Soldiers wanted to participate in worship on Sundays, but when that day was not honored it discouraged the men. James C. Bates recorded in his diary his constant desire to worship on the Sabbath and his disappointment whenever he could not. On September 29, 1861, Bates wrote, "Sunday again, my second Sunday in camp. As our Chaplain is sick we have no preaching today—after reading a while in my Bible concluded to attend preaching about a mile and a half from here—went & found a goodly number of soldiers from the different companies in attendance—after waiting two hours we were told that the preachers were sick."[80] His early responses were disappointment to the cancelation or absence of worship services on the Sabbath, but they changed to disgust as the war progressed. Bates later wrote to his mother, "You would hardly think that we knew this was a Sunday, if you were in camp a short time. All are as busily engaged at work as on any other day." His disgust soon turned to rage: "Sunday morning yet we are again on the march—I wonder if the Sabbath is as little respected by the northern as the southern army." When Bates finally worshipped on the Sabbath, it reminded him of his home and life before the war: "Sunday again—a beautiful bright sunny—sabbath this has been & always on such a Sabbath I do long to be at home with the loved ones—at Sunday school to see the bright shining faces there, & at church to see the faces there."[81] Worship on the Sabbath was just one activity that allowed Texans to cope with a soldier's life.

Prayer from home and by the soldiers boosted the morale of the men. Soldiers knew that their families and communities back home prayed for their safety and for victory on the battlefield. State governments organized days of thanksgiving and prayer. On January 14, 1863, "Governor Lubbock . . . issued a proclamation appointing the 4th *DAY OF FEBRUARY NEXT*, as a day of thanksgiving to Almighty God for his mercies and deliverances already vouched safe, with prayers, for their continuances to us and our children."[82] Local churches also helped boost the morale of the soldiers. The Little River Association of the Baptist Churches in Texas "resolved, that we affectionately ask the Churches belonging to this association to spend one hour on the Sabbath morning, of each of their regular meetings, in prayer and thanksgiving to Almighty God, for having given our brave soldiers so many signal victories on the Battle Field, and His special blessings for our ultimate success in the defense of our liberties, our religion and our country."[83] News of these acts of prayer and thanksgiving reached the soldiers through newspapers and letters from their families and communities.

Another way prayer helped the soldiers was through their personal communication with God. Before battles many men prayed for success, such as a soldier from Hood's Texas Brigade who wrote, "It seems to me that [McClellan] trusted in his powerful army for success. He had the best drilled men, the best arms the ingenuity of man could invent . . . drilled cannons & . . . even steel breast plates. Just think of his weak & feeble thrust in comparison to God's powerful arm of assistance. So I pray to God for success. I thank God for health and look to him for strength—turn me from God and I am a miserable wreck."[84] Another Texan, Jesse P. Bates of the 9th Texas Infantry, wrote to his wife, "Our god tells us if we pray for anything believing that we would receive it, we should have it."[85] Like the Sabbath, prayer reminded men of home and their families. A prayer James C. Bates heard provoked memories of home. He wrote in his diary that "after forming on prairie—a prayer was offered by [regimental chaplain] Rev

[T. A.] McIsh—eloquent fervor & full of faith in the justness of our cause. As it was the first prayer I had heard since I left home—many scenes & memories of bygone times revived."[86]

Soldiers prayed not only for themselves but for their families, friends, and communities. Throughout the war, while the soldiers were far from home, they prayed for the safety of those back home. J. C. Morriss of the 21st Texas Cavalry expressed his concern when he wrote, "I have my little family under His protection who never forsakes His trust."[87] Similarly, William Randolph Howell wrote, "I feel that the God of battles will protect you at home and me wherever I be."[88] Prayer for the protection of their families helped relieve the stress of the soldiers as they fought far from home.

In some cases the soldier off fighting in the war had to ease the burdens of family members back home who had lost a loved one to the war—reassuring them of God's support. In October 1863, Henry V. Smith of the 25th Texas Cavalry wrote home to console his sister over the death of her husband: "Trust on, it is all for the best and rest assured that whether we are able to see it or not, all was done by his kind mercy, and never fail to implore, constantly a throne of Grace, for His guidance and protection. He will be a husband to the Widow and a father to the orphan. Persevere and bring your responsible charge in the fear and admonition of the Lord. This is the great duty of life before you."[89] In the same letter, Smith demonstrated the role religion played in motivating men to fight by justifying their actions and, in most instances, helping maintain their morale throughout the war: "These are some of the greatest trials we are called upon to endure in this life, and lifes greatest mission to bear them all with Christian patience and resignation, trusting in the supreme wisdom and goodness of God—He will make all our afflictions less burdensome—and will temper all our trials and misfortunes so as to make them bearable. All we have to do, and must do is to trust Him and pray for a sufficiency of grace to enable us to understand and appreciate the mysterious ways of his mercy & goodness."[90] Throughout the entire war religion provided significant motivation for Texans by justifying killing and providing protection, answers to death, and the reassurance of prayer.

Another condition the Lone Star State shared with the rest of the South was the presence of a unionist minority. Because of their origins, a significant number of northeast Texans, Germans on the frontier, and to an extent Tejanos in the Rio Grande Valley were unionists. Northeast Texas contained a high percentage of settlers from free states and the upper South. Many of the Northerners were recent migrants, arriving in Texas in the 1850s, which did not give them enough time to assimilate Southern culture. Northern migrants in Texas, especially those from the border states, tended to follow Whig ideology, which stressed reverence toward the Constitution and the sanctity of the Union and

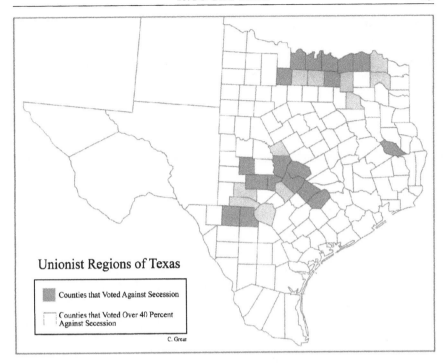

Unionist Regions of Texas

Counties that Voted Against Secession

Counties that Voted Over 40 Percent
Against Secession

C. Grear

obligation to preserve it. The isolation of North Texas and the frontier from East Texas, where Southern culture had its strongest roots in the Lone Star State, allowed these people to maintain their beliefs.

Additionally, the economic system of North Texas centered on raising corn and wheat—not cotton—creating little need for slaves on their farms. Many of these staple crop farmers saw the creation of the Confederacy as a direct threat to their way of life. Robert H. Taylor expressed his feelings in the McKinney *Messenger* on March 1, 1861: "In this new Cotton Confederacy what will become of my section, the wheat growers and stock raisers?"[91] People in North Texas and the German frontier remained isolated from the rest of Texas in the years before the war, and their ideology and low number of slaves influenced them to vote against secession and try to remain neutral in a state at war. Similar to these groups in their opposition to secession were Tejanos, who were commonly mistaken for unionists. Tejano opposition to secession and the Confederacy stemmed not from unionist ideology but from anti-Texas sentiments that remained from their mistreatment by Anglos during the Republic era.[92]

As the war progressed, unionists found it harder to avoid service in the Confederate army. Rev. Peter W. Gravis recorded the problems unionists had in remaining neutral in the war: "The year 1862 brought to the country circumstances of the most alarming character. . . . It became necessary for a man to either join the Confederate army or, if he was for the Union, to leave the state, or be ambushed or hung as an enemy of the South."[93] To avoid the pressures of conscription, some unionists joined the Union army, obtained positions in the U.S. government, or hid in their homes or the thickets of northeast Texas. Other unionists served the South because they felt that their beliefs were not important enough to risk losing their lives or homes to Confederate retaliation.[94]

James Lemuel Clark was a North Texan unionist. He had moved from Missouri to Gainesville, Texas, right before the war. He did not want to fight for the Confederacy, so to avoid service and save face in Texas he joined a state unit full of recent migrants from Missouri to fight Indians. When his unit received orders transferring them to Confederate service, Clark devised a plan to go back to Missouri to join state troops there and then desert and live with his mother's extended family. Once he arrived in Missouri, he decided not to desert because of the stigma of shame his family would have to endure. He decided instead to return to Texas. Wanting to stay in Gainesville, Clark signed up in a frontier unit but served only a short time before deserting again because the men in the unit did not trust him. For protection from the Confederates, he joined a unionist group and finally escaped Texas to Union-occupied Fort Gibson, where he joined the Union army as a scout. Life as a unionist in Texas was not pleasant, and as the war progressed so did their harsh treatment.[95]

In 1862 a large group of unionists began to form a peace party in North Texas as a response to the passage of the Conscription Act, which forced young men into the Confederate army. Most unionist activities took place in Cooke County and the surrounding area, where the party planned to raid local arsenals and promote a general uprising. When local Confederate sympathizers and officials uncovered these plans, they ordered Col. James G. Bourland and his state troops to arrest more than 150 people suspected of being involved in the plot. State troops escorted the prisoners to Gainesville, where the people of the city organized a "citizens court" overseen by Bourland and Col. William C. Young of the 11th Texas Cavalry at home on sick leave. The court found seven of the unionist leaders guilty of treason and immediately sentenced them to death. Before the disbandment of the court, the community lynched fourteen more and killed two who attempted to escape the panic. By time the bloodshed finally ended, forty-two people had lost their lives. Tales of these killings embarrassed the Confederacy about its mishandling of dissenters and fortified the Union's accusations of Southern barbarism. Remembered as the "Great Hanging of Gainesville," the event proved to be one of the greatest wartime atrocities suffered by American citizens in the history of the United States.[96]

Actions such as the Gainesville hangings made many unionists flee Texas to save their lives. Many did so, and many Mexican border towns, including

"The Great Hanging of Gainesville": This fanciful engraving was based on an account by Frederick Sumner. In fact, although the victims were all hanged from the same elm, they were executed singly or in pairs. Originally published in *Frank Leslie's Illustrated Weekly Newspaper,* February 20, 1864

Matamoros and Piedras Negras, along with interior cities such as Monterrey, filled up with Union sympathizers. Many other Texas refugees joined the Union army; 2,132 whites and 47 blacks fought for the Union in the 1st and 2nd Texas United States Cavalry.[97]

Two Texans, Edmund J. Davis and Andrew Jackson Hamilton, became brigadier generals in the Union army. Davis was born to Southern parents and lived in Florida until he moved with his family to Galveston in 1848. While living in Texas, he worked as a postal clerk, deputy customs officer, lawyer, district attorney, and judge of the Twelfth District Court. Initially he accepted Texas' decision to join the Confederacy but later criticized it, fearing it would create a huge public debt. In April 1861, Davis went to Washington, D.C., and successfully convinced Abraham Lincoln that he could rally unionists to retake Texas. With orders from Lincoln, Davis organized a regiment of Texas unionists who had fled to Mexico and New Orleans.

Hamilton was acting attorney general in Texas in 1849, and from 1851 to 1853 he served in the state House of Representatives for Travis County. During this time, he joined the "Opposition Clique," a political organization that opposed secession and the reopening of the African slave trade in Texas. In 1859,

Brig. Gen. Andrew Jackson Hamilton, Union military governor
of Texas and commander of the 2nd Texas Cavalry (Union).
Courtesy Library of Congress

Hamilton won election to the U.S. Congress. After the firing on Fort Sumter,
he returned to Texas to serve in the state Senate. By 1862, Texans were plotting
to murder the state senator because of his unionist sympathies and opposition
to secession. Fearing for his life, he fled to Mexico, where Washington, D.C.,
appointed him military governor of the Lone Star State. He rallied the support
of Germans and Mexican nationals to help form the 2nd Texas United States
Cavalry for the Union army. Late in the war Hamilton's Texas Cavalry invaded
South Texas and participated in the final battle of the Civil War, at Palmito

Ranch. Both Davis and Hamilton served terms as governor of Texas during Reconstruction. Similar to the rest of the South, Texas contained various sects of unionists within its borders.[98]

Other Texans from border states decided to return to their former homes to fight for the Union army. R. F. Bunting of Terry's Texas Rangers described this phenomenon when he discovered that "in the 1st Kentucky Federal cavalry —— Scott, who formerly lived in Texas on the Cibolo below Maj. Perryman's crossing, was Major, and the 4th Ohio regulars (cavalry) was commanded by Col. McIntyre, of Brenham, Texas. It was strange that Texans should thus meet each other face to face in deadly conflict."[99] Not all Texans were united in the cause of the Confederacy. Those with the strongest convictions took up arms against their state.

Southern nationalism was another similarity between Texas and the rest of the Confederacy. Early in the war, Texans believed that they belonged to a larger body, the Confederate States of America. Charles DeMorse, editor of the Clarksville *Northern Standard*, expressed this feeling in his column at the start of the war: "If the war comes, we have but to do our best to sustain the new Nationality; to sustain Southern credit for personal prowess and individual and aggregated chivalry."[100] Texans' feelings of Southern nationalism did not last long, though, because once they realized the hardships of war localism emerged. Texans did not forget who they were in the state before the war. Though two-thirds of the Texas population had recently migrated to the state, they inherited a strong sense of Texas nationalism when they arrived. Texas' history as a colony of American immigrants in the 1820s and 1830s, an independent republic, a state in the Union in 1845, and an independent again in the Civil War created a strong sense of localism and allowed people in the state to feel part of something unique. This inherited nationalism proved stronger than Southern nationalism.[101]

Accordingly, soldiers from the Lone Star State expressed a deep sense of Texas nationalism. Events such as the defense of the Alamo and the defeat of the Mexican army became important standards by which Texans measured themselves during the early antebellum period. Ben McCulloch used Texas nationalism, inspired by the Texas Revolution, to recruit soldiers to fight in Arkansas. In an advertisement in the *Navarro Express* he wrote, "Men of Texas, Look to Your Arms! Had we arms here, Arkansas could sustain herself! Texians! remember your former victories, and prepare to march to others. You won your independence from Mexico, and will again do it from a more tyrannical foe."[102] Paul O. Hébert, commander of the Department of Texas, used Texas nationalism to rally Texans against a Union invasion along the Texas coast. Hébert announced to the soldiers:

Look not to Richmond, there, for all your military inspiration and guidance. Remember the days of gone, when your own red right hands achieved your independence; and when some of your hardy sons are prepared to share in the glory to be soon in Virginia, Kentucky, and Missouri; and others guard the highway to the Pacific which they have won against superior arms and numbers; be it your portion of the duty which you owe to them and to yourselves to keep your soil free from the enemy's touch, and to preserve unsoiled the fame of the Texas Rangers.

Be ready at a moments notice to march, and wait for orders. Rely upon it, that I shall not fail to call you when needed; and when I call I know you will come I am to near to San Jacintos field, to doubt for a moment that, even against overwhelming numbers you will gladly rally to the defense of your homes, your families, and your blister's.[103]

The defense of the honor and reputation of the Lone Star State, established by their predecessors in the Texas Revolution and the Mexican-American War, motivated Texans in the Civil War to varying degrees. Tom Green, a popular Texas soldier who fought in all the state's major conflicts in the first three decades of its existence, wrote about how Texans behaved in times of need during the Republic era: "When a large portion of the country was menaced, volunteers were raised for short-term enlistment by official proclamations. . . . when the scene of hostilities were localized, a recognized leader of the community issued a call that none of his friends and neighbors could refuse."[104] Behavior such as this encouraged Texas nationalism because of the interdependence it created between Texans, especially by the beginning of the Civil War.

The effects of Texas nationalism were evident in the soldiers from the state. Victor M. Rose of the 3rd Texas Cavalry demonstrated the influence of the Lone Star on him when he wrote after the war, "To us, Texas was the 'nation'; to her alone we owed allegiance: we were *allied* with the other Southern States, not indissolubly *joined*."[105] Other soldiers wrote to their relatives back east about their new status as Texans. Josiah G. Duke of the 4th Texas Infantry wrote to his grandmother in Rutherford County, Tennessee, that he was "not boasting at all but I am glad that I can call myself a Texian for Texian soldiers never knew defeat that is the reputation we have and we intend to keep it."[106] Texas nationalism created a unique situation for soldiers from the Lone Star State; the sense of shared history provided an extra motivation for them to fight for their inherited state.

Texas nationalism also made Texas soldiers feel that they differed from their counterparts from other states. Texans felt that they stood apart, that they were tougher and more militant than the rest of the South. J. Sam Norvell expressed with an air of confidence that "there is a wide difference in the appearance of our troops and those from the 'States.' While we are dark and rough looking like we were prepared for almost anything the others are as fair and delicate as though they had never seen the sun in their lives."[107] Even though Texans boasted about their prowess, they did so because of state pride. Lawrence Sullivan Ross expressed his excitement that "Waco has done her duty in this War, and sent men who have bourne themselves bravely in Every Engagement, reflecting honor upon their Town & State, and sustained nobly, the reputation of the Texians."[108] John Mark Smither similarly boasted early in the war that "if we do get the chance with our fine Enfield rifles at them, we will show the 'Green Mountaineers' what the 'Lone Star Boy's can do for the honor of their state.' We may fall . . . but if we do, it will be where any man should be proud to die for their sunny home."[109] Later in the war, Smither wrote to his uncle, "I have fully done my duty in the cause of States Rights and for the honor of Texas."[110] Though Texans boasted about their differences with other states and expressed state pride, they were no different from men of any other state in this regard; it was common for men on both sides of the conflict to express pride in their regiment, state, and nation.[111]

Sources of pride and honor did not always originate from within units or states. It was also common for leaders to express pride in their soldiers to boost their morale. President Jefferson Davis lauded the Texas soldiers by associating them with famous members of a past army when he stated, "The troops from other states have their reputation to gain. The sons of the defenders of the Alamo have theirs to maintain."[112] By associating the Texas soldiers with the men who fought in the Alamo, Davis granted them membership in a prestigious group, which tended to boost morale in the soldiers because they themselves felt they were better soldiers. Other Southern leaders such as Gen. Robert E. Lee commented on the Texas soldiers to boost their pride. Lee once boasted about his Texas brigade, "Never mind the raggedness, the enemy never sees the backs of my Texans."[113] Even soldiers from other units commented on the martial abilities of Texans. While in Arkansas, William J. Whatley of Taylor's Regiment recorded the locals' remarks about Texans, including "They have a great deal more confidence in us than they have in their own troops."[114] On a darker note, when Texans marched through other states they were "respected as Texans, but it seems the people here have a different idea about Texans than they should." Capt. Robert Voight, a German immigrant to Texas noted, "They seem to think we are half-wild savages as long as they don't know us, but when we get to know them better, they sometimes even admire the fact that we can read and write."[115] Again, pride not only originated from the men and their state but also was the product of conscious actions by many people in leadership positions in various states who realized the influence of honor and pride on the effectiveness of the soldiers.

Reactions from the enemy demonstrate that the reputations of the rough and tumble Texans preceded them. When the men of the 17th Texas Cavalry fought Union soldiers for the first time in Arkansas, they soon learned how their enemy viewed them: "When the enemy first saw us, they thought we were 'Arkansawyers' and intended to fight them till the last, but when we raised the yell, their commander told them that 'they were the d-m Texans, to look out for themselves.'"[116] Even close encounters with the enemy produced unique responses. En route to Pleasant Hill, Louisiana, H. D. Pearce of the 16th Texas Cavalry came upon a wounded Union soldier. "When I went up to him he commenced to beg me not to kill him which vexed me to think that he had such a foolish idea about Texans; and replied, 'You fool! What would I want to kill you for? Don't you know any better than that?'"[117] The reputation of Texans was evident even after the fighting ended. John T. Stark of the 13th Texas Cavalry guarded Union prisoners who "are almost daily seen to have a wholesome dread of the Texians. some of them seem to think that we would murder them as fast as we could lay hand on them."[118] Reactions such as these reflected the pride Texans had in their martial abilities and directly influenced their motivation to fight—maintaining this hard-earned reputation of the men from the Lone Star State.

Besides state pride, the chance to fight alongside family members or friends encouraged a significant number of young Southern men, including Texans, to fight in the Civil War. Texans already had the desire to join the fray, but the opportunity to serve with their kin made it much more attractive. The men already knew each other and possessed strong bonds of trust and loyalty. Additionally, if they had a relative in a higher position it would increase their chances of obtaining a promotion to a higher rank. Texans tended to enlist together, like Drury Connally of Alf Johnson's Spy Company who had "four brother-in-laws in my mess"[119] or William Kuykendall who fought on the Texas frontier with the 1st Texas Cavalry with "four Kuykendalls on the Muster Rolls of the Company."[120] Men also recognized another advantage of having kin in their units: someone they could trust to care for them when they were injured or sick. In a letter discussing his two brothers' desire to join the Confederate army, Robert Ikard of the 19th Texas Cavalry wrote his father that "if they [the brothers] can't be together I want one or both with me, as we could be a great help to one another in sickness, for I see when a person is very sick & left if he has a brother along he is apt to be detailed to wait on him."[121] Fighting alongside kin not only encouraged Texans to join the army but gave the men a greater chance to survive the war, since they had somebody they could rely on to care for them if needed.[122]

Another similarity Texas shared with the rest of the South, and arguably one of the strongest influences on Texans' decision to fight, was the importance of defending the family. Southerners brought to Texas their ideas and strong feelings toward their kin. Familial ties in the South were arguably the strongest in North America and second only to the Highland Scots of the past. The Southern family was extremely strong during this time because of the lack of other strong institutions such as factories, public houses, fraternities, or theaters. Families in the North were important to their society, but because of urbanization and industrialization Northerners had other institutions to rely on and be influenced by. Instead of working in the fields with family members and relying on their extended relations during harvest season for additional help, Northerners relied solely on their immediate family and had other organizations, such as work and public houses, "pubs," to find support and solace. With the family being such a major influence on Texans, it proved to be a chief motivation for men in the state to join the Confederate army. Some Texans such as T. C. Mixson, who joined the 15th Texas Infantry, "never had any desire to be come a soldier had this been a war of mear conquest." The true motivation for Mixson to join the Confederate army was to defend "our homes, property, liberty our helpless Brothers and Sisters and our all."[123]

Southern families did not limit their bonds to their immediate family but retained strong ties to their extended family as well. Family hierarchy strengthened the ties of the immediate families to their extended members. In Southern families, both parents and grandparents held a tremendous authority over their children and grandchildren, even after they matured and had families of their own. Usually mothers and fathers expected other relatives to participate in the rearing of their children, further strengthening the familial bonds. The Southern family hierarchy developed because of its rural environment. In this atmosphere, the entire family did everything together, from working the fields and hunting to social events such as church services and parties. Everybody expected to be buried in the same place and, at the resurrection, anticipated seeing one another again. During the time they worked and played, the younger members of the family came to respect the older generation because of their skills and work ethic. From the elders' example, the younger generation realized that wisdom came from experience and learned to respect their parents' and grandparents' contributions to the family. Additionally, kinship groups had power and influence in their local region; they could rely on one another for financial support in times of growth or of need, and in the latter case they had emotional encouragement to persevere through their situation. This was evident throughout the Civil War when soldiers needed clothes and supplies the Confederate government or army could not provide. Lawson Jefferson Keener of the 2nd Texas Mounted Rifles observed, "The boys in much better health than I left them & in fine spirits but was very much in need of clothing, but the most of them have received their clothing from home at last with the exception of a few who have no one to make them."[124] Southern culture influenced Texans to believe that their prime duty was to help and protect their family members, both immediate and extended kin.[125]

There is also psychological justification for Southerners to defend their extended family members. According to Roy R. Grinker and John P. Speigel in their study on the psychological influences on men in combat, the motivation to fight in a war began

with the individual's past history and especially with his capacity to form identifications with other groups of people and to feel loyal to them. This process, as with any identification, is based on strong love and affection and begins very early in life. By identification is meant the feeling of belonging to, being a part of, or being the same as another person or group of people. The earliest identification made by an individual is with members of his family circle, and is at first confined to those that provide love and care, the parents, and especially the mother. Later the feeling of identity spreads to include both parents and then brothers and sisters and other members of the family. During childhood, the range of identification becomes constantly broader as the horizon of social contacts expands. Eventually, the school, then the community and finally the nation itself are included.[126]

Families are the first and the most important influence on how people identify themselves. It is only logical to think that family members will continue to be a very important part of a human's life. For Southerners, the ties were even stronger.

These bonds remained strong because Southern families tended to migrate and settle together. Kinship ties had a profound effect on Southern migration, which was almost exclusively westward. Close family ties, though very similar across the South, helped create one of the greatest differences between Texas and what became the Confederacy. Southerners moved to Texas from the old South for such reasons as soil depletion at home and the availability of cheap land in Texas—a place where sons who did not inherit the plantation could build their own fortunes, create for themselves and their families a better economic situation. Sometimes planters took over yeoman farmers' lands and forced them to go where land was cheap. When Southerners migrated and settled in Texas, they moved as a family unit because it increased their chances of success. They could rely on one another to help raise barns, rear their children, and provide assistance if someone was hurt or fell ill. They could even depend on one another for power, either economic through collective resources or political or physical because of their numbers. Kinship groups could even expand their influence and power through marriage to other groups. When a kinship group moved to a new region, usually a small group of the family chose to remain behind. In many cases the group that moved wrote back to the family members they left behind and in some cases attracted them to move to Texas.

Migration of these Southern families into Texas created a population boom. From 1850 to 1860, the Texas population increased 184 percent, from 212,592 to 604,215. Southern migrants tended to settle in lands that resembled the region they left because they already possessed the skills to farm that type of land and the proper tools to be successful. Consequently, people from one state would concentrate in a particular area of Texas. A pattern developed in which people from Tennessee settled in the black waxy prairie, Louisianans in the counties bordering the Gulf of Mexico, Georgians in the plantation districts in northeast Texas, Alabama in the inland counties east of the Tennesseans, Mississippians in western south-central Texas, and Kentuckians in North Texas. Within these regions families and friends settled together.[127]

While migrating from the South, travelers followed one of three routes—upper, middle, and lower. A tenth of the migrants followed the upper path, which originated in Virginia and North Carolina and traveled along the Ohio River and through Missouri. The middle route was the path for a third of the migrants. Originating in North Carolina, with some people from the bordering states, the path passed through Tennessee, Missouri, and Arkansas. This route provided most of the Tennesseans in Texas. Finally, there was the lower path, which originated in the Carolinas and passed through the states along the Southern gulf coast. The lower corridor was the dominant one, providing half of the migrants to Texas. These three routes allowed large numbers of Southerners and some Northerners to reach Texas.[128]

The migration of Southerners and foreigners to Texas in the decades before the Civil War dramatically altered the composition of the state's population, making it far different than the rest of the South. By 1860, the population of Texas had reached 604,215. Only a quarter of this number (153,043) could call Texas their birthplace, and a third (192,109) were Southern born. A very small fraction of Texans, less than 4 percent (21,712), came from the North, and a little over 7 percent (43,422) were foreign born. Of the foreign born, half were Germans, a quarter Mexicans, and a quarter Irish, French, English, and a mix of people from eastern Europe. One-third of the population (182,921) were slaves. No other state in the South had such a large number of migrants with very few natives within its borders.[129]

Since people from other parts of the United States had recently populated Texas, Texans identified almost as much with their former homes as with their new home. On the other hand, those who had lived in Texas the longest established a strong attachment to the state and the locality where they lived. How long a man had resided in Texas influenced his motivation to fight in the Civil War and, more important, where he wanted to fight. Migration had a direct impact on these decisions and created a special situation for Texas when the war started.[130]

Texas was similar to the South through its institutions and culture. Though these aspects of Southern life traveled a great distance to Texas, they remained intact because the majority of migrants to Texas came from the South. Southerners brought slaves, along with the fear of a slave revolt. Though the majority of Texans did not own a slave, nor have an opportunity to, they fought to keep the institution intact so they could maintain the social order of the South. In addition, they brought their culture of honor, which had a dramatic impact on their behavior. Honor motivated Texans to join the Confederate army to prove their manhood and kept the men in the army so they could maintain their honor. Religion dominated the lives of Texans and provided an outlet for stressful times and situations. It not only eased their minds about the safety of their loved ones back home but also alleviated the tension created by the prospect of death. The greatest attribute of Southern culture that remained very strong in Texans was the importance of family and extended kinship ties. Family was an important motivation for Texans to fight in the Civil War. Though Southerners brought these aspects to the state, other unique factors emerged from the history of Texas. Texas nationalism developed out of the Texas Revolution and a decade as an independent republic, and migration of families into the state in the decade before the war made Texas a mixture of people with multiple local attachments.

3

---∽∽∽---

DEFENSE OF THE
LONE STAR STATE
Why Texans Fought in the Trans-Mississippi

Texas, the home of my mother, the pride of my father, the guardian of my
sister and the home of my boyhood, God direct in the right, but right or
wrong, I fought for Texas and could see no honorable course for Texas men
but to stake their lives, their liberty, their all for Texas.

A. W. SPARKS, 9TH TEXAS CAVALRY

SINCE Texans lived in the westernmost state in the Confederacy, they had
many more options as to where they could serve than other Southern soldiers. Most Texans decided to fight in the trans-Mississippi—especially
Louisiana, Arkansas, Missouri, Indian Territory, Texas, Arizona, and New
Mexico. Compared to the Lone Star soldiers who rushed to serve in the East,
those wanting to stay west of the river were different in many respects. Generally, they had a stronger attachment to Texas because they either had lived in
the state longer or did not have as strong a connection to other locations. These
factors influenced Texans to enlist in Confederate units that would assure them
that they would stay and defend the borders of Texas, which included the land
north of the Red River, the coastline, the frontier, and the Southwest.

During the Civil War, the significance of events west of the Mississippi River
seemed to Col. William H. Parsons "small indeed by comparison with the more
imposing and dramatic events of the far east but momentous in results to the
fortunes of [the] Trans-Mississippi department, and especially to the fate of
Texas."[1] The importance of the Trans-Mississippi was not lost on any Texan,
even those who decided to go to the main theaters of the war east of Old Man
River. John W. Stevens, a soldier in Hood's Texas Brigade, noted in his reminis-

41

cences that "some [Texans] were not willing to go to Virginia to fight, but if any of Lincoln's Yankees put his foot on Texas soil they'd jes' show them what cold steel was made for."[2] There was no honor lost for the Texans who decided to remain behind and fight in the Trans-Mississippi theater to defend the people and places in Texas they held dear.

Throughout the war, many recruiters raised companies in Texas. In almost every case, the men knew which theater and often exactly where their unit would fight. Recruiters were smart enough to state in their advertisements for men where they planned to take them. Col. Edward Waller of the 13th Texas Cavalry Battalion advertised in the Houston *Tri-Weekly Telegraph* that he had "a call in today's for a regiment of Texas Rangers for the war, to serve under Van Dorn in Missouri."[3] Other recruiters advertised together, such as this advertisement in the Dallas *Herald:* "Gen. J. H. Rogers of Jefferson, who has just returned from Richmond has been commissioned to raise a regiment of infantry for service in Missouri. Mr. W. P. Crump has been commissioned to raise a battalion of mounted men for the same field of operations."[4] Some units even incorporated into their names the places they wanted to serve. The 3rd Texas Cavalry dubbed themselves the "South Kansas-Texas Regiment" because they wanted to campaign on the Kansas-Missouri border.[5] Since Texans knew where most units would fight, they joined the particular outfit that would guarantee them the opportunity to defend the locality they treasured most.

The Texans who enlisted in units raised to fight in the trans-Mississippi enlisted to defend the Lone Star State. To them such duty appeared more desirable than service in the East because they had especially strong connections to Texas. In other words, the locality they identified with the most was Texas. Many of these men, though born in other places, spent their childhood in Texas or lived in the state longer than the men who fought in other theaters. During this time the native and newly arrived migrants established businesses, families, and connections to their communities, creating a strong attachment to their current homes. Since their connection was strongest with Texas, their top priority was the safety of their state.

Texan soldiers' attachment to the Lone Star State can be measured by how long they lived in the state. The *Texas Confederate Home Roster* provides detailed histories, including origins, of Southern men and women who visited Confederate Homes in Texas for medical care. The average amount of time men serving in trans-Mississippi units resided in Texas was thirteen years before the start of the Civil War. Conversely, east of the Mississippi River men in both Terry's Texas Rangers and Hood's Texas Brigade on average spent only nine and a half years in Texas. Additionally, 21.4 percent of the men who enlisted in trans-Mississippi units were born in Texas. If you include the 13.4 percent who moved to Texas with their families when five years old or younger, this increases the percentage of those who would consider Texas their native state to 34.8 percent. This is even more significant when compared to the overall population of Texas in 1860, when just over a quarter of the population in the state, including women and children, were native to Texas. Compared to Terry's Texas Rangers (22.4 percent, including those who arrived at age five or younger) and Hood's Texas Brigade (20.2 percent), both under the average of the native population, there is a significant difference in the connection the men had to the Lone Star State.[6]

Texans were even particular about who they wanted to fight. Jesse P. Bates and the other men of the 9th Texas Infantry were upset they did not fight against Union soldiers in the first year of the war; instead, they fought Indians in the northeast and north-central part of the state. When the men received orders to march to Arkansas, they expressed jubilation because they no longer were fighting Native Americans but defending their homes in East Texas from the real enemy, Yankees. Other Texas units such as Polignac's Texas Brigade saw their morale soar when they too received orders to defend Texas instead of Indian Territory.[7]

Though prospects of Texans fighting in a major battle were less in the Trans-Mississippi theater than if they enlisted for service in the East, in many cases their desire to protect their hometowns outweighed their desire for martial glory. Most Texans with a strong attachment to the state feared invasion from the north, the west, and the coast. Some units, such as the 3rd Texas Cavalry, initially formed because of their fear that Kansas Jayhawkers would ride south to attack northern Texas.[8]

Texas soldiers shared many qualities and motivations to fight for the Confederacy. The most important difference between the men was where they wanted to fight. Though they chose different places, they had the same motivation to fight there—a connection to the location. Robert Cannon Horn of the 5th Texas Partisan Rangers was born in Wilson County, Tennessee, before he moved with his entire family, including his grandfather, cousins, and an old neighbor, to McKinney, Texas, in 1858, at the age of fourteen. Every person who had had a significant relationship with Horn lived in Texas, giving his adopted state the highest priority.[9]

Similarly, Newton Asbury Keen of the 6th Texas Cavalry, born in Harrison County, Illinois, moved to Texas in 1846 while a baby. Though not born in Texas, Keen had live there for fifteen years and came to see it as the only location he had an affection for. When the war started, the only locality Keen wanted to protect was Texas, and he enlisted in a regiment that promised him it would protect Texas by engaging the enemy in Missouri. Keen was not alone in his motivations. David Carey Nance, born in Cass County, Illinois, in 1843, moved to Cedar Hill, Texas, in 1852 at nine years old. Raised in Texas thereafter, he developed a strong loyalty to the state and gained many friends. Only eighteen when the war began, Nance's boyhood friend William T. "Little Will" Stuart convinced him and their friend "Lonesome John" M. Sullivan to join the 4th Texas Lancers, later officially called the 12th Texas Cavalry, for service in Arkansas.[10]

Many Texans had similar backgrounds, but one of the most striking examples is to be found in the story of the four Orr brothers, Henry, James, Robert, and Lafayette. They moved to Texas with their parents in 1854, the oldest being eighteen at the time and the youngest eleven. Since three of the four brothers were very young when they moved to Texas, they formed a strong attachment to the state. The oldest, Henry, had strong bonds with his brothers, so they all initially enlisted in the Ellis County Rangers, which eventually joined the 12th Texas Cavalry, to monitor Union troop movements in eastern Arkansas. One brother got sick, was left behind, and joined Churchill's Brigade to fight in Arkansas. All four joined outfits organized for the direct protection of their adopted state of Texas. From the beginning of the war, Henry stated that his main concern was the defense of Texas, which he called "the land of my friends, the seat of my affections."[11]

Henry's love and desire to defend Texas continued to be a major motivation for him throughout the war. Even after the initial shock of combat, he wrote from Searcy, Arkansas, "Oh! shall the foul foot of the invader even trace the soil of Texas and bring distress upon its people like they have here! God forbid that they may. I wish I were on its soil today to give my life if necessary for its defense."[12] In June 1864, Orr did not want to leave the trans-Mississippi and wrote to his sister from Alexandria, Louisiana, "I think our brigade is destined for some distant field, but where to I have but little idea. I hope we may go to north Louisiana or Arkansas, or to Texas."[13] As the war progressed, Henry's desire to protect Texas grew stronger. In the closing months of the war he wrote, "I must say that our late life in our own loved adopted state has been as pleasant as could be expected. How long we may continue in quiet is a question beyond my solution; may be for a good while. But it may be that the same may soon be broken by the advance of a brutal foe, and if such is the case, it will behoove us as soldiers in defense of *our state* and our Confederacy and as freemen struggling for independence to confront and if possible defend our country from every attempt of invasion, devastation, and ruin, which matter of course we may expect if the former is successful."[14] Texans whose strongest affection was Texas tended to want to stay and defend it directly.

In some cases Texans had connections to locations outside of Texas but within the trans-Mississippi. One soldier was Hartwell Bolin Cox of the 19th Texas Cavalry, who while in Little Rock, Arkansas, "saw some of our old neighbors and allso relation that belonged to another reg."[15] Similarly, Drury Connally, a soldier in Alf Johnson's Spy Company, fought in the state of his birth,

Arkansas. His departure from his home concerned his wife because she felt vulnerable with him away. Connally assured her: "You are now in the safest place in the Confederacy, for there is but little for them to go there after and it is too far from navigation."[16] Since he felt his home and family were safe in Texas, he would go to Arkansas to defend the kin who remained behind.

While in Arkansas, Connally discovered that Union soldiers had overrun his family's farm, which instilled a stronger resolve to fight in the Confederate army. In a letter to his wife he described his feelings: "I felt like I could meet them [Union soldiers] on any part of the ground. I felt like I had something more to fight for. When my sister and little nieces would hover around me and tell me how the villains had treated them, don't you know I am willing to stay and help to protect them. Yes, if it is God's will to take me off, let me be found between the enemy and my friends and relatives. My home and family is the most of my thoughts, but here is the place that I can best serve them now. Knowing what I do now, it would be no pleasure to be at home and my country liable to be over run, my children turned out to suffer for bread."[17] Connally vowed to defend not only his home and family in Arkansas but also his loved ones in Texas, by fighting the enemy in his former state. Similarly, Gus and George Creed, brothers from Missouri, enlisted in the 9th Texas Cavalry to protect their old hometown. They enlisted with their former neighbor, Ruben Rogers. Once in Missouri, the men followed the same pattern as Connally. They immediately sought out all the friends and relatives they had left behind when they moved to Texas.[18]

Attachments to Texas and an individual's community were not limited to the common soldiers; they extended even to the officers. Officers differed from enlisted men in generally being older and having more responsibilities in their lives, such as careers, businesses, and families. These made for stronger ties to Texas. Thus, they were protecting not only their hometowns but also their economic interests. Business was only one of several factors producing men loyal to Texas, but it was an effective one. Col. Trezevant C. Hawpe was one such man. A Dallas businessman and former city and county official, Hawpe raised the 31st Texas Cavalry in the Dallas area for the direct defense of Texas. He advertised in the Dallas *Herald* to raise a unit for the specific purpose of defending Texas. His advertisement put the matter plainly: "Who will defend Texas, Texans & Texans Alone."[19]

Another with commercial interests in Texas was Robert H. Taylor from Bonham. Taylor was a prominent lawyer and former member of the Texas legislature. He had lived in Texas for over a decade, having fought with John Coffee "Jack" Hayes in the Mexican-American War. A combination of living in Texas for an extended period and fighting to protect its borders created a strong connection with the state that influenced where he wanted to fight in the Civil War. In the winter of 1861/62, Taylor recruited the 22nd Texas Cavalry for twelve-month service to defend the northern Texas border by fighting between the Red River and Kansas.[20]

Additional officers whose strong connection to Texas influenced their decision to defend their state were James C. Bates and William Henry Parsons. Though born in Tennessee, Bates moved to Texas as a boy in May 1837. He spent most of his teenage years in Henderson, Texas, but moved back to Tennessee in the early 1850s to attend Bethel College. In 1856 he returned to Texas, where he lived in Paris until the start of the war. When the war started, he and many other men from his area answered the call of a recruiting circular that stated, "Said battalion, when organized will form a part of an army now being raised in Northern Texas for the defense of her Northern line, and to aid our friends upon the Missouri border."[21] Bates's initial desire was to join a unit that promised he could defend Texas.

Parsons had a similar background. Born in New Jersey in 1826, he moved to Montgomery, Alabama, as a child and remained there until he decided to fight in the Mexican-American War on the Texas front. After the war, he remained in Texas and married in 1851. Though Parsons still had a connection to Alabama, his love for Texas grew the longer he lived there, as he gained connections through marriage and friendship. Parsons's attachment to Texas is evident through the decisions he made after he raised the 12th Texas Cavalry. He was able to get orders to take his command to either Kansas or Kentucky. His loyalty to Texas made his decision easy; he wanted to defend Texas directly, and the only choice that gave him that opportunity was to fight in Kansas. Later in the war, Gen. Pierre Gustave Toutant Beauregard ordered Parsons to remain west of the Mississippi River because of the Union threat to Arkansas. Beauregard's orders pleased not only Parsons but also the men of his regiment, because they would fight in a place where they could stand directly between the foe and Texas.[22]

Among Parsons's men, Charles Morgan stood out as an oddity. Early in the war, Morgan, born in the Texas during the Republic era, received an officer's commission in Terry's Texas Rangers. He went east to fight because he was a young man of twenty-one and sought honor and glory in what most men thought would be a very short war. Once he realized that the war would not be over in a matter of weeks, he resigned his commission in December 1861 to return and defend Texas. He spent the remainder of his military career serving under Parsons, most of it fighting in Arkansas.[23]

Even some of the more prominent Texas officers, such as Lawrence Sullivan "Sul" Ross, the famed Texas Ranger who rescued Cynthia Ann Parker, and Ben McCulloch, felt the influence of their local attachment to Texas. Ross, born in Bentonsport, Iowa, in September 1838, moved to Texas with his family when he was one year old. By 1849 he was calling Waco his permanent home and

Texas his native state. His already strong attachment to the state grew in the first months of the war when in May 1861 he married Elizabeth Dorothy Tinsley from Waco. With these strong connections to Texas, Ross decided to join the 6th Texas Cavalry to fight under Ben McCulloch in Missouri. Ross wanted to keep the Jay-hawkers so busy "defending their own homes for the next six weeks, that they will not find time to plunder others."[24] In other words, he wanted to keep the enemy too busy defending their homes to have any opportunity to attack in Texas.

The man under whom Ross served, McCulloch, had a similar story. Being an influential Texan before the war, Mc-Culloch initially wanted to lead a Texas regiment to fight in Virginia for glory. When the Confederate government re-fused his request and he realized that the war would not be short, he wanted to

Brig. Gen. Benjamin McCulloch, commander of Indian Territory. Courtesy Library of Congress

command soldiers only in direct defense of Texas. McCulloch received what he desired when President Davis placed him in charge of "the district embracing the Indian Territory lying west of Arkansas and South of Kansas."[25] Davis's assignment to McCulloch was exactly what the Texan wanted because of his desire to defend the state from a northern invasion. As was the case with Ross, the length of time McCulloch lived in Texas directly influenced his connection to Texas and thus his decision of where he wanted to fight.[26]

Some Texans' attachment to locality was not merely to Texas generally but to a specific part of the state. Recruiters used this factor in their advertisements to raise units. In the Houston *Tri-Weekly Telegraph*, a recruiter advertised, "Companies Wanted Immediately, For a Confederate Regiment—A Regiment of Infantry to serve twelve months . . . in the defense of Galveston and the coast."[27] Calls for service on the coast were even made in Dallas, where an ad read, "Another Regiment—We learn that T[homas] C. Bass, of Sherman [Texas], has been authorized to raise a regiment of Infantry, for the coast service."[28] Texans knew which company to join if they wanted to defend the Texas coast.

Men across Texas had a strong desire to serve on the coast. Dr. John Claver Brightman from Fort Bend County expressed his intent in a letter to his mother: "I do not intend to go anywhere to fight unless the coast is invaded." Brightman's desire to fight only on the Texas coast came from his attachment to Galveston. Born in Floyd County, Indiana, in May 1819, he moved to Galveston in 1843. He joined the 35th Texas Cavalry, also known as Brown's Regiment, to defend the only area of Texas he had a strong connection to, his hometown of Galveston.[29]

Other men who wanted to defend the Texas coast had similar backgrounds. Andrew Neill and Robert W. "Dick" Dowling were both born outside of North America, and their only attachment on the continent was to the Texas coast. Neill was born in Scotland and moved to the United States as a young man, where he studied law in Virginia, practiced law in Mississippi, and finally settled down in Guadalupe County, Texas, in 1836. The Scotsman led an interesting life in the Lone Star State before the war. In 1842 a Mexican force under the command of Gen. Adrián Woll invaded San Antonio, capturing Neill and imprisoning him in Mexico City. He escaped his Mexican captors and later became a prominent figure in the state, serving as grand master of the Masonic Grand Lodge of Texas and nearly gaining the Democratic nomination as a candidate for lieutenant governor. During the war Neill resisted joining the Confederate army until it appeared that there would be a coastal invasion of Galveston, thus threatening his home and family. This threat compelled him to enlist in the 1st Texas Partisan Rangers, a unit that would defend his trans-Mississippi home region and the Texas coast.[30]

Lt. Richard "Dick" Dowling, Confederate commander of the Davis Guards at the Battle of Sabine Pass. Courtesy Louisiana and Lower Mississippi River Valley Collections, LSU Libraries, Baton Rouge, La.

The more famous Dowling was an immigrant to Texas who likewise wanted to defend the coast. Born in County Galway, Ireland, Dowling moved to Texas when he was twelve and settled in Houston in the early 1850s. Once there, he established strong connections to the city when he married a local girl and opened a saloon. Some of his relatives from Ireland also settled in the city on Buffalo Bayou. Before the war, Dowling served in the Houston Light Artillery, and in 1860 he helped organize the Davis Guards with the help of his in-laws and relatives. Dowling and the Davis Guards joined the Confederate army to defend the Texas coast, more specifically the port cities of Houston and Galveston. Their actions in the Battle of Sabine Pass immortalized these Texans because they defended the small pass between Texas and Louisiana from a large Union naval flotilla with only six cannons positioned on an earthen fortification. Jefferson Davis memorialized the battle after the war when he called it the Thermopylae of the Civil War. The Texas coast was the only place in the United States that Neill and Dowling identified with, which influenced them to defend that specific location during the Civil War.[31]

Some men, like Noah B. Cox of the 35th Texas (Brown's) Cavalry, who eventually received orders to defend Louisiana, wanted to fight in another unit near their homes. On hearing that John "R.I.P." Ford had launched a campaign to push Union soldiers out of the Rio Grande Valley, Cox wrote Capt. R. W. Hargrove, "I would respectfully ask to be exchanged from your company, to company, Col Ford's command—for the reason that my home is on the Rio Grande and I have a large number of Beef Cattle there and no one to take care of them and I wish to save as many of them as I can and turn them over to the Commissary Dept there, and thus not lose them entirely as I will if I have to remain here."[32] Cox wanted to be near his home to protect as well as assure that his ranch would not fall into neglect. Fighting in a unit destined for that region was his only desire that late in the war.

Most of the time, the men who enlisted in units to defend Texas were able to stay in the region they desired. In other cases, Texans received orders to fight east of the Mississippi River after they organized. Though it would seem that all the soldiers would object, only a few did. Most Texans did not complain about their transfer, because after the initial months passed they realized that there was no immediate threat to Texas. Those who had the strongest attachments to Texas became demoralized and sought ways to get back across the river. The rest of the Texans marched to other regions of the South, though they confessed in their letters and actions the specific regions they desired to serve near their old hometowns and areas where their relatives lived.

Early in the war, some men in the 10th Texas Cavalry and the 2nd Texas Infantry wanted to serve on the Texas coast, where they felt there was an imminent threat. Their hopes of defending the shore ended abruptly when they received orders to serve east of the Mississippi River. Initially they made no protests, but some had major reservations. The Texans followed their orders because they felt that doing so was their duty and that their assignment would be temporary since, in their minds, the war would not last long.[33]

Men in the 10th Texas Cavalry enlisted under the promise of serving on the Texas coast. Just after they were sworn into the Confederate army, their first orders came as no surprise. An "Order come this evening," wrote John Allen Templeton on October 11, 1861, "that we are to go to the coast."[34] After receiving this order, the men assumed that they would stay in Texas, but they understood wrong. Months later, in February 1862, to their dismay they received orders to march to Little Rock, Arkansas, and soon thereafter joined Beauregard's army in Mississippi. Some men in the 10th deserted or received transfers out of the unit and never left Texas, but most followed their orders to march to Mississippi — not without some protest and complaints.[35]

Almost immediately after their arrival on the far bank of the Mississippi River, some of the men — especially those who had lived most of their lives in Texas — wrote home complaining of their orders. For example, John Allen Templeton, whose family moved from North Carolina to Texas when he was two, wrote in a letter to his father, "I think I will be home In the course of a few months as I am exempt from military duty according to the new military law [Conscription Act], and I am not going to volunteer so far from home when there will be need for men on the frontier of Texas and on the coast. I have not found out at what time I will get off but be assured that it will be at the earliest period for there is no telling at what moment the enemy will be spoiling Texas; & if they should get there I want to be close by."[36]

Templeton was not the only Texan in the 10th who wanted to leave. Almost a year later his "Cousin Frank [said] he is going to work for a transfer or his Father is going to rather and wants me to get one and to go with him. He intends going to the coast of Texas and get into artillery service. I would be glad to make such an exchange if I could just get on Texas soil if nothing else."[37] John continued to pursue his desire to return to Texas, because according to him, "Nothing would please me better than to get a swap to Johnson's Co. so then I would be where I want to be."[38] Even though he wanted to leave the regiment to return to Texas, he rationalized his stay east of the Mississippi: "I had rather meet them here than in Texas as this country is already ruined."[39] Like other motivations, his willingness to fight outside of Texas against his wishes lasted a short time.

Another Texas regiment raised to fight in the Lone Star State was the 2nd Texas Infantry. The primary desire of the men in this regiment, dubbed the "Galveston Regiment," was to defend the Texas coast. Their connection to the coast is evident in the backgrounds of the men who composed the regiment. Dr. Ashbel Smith came to Texas from Hartford, Connecticut, to fight in the Texas Revolution. During the Republic era, Smith served as surgeon general of the Texas army. Though an abolitionist and still strongly connected to his former state of Connecticut, he organized Company C, better known as the "Bayland Guards," when the Civil War began specifically for the defense of the Texas coast. Smith had a strong desire to protect his home, the most vulnerable area of Texas, from the Union navy. Born in Connecticut, he did not have any affinity to the rest of the South, just to his adopted state.[40]

Another member of the 2nd Texas with a similar background was J. Henry Cravey, who moved to the Lone Star State with his family from Georgia at the age of five, too young to remember his old hometown. He too had no local interest in the war other than protecting Texas itself. An interesting Texan in the regiment was Maurice Kavanaugh Simmons. Born in Halifax, Nova Scotia, in 1824, Simmons moved to Texas in 1834, when he was ten. From that time to the start of the Civil War, Simmons's attachment to Texas grew. He served in the Mier expedition and fought in the Mexican-American War, where he lost a leg. Simmons's attachment to Texas and desire to protect his adopted state was strong enough to volunteer to defend its coast even though he had only one leg. All of these Texans had few if any strong connections to the rest of the South. Their desire to join the Confederate army was more about directly defending their present homes in Texas from a Union invasion than defending any other place or idea, including proving manhood or winning glory on distant battle-fields.[41]

In some instances, Texans with strong desires to defend Texas served east of the Mississippi. In these cases, "recruiting colonels," officers who organized regiments, wanted to fight in a distant theater of their choice and took units raised for state service and marched them away to the far corners of the Con-federacy. The 2nd Texas Infantry was a good example of this phenomenon. The recruiting officer of the 2nd Texas was Col. John Creed Moore. Born in Hawkin County, Tennessee, in 1824, he graduated from West Point and was a professor at Shelby College in Kentucky at the on-set of the war. In the early months of the war, the Confederate government made him a captain in charge of artillery along the Texas coast. In the process, Moore received command of the 2nd Texas and was able to get orders to move the men east of the Mississippi, where he had his own desire to defend Kentucky and Ten-nessee.[42]

Though the majority of the men of the 2nd Texas Infantry wanted to serve in their home state, Moore led them to the east bank of the Mississippi. Initially he did so without informing them of his plans. The men in the ranks thought, even after they left the Texas coast, that they would shortly return after a brief sojourn east of the river. According to J. M. Hatchell, "The supposition is after getting togather at Shreveport and get armed we will go to

Brig. Gen. John Creed Moore, com-mander of the 2nd Texas Infantry. Courtesy Library of Congress

Vicksberge and join Van Dorn's command but there is no certainty in that before going may be ordered to Galveston."[43] En route to the Mississippi the men
developed the idea that Moore was taking them to the other side of the river,
but they still clung to the hope that, after receiving arms, they would return to
the Texas coast. The 2nd Infantry never received a transfer back to Texas. After
the siege of Vicksburg, they surrendered to the Union army and were paroled,
pending an exchange of prisoners. Once exchanged, the regiment reorganized
in the Trans-Mississippi Department and spent the balance of the war in the Rio
Grande Valley and on the Texas coast.[44]

Not all Texans became demoralized with the transfer of their unit to another
theater. Men from the 3rd, 15th, and 9th Texas Cavalry provide some insights
about Texans whose highest priority was to protect their native state. Generally,
these Texans were not upset about receiving a transfer to another region of the
war, as long as they had some tangible connection to it. Men in these regiments
showed that, though they wanted to protect their interests in Texas, they also
did not object to fighting in other regions, as long as they were near their old
hometowns or kin. To a lesser extent, men like Lt. Col. William Quayle of the
9th Texas Cavalry, who had little to no connection to the East, found ways to
return to Texas. After the Confederate army implemented the Conscription Act,
Quayle declined "re-election on account of his health & especially his sight,"
along with "many of the old officers . . . that they might be discharged." Unlike
most of the men in the 9th Cavalry, the officers simply returned to Texas to defend their homes.[45]

The men who decided to remain with their regiments east of the Mississippi
did so to protect their attachments in the region. For example, Douglas John
Cater was born in 1841 in Sparta, Alabama, and moved with his family to Harrison County, Texas, when he was five years old. By 1848 his family had moved
to Mansfield, Louisiana, where he grew to manhood. Before the war started,
Cater left his parents' home to live in Rusk County, Texas. Being a typical young
man looking for independence, he decided to join the 3rd Texas Cavalry and
not a Louisiana unit because "I was now separated from my parents, brothers
and sisters, and they had learned to bear this separation." When the 3rd Cavalry
crossed the Mississippi River, Cater met his brother in a camp and transferred
to his sibling's unit, the 19th Louisiana Infantry.[46]

Cater was not demoralized by his transfer, especially when he received
orders to march to Mobile, Alabama. Cater and his brother, both born in Alabama, wanted to revisit their birthplaces and see the relatives who remained
in the region, especially their cousin Doug and his wife. "In September," Cater
wrote, "I obtained my first leave of absence. This was a seven day furlough, too
limited to allow a visit home, so I used it in visiting relatives, some at Burnt
Corn, and some friends of my father at Sparta, all in Conecuh County, Alabama.

I was born in Sparta twenty-one years before this visit, and I wanted to see the old town." During this trip, he visited his cousin and uncle and joined them for a deer hunt.[47]

Through the war Cater visited his family and birthplace many more times. During Christmas of 1862 he received another furlough and visited his cousin Lawrence and an old family friend. Again in February 1864 he had an opportunity to visit kin in Sparta. During this trip he visited additional family members and friends. The aspect of his visit that stood out most was the condition of Sparta. Cater was clearly upset that the place of his birth had fallen into neglect because of the war. Though his attachment to the trans-Mississippi was the strongest, Cater's transfer to Alabama did not upset him because of his birthplace and family in the region.[48]

Men in the 9th Texas Cavalry, organized to defend North Texas by fighting in Missouri, were Texans whose first priority was to defend the Lone Star State, but their transfer east of the Mississippi produced little demoralization. Once transferred to the Western theater, Capt. John Germany was eager to get a furlough so he could visit all of his relatives in Mississippi, Alabama, and Georgia.[49] James C. Bates, the Tennessean who attended Bethel College, did not object to fighting in his old state of Tennessee, because of the number of relatives who still lived there along with friends he made during college. Bates wrote to his sister in April 1863 about these connections, listing half a dozen Tennessee friends and cousins he had recently visited and noting that there were "several others." Bates remained in good spirits while defending his old hometown and alma mater.[50]

Bates and the other Texans in the 9th Cavalry enjoyed their stay in Tennessee and became demoralized only when they received orders transferring them from their old native state to Mississippi. Bates recorded the men's objections to their transfer in a letter to his mother: "We left our camp at Spring Hill on yesterday, and are now enroute for the 'land of all abominations' [Mississippi]. I hoped when we left there that we had bidden a final adieu to the hated state & yet hope we will not have to remain there long." Bates continued, "I never regretted to leave any place as much as Murry [Maury] Co[unty]. Besides having much better fare ourselves and horses, we received more kind treatment during one week of our stay there, than the whole time we were in the land of niggers and swamps."[51] Though in the initial months of the war the men of the 9th Cavalry wanted to defend only their home state, they, like many other Texans, made exceptions when they received transfers to other theaters of the war within which they had strong local attachments.

Texans in the 15th Texas Cavalry experienced the same influences, especially Lt. Robert Marion "Bob" Collins. Born in Cleveland, Tennessee, in 1838, Collins moved to Texas in 1852. A year after the war commenced he joined the 15th Cavalry to fight in Arkansas, but the Union army captured him and his regiment in the Battle of Arkansas Post. After their parole, the regiment received orders to join Granbury's Brigade in the Western theater. Though his capture at Arkansas Post demoralized him, the prospect of fighting in east of the Mississippi did not. Collins wrote that he had "secured a kind of underground leave of absence for the purpose of a few days visit to his old home near Cleveland, Tennessee. We had left there when only twelve years old, and it seems hard for kin folks and acquaintances to realize on return a great big young man in a Confederate uniform."[52] Many Texans with attachments to other localities, though not as strong as those to Texas, served proudly in those locations until certain events influenced them to change their priorities (see chapter 5).

Some Texans joined units that the Confederate government could not remove from the state. These consisted of the home guards or soldiers organized to round up conscripts and deserters. The composition of these units was mainly young men and boys eight to sixteen years old. These young, immature boys exploited the responsibilities given to them by the state. In their service, the Texas home guards did not discriminate between friend and foe but harassed both alike, winning the nickname "heel flies," the annoying insects that flew at the heels of cattle.[53] Even soldiers returning home on furlough were not immune, for the home guard frequently forced them to turn over their money, horses, and arms. They were harsher on the civilians; they not only stole from locals but subsidized their meager pay through bribes.[54] Some men accused home guards of being organized as "a harbor for those who are trying to evade the service."[55] Commanders such as Col. James Bourland even acknowledged that "in the organization of the militia you were forced to take all as they come, and among that number was bound to be a great many bad men who had resorted to the frontier for the purpose of evading the Confed. service and in fact all the service they could. And I think the good men of your command are bound to acknowledge this as a fact."[56]

In some rare examples home guard units were not as rowdy. A few companies in San Antonio filled their ranks with men over age fifty, and one was even commanded by a man in his eighties. "Among them are men of San Jacinto, of the Santa Fe expedition, the Mexican war—men who have been captains, colonels, judges, senators, members of Congress, and who have sons and grand-sons in the army—all standing side by side, going through the drill of the soldier," noted the Houston *Tri-Weekly Telegraph*. Others had more pressing matters than to engage in bad behavior. Home guards such as the 13th Brigade Cedar Hill Cavalry organized themselves to serve exclusively on the frontier. According to Capt. Richard Sullivan, they were not meant to "be taken out of the State of Texas nor marched South or East, except by a two third vote of the company."[57] Very few men outside those who lived on the frontier would agree to terms like these.

Home guards were not the only Texans to defend the frontier. From the start of the war, there was a great need to defend the western frontier and North Texas from Indian depredations. Decades before the war, Texans established "ranging companies" to quell Indian problems. In this service, many Texans gained military experience and made a profession of fighting Native Americans. Starting around 1856, Indian hostilities mainly by Comanches and some Apaches, Kiowas, Lipans, and Kickapoos increased on the Texas frontier with the encroachment of white settlement. In response, the U.S. Army sent more cavalry units to protect the ranches and homes in the areas. With the removal of U.S. cavalry units from Texas forts at the outset of the Civil War, as early as April 1861, Comanches pushed many settlers from the frontier to East Texas. Texans enlisted in frontier units to push Native Americans back west, in many cases to eliminate this threat to their homes in both West and North Texas and their future.[58]

Many Texans served in Confederate and state units stationed on the frontier. Their motivation to fight Native Americans instead of Yankees was the result of local attachment. Most of the men who enlisted in frontier units did so for two main reasons: Before the war they fought Indians, and the war created an opportunity for them to continue fighting them; and they lived on the frontier and wanted to defend their families and homes against Indian raids.

Even among Texans who did not have homesteads in West Texas, most had experience fighting Native Americans before the war. Leading the charge was Henry McCulloch and the men of his 1st Texas Mounted Rifles, a regiment organized expressly to defend the Texas settlements on the frontier. McCulloch had lived in Texas for more than twenty-five years before the Civil War and gained experience fighting in the Mexican-American War and as a Texas Ranger. As commander of the 1st Mounted Rifles, he continued his career as an Indian fighter, as did many of the men, whom he ordered to "severely chastise"—in other words, kill—any Indian seen. When the war broke out, McCulloch had trouble recruiting Texas frontiersmen for a regiment to defend the frontier. His problem was not finding frontiersmen willing to join the regiment to fight Indians but convincing them to travel to San Antonio to organize, leaving their homes and families exposed to Indian raids.[59]

Many Texans in the 1st Mounted Rifles had backgrounds similar to that of their commander. Men such as James Buckner "Buck" Barry, born in North Carolina in 1821, settled on the Texas frontier in 1845 in his early twenties and joined the Texas Rangers. Throughout his adult life in Texas, he either lived in danger of attacks by the Comanche or was employed by the state to fight Indians. When the Civil War broke out, Barry continued to fight Indians as a soldier in the 1st Mounted Rifles.[60]

Other men in the 1st Mounted Rifles, like William A. Pitts, Edward Burleson, and Thomas C. Frost, could relate to Barry's background. Pitts, born in Washington County, Georgia, in 1830, migrated to Texas when he was sixteen and spent most of his life as an Indian fighter. Similarly, Burleson migrated to Texas with his family from Tennessee in 1830 at the age of four. Once he reached adulthood, he became a Texas Ranger and spent most of his adult life fighting Native Americans on the frontier. Frost, born in Bellefont, Alabama, also fought Indians after moving to the Texas frontier in 1854. These Texans, though they had connections to other places in the South, wanted to continue their campaign against the Native Americans because Indian raids on the frontier directly threatened their homes and produced a deep-seated animosity. Threats to their families and hatred of Native Americans contributed to some Texans' apathy toward fighting in any other theater of the war.[61]

Most men of the regiment came from the frontier and had experience fighting Native Americans. Men such as Sidney Green Davidson, elected by his company to be 1st lieutenant, desired to defend his home on the frontier. Since they served near their homes, the regiment had a low desertion rate, an average of 3.8 percent throughout its existence. The composition of the 1st Mounted Rifles differed greatly from that of other Texas units. The regiment contained a large number of northern-born men (14 percent) and immigrants from foreign countries (21 percent), a rarity among Confederate units from Texas. An example of a common Texas unit was the 14th Texas Infantry, 2 percent of whose men were northern born and barely over 3 percent immigrants. Most of the men in the 1st Mounted Rifles did not have a strong connection to the causes of the South, but they had a strong affinity to their homes and families living on the Texas frontier.[62]

The 1st Texas Mounted Rifles disbanded in April 1862 when its one-year enlistment expired. A contributing factor to the disbandment was the Confederate defeat at Pea Ridge, Arkansas. Before Pea Ridge, Texans did not worry about major threats from the Union army. That battle, occurring just a month before 1st Mounted Rifle enlistments ran out on March 7 and 8, 1862, signified for the first time that Texas was vulnerable to a Northern invasion. Pea Ridge influenced the men in their choice of where to serve after the 1st Mounted Rifles dissolved into the 3rd and 8th Texas Cavalry battalions to patrol against dissenters, mainly German unionists, in Texas. The army reconstituted the regiment in May 1863 as the Texas 1st Cavalry to defend Texas from a Union threat from Louisiana.[63]

John Robert Baylor, commander of a detachment from the 2nd Texas Mounted Rifles stationed in Arizona Territory, embodied the desire of a Texan to continue his profession as an Indian fighter during the Civil War. Born in Paris, Kentucky, in 1822, Baylor moved to frontier Weatherford, Texas, in 1840. As with most men living there, he was as an Indian fighter. When he first moved to Parker County in 1855, Baylor received a commission as a special agent with Comanches at the Brazos Indian Agency. Baylor proved to be inefficient as an agent because of his lenient attitude toward the Comanche. The Comanche in turn took advantage of his demeanor by committing numerous raids and murdering many frontiersmen living in the area. Baylor's ineffective leadership led to his dismissal from his post. Unwilling to accept responsibility for his own failure, Baylor blamed the Comanche for ruining his career, which contributed to a deep-seated hatred. This hatred led to a new career as an Indian fighter in the years leading up to the Civil War. Though not the sole reason he joined the Confederate army, fighting in Arizona and New Mexico gave Baylor the opportunity to continue fighting Indians without the interference of the U.S. Army and the reservation system in Texas. With the removal of the cavalry from Texas forts and reservations, Baylor could kill Native Americans with few, if any, repercussions.[64]

When the war began, Baylor received a commission as lieutenant colonel of the 2nd Texas Mounted Rifles. He accepted his appointment and then requested that the detachment of the regiment he commanded serve on the frontier because he was familiar with the terrain, and in the process he could secure the frontier forts. The men of the 2nd Mounted Rifles enlisted to occupy these forts because of their hatred of Indians. According to Enrique B. D'Hamel, a Cuban immigrant in the 2nd Mounted Rifles, "Most of the men had been Indian fighters."[65]

Baylor's desire to exterminate Native Americans appears in an order he issued on March 20, 1862. On that date Baylor issued an order to Capt. Thomas Helm, guarding the Pinos Altos mines, to exterminate all Native Americans in the region. Baylor wrote:

I learn from Lieut. J. J. Jackson that the Indians have been in to your post for the purpose of making a treaty. The Congress of the Confederate States has passed a law declaring extermination to all hostile Indians. You will therefore use all means to persuade the Apaches or any tribe to come in for the purpose of making peace, and when you get them together kill all the grown Indians and take the children prisoners and sell them to defray the expense of killing the Indians. Buy whiskey and such other goods as may be necessary for the Indians and I will order vouchers given to cover the amount expended. Leave nothing undone to insure, and have a sufficient number of men around to allow no Indian to escape. Say nothing of your orders until the time arrives.... To your judgment I intrust this important matter and look to you for success against these cursed pests who have already murdered over 100 men in this territory.[66]

The planned ambush never came to fruition, but the resourceful Baylor conceived other plans. In another instance, he and his detachment of the 2nd Texas Mounted Rifles planned to give Native Americans in Arizona poisoned flour in an attempt to eradicate them. Though these plans never developed, the actions of Baylor and the men of the 2nd illustrate the desire of many Texans to continue the fight, started decades before the Civil War, against the Native Americans on the frontier and eliminate their immediate and future threat to the Lone Star State.[67]

Before the Civil War, frontiersmen lived in relative isolation from Texas society and, more important, from East Texas markets. Since there were no major rivers on the frontier, the settlers could not grow cotton or other cash crops and expect to earn a profit. Instead of relying on the markets, the frontiersmen looked to earn money from selling agricultural products to the local U.S. Army forts. Their whole existence on the frontier relied on the forts' economy and the protection the soldiers stationed there provided. Though life on the frontier revolved around the forts, most of the frontiersmen who voted for secession did so because they felt the fort system was not effective enough against Indian raids. They were willing to try another government in hopes that it would protect them better. Essentially, the desire for the protection of their homes and families from Native Americans overrode the economic prosperity they enjoyed in the years before the Civil War began.[68]

Texans living on the frontier demonstrated a strong desire to defend the area they had the strongest connection to, which at the time Native Americans threatened. Men from Blanco County in 1861 showed this clearly when they stated their reasons for enlisting in the state militia: "for the purpose of drilling and defending our settlement and immediate frontier from the depredations of the Indians or invasion of the Black Republicans."[69] The men from Blanco County demonstrated their priorities at the onset of the war. Since Texas was relatively safe from Union attacks, the main concern of the men on the frontier was to protect their homes against Indians.

Brig. Gen. James Webb Throckmorton, commander of Texas' First Frontier District. Courtesy Library of Congress

Similarly, the men in the 11th Texas Cavalry enlisted to defend North Texas from both Indian raids and Yankee invasion. Recruited by Col. William C. Young, the regiment contained a large number of men who opposed secession but fought for the Confederacy to defend their homes and families, including such prominent unionists as James Webb Throckmorton. Men from Collin County organized their cavalry unit to form a "military company for the protection of [their] homes and [their] rights."[70]

Soon after its organization and introduction to state service, Young received orders that the regiment belonged to the Texas force under the command of Brig. Gen. Ben McCulloch in Arkansas. Young made requests to Richmond, McCulloch, and Texas governor Edward Clark that his command remain in the trans-Mississippi so they could be available to defend their homes in North Texas. Clark assured Young that the regiment would remain close to the region, which provided relief among the men in the ranks until the introduction of Brig. Gen. Paul O. Hébert as commander of the Department of Texas. Hébert revived the anxiety of the men when he quickly transferred Young's regiment into the Confederate army with no guarantees about where they would serve. Men in the ranks reacted quickly to these changes; one-fifth of the regiment hired substitutes and others deserted. Six months later the regiment marched to Missouri and eventually to Mississippi, where they received orders permanently assigning them to Maj. Gen. Joseph Wheeler's cavalry corps. Pulled away from their homes in North Texas and with no real desire to fight for secession, men began deserting and hiring substitutes at an alarming rate. Within three months of leaving North Texas, the regiment lost nearly two-thirds of its men, including Young, and other officers serving with the 11th Cavalry such as Throckmorton joined the 6th Texas Cavalry. Though the men left the Confederate army, they did not shirk their martial duties. Most of them returned to defend North Texas as state troops, partisan rangers, or Bourland's Border Regiment to fight on the frontier. Young became a prosecutor in the great hangings in Gainesville until outlaws murdered him, and Throckmorton helped organize the 2nd Texas Partisan Rangers to defend North Texas. The actions of the soldiers of the 11th Texas Cavalry clearly demonstrate the lengths Texans would go to defend a particular locality dear to them during the war.[71]

Other units from less threatened regions were more flexible about where they would serve in the state, such as the 8th Texas Cavalry Battalion, which was organized by Jean Francois "Frank" van der Stucken, a German who settled in Castroville in 1846, later moved to Fredericksburg, and actively recruited Germans from Gillespie County. The battalion had two main purposes in Texas: to help the home guard protect frontier settlements, and to assist the Confederate army in defending the coast. To enable the battalion to perform these duties, the 8th's headquarters was at San Antonio Springs, present-day Pedernales Falls, a location equidistant from the frontier and the coast. Other men from the 1st Texas Mounted Rifles continued to serve in the army as part of the 3rd Texas Cavalry Battalion, which guarded the Texas coast.[72]

Where the men came from determined which of the two units they joined.

William Kuykendall, who lived in coastal Jackson County before the Civil War, exemplified those who decided to defend the coast after their one-year enlistment expired. When hostilities started, he rushed to join a company with family members and other Jackson County men. Organized in Victoria, his company became Company D of the 1st Texas Mounted Rifles and eventually joined the 3rd Texas Cavalry Battalion. The men had different expectations for themselves when they enlisted, as noted by Kuykendall in his diary. On receiving orders to defend the coast as part of the 3rd Cavalry Battalion, Kuykendall wrote, "When we [Company D] enlisted in the service we expected to be sent to the seat of war [Texas coast]. . . . Instead we had been kept against our earnest protest on our Southwestern frontier where no enemy had polluted our soil and we were greatly chagrined. . . . we were enthused with the prospect of realizing our ardent wish to be ordered to the front [Texas coast]."[73] Kuykendall's attachment to the Texas coast influenced him to join the 3rd Cavalry Battalion and protect the people and area he held dearest; eventually he fought in the Battle of Aransas Bay, on April 22, 1862.[74]

Though the 1st Texas Mounted Rifles dissolved, defense of the frontier continued. Gov. Francis Richard Lubbock replaced the 1st Mounted Rifles with the Frontier Regiment, under the command of Col. James M. Norris, a frontiersman from Coryell County, Texas. Nine of the regiment's ten companies contained men living on the frontier. All the men of the Frontier Regiment camped near their home counties in order to protect them. According to the weekly Austin *State Gazette*, "The company for the Frontier Regiment . . . is made up of our best Indian fighters now on the frontiers, the largest portion of them has been in many an Indian encounter in the last two years. With such men in the field we think that there will be some Indians lose their top-knots during the coming spring and summer."[75] These men defended the most important strip of land to them. From this location they defended their homes on the frontier from Native American raids. To keep the Confederate government from conscripting them into the regular army and removing them from local defense, the state government passed the 1863 Frontier Defense Act. The act made an exemption for the men fighting in local militias from the Conscription Act, thus assuring the men in the Frontier Regiment that they would continue serving near their homes.[76]

The Frontier Regiment proved effective against Native Americans, but by 1863 it began draining the Texas Treasury. To save funds, Lubbock wanted to transfer the Frontier Regiment to the Confederacy but retain control of the men. In this manner, the Confederacy would financially support the regiment but have no authority to order them off the frontier. The Confederate congress agreed with Lubbock's idea, but Jefferson Davis rejected it, declaring the proposal unconstitutional. Texas finally agreed to transfer the regiment to the Confederate army, but only after it "organized state militia companies" to be "assisted by Bourland's Border Regiment" serving in Indian Territory. The state militia, better known as the Frontier Organization, consisted solely of frontiersmen who had not joined the Confederate army. Since the men in the Frontier Organization were older than most units, the average age being thirty-three, they had more to defend on the frontier because they were fathers and had a stronger connection and more responsibilities to their immediate location. By early 1864, the Frontier Organization was stretched too thin to defend the frontier effectively. Despite these odds, the men fought the best they could to defend their property and families on the frontier.[77]

Brig. Gen. Henry Hopkins Sibley, commander of the New Mexico campaign. Courtesy Library of Congress

Not all Texans had a purely defensive attitude about their homes and families. Some Texans took the offensive, most notably the men of Sibley's Brigade and the 2nd, 4th, 5th, and 7th Texas Mounted Rifles. Before the Civil War, Henry Hopkins Sibley served in the U.S. Army in New Mexico. After the opening shots of the war, he went to Richmond with a plan to raise Texas troops to invade and capture the Southwest. Sibley presented his idea to President Davis, who approved his plan because it would bring the people of the territories, the gold in California, and major ports along the Pacific Ocean into the Confederacy. Most Texas soldiers who enlisted in Sibley's Brigade for the expedition west knew what it entailed.[78]

Officially, Sibley stated that he only wanted to capture New Mexico, but many of his men alluded to other plans. Texans boasted that they would not stop there but continue to California and northern Mexico. They claimed Sibley's main objective was to capture California so the Confederacy could divert the gold deposits from the Union and make the naval blockade impossible by acquiring two seaports on the Pacific Ocean. Capt. Theophilus Noel of the 7th Texas Mounted Volunteers believed that the destination of Sibley's brigade was Tucson, Arizona, where they would meet Southern sympathizers from California and "switch off down in and take Sonora, Chihuahua, Durango, and Tamaulipas in Mexico and add them to the Confederacy."[79] Trevanion Theodore Teel of

Sibley's Brigade also wrote, "As soon as the Confederate army should occupy the Territory of New Mexico, an army of advance would be organized and 'on to San Francisco' would be the watch word."[80]

The defense of Texas further encouraged men to enlist for Sibley's expedition. An article in the Houston *Tri-Weekly Telegraph* elaborated on this point:

... the Federals have us surrounded and utterly shut in by their territory, with the privilege of cutting us off from commerce with the Pacific as well as with Northern Mexico. They confine slave territory within a boundary that will shut us out of 3/4 of the underdeveloped territory of the continent adapted to slavery. They also render it utterly out of the question in future years to take advantage of the changes in our neighboring Republic and add to our Confederacy those rich states of Mexico, so necessary to our future development. They destroy all prospect of a railroad to the Pacific for us, and thus make our commerce forever tributary to them. We must have and keep . . . [New Mexico] at all hazards.[81]

In response to this fear, Sibley's men wanted to conquer the American Southwest and eventually incorporate Central America and the islands in the Gulf of Mexico into a Southern slave empire to ensure a bright future for Texas. It is speculation to assume that Sibley secretly harbored these plans, but many of the Texans for the expedition were eager to capture these territories.[82]

How did fighting for home and hearth influence these men to enlist in this endeavor to capture New Mexico and potentially the American Southwest and northern Mexico? It influenced Texans because of their attachment to the Lone Star, backgrounds as Indian fighters, the opportunity to serve with kin and friends, the effects of the institution of slavery, personal background and place of birth, and notions of manifest destiny. Though not the only rationale, these factors influenced Texans to enlist in Sibley's Brigade, organized specifically to campaign in and conquer New Mexico. The men's attachments to Texas can be measured by how long they lived in the state. Just like other Texans serving in the Trans-Mississippi theater, the average amount of time the men of Sibley's Brigade resided in Texas before the war was thirteen years—four years greater than the men who enlisted for the East. Sibley's men spent more time in the state, giving them a greater attachment to its future. Additionally, 14.3 percent of the men who fought in New Mexico were born in Texas. If one includes the 26 percent who moved to Texas with their families while five years old or younger, this increases the percentage of those who would consider Texas their native state to 40.3 percent, 7 percent higher than all the men who served in the trans-Mississippi and 15 percent greater than the total native Texas population. Compared to Terry's Texas Rangers (22.4 percent, including those who arrived at five years or younger) and Hood's Texas Brigade (20.2 percent), there is a significant difference in the

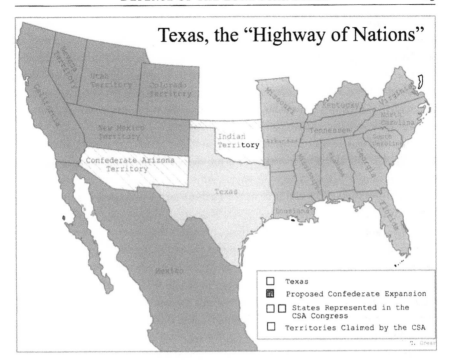

Texas, the "Highway of Nations"

men's attachment to Texas. Since the men in Sibley's Brigade generally lived in the Lone Star State longer than their counterparts fighting east of the Mississippi River, their main priority was to their native state and its future.[83]

Local attachment fueled the idea of conquest; if the Confederacy expanded its borders to the south and west, it would ensure the security of Texas by pushing enemies farther from its borders. In addition, the state not only would become the corridor for travel between the old South and the conquered territory, but it would benefit economically through trade as the avenue for the flow of raw material from Mexico and the American Southwest, including the ports on the Pacific Ocean. The inclusion of ports would not only break the Union blockade but create greater opportunities for foreign countries to recognize the legitimacy of the Confederacy.[84] Col. James Reily, commander of the 4th Texas Mounted Volunteers, stated this idea best when he wrote, "We must have Sonora and Chihuahua. . . . With Sonora and Chihuahua we gain Southern [Baja] California, and by a railroad to Guaymas render our State of Texas the great highway of nations."[85] Texans took the offensive early in the war to promote the future of the South and, more important, of Texas.

The first regiment organized to fight in the West, later attached to Sibley's Brigade, was Baylor's 2nd Texas Mounted Rifles. Though raised at the start of the war to occupy the forts abandoned by U.S. soldiers, they had other motivations to enlist in the 2nd Texas—to fight Native Americans in West Texas and the Southwest and gain control of and annex Arizona Territory. Months later Sibley organized the 4th, 5th, and 7th Texas Mounted Volunteers for the sole purpose of invading New Mexico. Once he and his men reached New Mexico, the 2nd Texas Mounted Rifles joined his ranks, along with two companies of Arizona soldiers, the Arizona Rangers and Arizona Guards.[86]

After the 2nd Texas occupied the forts in West Texas and started their campaign against the Indians, recruiters for the three original regiments of Sibley's Brigade began enlisting troops in August 1861. Sibley's recruiters raised most of their companies after the first major rush to join Confederate units, which left many counties depleted of men. This changed the dynamics of Sibley's regiments, because many of the men in the companies did not come from a specific county but rather from an entire region of the state, mostly from eastern and central Texas. Typical Confederate units began their organization at the company level. When enough companies organized, they combined themselves into regiments and then brigades, essentially from the bottom up. The organization of the companies for the New Mexico campaign differed. Sibley's Brigade was formed from the top down, with the commissioning of brigade and regimental commanders before any men enlisted into companies. To recruit men into the brigade, Sibley established a contract system of enlistment to get men into the ranks quickly. This contracting system granted a captain's commission to those who recruited enough men to form a company. If a man failed to recruit enough men, he simply did not receive a commission and enlisted as a private. These prospective captains attracted a sundry of men through many means. They even resorted to bribing men in standing units raised to fight elsewhere to join their company for the New Mexico campaign.[87]

The prospect of fighting alongside family and friends, though not uncommon, inspired some men to enlist in Sibley's Brigade. By joining with kinship groups and social circles, they could count on the bonds of trust and relationship already established to provide some comfort when they were injured or ill. Many men transferred from other units to Sibley's Brigade for this purpose. As a future company of the 4th Texas Mounted Volunteers passed through Huntsville, Henry C. Wright "met an old friend—John T. Pope. His father's family lived in Polk County and he had two uncles and several cousins in our company, besides many friends of whom I perhaps was the closest. He had enlisted in a company there but he at once withdrew and joined in with us, to my great delight."[88]

Even slavery motivated Texans enlisting to fight in New Mexico. Some thought that the social order established by slavery was best for the future of their state, and, more important, for the future of their hometowns and families.

As long as they could maintain the social order, the localities to which they had established attachments would flourish in safety. John Marshall expressed his belief in maintaining the social order in his newspaper, the Austin *State Gazette*, when he wrote, "It is essential to the honor and safety of every poor white man to keep the negro in his present state of subordination and discipline."[89] Trevanion Theodore Teel of Sibley's Brigade expressed the motivation slavery provided the men when he wrote, "California had to be conquered, so that there would be an outlet for slavery. . . . [By conquering the Southwest] there would be plenty of room for the extension of slavery, which would greatly strengthen the Confederate States."[90] Even Charles Stanfield Taylor, a native of England and member of the 2nd Texas Mounted Rifles, enlisted because he "heard the abolitionists were going to take Ft. Bliss."[91] Texans fought not so much for slavery as for the social order it provided for Texas and the South. Fighting for this cause legitimized what the soldier was doing because he believed he was furthering the goals and interests of Southern society.[92]

The personal backgrounds of individual soldiers also contributed to their decision to fight in New Mexico. Sibley's men had a wide variety of backgrounds, ranging from fighting for Texas independence to personal tragedy, and many had an attachment to the North. Thomas Green, colonel of the 5th Texas Mounted Volunteers, serves as the epitome of a Texan. He fought for Texas independence and defense of its sovereignty during the Republic era. Though born in Amelia County, Virginia, in 1814, he was three years old when his family moved to Tennessee, where he lived until adulthood. On Christmas Day of 1835, Green entered Texas to participate in its war for independence from Mexico. He quickly enlisted in the army to fight for Texas and never stopped defending his adopted land. Spending most of his adult life in Texas, he developed an extremely strong connection to the Lone Star State.[93]

Personal calamity also influenced men to join Sibley's expedition. Some, such as William Randolph Howell, had been unlucky. Born and raised in South Carolina, Howell moved to Texas at eighteen years of age after attending Furman University. One year later, the war broke out. Howell wanted to defend his native state of South Carolina by joining the 4th Texas Infantry, which had orders to march to Virginia. But before his regiment left Texas, Howell fell ill and had to remain behind. His opportunity to fight in the East was lost when the Confederate government prohibited any more Texans from joining the three infantry regiments in Virginia. After recovering from his illness, Howell wanted to join another unit that could promise adventure and a chance to fight Yankees. He knew that his last chance to fight Yankees early in the war would be to join Sibley's Brigade.[94]

A different form of personal calamity affected Alfred B. Peticolas. He chose to fight in the Southwest because he did not want to be reminded of his hometown or the memories it contained. Born and raised at Richmond, Virginia, Peticolas moved to Victoria, Texas, in October 1859. Though he had a strong devotion to the East, he refused to return to defend Richmond. A girl back east had broken his heart by rebuffing his marriage proposal. His heartache influenced him to want to fight as far away from his rejected love as possible.[95]

Place of birth was another common factor of the men's backgrounds that influenced them to enlist for the New Mexico expedition. Some in Sibley's Brigade had a strong attachment to areas other than the South. A significant number were born in foreign countries or the North, especially when compared to other Texas units. Of the men in Sibley's Brigade, 10.5 percent were born in the North and 11.7 percent outside North America, mostly from Europe, especially Germany, and some from Canada, Mexico, and Cuba. Additionally, the brigade contained two companies of the 4th Texas Mounted Volunteers that were composed solely of Germans. The significance of this is best seen when compared to other units from Texas, such as Terry's Texas Rangers and the Grapevine Volunteers, unique in becoming the nucleus of a regiment from another state, the 7th Kentucky Cavalry Regiment. In each of these units the percentage of Northern and foreign born are significantly lower. Only 4.25 percent of Terry's Texas Rangers were born in Northern states or other countries. The men of the Grapevine Volunteers, raised around Grapevine, Texas, were only 5 percent from free states and 1 percent from outside the United States. Significantly more Texans born outside the South fought in the New Mexico campaign.[96]

Texans with strong connections to the North had to fight for the South or risk losing their homes, businesses, farms, and way of life. Though pressured they could decide which theater best suited their interests and protect their adopted state without risking the guilt of killing somebody from the region to which they had an attachment. The commanders of Sibley's regiments provide excellent profiles of this influence. Col. James Reily, commander of the 4th Texas Mounted Volunteers and later commander of the Frontier Regiment, was born in Ohio and moved to Texas during the Texas Revolution. William Steele, colonel of the 7th Texas Mounted Volunteers, along with Lt. Col. John Schuyler Sutton and Sgt. Morgan Wolfe Merrick serving under him, were other Texans born in the North, all from New York.[97]

Some of the enlisted men, such as George T. Stansbury of the 2nd Texas Mounted Rifles, were born in the North. Stansbury was a native of Ohio and was actually visiting his boyhood home in the Buckeye State at the start of the Civil War. When he returned to his home in Texas, Stansbury decided to enlist in the Southern army, but he based his decision on a desire to not fight his fellow Ohioans and to go somewhere he had never been, the West. Stansbury recorded his motivation in a letter to Jenny Gordon of Cincinnati, Ohio: "Among the first Companies in the state and the first organized in Houston was Stafford Ranger

Organized in April 1861 and advertised to start for the frontier. . . . I had long entertained a desire to visit the far west and see with my own eyes that Eldorado of the sport." Henry C. Wright of the 4th Texas Mounted Rifles was also an enlisted man of northern birth. Born in New York City in 1840, Wright moved to Texas when ten. Fighting in the West reduced the chances that Stansbury and Wright would fight their fellow statesmen. Joining Sibley's Brigade allowed them, to an extent, to remain in favor with their friends and family back home in the Yankee states.[98]

Some men born in the South who later moved north lost their attachments to the rest of the South because of the time involved and family squabbles. J. W. DeWees of the 7th Texas Mounted Volunteers was born in Grayson County, Kentucky, in 1838 but moved with his parents to Wayne County, Illinois, when he was only a year old. According to DeWees, "When I was 17 years of age my father and I visited my grandmother in Kentucky where I was born and where my parents had a large connection of Kinsfolk. Our wearing apparel on this occasion was principally made from raw material on my mother's loom and spinning wheel, but old Kentucky had by this time outgrown many of the former customs and our visit was not as enjoyable as it otherwise might have been." The ridicule DeWees and his immediate family received was enough for them to break off ties with their Southern relatives after their visit. He remained in Illinois until his mother's death in 1858. The following year, the Illinoisan moved to Texas with his uncle and several neighborhood families and established a homestead in Wise County. When "secession came up," DeWees cast his "vote against it, but when Texas went out of the union I enlisted in a brigade of cavalry being made up at San Antonio, not for the purpose of killing men, but that I might be able to see New Mexico and Arizona as the object of the Sibley Expedition was to take and hold that territory for the Confederacy till the close of the war." With his connection to Kentucky severed, thoughts of adventure in the West influenced DeWees to enlist in Sibley's Brigade.[99]

Edward Burrowes is one of the finest examples of a northern-born Texan fighting for the Confederacy. Born in New Jersey, Burrowes developed a fondness for Texas, where "he was tending to his little stock of Cattle faithfully, [and] had bought a piece of land [and] built a house." To maintain his new way of life, Burrowes decided to fight for the Confederacy. He had to make a hard decision about where to fight because "he loved his Mother, and the land of his Mother, the Flag of that land, but no one dreamed that there would [be] a two or three years future of Bloody War extending to such wide bounds," and he did not want to risk killing anybody from his former state. Torn in his decision, he finally decided, "I love my country . . . but all the boys are going. . . . I shall not be likely to fight New Jerseymen in New Mexico."[100] Texans of northern birth enlisted in the Confederate army to fight in New Mexico because of the attachment they developed to the Lone Star State and to protect their future in their adopted state.

Northern and foreign-born men shared many of the same Southern sentiments that caused native Texans to join the war effort. Ideas such as state's rights and slavery influenced foreign immigrants to join Sibley's ranks. Henry C. Wright, born in New York and not arriving in Texas with his family until 1855, expressed this influence when he wrote in his reminiscences about the Civil War, "It took but a very little while for my mind to grasp and appreciate the Southern ideas of the State's rights and the white man's supremacy."[101] Wright, along with other Northern men, adopted Southern views after realizing the prevalence of these ideas in Texas.

Though most foreign immigrants had no contact with these ideas until they arrived in Texas, their time in the state gave them exposure to Southern culture. A German in Sibley's ranks, Ferdinand Boesel, expressed similar feelings when he wrote a letter to his family back in Germany. He blamed the war on the "the North," because "it is not fighting to save the Union, but rather to set 4 million blacks free, so the blacks can subdue 6 million whites. The blacks have an easy life compared to a day laborer in Germany. Without slaves, the South would be a desert, but with free blacks, no white man can live there. . . . We are fighting for our rights; the Union is lost."[102] Time spent in Texas allowed both Northerners and foreign immigrants to become influenced by ideas that permeated the Lone Star State and the South.

Other factors directly influenced those born outside the South to fight in New Mexico. Though these men had attachments to Texas, they were careful in their decisions to enlist and where to fight. The Texans who enlisted in Sibley's Brigade came from all areas of Texas except the northern part of the state. North Texas was an area of the state with a high percentage of northern-born residents with Whig ideology. Central Texas and the frontier of the Hill Country also had a large number of unionists. The Germans in Central Texas, surrounded by Southern-born Texans, felt the pressure to enlist or face the consequences from their neighbors. Ferdinand Jacob Lindheimer, the editor of the German-language newspaper *Neu-Braunfelser Zeitung,* appealed to the citizens of New Braunfels to vote for secession through an editorial: "Since it is undeniably foreseeable that Texas will secede from the Union. . . . all questions cease as to whether it would be to the advantage of Germans here, if Texas secedes or stays in the Union. The only practical question remaining is: How shall the Germans at secession of our State conduct themselves."[103] Those born outside the South enlisted not just for their future but for the future of their community and family.

Additionally, Germans wanted to join the ranks of the Confederate army to prove their loyalty to their state and the South with the least amount of risk of death or injury. New Mexico appeared to be the best theater of the war to fulfill these needs. Baylor's bloodless victories early in the war provided the evidence they needed. Reports reached Texas quickly of Baylor's capture of Mesilla, Arizona (in present-day southern New Mexico), and of approximately five hundred Union soldiers and three howitzers near San Augustín Springs. When those not born in the South felt the pressure to enlist, Sibley's expedition into New Mexico appeared to be the best solution, since they did not have to fear fighting somebody from their birthplace, could appease the suspicion of their neighbors, and could protect their homes, families, and way of life, all without the perceived threat of losing life or limb.[104]

Finally, ideas of manifest destiny proved to be a very influential motive for Texans to conquer the Southwest and northern Mexico. This concept was not new to Texas when the Civil War started; Texas had attempted to expand its borders during the Republic era. The concept included the desire to spread democracy and civilization across the world, which directly influenced Texas expansionism. The Dallas *Herald* on February 29, 1860 stated, "Let these Texans range on the Mexican Frontier and infuse some of the Anglo-Saxon ideas of progressiveness into the stupid, leaden souls of the people—and then the world will notice a change."[105] A contributor to the *Texas Almanac* described Texans as "men who . . . beat back, step by step, the treacherous and bloody savage, and open the highways of civilization into the unknown desert."[106] By spreading their definition of civilization, Texans could broaden the physical, political, and economic influence of Texas.

During the Republic era, Texas citizens talked of expanding to the Pacific coast. For economic reasons, Texas wanted to acquire a port city on the Pacific Ocean. According to the Columbia *Telegraph and Texas Register,* a newspaper in the then capital of Texas, "The army of Texas will display its victorious banner west of the Rio Grande, and when once its conquering march shall have commenced, . . . the roar of the Texan rifles shall mingle in unison with the thunders of the Pacific."[107] To reach the Pacific Ocean, Texas launched the Santa Fe expedition of 1841 to bring New Mexico into its control and justify its claim to the land. Though the expedition was a complete failure and a major embarrassment to the state, Texans continued to want to maintain a claim on the land of eastern New Mexico and made two more attempts to acquire that land before the Compromise of 1850 ceded the territory to the federal government and eventually to New Mexico. The loss of New Mexico upset some Texans, such as John S. Shropshire of the 5th Texas Mounted Volunteers, who saw the war as an opportunity to regain the lost territory. "Men & nations fight for principle. The U.S.A. spent millions of money to buy this country from Texas (I mean New Mexico) & then spent much money & life to whip it from Mexico & after all a country was acquired which would impoverish any private individual to own. Our people fought for principle and took the country for spoils, & got cheated."[108]

During antebellum statehood, manifest destiny and Southern nationalism were closely linked as Texans desired to expand the South into the Caribbean and Latin America. The *State Gazette* asked its readers, "Shall we not go on in the attempt to acquire Cuba, and thus prepare the way for an inevitable decree of destiny in the final annexation of the rest of the Antilles?"[109] The *Gazette* also wrote, "The child of today will live to see the boundaries of a Southern Republic gradually extended over Chihuahua, Sonora, and Lower California. Our ships will whiten the Gulf of California and the Pacific as well as of Mexico and the Atlantic."[110] Texans wanted to expand into Latin American territory because the Missouri Compromise limited their expansion of slave territory into the unorganized areas of the United States.

Texans' desire to expand into Latin America increased as the Civil War approached because of the activities of the Knights of the Golden Circle, a vehicle of Southern manifest destiny.[111] Founded by George Bickley in 1855, the Knights wanted to "take up the line of march," to "take possession of states of Tamaulipas, Neuava Leon, Coahuila, and Chihuahua, and of them organize a Government, thereby forming . . . a nucleus around which our valiant Knights would soon rally" in order to expand the borders of the United States and extend slavery into Latin America.[112] Under Bickley's leadership, the Knights wanted to establish Havana, Cuba, as the center of a slave empire that would reach 1,200 miles in every direction. The empire would include the old South, all of Central America, and the northern tip of South America so the South could control "the cotton lands of Mexico" and "the rich resources of Mexico and South American States." This land could "thus be developed for the benefit of the Southern Confederacy."[113]

Though the Knights were a Southern organization, Texas provided the strongest support. Not only was the Knights of the Golden Circle headquartered in San Antonio, but the largest number of members resided in Texas. These large numbers were extremely helpful to Texas when it seceded because the state needed a way to secure itself from the large number of federal troops in San Antonio and the frontier forts. Approximately 150 Knights helped Ben McCulloch capture the federal military headquarters at the Alamo in San Antonio, and many of these men formed the nucleus of numerous Confederate companies, especially those that fought in New Mexico.[114]

At the onset of the Civil War, these ideas of expansion did not end but grew under the leadership of Sibley, who had spent most of his military career in Texas, gained an affinity for the state, and was influenced by the Texan desire to expand its borders. Soldiers from Texas agreed with Sibley's plans of conquest because they mirrored their own expansionist ideas. Influenced by ideas of manifest destiny, Texans wanted to spread their own brand of civilization and the authority of Texas and the South. At the same time, Texans believed they were serving their own interests and those of their state and improving the lives of their families and hometowns.[115]

Texans' strong devotion to the Lone Star State influenced them to stay in the trans-Mississippi to defend its borders. A majority of the men who stayed in Texas had a stronger connection to the state because they had lived there longer and developed attachments through businesses and families. Where in the trans-Mississippi they wanted to fight depended on their surroundings and past. Those in East Texas or the northern border area wanted to fight in Arkansas and even in Missouri to keep the Union army as far away as possible. Those living on the coast wanted to keep the Union navy and army at bay. Frontiersmen had a strong desire to defend their homes and families from Native American raids. Men in Sibley's Brigade wanted to ensure a bright future for Texas as a corridor to a Southern empire in Latin America. All of these factors influenced men, as A. W. Sparks of the 9th Texas Cavalry stated, to fight for "Texas, the home of my mother, the pride of my father, the guardian of my sister and the home of my boyhood, God direct in the right, but right or wrong, I fought for Texas and could see no honorable course for Texas men but to stake their lives, their liberty, their all for Texas."[116] The defense of Texas was these men's top priority throughout the war. William Randolph Howell stated this idea best when he wrote, "How blessed are the people of Texas! and how thankful am I that those I so much love are not in the enemy's lines and are unacquainted as yet with the horrors of war and the thought that, when I am suffering and exposing myself here, I am driving the enemy away from Texas and its loved ones."[117]

4

DEFENSE OF THEIR FORMER HOMES

Why Texans Fought East of the Mississippi River

Lincoln's hordes have invaded the soil of Va. I felt it my duty to take
up arms in defence of this the state of my birth. . . . If there is one thing that
I am proud of, it is being a Virginian, and a Texan!

CHARLES TRUEHEART, ROCKBRIDGE ARTILLERY (VIRGINIA)

THE majority of Civil War battles were fought east of the Mississippi River, and Texans participated in almost every engagement. Approximately a quarter of all units raised in Texas fought east of Old Man River. Most of these soldiers had their origins in one way or the other from that region, having recently moved to Texas and leaving extended families behind; thus they had multiple local attachments.

One of the strongest motivations for Texans to fight east of the Mississippi was their desire to protect localities they had developed a commitment to, including the hometowns, family members, and friends left behind. Since a majority of Texans migrated from the East, many had more than one hearth and home, and most still had a "home" in the state they moved from, metaphorically and sometimes physically. These were the homes where they had grown up and the areas where their parents had raised them. In some cases, parents and extended kin still inhabited the old home east of the Mississippi, forming a continuing, loving connection with the Texas soldier. Texans had to make a decision about which location they wanted to protect—Texas or their hometowns in the East.[1]

At the beginning of the war, Alexis T. Rainey, a soldier in the 1st Texas Infantry, expressed what many thought, that "no one here believes that Texas will be invaded."[2] Their former home states back east differed from Texas in being under a more immediate threat by the Union army. These attachments influenced Texans to leave their immediate families in the Lone Star State, to fight east of the Mississippi River to defend their old hometowns and kin. Men in such famous Texas units as Hood's Texas Brigade and Terry's Texas Rangers and lesser known organizations like the 7th and 9th Texas Infantry and Waul's Texas Legion answered the call to enlist in distant theaters. Some men such as those in the Grapevine Volunteers and others like Charles Trueheart and Adam Rankin Johnson went as far as enlisting in regiments from their former states.

Even though local attachments provided one of the strongest motivations for Texans to enlist, they are not the only reason Texans fought east of the Mississippi. Youthful ambitions were significant in the recruitment of men to fight in the East. Texas was a state of young people, especially the native born. An obvious illustration of the youthful nature of the men born in the Lone Star State is that only one native, Felix Huston Robertson, reached the rank of brigadier general, and he was the youngest of all Confederate generals. Of the Texans who fought in the Virginia theater early in the war, the average age of privates and noncommissioned officers was less than twenty years, and company grade officers averaged less than thirty years. The youthfulness of the men who joined the ranks of the units marching east was even noticeable to the men themselves. L. B. Giles, a member of Company D, 8th Texas Cavalry, more commonly known as Terry's Texas Rangers, noted that the enlistees were "all young, in their teens and twenties."[3] David Cary Nance's pen expressed the thoughts of young men with the opportunity to experience adventure: "But like all boys in Early life, I loved adventure, so that when the first call came for volunteer troops I was crazy to go yes, crazy, for that is the only way to describe a boys sentiment when he is anxious to go to war."[4] Youthful excitement was common in the Civil War, and many of the soldiers who fought east of the Mississippi described their units' youth and enthusiasm to reach the front lines and experi-

Brig. Gen. Felix Huston Robertson, the only native-born Texan general. Courtesy Historical Research Center, Texas Heritage Museum, Hill College, Hillsboro, Tex.

ence combat with the enemy. According to chaplain Nicolas A. Davis of Hood's Texas Brigade, Texas soldiers in the East "were representative men from all portions of the State—young, impetuous and fresh, full of energy, enterprise, and fire—men of action.[5]

Other young men caught up in the excitement of secession belonged to Company E, 1st Texas Infantry, better known as the "Corsicana Invincibles," and Company I, 4th Texas Infantry, the "Navarro Rifles," both from Navarro County. Both companies felt the frenzy and patriotism of secession. Young men volunteering to fight in a war are prone to seek adventure and something different from their lives as adolescents. This is true of most people throughout time, because human beings love spectacles and fear that if they do not participate they will miss seeing something unique. The desire to witness the spectacle of warfare affects the young more than it does older, more experienced, members of society, because there are many more sights and events that they have not yet experienced. This is especially true for young men from rural areas who rarely travel far from their homes. In addition, young Texans were anxious to fight and felt dishonored if they did not receive the opportunity to prove themselves, since they had had very few opportunities in their short lives.[6]

Relatively few of the young Texans who enlisted had wives or children. This lack of responsibility not only allowed these men to join the army but gave them the flexibility to fight far from home. Dr. Thomas B. Greyson explained this motivation late in the war to his wife: "The young men—by which I mean the unmarried—of this command have within the past few days become impressed with the belief that it is their duty to make an exertion to get on the other side [east] of 'the big river.' They say and rightly too . . . that on the other side the service is active, and that the country needs all the aid that can be afforded on that side."[7] Another soldier, Benjamin Marshall Baker of Company B, 5th Texas Infantry, noted, "I laud my friend, W. J. Darden, Esq., . . . As he is the only married man in the company"[8]

Older men who wanted to raise units did not ignore the fact that young Texans enthusiastically enlisted to fight in the war. Col. Matthew F. Locke knew of the men's eagerness to fight when he raised the 10th Texas Cavalry Regiment in Goose Lake, Texas. "I believe," wrote Locke to his wife, "that there will be little difficulty getting a Regiment if I can promise them a prospect of fighting soon."[9] Once this promise reached the ears of young Texans, they flocked to recruiters because they were afraid that the war would be over before they could participate in combat. Alexis T. Rainey expressed this belief when he wrote, "The current opinion is that the war will be a very short one."[10] Many Texans expressed this fear. John W. Stevens, who fought in Virginia with the Texas Brigade, wrote, "If we did not hurry up, the fight would be over or declared off before we could get there. Our patriotism was just bubbling up and boiling over and frying and fizzing, until it required all the military skill the chief commander could exercise to hold the boys down until Jeff Davis should call for us."[11] Normally, young men joined units raised where they lived, but, if their communities were too small to recruit a company, they would go elsewhere for an opportunity to enlist. David H. Combs and Charley McGhee, for instance, traveled to another town to join Terry's Texas Rangers. "I was very fearful the war would be over before I saw a live Yankee. So Charley McGhee and I went fifty miles from home to join a company."[12]

With all their enthusiasm, the young men needed a place to fight. Northern Virginia immediately became the most important battleground in the Civil War. John C. Porter, a sixteen-year-old native Texan in 1861, recorded the enthusiasm of the men in his hometown of Shelbyville when news of the start of war arrived. "Pretty soon . . . companies began to organize to repair to the seat of war, who, as a general thing, were in a great hurry, and a little jealous of the Virginia troops for fear they would whip the fight and get the glory before they, the Texas troops, could get there."[13] Not wanting to be left out of the conflict influenced Texans to rush to Virginia.

The desire to protect the symbols of their newly formed country from the enemy also contributed to their motivation to fight far from home. National capitals proved to be the most obvious symbols of the countries, and their capture became a major priority. The need to defend and take symbols contributed to Texans' desire to fight in Virginia because that was where the most fighting would occur. Since Richmond, Virginia, the Confederate capital, needed soldiers for its defense and required soldiers to attack and take Washington, D.C., the Confederate government asked for twenty companies of Texans. In its precarious situation, fearing imminent Union attack, Richmond needed these men immediately. Texans were more than willing to serve in Virginia, and thirty-two companies of them rushed to join the fight.[14]

To raise these companies, the Confederate government advertised in newspapers to attract men to the region. During this period, very few copies of distant newspapers reached Texas, but other newspapers copied the advertisements and reprinted them in other states. Over time, they eventually reached the Lone Star State. An example of this call for troops appeared in the June 22, 1861, edition of the Marshall *Texas Republican*: "The Last Richmond [Va.] Enquirer contains an editorial article eulogizing Texas for the promptness, patriotism, courage and humanity displayed by our people during the present struggle and stating that one or two regiments from this State are much needed and will be received."[15] The promotion proved effective. Company E, 1st Texas Infantry, soon to be known as the "Marshall Guards," were soon on their way to the Old Dominion. In general, men who responded to this call would form the most famous of all Texas units, John Bell Hood's Texas Brigade.[16]

Hood's Brigade comprised the 1st, 4th, and 5th Texas Infantry along with the 18th Georgia Infantry and the 3rd Arkansas Infantry. The companies within the Texas regiments came from distinct areas of the state. Most of the men who served in the 1st Texas Infantry came from East Texas, those who served in the 4th Texas Infantry came mainly from Central Texas with a smaller number from East Texas, and the men in the 5th Texas were divided evenly between both regions. Among the Texans of Hood's Brigade, approximately half called Southern states east of the Mississippi River their birthplace and childhood home. Compared to Texans who enlisted in regiments serving in the trans-Mississippi, which had a similar percentage of men from the region, Hood's men had lived for three fewer years in Texas, on average. A smaller percentage of the men serving in Virginia, over 7 percent, had moved to Texas by their fifth birthday, compared to 12 percent of the men who remained behind to defend the Lone Star State. The soldiers remembered their old homes. Consequently, a greater number of these Texans had a stronger attachment to the their states of origin than those serving west of the river. Their connection to the land east of the Mississippi, combined with living in Texas for less time and thus having fewer opportunities to develop strong attachments to their new locality, contributed to their desire to fight in the Eastern theater of the war—the only one threatened by the Union army early in the war.[17]

This influence reveals itself in the histories of the individuals who initially commanded the Texas Brigade, raised the companies, and enlisted to fight. The first commander of the brigade was Louis T. Wigfall. Born in Edgefield, South Carolina, in 1816, Wigfall migrated to Texas in 1848 after becoming bankrupt. In the Lone Star State he established a law office and entered politics; eventually he was elected as a U.S. senator for Texas. Wigfall was present when the Confederates fired on Fort Sumter, on a ship in Charleston Harbor. Without authorization, he was the first man to issue terms of surrender to the Union fort. Wigfall's terms were declined, but his desire for martial glory led him to pursue a military career. After Fort Sumter he received a commission as colonel of the 1st Texas Infantry, and soon thereafter he became a brigadier general and the first commander of the Texas Brigade in the Confederate Army of the Potomac (later called the Army of Northern Virginia). Though Wigfall had lived in Texas for more than ten years before the war, he returned to protect the state of his and his wife's birth, South Carolina, by fighting and possibly defeating the Union army in Virginia before it had a chance to advance south to the Palmetto State.[18]

Once the general learned that the Permanent Confederate Congress was organizing, he resigned his commission to venture back into politics as a senator for Texas. In this role he continued to protect South Carolina and his adopted state of Texas through the Western Concentration Bloc, an informal group of

Brig. Gen. Louis T. Wigfall, Confederate senator from Texas.
Courtesy Library of Congress

politicians and officers who opposed Jefferson Davis's strategy of a cordon defense of the West. These men advocated the concentration of western manpower
to defeat the Union threat to the central corridor of the South, which extended
from the lower Appalachian Valley of Virginia to Atlanta and to Nashville, an
area that included South Carolina. Though the strategy would leave some territory vulnerable, the prospect of destroying the Union army and ridding the area
of its threat through a complete victory for the Confederacy was their ultimate
goal. Wigfall expressed his belief in this strategy in a letter to Joseph E. Johnston,
one of the generals in favor of the concentration strategy:

If I had control of the army every soldier from Arkansas and Texas should be brought
at once to this side [east of the Mississippi River] so that [Braxton] Bragg might at once

crush [Don Carlos] Buell. The debate was published and I have to see the first man from Texas who does not approve my course. . . . The valley of the Mississippi should be the échequier of operations and the armies of the West should be under one head. On whichever side of the river the enemy appears, he should be met with our whole force, and crushed. If he appears on both sides, concentrate on one, and crush him there, and then cross and crush him again.[19]

Though the strategy was never realized, the effort Wigfall exerted in its advocacy demonstrated his devotion to protecting the two locations dear to him, South Carolina, the land of his birth, and Texas, his adopted state.

Wigfall was not the only officer with multiple local attachments. Another example is John F. Marshall, who was born and raised in Charlotte County, Virginia, and moved to Texas in 1852 after living in Shelbyville, Mississippi, for two years. In Texas, Marshall became a half partner and editor of the *State Gazette*, a newspaper based in Austin. Marshall enlisted in the war as a private in the 4th Texas Infantry but received a promotion to lieutenant colonel by Jefferson Davis, a personal acquaintance, in "the spirit of political favoritism." When John Bell Hood received his promotion to brigadier general and replaced Wigfall as commander of the Texas Brigade, Marshall became the commanding colonel of the 4th. Like Wigfall, Marshall returned to fight in the region which, as a youth, he had called home. Unfortunately, he died from a gunshot wound to the forehead in his first engagement, at Gaines Mill.[20]

The motivation for Texans to defend their original hometowns was not limited to high-ranking officers but extended to company-grade officers such as George T. Todd. During the war Todd was a company commander in the 1st Texas Infantry. Born in 1839, in Matthews County, Virginia, Todd migrated to Texas as a child in the early 1840s. Yet he never severed his ties to Virginia. When he came of age, he chose to attend college at Hampton Academy, just across the Chesapeake Bay from where he grew up, for his first three years, then transferred and graduated in 1860 from the University of Virginia, rejuvenating his attachment to the state. That same year he returned to Texas, where he studied law and was admitted to the bar. The combination of being born in Virginia and spending his college years in that state influenced his decision to leave his immediate family behind in Texas to defend the Old Dominion.[21]

Other Texans had strong connections to Virginia. Asa Roberts, of the 4th Texas Infantry, born at his grandfather's house in Madison County, Virginia, did not move to Texas until 1858. When the war began, he came back to Virginia to defend his old hometown and protect his grandfather, who during the war nursed Roberts to health when he was stricken with typhoid fever. Other Texans included Frederick S. Bass, commander of Company E of the 1st Texas Infantry and later colonel of the regiment, a graduate of the Virginia Military Institute; William H. Hamman, of the 4th, who graduated from the University of Virginia before moving to Texas in early 1858; James D. Roberdeau of the 5th Texas Infantry, who was born and raised in Fairfax County, Virginia, before moving to Texas in 1858; and John Robert Keeling, whose family's roots in Virginia extended back two hundred years before the war.[22]

These Texans originally from the East never lost their connection to their old home states. While riding to enlist in the Confederate army, Pvt. William Randolph Howell wrote that "we crossed the Guadalupe River just this side of town, in a ferry boat, across a mill dam, with an old fashioned grist and saw-mill which make me almost feel myself in old South Carolina." Howell, born in Union Court, South Carolina, in 1842, attended Furman College and did not come to Texas until 1860. When war broke out, he joined the 4th Texas Infantry for service in Virginia but stayed behind because of sickness. By time he recovered from his illness, the Texas companies in Virginia were full and would not allow any more men to join. Prevented from fighting in Virginia, Howell enlisted in Sibley's Brigade, the only units being raised at the time. His attachment to his native state continued to be strong even after moving to Texas, and his letters demonstrate that "old South Carolina" was still very much in his thoughts.[23]

Although many men in the Texas Brigade came from Virginia or South Carolina, a significant number came from other states in the region as well. One of these was Edward D. Ryan, captain of Company E, 4th Texas Infantry. Born in Alabama in 1837 and raised there, Ryan migrated to Texas in the late 1850s. Twenty-four years old when the war began, he left his new state to defend the one he left behind. At that time the best place to prevent Northern soldiers from entering Alabama was to fight them in Virginia. Another officer with a similar situation was Robert M. Powell. Born in Montgomery, Alabama, Powell migrated to Texas in 1849. He enlisted to fight in Virginia as a soldier in Company D of the 5th Texas Infantry when the war started, and later he commanded the regiment. Edward Richardson Crockett, born in Decatur, Alabama, signed up to fight in Virginia with Company F, 4th Texas. His eastern roots influenced him to seek service in Virginia. Similarly, two Alabama-born brothers, Robert and Billy Gaston, moved to Tyler, Texas, in 1849 but enlisted in the Virginia-bound 1st Texas Infantry. These men believed that by confronting the enemy in Virginia they could keep them away from their native states.[24]

Many Texans believed that they were defending the Lone Star by fighting in Virginia. John Marquis Smither epitomizes that notion. Born in Walker County, Texas, in 1845, Smither enlisted in Company D of the 5th Texas Infantry. His motivation to fight is found in a letter written to his mother on February 27, 1862, from Virginia. Smither wrote "that although fighting in Virginia I was striving to maintain the honor and in defense of 'Texas my native land; my home.'"[25] Though he had few ties to Virginia or the East Coast, he still believed that the fighting in the East was important to the future of his state and hometown.

Smither represents the young men who had no direct connection to the East but instead enlisted in the war early because they believed that it was better to fight the enemy in Virginia than to engage them in Texas. Henry V. Smith of the 25th Texas Cavalry also demonstrates this idea. In a letter to his parents while camped at Chattanooga, Tennessee, Smith wrote, "How thankful to God that, if our fathers husbands and sons are and must be engaged upon the battlefield our homes and innocent one are far away for personal harm and danger."[26] By fighting where the enemy was—in the East—Texans hoped to keep them busy there and thus prevent them from invading the Lone Star State.

The desire to fight alongside and protect family and friends was another motivating force for men joining units slated to fight east of the Mississippi. Men tended to join Confederate units with other family members, especially if the recruiting officer was kin. Others were concerned about family and friends they had left behind. Campbell Wood, born in Alabama, joined "the Waverly Confederates," later becoming Company D, 5th Texas Infantry, which his brother-in-law Robert M. Powell raised. Others such as C. S. Worsham wrote about their desire to fight alongside relatives. Worsham wrote home that "I have been transferred from the 2nd to the 4th Texas Regiment so that I could be with brother James & Ed."[27] Sometimes this was only a temporary motivation. Capt. George W. O'Brien enlisted for the war because his relative, Capt. King Bryan, raised a company that became Company F of the 5th Texas Infantry. Unlike most of the men who fought in the Eastern theater, O'Brien had no formal ties to the East Coast, having been born in Vermilion Parish, Louisiana. The main influence in his joining the 5th was his kin, Bryan, and his good friend and neighbor William A. Fletcher, who helped influence him to join the unit. Though joining a company raised by kin motivated O'Brien to enlist in a unit destined for the East, his desire to defend his native state of Louisiana overcame his desire to fight in Virginia. After three months, O'Brien returned to Texas, where he served throughout the remainder of the war with the 11th (Spaight's) Battalion of Texas Volunteers.[28]

Most men who enlisted to fight in Virginia had direct ties to the East through family and friends, or through the influence of family and friends in Texas. Theophilus Perry and several of his cousins enlisted in the Marshall Guards with the idea that by fighting in Virginia they would be protecting other family members who still lived in North Carolina. Some of Perry's relatives even joined and fought in North Carolina regiments alongside their Texas kindred. The connections affecting Perry were even stronger than those of the average Texan, since he fought both alongside kinsmen and in defense of his family in North Carolina.[29]

Another way familial ties influenced Texans' decisions to fight in Virginia is evident in the actions they took once they arrived in that region. Many visited their extended families and old homes in the Eastern theater. Though born in Alabama, William H. Lewis had relatives in Virginia. Accordingly, Lewis looked out for news and updates that he could relay back to Texas. He wrote to his mother, for instance, "One of our Virginia cousins came over to see me a week or so ago. His name is Murrie S. Anderson a son of cousin Lucy Anderson of Ablemarle Co. Va. . . . His mother has been very kind to me indeed I have never had the pleasure of paying her a visit—but intend to do so the first opportunity."[30] James T. Hunter, of the 4th Texas Infantry, had similar desires. Hunter wrote to a friend, "I was very anxious to have gotten a short furlough to visit my friends in Buckingham and Appomattox Counties this winter."[31] Other transplanted Texans visited their childhood homes and wrote nostalgically to their families about what they had left behind before they moved to Texas. C. S. Worsham wrote to his mother that "I am right here at my old home."[32] While on furlough in Macon, Alabama, his hometown, Robert T. Wilson of the 5th Texas Infantry informed his siblings in Texas, "I am at home at this time I hav bin home a month."[33] Having family, friends, and childhood homes near the battlefields influenced many Texans to leave the Lone Star State to defend these locales.

Rufus King Felder offers another example of the influence of multiple local attachments. In 1855 at the age of fifteen, Felder moved to Texas from South Carolina with his cousin Miers, leaving behind a large number of family members. When the war started, both Felder and his cousin enlisted in Company E of the 5th Texas Infantry, originally known as the "Dixie Blues." They fought for the Confederacy and for Texas, but they had a more immediate desire to defend their extended family back east. In letters to his family in Texas, Felder described a visit to relatives and friends in Orangeburg, South Carolina, while en route to Chickamauga, Georgia, from Virginia: "Things had changed so much in the family it did not seem natural, Cousins John and Sam are no more and cousins Eugene and Adella have moved off, and Ed is in the service. I did not see any of the family except cousin Lon."[34] Another letter further reveals his concern for his extended family. On February 23, 1865, he wrote his sister, "The insolent foe have dared to march through the very heart of South Carolina & I have no doubt committed depridations on the property, if not on the persons of our dear, but unfortunate relatives. God grant that they may have been spared and that the scenes of our childhood of our noble ancestors not desecrated by the [ill.] of our brutal enemy."[35] This connection influenced Felder's decision to leave his immediate family in Texas and go to Virginia to keep the Yankees from reaching the extended family, friends, and hometown he left behind in South Carolina.

Not all Texans who enlisted early in the war fought in Virginia. Another famous regiment of Texans, the 8th Texas Cavalry, more commonly called "Terry's Texas Rangers," named after its first colonel, Benjamin Franklin Terry, fought

Rufus King Felder and his cousin Meirs, Company E, 5th Texas Infantry. Courtesy Historical Research Center, Texas Heritage Museum, Hill College, Hillsboro, Tex.

between the Mississippi River and the Appalachian Mountains. Though the men enlisted under the promise of fighting in Virginia, they later received a transfer to Kentucky. These Texans experienced the same motivation to defend their former homes as the men in Hood's Brigade.[36]

The organization of Terry's Texas Rangers began at the conclusion of the first battle at Manassas, when Thomas Saltus Lubbock, brother of future Texas governor Francis Richard Lubbock, along with Benjamin F. Terry and John A. Wharton arrived in Virginia early in the conflict and asked if the Confederate army in the Old Dominion needed some cavalry troops from Texas. All three men had physical and emotional ties to places east of the Mississippi River. Lubbock, born in Charleston, South Carolina, in 1817, moved to Louisiana as a young man in 1835 and then to Texas during its revolution as a member of the New Orleans Grays. Wharton was born in 1828 in Nashville, Tennessee, and his parents brought him to Texas as an infant. He attended the University of South Carolina and eventually married the daughter of that state's governor, creating a lasting loyalty to the Palmetto State. Sometime between 1848 and 1850, Wharton returned to Texas, opened a law practice with Clint Terry, Benjamin Terry's brother, and became the district attorney for the First Judicial District in 1858. Benjamin Terry had a similar background. Born in 1821 in Russellville, Kentucky, he arrived in Brazoria County, Texas, at the age of ten. As an adult, he became a successful sugar and cotton planter in Fort Bend County, Texas. The eastern connections of these three men certainly influenced the formation and history of the regiment.[37]

All three were optimistic about receiving permission from President Davis and "the Secretary of War to raise a regiment of mounted rangers for service in Virginia."[38] With authorization, they returned to Texas to recruit their regiment. Their advertisement in the Dallas *Herald* on May 8, 1861, appeared under the bold title "Texas Guerillas HO! To the Rescue!" The ad called for "volunteers to form an independent company to go to Virginia, to aid and assist in the great drama that is about to come off in that State." Similar advertisements appeared in other papers across the state.[39]

Once Lubbock, Wharton, and Terry raised enough men to form a regiment, they marched toward Virginia. The Texans' dreams of getting into the war quickly ended in the fall of 1861 as they passed through New Orleans. In the Crescent City, the men heard news that they were no longer going to Virginia; instead, they received orders to march to Bowling Green, Kentucky, to join Gen. Albert Sidney Johnston's Army of the Mississippi. Johnston, the highest-ranking Texan in the Confederacy and a former brigadier general of the Army of the Republic of Texas, requested that the government transfer Terry's Texas Rangers to his command, thus upsetting many of the men, especially those who had dreams of fighting in Virginia. In his diary, James Knox Polk Blackburn expressed his disappointment when he received news that they were not going to Virginia: "This change of destination brought deep disappointment and displeasure to everyone, as their hearts had been set on going to Virginia."[40] Another Ranger, John W. Hill, agreed with Blackburn's dismay in a letter to his mother: "We received orders last knight by Telegraph to go to Kentucky instead of Virginia We will leave here in the morning for Nasvile Tenesee where we will be mounted There is som dissatisfaction among some of the Companyes as to the change of our servise from Virginia to that of Kentucky."[41] Though the men were upset about the transfer, they grudgingly marched to the Blue Grass State.

The regiment was transferred for two reasons. First, Terry and Johnston were not just old friends but owned neighboring plantations in Fort Bend County, Texas. Familiar with Terry, Johnston was more than willing to request his friend and somebody he trusted to transfer to his command. Second, the end of Kentucky's declared neutrality made the Western theater vulnerable to Union invasion. Though the Rangers may have been upset about losing the opportunity to fight in Virginia, they would have their chance to prove themselves sooner than they thought, and other motivations would quickly emerge. Unlike Lubbock and Wharton, most Rangers, including Terry, came from states in the Western theater. In comparison to Hood's Brigade and Texans serving in the Trans-Mississippi theater, 10 percent more men came from the east of the Mississippi, almost 60 percent. Additionally, they spent less time in Texas, a year less than the average for Hood's men and four less than those serving west of the Mississippi. The difference is more pronounced in Terry's Texas Rangers because it was raised later than Hood's Texas Brigade, which increased opportunities for men not solely looking for adventure and with stronger ties to the East to enlist in the former unit.[42]

The original leaders of the regiment, Lubbock, Terry, and Wharton, did not spend much time with the Rangers, and thus they had little influence on the unit after the first months it arrived in the Western theater. Lubbock fell ill when the regiment reached Nashville and died soon thereafter. Terry led the regiment in its first engagement at Woodsonville, Kentucky, and was killed in a charge against the enemy. Wharton became the next commander of the regiment but received several promotions and a transfer to the Trans-Mississippi theater.[43]

After the departure of the three original leaders, Thomas Harrison eventually led the regiment. Harrison, initially a major in the regiment, received a promotion to colonel in late 1862. Born in Ruhama, Jefferson County, Alabama, in 1823, Harrison moved with his parents to Monroe County, Mississippi, where he spent his formative years. By 1843 he had moved to Brazoria County, Texas, but for only a brief time before moving back to Mississippi. After serving in the Mexican-American War, Harrison returned to Texas and was living in Waco when the Civil War broke out. Though born in Alabama, his strongest emotional connection was with Mississippi, and by serving in Terry's Texas Rangers he could be satisfied that he was protecting both localities by blocking the Union advance through Kentucky, the main threat to the two states at the time.[44]

Other men in the ranks had a direct connection to the region. Men such as James Knox Polk Blackburn, born and raised in Maury County, Tennessee, in 1837, did not move to Texas until 1856 at the age of nineteen. George Washington Littlefield, born in Panola County, Mississippi, June 21, 1842, was eight years old when he and his family moved to Belmont, Texas. Another Texan, G. L. McMurphy from Galveston, was a native of Rome, Georgia. During the war he noted every time he met soldiers from his former state, including "old friends in [Clinch] Rifles." He also visited familiar homes when he passed them, such as "Wm [Poullain's] place." On his arrival, McMurphy "learned from neighbors he was dead & that the plantation has been sold." All three men had direct ties to the many different regions within the Western theater of the Civil War.[45]

Like those men who joined Hood's Brigade, Terry's Texas Rangers fought to defend family, friends, and the hometown they left behind when they migrated to Texas. Ephraim Shelby Dodd was born and raised in Richmond, Kentucky, and did not move to Texas until late 1860. While in Kentucky, Dodd "went over to Cousin Mec's to take dinner." Aside from visiting family members, Dodd went back to his old hometown to visit friends: "I went down to our old stamping ground to-day. I stopped to see Miss Eugenie Holt; had just returned from visit to Marietta and was looking very pretty." He then continued to see several more people from his hometown. Some of these people and places include, once again, extended family members: "Went to Grandpaps . . . and got breakfast."[46] Words and actions of the men of Terry's Texas Rangers exhibit the influence of local attachments on the Texans' decisions of where they desired to fight and if they wanted to continue the struggle.

The effects of multiple local attachments were not limited to these famous units but extended to other Texas troops that crossed the Mississippi River. Two regiments raised in the early months of the war with a strong desire to defend locations east of the river were the 7th and 9th Texas Infantry. The majority of these men purposely organized to fight in the Western theater of the war, because they had an interest in defending kin and localities in the regions they fought.

Texans of the 7th Texas Infantry and its commander Col. John Gregg had a strong desire to protect localities to which they had an attachment. Born and raised in Alabama, Gregg moved to Texas in 1855 and settled in Leon County, where he established a law practice. When the war began, Gregg toiled with Hiram B. Granbury to raise a company of Texans from Waco and the surrounding area. Once they recruited most of the men, Gregg traveled to Richmond and wrote to Confederate secretary of war Leroy Pope Walker, requesting that

Col. John Gregg, commander of the
7th Texas Infantry. Courtesy Library
of Congress

the government formally muster his companies into the Confederate army. Gregg wrote, "I ask for an order, that these companies, to such a number as will form a regiment, be brought to the seat of war."[47] Gregg wanted his regiment to serve east of the Mississippi River, because at that time, July 1861, the only "seat of war" was in Virginia. One could surmise that Gregg had no objections to serving east of the Mississippi River and can conclude that the prospect to be back near his old hometown pleased him. Gregg was not specific about where he wanted to serve and did not have to be, because early in the war he could defend Alabama by fighting the Union army in Virginia.

Gregg did not hide his desire to fight east of the river from his men; it was common knowledge to the Texas soldiers in their recruitment camps. The men enlisting in the 7th Texas Infantry knew before they joined which theater they would fight in. According to Edward Thomas Broughton II, the unit still accepted men into the ranks when they knew which theater the Confederate government would assign them to fight in. Broughton stated, "The company is getting along well. It is not very full. I have no doubt I will be able to fill it by the time I get to Marshall. . . . write to me at Corinth, Mississippi." Almost a month later Broughton again wrote, "I have been laboring every day since I reached Marshall, recruiting for my company. . . . We have been ordered to Memphis, Tennessee."[48] After Gregg received the orders he requested in Richmond, he traveled with his wife, Mollie, to Decatur, Alabama, where her family lived, to leave her there until he could return with his unit. After saying his goodbyes to Mollie and her kin, he returned to Texas to finish organizing his regiment and marched them to Kentucky.[49]

Gregg was not the only man in the regiment who had a connection or kin in the Western theater. Other men included the aforementioned Broughton, born in Monroe County, Alabama, in 1834. He did not migrate to Texas until the 1850s; he then served as a lawyer in Athens, Texas. Another Texan with strong connections to the Western theater was Thomas Oscar Moore. Born in Oxford, Alabama, in 1842, Moore moved to Hays County, Texas, in the fall of 1855. His migration to Texas did not sever his connections to Alabama, because even at a young age he helped his father drive teams to Alabama. When the war started, it made sense to a nineteen-year-old to enlist in a unit that could put him in a position between the enemy and his old hometown. Another nineteen-year-old, Linson Montgomery Keener, had moved to Rusk County, Texas, from Macon County, Alabama, in 1849 at the age of seven. He wanted to fight in Virginia with Hood's Brigade but was severely disappointed when he fell ill and missed the roll call for the company. Instead of remaining in Texas, he joined the 7th Texas Infantry so he could fight east of the river.[50]

Having kin on the east side of the Mississippi gave these Texans some advantages that others could not enjoy. If the men lacked supplies, they would call on their family and friends to help. Gregg did this when he needed a horse. In response to his request, "Mr. Callahan who is up from Decatur, Alabama," came "with a horse for Col. Gregg."[51] Linson Keener expounded on this advantage in reminiscences he wrote with the help of his wartime letters: "I have been to see our Relatives in Ala & Geo only once yet. I believe I wrote of that in my other letter. I find it a considerable advantage to have Kin folks on this side the river & am very liberal in sending to them for clothing, eatables, &c. I recd a nice box of provisions from Grand Ma Stinson yesterday."[52]

The gifts and provisions did not end in the field but were also sent to men in prison. After the 7th Infantry's capture at Fort Donelson, Khleber Miller Van Zandt wrote of the support his kin east of the Mississippi provided. "I have a good many books sent to me by Dave Lipscomb and Mr. Clough's relatives and Uncle Lipscomb."[53] Later that month he explained that "I have rec'd letters too from Cousins Anne and Jennie Lipscomb and from Mr. Clough's father and brother Jos."[54] Not only did Texans' extended families motivate them to fight for their old hometowns, but the people they protected reciprocated with generosity of their own.

Family, once again, proved to mean more to the men of the 7th Texas Infantry than just a luxury in the East; it proved to be a factor in their decision to participate in the war. This is noticeable in the letters they wrote home detailing the visits they made to family members while on furlough or the visits their kin made when they were camped nearby. Van Zandt had several family members visit him while camped near his alma mater in Franklin, Tennessee. "Cousin Lauren Billingsley and Miss Callie Barnes came down from Nashville to Trenton" near where the 7th Infantry camped for the night. Van Zandt visited relatives as well, including his in-laws. He summed up the importance of family to the lives of Southerners in a letter to his wife: "I feel thankful indeed to our Heavenly Father to know that while so many unhappy changes have been made in many loving family circles that our own little flock remain preserved and protected."[55]

Men changed their minds about where they wanted to fight when a new theater opened closer to the place they had an attachment to. In September 1861, Kentucky removed its mask of neutrality and officially joined the Union states. The opening of a new front influenced Texans to reconsider their choices. Members of what would become Hood's Texas Brigade who had family in Kentucky had joined because at the time Virginia was the only battlefront that threatened their extended families and hometowns. Only a few of these men had the opportunity to change their minds before they officially joined their regiments in Virginia. A couple of fortunate young men got this opportunity in Louisiana when they happened to see the men from the 7th Texas Infantry. Van Zandt explained that "Billy Thompson and Isaac Johnston's son Wesley passed us in the stage on Sunday night on their way to Richmond Va. to join the Marshall Guards, but on Monday night they came into our camp and asked to be taken into our Company and they are now with us."[56] Later in the war men in the 7th Texas Infantry actively pursued family members in other units to join theirs. Van Zandt explained to his wife, "Your Pa left this evening for Richmond to see your brother. He will try and have him transferred to our Company. I sincerely hope he may succeed."[57]

Similarly, the men of Sam Bell Maxey's 9th Texas Infantry desired to defend their former homes. Born in 1825 to a prominent Kentucky family, Maxey raised

Maj. Gen. Samuel Bell Maxey, commander of the 9th Texas Infantry and later Indian Territory. Courtesy Library of Congress

the 9th Infantry to serve in the Western theater. When Albert Sidney Johnston requested his command, the Kentuckian was overjoyed. Like the men of the 7th Infantry, those of the 9th knew which theater they would serve in. Charles Samuel Dyers explained to his wife, "We are camped twelve miles east of Little Rock on our way to Memphis. We don't know where we will be ordered to but expect to go to Kentucky."[58] The men did not know the specific place they would be stationed, but the specifics did not matter as long as they were between the enemy and their old hometowns.

The 7th Texas Infantry demonstrated the same desires by visiting family members and old friends en route to the front. Some of the men's families were not in one place but spread across the South. Charles Samuel Dyers knew his regiment had received orders to fight in Tennessee, but he still took the time when the regiment camped near Little Rock to stay with his "Father and Mother two nights and a piece. I stayed one night with Uncle John Easley."[59]

Soon after crossing the river, the men searched for their kin in the region the first chance they got. In February 1862, after the 9th Texas Infantry settled into its camp in Tishomingo County, Mississippi, James K. Street inquired about where his grandmother lived and discovered he was within eleven miles of her house. He hastily received a furlough and went to see her. When he arrived, she was at Uncle Abner's farm along with other kin including his Uncle Albert and Uncle D. Street's inquiries about family members did not end there, and he was pleasantly surprised to meet kin he never knew existed. Street explained to his wife, "As strange an incident as this occured with me to-day—after preaching this evening I was sitting down

James K. Street, 9th Texas Infantry. Courtesy Southern Historical Collection, University of North Carolina at Chapel Hill

talking with some gentlemen—one spoke to a young man sitting by and called him Street." The Texan remarked to the young man that that was his name, and commented "that I never knew any of my fathers relations, that I had an Uncle who lived in Lincoln Co, Tenn named Walter Street. 'Well sir,' said he 'that was my father'—so you see I have very unexpectedly met with an own cousin—the only one of my father's connection I have ever seen—his name is Columbus."[60]

Stephen Bullock was another man from the 9th Texas Infantry who wasted no time looking for relatives. The Texan wrote to his brother in Hood's Brigade, "I can inform you that we have got back in old mississippip [ill.] the old red hills an [ill.] trees looks very natural. I have a notain If we stay here very long and I git the Chance I will be over in Old Carol County and see the folks."[61] Jesse P. Bates experienced something similar. While camped at Shelbyville, Tennessee, Bates wrote to his wife Susan that "I have seen Alton McCaleb and John Kelley. Alton is in the same company with Cochran's boys. They are all well as far as I know. Baird and Beverly Wack was well when I last seen them. John Harberson is in the same company with Cochran's boys also, Wm. and Sam Baker." All the individuals Bates mentioned to his wife were old friends of theirs from Anderson Bend in Hickman County, Tennessee. McCaleb and all the men serving with

Jesse P. Bates, 9th Texas Infantry. Courtesy Historical Research Center, Texas Heritage Museum, Hill College, Hillsboro, Tex.

Cochran's boys belonged to the 11th Tennessee Infantry. It was no coincidence that he met those people there since Shelbyville is just southeast of Hickman County. His concern for old comrades influenced Bates to fight east of the Mississippi.[62]

Maxey demonstrates most clearly the desire of any man from the 9th Texas Infantry to defend his former home east of the river. After the demise of Gen. Braxton Bragg's Kentucky campaign, Maxey expressed his dismay at not being able to defend his native state. He wrote to his wife back in Paris, Texas, "I can but look on the Kentucky campaign as very unfortunate. The State is lost to us forever. . . . It was a cherished ambition with me to aid in redeeming my native State. That dream has fled. . . . I was ordered to Danville just where I want to go."[63] Danville is almost one hundred miles northeast of his childhood home in Tompkinsville, putting him directly between the enemy and his hometown. The bonds between the Texans and their kin remained strong in spite of years of separation—strong enough to motivate men to defend their kins' lives and property as long as their immediate families were safe in Texas.

Another unit destined to fight east of the Mississippi River was Waul's Texas Legion, commanded by Col. Thomas Neville Waul. Waul spent most of his adult life, twenty years, working as a lawyer and district attorney in Grenanda, Mississippi. In 1850 he moved to Gonzales County, Texas, where he lived until the war. In the spring of 1862 he organized Waul's Legion to fight on "the eastern side of the Mississippi river if the passage is at all practicable," because of his knowledge of the region.[64] Some of his men had strong ties to the region, such as L. D. Bradley and Dr. E. Randall. Bradley initially enlisted in the 11th Texas Cavalry but transferred quickly to Waul's Legion when the regiment experienced problems east of the river. Both Bradley and Randell were natives of Alabama, and serving in Waul's Legion provided them the opportunity to be near their old communities. Once the unit finished organizing, it crossed the Mississippi River. Later, when Union Maj. Gen. Ulysses S. Grant threatened Vicksburg, Waul requested permission for the men to camp at Grenada, just outside his old house. Not only did Waul receive orders to fight in a specific region, he was able to get his men to defend his old home. The Legion later fought at Vicksburg, where it surrendered.[65]

Another Texan with a strong connection to the East was Thomas J. Stokes of Granbury's Brigade. Born and raised in Georgia, near Resaca, Stokes frequently wrote home to his half-sister about his life and thoughts in the army. As he neared Resaca he wrote to her that "it grieved my very soul to think of the sad fate which awaited it when the foul invader should occupy that 'vale of beauty.' . . . Right here, with a thousand recollections of bygone days crowding my mind, in the valley of my boyhood, I felt as if I could hurl a host back." Stokes described his main motivation for joining Granbury's Brigade as keeping his old hometown as safe and beautiful as it was in his memories.[66]

Some Texans were not as fortunate to defend their former states. Enlisting with high hopes of fighting east of the Mississippi River, James A. Tabb joined the 18th Texas Infantry eager to

be assigned to Mississippi, which is the land of my birth, and in its bosom lies the cold and silent frame of my mother, brothers four and many kindred and friends. Not resist a foe that is trying to overrun such a country as that! 'Tis folly to think of staying at home when our lives, fortunes and our sacred honor is at stake; when our peace and prosperity is about to be taken away from us; when our wives and children are menaced with insults; and any lady that falls into the hands of the invading foe is basely insulted and cruelty used. I say it is folly to think of staying at home. I had rather die the death of a soldier a thousand times than to live to see my wife and baby, my sisters and friends, [ill.] my portion of the Confederacy thrown upon an equality with the thoughtless negroes, or to live under Lincoln's administration.[67]

Unfortunately for Tabb, his regiment never crossed the river, and he lost his opportunity to defend the state of his birth and land of his relatives.[68]

Texans also met others from the Lone Star State east of the Mississippi, and not all of them belonged to Texas regiments. "There is a great many Texans in other regiments," wrote A. J. Coffman. "I m[e]t up with old friends & relations" while camped at Corinth, Mississippi.[69] Some Texans joined other state units that were several states away, like Silas Keen, whose brother "obtained a transfer . . . from Company 'C' Sixth Texas to his Ky [Kentucky] battalion."[70] In Virginia, Thomas J. Goree also noticed that "there are a great many Texans scattered about. . . . William Hume of Huntsville is also here. He belongs to a Mississippi Company. John White of Huntsville is here with an Alabama Company."[71] These are a few extreme examples of Texans' continuing attachments to locations outside the state that led them to not only leave the Lone Star State but join another state's unit. Sometimes whole units fought for another state, such as the Grapevine Volunteers, a squadron from Tarrant County that traveled to Kentucky to enlist en masse in a Bluegrass regiment, or individuals such as Charles Trueheart, Thomas Goree, and Albert Rankin Johnson. Their experiences and stories of raising units and fighting for other states illustrate the extremes some men took to protect their former homes.

The commander of the Grapevine Volunteers was Capt. Richard Montgomery Gano, whose life and career before the war influenced the origins of the squadron. Gano was born in Bourbon County, Kentucky, on June 17, 1830, to Elder John Allen Gano and Mary Catherine (Conn) Gano. When he was twelve, his parents sent him to Bacon College in Harrodsburg, Kentucky, for schooling. He finished his studies in 1848, at the age of seventeen, at Bethany College, Virginia. After graduation, he attended Louisville Medical University, and two years later at

Brig. Gen. Richard Montgomery Gano, commander of the Grapevine Volunteers and Gano's Brigade. Courtesy Historical Research Center, Texas Heritage Museum, Hill College, Hillsboro, Tex.

the age of twenty he received a degree in medicine. He moved to Louisiana, where he practiced medicine for several years. In March 1853, two years after moving to Baton Rouge, he married fellow Kentuckian Martha J. Welch. By 1857 he and his wife had moved to Grapevine in Tarrant County, Texas, and by 1860 he had earned many different titles: doctor, successful businessman, Indian fighter, honored soldier, and elected representative of Tarrant County in the Ninth Texas Legislature.[72]

Almost a week into May 1861, news reached Tarrant County of the Confederate attack on Fort Sumter and Lincoln's call for volunteers to suppress the rebellion. When men in Tarrant County heard this news, they rushed to join military units. Gano's position as a representative in the Texas legislature and his other professions proved helpful in raising a group of volunteers.[73]

In early May, Gano started to organize two companies, which would later form a squadron of cavalry. Gano's prestige and his direct involvement in recruiting the men for the squadron gave him an advantage when it came time for the unit to elect a captain and its officers. Throughout most of the South, it was customary for the men to elect their leaders. The man who had the most prestige and was the most active while organizing the unit was usually elected commanding officer. On June 1, 1861, the men of Gano's squadron elected him captain of Company A and squadron commander and elected John M. Huffman captain of Company B. They were not immediately mustered into the Confederate army. Instead, Gano and his men enlisted as state troops to protect Tarrant County and the surrounding area. Many military units formed in the South first mustered into state services before applying to join the Confederate army. On June 28, Gano's squadron officially entered state service as the Grapevine Volunteers, named for the location where they enlisted.[74]

The average age of the men who volunteered to fight for Gano was older than in other units raised in the South. Across the Confederacy, the average enlistee was in his early twenties, although some were in their late fifties and the youngest were around sixteen. The average age of Gano's men at the start of the war was around twenty-five years, one year above the Confederate mean age of twenty-four, with the oldest being Pvt. Hugh Roberts at the age of forty-seven. Consequently, most members of the Grapevine Volunteers did not enlist because of the youthful ideals of adventure.[75]

Soldiers of the Grapevine Volunteers also had recently moved to Texas. The majority of Tarrant County's population were migrants from the upper South, especially Tennessee and Kentucky. As new residents, these men felt the strong pull of previous local attachments, intensified by kinship ties. Only 1 percent of the Grapevine Volunteers had been born in Texas, 1 percent came from foreign countries, and 5 percent came from free states. An overwhelming majority of the men, 93 percent, had come from the rest of the South. More specifically, 26 percent were from the lower south and 67 percent from the upper South. These origins were significant when men decided which military unit to join; most, like James Blewett, who "was born in Warren co., the state of Kentucky," wanted to enlist in a unit whose organizer could promise they would have the opportunity to join an army and defend their extended families in the Western theater.[76]

With his two companies organized, drilled, trained, and armed, Capt. Gano finally had his men ready for military action in 1862. In early March, they patrolled the northern Texas border at Clarksville, Red River County. At that time he received orders from Gen. Albert Sidney Johnston, a fellow Texan, personal acquaintance of Gano, and commander of the Western theater, that the Grapevine Volunteers be mustered into the Confederate army. Gano and his men were to meet Johnston at Bowling Green and serve as scouts for his headquarters. Excited about the opportunity and the prestige of serving as scouts to the highest-ranking Texan in the Confederate army, Gano immediately resigned his position as representative for Tarrant County and mustered his squadron into Confederate service. Gano and his men marched to the nearest Confederate government office, at Witts Mill, Dallas County, Texas. When they finally arrived, on March 6, 1862, they immediately enlisted in the Confederate army for twelve months. The men of the Grapevine Volunteers had a strong desire, if not duty, to defend their parents, grandparents, aunts, and uncles left behind when they moved to Texas.[77]

In the process of getting their men enrolled in the Confederate army, Gano and Huffman advertised in the Dallas *Herald* on January 28, 1862, to fill the openings in their squadron created by men receiving transfers to other units or who had to return home because of illness: "Doctors J. M. Huffman and R. M. Gano, have authority to muster into Confederate service, two companies as a cavalry squadron, to be marched by Little Rock, to Memphis, and thence by cars to Bowling Green, Ky." Not merely making a call for men in Texas to join the Confederate army, this advertisement made a specific call for men who wanted to serve in Kentucky.[78]

For months Gano had been writing to the secretary of war, Leroy Pope Walker, to ask for a permanent assignment in Kentucky after the death of Johnston. In one letter Gano stated that he and his men should be transferred because he had firsthand knowledge of the state and surrounding region. Gano expressed these desires clearly in two letters he wrote while en route to Johnston's command. He tried to get his men attached to the command they desired in the Western theater, arguing that since he had spent his childhood in Bourbon County, gone to school nearby in Harrodsburg, and married a local girl, "I have a knowledge of the country that would aid us greatly in the service of my beloved country. If we should succeed in driving the enemy back out of my native state." The captain was not above the use of flattery: "We hope to vie with

Captain [John] [Hunt] Morgan's Squadron for honors and laurels. We expect a place in your command, and do not let us be disappointed. . . . I shall never get over it if we are placed anywhere else. I used that as an argument in raising the squadron and the consequences was your warmest admirers flocked to us and we must not be disappointed. All we want is that place."[79]

Gano emphasized his men's desire to defend a specific region of the Confederacy, the upper South—especially Kentucky and Tennessee—the area where most of them had been born and where their extended families lived. In another letter, the Texas captain repeated the theme: "I am well acquainted with all central Kentucky and upper Tennessee. . . . We can under Genl B[reckinridge] who knows well the section of country I am acquainted with, render to our country efficient service."[80] Gano and his men got their wish and received orders to join Col. John Hunt Morgan's command. They would fight under Morgan for almost two years, participating in almost every fight as the nucleus of the 7th Kentucky Cavalry. While the unit was fighting in Kentucky, Gano visited his parents behind enemy lines and members of his family still living in the region. Frank and John A. Gano joined his regiment to serve alongside their kin. Additionally, John M. Huffman rose through the ranks and received command of the 5th Kentucky Cavalry.[81]

Many Texans enlisted as individuals in the regiments of other states. One example is Charles Trueheart, who was born in Virginia but moved to Texas with his family as a child. At the outbreak of the war he was studying medicine at the University of Virginia and "felt it my duty to take up arms in defence of this the state of my birth." Initially Trueheart enlisted in a company formed by students at his university, but eventually he transferred to Rockbridge [Va.] Artillery because "a large num[ber of my] college mates belong to it. . . . So I [have] a number of friends and kin to [keep me] company." Another influence on his decision to defend Virginia was his extended family. Throughout the war he constantly visited his kin; he reported to his family in Texas that "all of our kith and kin there abouts were as well as usual." Even though he spent most of his life in Texas, he had a profound devotion to Virginia because he was born there, was attending college there, and had extended family there. He even claimed, "If there is one thing that I am proud of, it is being a Virginian, and a Texan!"[82]

Maj. Thomas Goree had a Civil War career similar to Trueheart's. A native of Marion, Alabama, who attended Howard College, he moved with his family to Texas, where he graduate from Texas Baptist Educational Society (present-day Baylor University) in 1856. On graduating he became a headmaster of a male school in Washington, Texas, and later practiced law in Montgomery County. When the war began, he accompanied the three organizers of Terry's Texas Rangers to Richmond. Though he desired to join the Rangers, his true goal was to receive an appointment as a volunteer aide on Brig. Gen. James Longstreet's

Col. Adam Rankin "Stovepipe" Johnson, commander of the 10th Kentucky Partisan Rangers. Courtesy William C. Davis

staff. By serving in Virginia and fighting under a fellow Alabamian, Goree could defend his native state of Alabama and his relatives in the Old Dominion. While serving in Virginia he spent considerable time visiting relatives and old college friends. He made one trip to visit his cousin David Scott. Another day he "saw George D. Johnston (an old schoolmate at the Howard) Sad Hinton, Lew Sewell, Sel Evans, and several other boys that I used to know about Marion." Goree made the conscious decision to defend Alabama and his relatives in Virginia by serving in Longstreet's command.[83]

The most notable Texan to enlist in another state's regiment was Adam Rankin "Stovepipe" Johnson. Born in 1834 and raised in Henderson, Kentucky, Johnson moved to Burnet County, Texas, at the age of twenty. In Texas he surveyed the frontier and worked on the overland mail route, but he found no success in either. When the Civil War began, Johnson had few material possessions in Texas and sought to do as his friends "Helm and Barnet," who had "returned to their native States." People pleaded with him to stay because he had just married a sixteen-year-old Texan, but that was not enough to hold Johnson in the state. He decided to protect his native state of Kentucky and, more important, the town of Henderson in western Kentucky on the border with Indiana, where his parents still lived. He made arrangements for the safety of his wife in Texas and left for Kentucky.[84]

According to Johnson, once in Kentucky, "I determined first to pay a visit to my father and mother, in Henderson. . . . Henderson was occupied by Northern troops."[85] Johnson, alarmed by the Union occupation of Henderson, sought to join a Confederate command that would promise to stay in western Kentucky so he could protect his old hometown and family in the region. The first commander he met who made this promise was Gen. Nathan Bedford Forrest. After an elaborate conversation with the general, Johnson told him, "I wish to go to Henderson, Kentucky." Forrest responded, "I want to go there, too, and we will go together."[86] Forrest kept his promise, and soon thereafter the unit scouted the area just south of Henderson, where Forrest and his men, except Johnson, fought their first engagement at Sacramento, Kentucky.[87]

Johnson missed the fight because Forrest's men could not reach his hometown for two days, and being too impatient Johnson left for Henderson with an old schoolmate who still lived there. Impatience cost Johnson his opportunity to fight Union soldiers, but it did not matter to him because his main priority was to visit his family and assure himself that they were safe, though they were behind Yankee lines. Johnson eluded the enemy and described his homecoming through the emotions that every family member felt: "We entered Henderson without interruption, and after five or six years' absence, I was soon in the arms of my dear mother." Besides seeing his sister and mother, Johnson visited old schoolmates and his brothers. His homecoming was bittersweet because he knew that he could do nothing at that moment to rid his beloved hometown of the enemy's forces, but it fueled his desire to do what he could.[88]

Albert Sidney Johnston cut the Texan's visit short by issuing orders to Forrest "to hold his command in readiness to move to Fort Donelson." Johnson's reaction was typical of a man with a deep-seated desire to protect his hometown and family. "I was greatly disappointed," he wrote, "for I had anticipated capturing the blue-coats or driving them out of my native town."[89] Though he did not want to obey the order, he left his hometown to fight in the battle at Fort Donelson and accompanied Forrest when he made his escape from the encroaching Union force.[90]

Johnson remained with Forrest as a scout until another threat arose against Henderson. As soon as he and other men from Henderson discovered the arrival of the Union provost guard in Henderson, approximately eighty men, they attacked them and quickly retreated from the town to a nearby family friend's farm to hide from any Yankee retaliation. In the fight, the men killed a captain and a lieutenant and wounded nine privates. Knowing that they could not rid Henderson of the Yankee presence, the men remained outside the town, vigilant to any further threats.[91]

The Texan continued to be extremely sensitive to any perceived threat to his hometown and family. Soon thereafter, Union authorities in Louisville, Kentucky, sent a cavalry regiment to Madisonville with orders to burn the houses of all citizens sympathetic to Confederates. Johnson feared for the safety of his hometown and especially his family, who had given him aid. In an extraordinary response to the threat, Johnson did the unimaginable: he raised a Confederate unit behind enemy lines to protect western Kentucky. Initially, he attracted enough men to create a battalion, dubbed the "Breckenridge Guards," but eventually he raised enough for a regiment that became the 10th Kentucky Partisan Rangers. This Texan not only crossed the Mississippi River to defend his hometown but created a regiment of Kentuckians. While raising the unit, he made an attempt to draw more Texans to Kentucky through a December 10, 1862, advertisement in the Austin State Gazette, to "raise another company of Texas

Rangers to serve in Tennessee or Kentucky under the celebrated A. R. Johnson of Burnet County, Texas, now commanding a brigade of Kentucky cavalry."[92]

Johnson was an extreme example of the Texans who crossed the Mississippi River to defend their old hometowns and kin on the east side. Time and again, Johnson returned to western Kentucky to drive Yankees out of the region and ensure the safety of his parents and sister. When he received orders to leave the region by superior commanders, he would find ways to keep his men in the region. For example, according to Johnson, Gen. Braxton Bragg wanted Johnson's command to remain with his army and ordered all unattached units to fall under his authority. Johnson felt that Bragg would pull him from western Kentucky, so he again sought a command that could guarantee he could remain near his native town. His wishes were fulfilled when Gen. Morgan offered him command of one of his two brigades. Johnson quickly agreed and returned "to my old department of Western Kentucky." In addition, whenever he could not find a local solution to remain in western Kentucky, Johnson was not afraid to look to the seat of the Confederate government. As soon as he felt he was too far from Henderson, he sent letters to Richmond, particularly to Sen. Henry Burnett and Col. William Preston Johnson, two of his old Kentucky friends, and "presented to them urgent reasons for my return to this special territory."[93] Not all Texans were as adamant about a specific location as Johnson, but the influence was still present in most Texans fighting east of the Mississippi.

Texans' desire to fight in the Eastern and Western cis-Mississippi theaters stemmed from a combination of many motivations. A little-studied influence on Texans to join, fight, and stay east of the Mississippi is found in their attachments. Since many Texans had family members, friends, and homes on the other side of the river that appeared more vulnerable to the Yankees than their present homesteads, many enlisted in the Confederate army to defend these attachments. This motivation is more pronounced in Texans than in men in other Southern states such as Georgia and South Carolina. Most other Southerners did not have any real desire to travel hundreds of miles to fight in the trans-Mississippi, because they had only one hometown and it was east of the river. Texans, on the other hand, such as those who fought in the Texas Brigade, Terry's Texas Rangers, the 7th and 9th Texas Infantry, and the Grapevine Volunteers wanted to defend many different locations, and where they chose to fight depended on the attachments in their lives and the strength of the connection they had to them. Texans enlisting to fight east of the Mississippi did not make their decisions lightly; they had a strong desire to protect the families, friends, and hometowns they left behind in those localities.

5

DEMORALIZATION AND DESERTION

Why Texans Returned to the Lone Star State during the War

Perhaps we who are from Tex and Ark may recross the River—God
send the great blessings. I am truly sick of this side, and the vast Army
here. We fare much better when off to ourselves. General Price has gone to
Richmond for the purpose, I think, of getting his troops transferred to the
other side of the River again—his men, as well as those from Texas are
not satisfied here. I would give almost any consideration to touch
the West bank of the Miss River again.

LAWRENCE SULLIVAN ROSS, 6TH TEXAS CAVALRY

A
S the Civil War stretched into a second year and then a third, Texans'
priorities began to change. The men began contemplating whether they
wanted to continue the struggle. Early in the war, soldiers expected the
conflict to be brief, so when Texans received orders transferring them to
the east bank of the Mississippi River there was little opposition. But as the war
progressed, many Texans wanted to return to the Lone Star State, especially
when there was a perceived threat to their homes, wives, and children.[1] Texans,
though highly motivated to fight for the Confederacy, succumbed to the same
despair that many Southern soldiers experienced when the war reached the
doorstep of their homes. The despair Texas soldiers experienced was amplified
for many reasons, including the hardships of soldiering; letters from home detailing the privations of their wives, children, and family members; loss of their
horses; and, most important, the imminent threat to their hearth and home in
the Lone Star State.

Though Texans succumbed to the same influences that affected other Confederate soldiers, they experienced them differently because of the effects of
multiple local attachments. Texans who were recent immigrants to the state, as
most were, had more than one hometown or county. The desire to defend the

place of their birth was initially a significant motivation for many Texans to fight east of the Mississippi River, but the desire to protect their adopted homes influenced them to return to Texas. Though the men left Texas to defend their old hometowns to the East, their attachment to the Lone Star State never wavered. "Back in Tex how I love to think of my own loved Tex," wrote James K. Street of the 9th Texas Infantry. "But what makes it *peculiarly* dear to me, is 'The loved ones at home' are there."[2] When their adopted state faced a serious threat to its security in 1863, Texans begin to reprioritize their motivation to fight for the Confederate cause. No longer was it to protect their extended families east of the Mississippi River but to defend their homes and immediate family, because the North finally threatened them. The danger the Union army posed to Texas during the latter half of the war had a devastating impact on Texans' morale.

John Baynes, a scholar of morale and motivation, argues that a soldier's spirit "is concerned with the way in which people react to the conditions of their existence." Maintaining morale is extremely important in warfare, even more important than tactics, because commanders have difficulty getting soldiers to fight well if their hearts are not in the conflict.[3] When the Civil War began, morale was not a concern for the commanders, because the men's heads were full of romantic ideas of battlefield glory. The romance of warfare quickly dissipated once men experienced combat. A "Letter from the 2d Texas Regiment" appearing in the Houston *Tri-Weekly Telegraph* on July 16, 1862, demonstrated that the realization of war had reached Texas soldiers. In the letter, an unnamed soldier wrote that the "romance of soldiering has pretty nearly worn off, and it has become reduced to facts and figures."[4] Another Texan, John Allen Templeton, expressed a soldier's reaction to the hardships of war: "I must acknowledge that farming is a tolerable hard way of living but 'soldiering' is much harder. It is true that while an army is stationed at one place any length of time it is not so hard—but no telling at what moment we may be ordered on a long march to go to a fight. In marching & fighting there is but little fun."[5] Even the act of drilling in camp discouraged some men, as Samuel A. Goodman Jr. of the 13th Texas Infantry reported graphically in a letter to his parents: "We drill four hours each day under our devil deserving would be Luientenant Great Goodgame. . . . a bigger shit ass never aspired to a position among men than he is."[6]

Texans in the army endured a difficult situation in combat with their lives in peril and witnessed the atrocities of war. When the men "saw the elephant," they realized that the romantic descriptions of war were false. Few soldiers record these feelings, especially in letters back home, because they did not want their loved ones to worry about their safety or consider them cowards or dishonorable. The carnage of warfare and its impact on the minds and bodies of the young men involved led them to see their motivations to fight from a new perspective. William Kuykendall of the 1st Texas Mounted Rifles recorded his feelings of combat in his diary: "I had now seen 'grim-visaged war' with its masque off. How dreadful in its horried features, a regular charnel house of death. . . . The very atmosphere protested as the foul stench from decaying men and beasts filled the nostrils. Friends whom I had left but two short months before in health and strength in full enjoyment of 'vigerous' manhood had immolated themselves on the altar of their country."[7] Scenes of death and destruction, though rarely acknowledged, had a dramatic impact on the morale of Texas soldiers in the Civil War.

Though the soldiers' enthusiasm diminished, the men continued to fight, but not for the same reasons many of them had enlisted. As the Civil War became protracted, some of the initial motivations of the soldiers disappeared. Texans' motivations changed, especially those of the men who enlisted to fight east of the Mississippi River. Men with few or no ties in the cis-Mississippi were the first to reprioritize their motivation. Early in the war, Robert Hodges, born in Galveston two months after the fall of the Alamo, enlisted in Terry's Texas Rangers to fight east of the Mississippi but eventually transferred into the 24th Texas Cavalry. When he realized that the war would not end in a matter of months, he began searching for a way to get back across the Mississippi. In December 1862 he asked his father to "go to Brown's battalion you can perhaps find some one there who would be willing to exchange with me as I have no doubt. There are many there who would prefer this service to that of Texas and Col. Wilkes [said] that I can exchange or get a transfer in that way."[8] As Texans lost the illusions that had initially motivated them to fight, they had to resort to their basic instincts—the desire to defend their wives, children, and their adopted state—before the Union army could harm the people and land they loved. When morale plummeted, those instincts influenced Texans to recross the Mississippi through any means available, whether it be transfer or desertion.[9]

Other reasons morale dropped among the Texans included military discipline, lack of supplies, disturbing letters from home or no letters at all, conscription, and dismounting. Army life and the restrictions within the organization surprised many Texans. Texans, like Southerners generally, were not used to strict segregation within white society. Most Southern whites recognized the differences between the classes, but they did not recognize any significant social stratification among those in their own race, with the exception of Germans and other immigrants from Europe. Their identity as white men, socially equal to all men of the same complexion, was something Texans took for granted before the war and expected to continue through the duration of the war. Army organization and the war disrupted these notions with the distinctions between officers, noncommissioned officers, and enlisted men. These distinctions, combined with army protocol and military discipline, upset many of the soldiers as they fought far from home. Many Texans complain to their loved ones back home, "We don't have any liberties at all."[10] The men felt that the Confederate army violated their social standing and identity as free men.

Restrictions placed on them affected everything from leaving camp to visit friends and family to the portioning of food—simple actions that reminded them of how they treated slaves back home. Consequently, many men related their treatment in the army to the institution of slavery. A cavalryman of the 17th Texas, Gil McKay, relayed these feelings to a friend when camped at Searcy, Arkansas: "The idea of weighing out a certain quantity of meal and meat for 'white men,' say three-quarters of a pound of meat, and a pound of meal or flour a day for each man, struck me with considerable force. It reminded me of what I had often seen overseers do on plantations in Texas."[11] Another member of his regiment went as far to comment, "We are not as free as the negros are."[12] Resentment brewed against the Confederacy. Alexander C. Crain of the 2nd Texas Partisan Rangers noted it well in a letter to his wife: "This regment will go to Port Hudson in five days I dont much like to go but I have to do a heep of things that I dont like I never vowed untill now that white men could be made a negro of. . . . I would like to fight for my Country But this being so confine under a Master I dont like."[13] Crain felt that the Confederate army violated his freedom to go where he pleased, which he easily related to the Southern institution that placed the same restrictions on slaves.

As the war progressed and defeats and casualties mounted, some Texans desired to exchange the bondage of Africans for their freedom and protection of their homes. Thomas J. Goree exclaimed in a letter to his sister that "we must have *more* men, and the places of detailed men will have to be supplied by negroes—and, if needs be, I say put the negroes in the ranks and make soldiers of them—fight negro with negro. I believe they will fight as well or better for us than for the Yankees, and we had better even free the negroes to gain our own independence than be subjugated and lose slaves, liberty, and all that makes life dear."[14] Desperation filled the minds of Texans, changing their priorities from their initial motivations to protect slavery to those closer to home.

Hardships of war test the mettle of any soldier. Studies of morale in war have shown that the spirit of men drops if they are not given good food, proper rest, mail from home, medicine and medical care, and supplies such as clothes, cooking utensils, blankets, and tents. Soldiers can go for periods without these, but not for long. Texans experienced all these hardships. A member of Hood's Texas Brigade, Thomas L. McCarty, wrote, "Our brigade has suffered heavily, and particularly for the necessaries of life, and clothing and shoes. The men are ragged, hatless, and shoeless, fed the greater part of the time one-fourth of a pound of bacon a day, and corn meal and nothing more."[15] In one case troops on Galveston Island received such poor beef that "they buried it with the honors of war."[16]

Early in the war some men, such as William G. Young of the 15th Texas Cavalry, made light of the privations of soldiering: "I had no idea that I ever would become so contented in the army but I do believe it is the happiest life a man can live. After all, we get nothing to eat and but little to wear, have to work hard all the time, get no pay for it, only kicks and cuffs from all the officers, and dang me if this is not enough to make a man be content, he is very hard to please."[17] After prolonged periods of hardship, some men even considered desertion, like the men of the 17th Texas Infantry camped at Pine Bluff, Arkansas, in March 1863. D. E. Young wrote to his wife, "Some Weaks we have plenty and others we have non So you see that it is a feast or a famon with us and that is the reason thaire is so much sicness heare when tha get something to eat tha nerly kill themselves eatine thair is great dissatisfaction among the soldiers som of the Regiment talking about going home if tha don't do beter tha have Promist to do all tha can."[18]

Over time, the conditions in the Confederate army worsened and Texans began to desert. John Simmons of the 22nd Texas Infantry wanted peace to exist between the North and the South, "for we live horrible. We have nothing but bread to eat. We scarcely ever get any meat to eat at all—probably one pound in ten days. The old poor beef we buried in the honors of war, and we declared we would receive no more until after the first of June; consequently, we have to live on dry bread. Our men are deserting daily."[19] Letters describing men deserting their units because of the hardships of war reverberated through the Confederate army. Davis Cook, a soldier in the 35th Texas Cavalry, described the impact of the lack of food and supplies for the men and their horses: "There is a great deal of dissatisfaction with the soldiers. There was 12 deserted the company last week."[20] Some of the most patriotic Texans, not wanting to desert, began to wish for death to relieve the burden of the misery they were suffering. Isaac Dunbar Affleck of Terry's Texas Rangers lamented, "When my mind runs as it does to night—and it often does, I often wish that I had been one that first died for our country in defence of our liberty, then I would not have had to endure all the privations, and sufferings that I have had."[21] When the authorities in Richmond could not provide Texas soldiers the basic needs and comforts for long periods of time, the soldiers' priorities changed and the men escaped their feelings of vulnerability by simply leaving the army for home, where they knew they could be cared for and feel assured that that community would survive while the army was disintegrating.

Mail was essential to the morale of Texans fighting far from home, but it proved to be a double-edged sword. They wanted to hear about the lives of their families back home and constantly asked their loved ones to write. "Write to me often as you can," Alexis T. Rainey urged from Virginia. "You have no idea how much pleasure it gives me to read a letter from my sweet little wife."[22] Another Texan, T. A. Williams of the 3rd Texas Cavalry, complained to his wife, "When you receive this letter, write to me. I have wrote 4 letters and I have no answer yet. Write soon."[23] Even if they never left the state, Texans like P. H. Hill of the 4th Texas Arizona Brigade still longed for letters from home. As Hill wrote from Brownsville, "I want you all to write to me as soon as you get this for I am very anxious to hear from home."[24]

Loved ones back home had trouble comprehending the ideology that drove the men to fight. The main concerns of civilians were what happened on the home front during the war, such as food shortages, inflation of currency, and conditions of their town and farm. People back home expressed these concerns constantly in their letters, ultimately damaging Texas soldiers' morale. Letters showed wives fearing they would become widows and their children grow up without fathers. Parents suffered loneliness and missed their children. The war destroyed many of these letters from home; soldiers would throw them away, or more commonly the letters were lost during an engagement or stolen when left behind in camp. Their content, however, is often clear from the soldiers' responses. Elijah P. Petty of Walker's Division wrote to his wife, "Cheer up, dont despair or be discouraged. Keep all things right and when I give the infernal Yankees their just deserts I will return home to cheer up your spirits and make home happy once more."[25] Col. William P. Rogers of the 2nd Texas Infantry wrote to a friend about why he was fighting in the war against the wishes of his wife and children: "As for myself, I have many strong reasons to urge me to Texas, but my duty to my oppressed and bleeding country is superior to the claims of wife and children, for it is for their sakes, for the peace and quiet of my own home as well as others that I am here and here I will stay until I can return and say to wife, children and friends, 'You have a country'—'it is free.'"[26]

Sometimes parents asked their children to return home, as did the mother and father of Benjamin F. Burke of Terry's Texas Rangers. Burke replied to his parents, "You asked me to try and get a discharge and come home. . . . It is true I would like to go home and see you all but I don't think it becomes any good Southern soldier to want to get a discharge and quit the service in this critical time."[27] Whether letters came from wives or parents, they had a direct influence on the men fighting in any theater by creating a difficult situation for them: Should they obey the army or their loved ones and leave their units?

Some Texans deserted because they received letters from home detailing the poverty and starvation their families had to endure. In Indian Territory, Robert Cannon Horn of the 5th Texas Partisan Rangers penned, "I shall never forget one poor soldier named McDurmitt. . . . It was very dry in Texas. His wife wrote him that there was no water in several miles of her and that she had no way of getting her children to water and food. . . . Then he went home without leave, moved his family to where there was water, and later came back. He was shot as a deserter."[28] John Simmons of the 22nd Texas Infantry witnessed a similar event in Arkansas: "The time is fast coming when everything is becoming demoralized. If a man . . . wants to go home after being absent from his family a long time, if his family should be in a suffering condition and he attempts to go home, he is taken before the whole army publicly and made to kneel down and be shot like a brute. Last Friday that very thing was done; two poor men were shot."[29]

Mothers and sisters also wrote their loved ones trying to coax them out of the army. In a letter to his sister, John B. Long commented about other men's desire to return home. Long wrote, "In one letter that I saw which was written by an older lady to her son. She said to him, my son, come home if you can possibly get off for I believe you are battling on the wrong side." In another letter a young lady wrote to her brother to convince him to come home, rationalizing that the war appeared to have no end and the Confederate army already had enough men in its ranks.[30] It is not known if those men deserted.

Letters of stolen love also impacted the morale of men fighting far from home. Separation from sweethearts strained relationships, and the young ladies back home began seeking new courters. News of these choices reached the men on the warfront. According to 1st Lt. Watson Dugat Williams of Hood's Texas Brigade, "Some of the boys who left Liberty [Tex.] with a hope of turning their sweethearts into wives are becoming very much alarmed—afraid they will take advantage of their absence and get married to some 'home soldiers.'"[31] Later in the war, women back in Texas began marrying men on the home front, which angered the men in Virginia. "I pity the boys that are away off here in Virginia. I don't think the home soldiers have much regard for the 'prospects' of their less fortunate brothers-in-arms who are too far away to attend to their own cares. I mean the Matrimonial prospects. Take Messrs Shaw and Buford for instance and while I cannot in the least bit blame either of the young ladies or the gentlemen yet I should feel right queer if, because I was too far away from home to see my interests, some Sunday Soldier should cut me out."[32] Texans who already felt powerless over their future now had to deal with the sting of lost love to men back home taking advantage of their absence. Overall, letters from home had a deep impact on the morale of Texans and other Confederate soldiers during the war, but they were not the only negative influence on the men.

The Conscription Act of 1862 also contributed to the problem of desertion in the Confederacy. The Confederate Congress passed this law to keep men who initially enlisted for only twelve months in the army for the duration, to organize the army more efficiently, and to distribute the burden of the war on all the states evenly by forcing able-bodied men between the ages of eighteen and thirty-five to enlist. Though intended to strengthen the military, in some ways it did the opposite. It dragged men into service who were not devoted to the cause. Northerners, Germans, Tejanos, and Irishmen were some of the unwilling conscripts. Consequently, these uncommitted recruits made poor soldiers for the Confederacy.[33]

An interesting aspect of the Conscription Act was the thirty-day grace period given to men to volunteer and retain the privilege of electing their officers and choosing their branch of the service. It gave men the opportunity to join the army without the stigma of being drafted. Texans rushed to volunteer so they could avoid the double disgrace of conscription and being forced to serve in the infantry. "If we have to stand a draft," W. S. Howell wrote to his brother in Sibley's Brigade from his home, "I think I will be compelled to volunteer. Every person that can make arrangements to enlist is trying to do so."[34]

Conscription also denied men the choice of unit. Recruiters in the spring of 1862 understood how important it was to the men to choose which company to join and used it to attract men to their units. One such man was newspaper editor Charles DeMorse, who used the looming threat of the draft to raise the 29th Texas Cavalry. In his newspaper, the *Standard*, DeMorse advertised that if men did not rush to join his unit before May 15 they would have no choice of their branch of service or their officers.[35] An advertisement in the *Bellville Countryman* stressed that the men better join before they could no longer choose their branch of service: "Now boys is perhaps the last chance you will have to go into service on your own terms. Who responds?"[36] The Houston *Tri-Weekly Telegraph* also called for men to volunteer before the Conscription Act took affect. The newspaper stressed that "the regiments now in process of formation within the State, will be filled up without delay. The desire to avoid the conscription will drive nearly every man if able to it into the ranks of these regiments, where he will have a vote for his officers."[37] Others, such as Col. Rueben R. Brown, used the *Tri-Weekly Telegraph* to try to pressure men to join: "Col. R. R. Brown, who has a battalion of cavalry, (not infantry, as we before reported) has authority to fill it up to a full regiment. . . . This is about the last chance for cavalry service now to be found."[38]

Without their consent, the act extended the service of currently enlisted soldiers for three more years. The angered ranks believed that the government could not compel them to stay in the army past their original twelve-month enlistment. With feelings of betrayal, soldiers who enlisted in 1861 and early 1862 had lively discussions about conscription. "The Conscript Act," Henry Orr explained, "is the sole topic of discussion in camps—it has many opponents."[39]

Young men disgruntled about their assignment to fight east of the Mississippi River saw an opportunity to leave their units with the passage of the Conscription Act. Since existing units had to reorganize under the act, the men thought they had found a loophole in the legislation. John Allen Templeton, who was sixteen years old when he enlisted in the 10th Texas Cavalry, thought he "was entitled to a discharge by the Conscript Law" because he was not yet eighteen. Templeton had been upset with the Confederate army because he enlisted to fight on the Texas coast but was now in Chattanooga, Tennessee. Though the discharge never occurred, Templeton remained hopeful and fought with the 10th Cavalry until Union troops captured him at the Battle of Chickamauga on September 19, 1863. He served out the rest of the war at the infamous Camp Douglas in downtown Chicago.[40]

Many commanders did not like to receive conscripts, believing them to be lacking in valor and devotion to the cause. Col. William P. Rogers of the 2nd Texas Infantry wrote to his wife, "Lt. Col. Smith goes to Texas this evening in search of conscripts for my Reg—which I hope he will not get, for I do not want them."[41] On the same day, Rogers wrote to Dr. William McCraven, "I will not have them [conscripts] if I can help it. I do not want to command men who have been passed by law into the ranks—no give me the brave men who made a free offering of their services to their country rather than take them I shall ask that my regiment be reduced to Battalion and my rank to that of a Major, not withstanding my Cols. spurs were won at Shiloh and Farmington. If they still force them upon me, I must take the fellows and do the best I can with them."[42] Others such as Capt. Bryan Marsh, commander of Company C of the 17th Texas Cavalry who later gained fame as a Texas Ranger, found a solution to the conscription problem that appeased the original enlistees in his company. The original men in the company recently had received orders to dismount. Upset about their situation, the men wanted out of the army, which Marsh aided. Whenever conscripts arrived in their camp, Marsh became "buisey makin out discharges for the nonconscripts in my company & trying to get them off." Essentially he attempted to replace all the original volunteers in his company with conscripts so the two groups did not have to serve together and the men he respected could return home or join a mounted cavalry unit.[43] Overall, officers feared that conscripts would hurt the morale of the early volunteers.

Texas veterans felt the same way about conscripts, believing that the reluctant soldiers' failure to enlist early had hurt the Southern cause. "Bill had been one of the first to respond to his State's call to arms," wrote Ralph Smith, a young man in the 2nd Texas Infantry. He continued to explain "that the only cause for our failure to crush the United States and end the war in a year was a mortifying fact that there were thousands of able-bodied men in the South who not only refused to volunteer but were skulking in the brush to escape being conscripted. He could not abide a conscript, his idea being that a man who had to be forced into the army would not fight and was good for nothing but to dig trenches after he got there."[44] Others, like Benjamin F. Batchelor of Terry's Texas

Rangers, were "sadly disappointed by the meagre result & poor material" of the conscripts and measured their worth as "one veteran volunteer soldier is worth 20 of them."[45] Some of the veteran's responses were comical. A soldier in the 9th Texas Cavalry felt that Texans who refused to join "ought to live in the swamps of Arkansas the balance of their days without ever seeing the face of a woman."[46] This condemnation does appear too harsh.

It offended some Texans to serve next to men forced into the army. Ralph J. Smith of the 2nd Texas Infantry recalled the relationships between volunteers and conscripts. "Conscripts and volunteers being actuated by different motives, interfere and hinder each other like a Team composed of a lazy mule and a spirited horse, when combined in the same regiment. Our conscripts never amalgamated with the 'boys' as the Colonel always called the remnant of the original volunteers, which was no doubt rather our fault than theirs, for we considered ourselves their superiors, an opinion even in which our officers shared."[47] Elijah P. Petty elaborated on the inferiority of conscripts when he wrote to his daughter, "If it was not for the Army I mean the Volunteer Army not conscripts & drafted men and feather bed soldiers but the Army I would loose all hope of the Confederacy."[48] Hood's Texas Brigade's rank and file also had strong opinions about conscripts. James T. Hunter of the 4th Texas Infantry wrote, "My company now has 70 men, all well and hearty, ever in good spirits and are worth more than a Regiment of your Reconstruction Texas Conscripts."[49] Volunteers' feelings about conscripts had a dramatic impact on their attitude toward the army and the cause they fought for.

Some Texans hated the Conscription Act because it would force their younger siblings into the war. Having already experienced the hardships of war, they did not want to see their younger brothers and cousins go through the same events. In a letter to his sister, John Wesley Rabb of Terry's Texas Rangers asked her to "tell Virge not to leave there upon any consideration to go to the war. Tell him not to enlist till just before they go to draft him and only enlist for Texas service and for as short a time as possible."[50] Overall, Texans disliked the draft because it forced unreliable men into the army and required their younger siblings to enlist and experience the same hardships they had already endured for a year. As a result, veterans deemed a large number of men in units raised during conscription, such as the 22nd and 34th Texas Cavalry, "unreliable and to some extent disloyal."[51]

Another unpopular aspect of the Conscription Act was that men were not able to pick the branch of service they wanted to serve. In 1862 conscription increased enlistment into cavalry regiments because Texans feared that if they waited too long the army would draft them and forced them into the infantry. Men raising units made use of this in their recruiting advertisements. "Last

Chance—," an advertisement read in the Dallas *Herald,* "For men to join a Cavalry Company which will not be dismounted during the war."[52]

Of the various branches of the army, Texans preferred service in the cavalry. Gov. Edward Clark summed up Texans' desire for mounted service: "The predilection of Texans for cavalry service—founded as it is upon their peerless horsemanship—is so powerful that they are unwilling, in many instances, to engage in service of any other description, unless required by actual necessity. This passion for mounted service is manifest in the fact, that no call for cavalry has yet been made which has not been complied with almost instantaneously, and there are companies of this character now throughout the state which are eager for service."[53] Soldiers such as L. B. Giles of Terry's Texas Rangers expressed this strong desire to serve on horseback when he wrote, "The supreme desire was to get into the war in a crack cavalry regiment."[54] William A. Jones of the 12th Texas Cavalry warned his friend John that "if you go to the War, don't go as infantry, for I had rather be a negro and belong to a good man than to belong to the infantry."[55]

Texans' preference for cavalry is apparent in the disproportionate number of the mounted units from Texas in the Confederate army. In 1861, Texas raised sixteen regiments, three battalions, and three independent companies of cavalry compared to seven regiments and four battalions of infantry, about two and a half cavalry units to every infantry organization. Francis R. Lubbock wrote to secretary of war, Judah P. Benjamin, that "efficient cavalry . . . [could] be obtained from this state [Texas] almost to the extent of the male population, but infantry is difficult to furnish."[56] By 1862 the Confederate army was employing underhanded tactics to raise more infantry in Texas. According to Frank M. Files, "It was impossible to get a Texan to join the infantry." To get Files to become an infantryman, enlistment officers used a method "to organize a cavalry troop and them dismount them." Texans "sure did kick when they found they had been tricked." Compared to other states in the Confederacy, such as Virginia, which had twice as many infantry units, Texas differed dramatically in its preference for the cavalry.[57]

Throughout the war, Texans maintained their affinity for serving on horseback. John Wesley Rabb of Terry's Texas Rangers wrote to his mother about his little brother: "Virge, I suppose is in Lt. Mooer's company. A Lieutenant, but he has to walk. I wood rather be a corporal in Company 'F' of the Texas Rangers than to be first Lieu in a flat foot company."[58] In 1862, Richard M. Gano's Grapevine Volunteer squadron "had the alternative presented us, either to be dismounted or to go to Morgan, and act with him as partisans." The Texans felt they had only one choice: They "gladly chose the latter . . . and went on our way rejoicing to Chattanooga, Tennessee" to join Morgan's Brigade.[59]

Though Texans enlisted in cavalry units, they did not always stay mounted. Logistical problems forced the government to dismount fifteen regiments temporarily and dismount seventeen of the fifty-three Texas cavalry regiments permanently, 60 percent of their mounted forces. East of the Mississippi River all but one regiment, Terry's Texas Rangers, received orders to dismount and surrender their horses. Initially, Texans were not very upset, believing their dismounting was only a temporary arrangement. Jim Watson of the 10th Texas Cavalry wrote, "Our Regiment was very much opposed to dismounting until we got here and the General said that it was impossible for us to get forage for our horses and we concluded rather than disband and go home that we would dismount and take it afoot."[60] James C. Bates had a more pessimistic view of their dismounting. He wrote in his diary, "Order from Van Dorn read dismounting us temporarily—only for the emergency. Think the emergency will last the remainder of our term. Some dissatisfaction but most of the men are willing to do anything for the best. I had rather remain cavalry—but am willing to serve my country in any capacity in which I can be most useful."[61] Others such as Thomas H. Seeley remained hopeful: "I am in hopes we will soon be moved up in the interior of the State and be re-mounted."[62]

Texans did not always have as good a reaction to dismounting. "We are dismounted," wrote Joseph David Wilson. "I hate it verry much but I can not help it."[63] Texas soldiers resented orders to dismount because they felt betrayed by the Confederate army. They believed "this order [was] a breach of faith, totally at variance with [their] contract."[64] Dismounting affected not just individual Texans but also groups, as described by William G. Young of the 15th Texas Cavalry: "Our boys all look down-spirited. The cry is when shall I be mounted on a horse again. The Lord send how soon it may be, for a man is as low down as he can get when he has to go as infantry."[65] L. D. Bradley of Waul's Texas Legion commented in a letter to his wife that "cavalry who have been dismounted— have deserted."[66] Dismounting embarrassed Texans, because they felt they had lost their higher status in the army as cavaliers, being relegated to same level as the common infantry soldier.

When ordered to dismount, Texas soldiers gave up something more important than a pet; they lost an animal they considered their comrade in arms. James C. Bates had an emotional parting with his horse: "Today . . . a detail of seven men left for Texas—it seemed like parting with an old friend to see my horse leave. He has carried me so long & so willingly—& through so many dangers that I was loath to give him up. If I should live through the war I will keep him for the noble service he has done."[67] The men were losing more than just a mode of transportations; "they were to part with their best friends and companions, their faithful horses." A. B. Blocker of the 3rd Texas Cavalry described this relationship between the men and their horses as "a good one, that only those who know by experience can appreciate. The boys of the 3rd Texas were too patriotic and too good soldiers, now, to more than express their regret at having to part with their loved horses, and there were many tearful eyes when they delivered them to the men that had been detailed to take them home."[68] Service in the cavalry was important to Texans, and parting with their horses meant losing an animal they had constantly relied on to that point in the war.

Initial reactions to losing their horses were relatively mild compared to their outrage when they realized that the dismounting of Texas cavalry units was to be permanent. From that point on, even the idea of dismounting created waves of desertion among cavalrymen. Henry Orr described the strong reaction in Parsons' Brigade. "Among those to be dismounted," Orr wrote, "there is great dissatisfaction and some of them have started home."[69] Alexander C. Crain of the 2nd Texas Partisan Rangers noted that "we have lost a great many of our boys Since we were dismounted."[70] Other men, such as privates G. G. Pierce and J. A. White in the 10th Texas Cavalry, volunteered to take the horses back to Texas. Pierce and White took advantage of their responsibility and never returned to their regiment. Even officers left their units after receiving orders to dismount. Officers did not have to desert like enlisted men since they had the option of resigning their commissions. Many officers left their dismounted commands only to join another unit that had kept its horses.[71]

Desertion was not the Texans' only reaction. Lt. Robert M. Collins of the 15th Texas Cavalry elaborated on his regiments' thoughts and reactions. "He [Col. George H. Sweet] had a hard time breaking five thousand wild Texans into the infantry harness. Fact is, we were all mad because we had been dismounted, having had our hearts set on doing our soldiering on horseback, and the boys very unjustly charged all this misfortune and hard camp duty, drilling, strict guard duty, etc. to Col. Sweet." In retaliation, the Texans shaved the mane and tail of the colonel's horse.[72]

A few men experienced a deep depression at the change: "Garner came into camps a few days since, yet unwell. . . . I think he has got the Hippo the worst of any man I every saw. He is grieving because he had to be dismounted."[73] Other men had reactions that were far more dramatic and painful. Some Texans knocked out their front teeth so that they could not bite and tear the paper cartridges used by foot soldiers. Some in the 10th Texas Cavalry knocked out their teeth to receive transfers out of their dismounted regiment.[74] Depression and physical mutilation, though not the rule, are common reactions of people after they lose a beloved animal or their position of prestige.

Some were more radical when they lost their horses. After six months without their horses, the men of the 6th Texas Cavalry mutinied. They vowed that they would not obey orders until officers reunited them with their mounts. Newton Asbury Keen wrote, "They wanted to send our horses down the southern part of the state [Mississippi] to winter them and continue us as infantry. Now this did not suit at all and a general row was about to get kicked up. They sent General [John W.] Whitfield over to us, who made us a fine speech, but strange to say when he was through, the boys with one united to shout 'Horses, horses we must have.' He threatened to take our arms from us and put us all under arrest, but we still shouted 'horses,' and further he was informed two hours afterwards the horses were sent."[75]

When dismounted, Texans sometimes reacted violently to get their horses back. Yet nothing brightened their spirits more than receiving orders to remount. James C. Bates wrote to his mother that "the boys are half crazy to get them" when he received news that his regiment was to receive horses again.[76] Other Texans expressed their joy. "How bully I felt when I got on my horse," wrote Newton A. Keen of the 3rd Texas Cavalry. "Our horses were not in good fix at all. . . . But a pair of ribs between ones legs felt very whole some at the time."[77] For some of the men, it renewed the desire to fight. David Grisom wrote home when he heard news of the remounting of his regiment: The "boys are in better spirits now than they have been since we left home. . . . none of us want to come home until we run the last Fed from our soil. You need not look for me until our little confederacy comes out in flying colors. . . . I am content to remain in the army."[78]

Returning horses to Texas soldiers helped keep some of them in the army, but other influences demoralized them, creating a strong desire to return home. The greatest influence on their morale seemed to involve threats to their homes in Texas. Terrorization by Indians and deserters on the frontier and major Confederate defeats and occupations in the Trans-Mississippi and Western theaters were perceived by Texans as threats to the safety and security of Texas. Five battles that had the strongest impact on Texans' morale were those at Pea Ridge, New Orleans, Galveston, Vicksburg, and the Red River Campaign. These defeats symbolized a new threat to Texas since they allowed the Federals to range closer to their state and cut off the Trans-Mississippi Department from the rest of the Confederacy. The feeling of isolation from their homes in Texas became apparent to Texans when they lost control of the Mississippi River. This new threat to the Lone Star State sparked waves of desertion.[79]

In the midst of fighting in different regions far from home, Texans maintained a strong connection to their home state and always pined to hear news from the home front. As in all wars, rumors spread fast and were mostly inaccurate or wrong. Ever worried about home, Texans remained vigilant toward rumors about a Union invasion of the Lone Star State. Even early in the war gossip existed. Some was completely false, such as the news Gil McKay of the 17th Texas Cavalry heard while in Searcy, Arkansas. He wrote to a friend "that the gunboats had shelled Marshall and were on their way to Tyler."[80] Others rumors proved to be true, such as the one spreading through Camp Shavetail in Arkan-

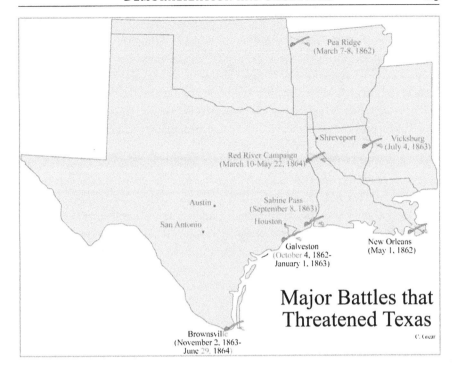

Major Battles that Threatened Texas

sas about the Union occupation of Galveston. Whether the perceived threats to the home and loved ones were true or false, Texans remained vigilant.[81]

Men reacted strongly to these rumors because they witnessed the death and destruction armies produce. In Wartrace, Tennessee, Erasmus E. Marr of the 10th Texas Infantry was comforted in the thought that "Texas is the most fortunate state in the confederacy on account of its distance from the seat of war and of consequence has never been over run by large armies and been subjected to worse cavalry raids If you could but see a country that has been like subjected you would be thankful that it was your lot to be elswhere. . . . west of the mississippi to us is nearly a sealed book."[82] Other soldiers described the destruction in greater detail. Writing to his wife from Boils Parrish, Louisiana, Alexander C. Crain of the 16th Texas Cavalry noted that "the fences the stock cattle and hogs and horses are in the cotton fields Destroying the entire crop the Yankees destroyed all the Shugar and the Shugar Mills in the Country and the (Sitizens) Burnt all the cotton you all no nothing about trouble to thoes people."[83] Not wanting their families to experience such destruction and possibly lose everything they worked for before the war, Texans returned west to protect their now threatened homes.

News of Indian raids and bands of deserters on the frontier chilled the spines of Texans fighting far from home. It instilled a sense of vulnerability for the families they left behind. There was news from the frontier that "one band [of Indians] crossed Red River.... Another party showed themselves in Jack County at the same time, who stole some twenty horses, severely wounded a young lady in each arm and in the breast."[84] Texas leaders took notice of these events. Gov. Francis R. Lubbock commented to President Davis that "the very counties now being ravaged have supplied not only companies, but battalions to the CSA service."[85] The governor then feared "this may be attended with bad effects upon our frontier men who are in the army."[86]

Compounding the problems with Native Americans was the accumulation of deserters on the frontier. William Quayle, commander of the First Frontier District, reported to Henry McCulloch that "the citizens are being killed and pillaged both by Indians and Confederate soldiers. We are certainly in a lamentable condition."[87] At one point in the war, John "R.I.P." Ford, superintendent of conscripts in Texas, estimated that around a thousand deserters hid in the thickets of North Texas. The situation on the frontier became so grave that McCulloch employed Col. William Quantrill and his raiders to round up deserters. Unfortunately, this proved to be a bad idea, since the partisans robbed and pillaged Texans themselves. Concern about the frontier spread across the South, and Texans took notice. John Allen Templeton, fighting east of the Mississippi in the 10th Texas Cavalry, told his brother, "there will be need for men on the frontier of Texas and on the coast."[88] Others such as Maj. Gen. Samuel Bell Maxey returned to the Lone Star State to protect North Texas from the threat of Indians and a possible Union invasion through Indian Territory. Even as far as Virginia, Texans such as Charles L. Martin took actions to protect their frontier homes. A native-born Texan and citizen of Seguin, Martin resigned his commission as 1st lieutenant in the 4th Texas Infantry and wrote to Governor Lubbock that "I thought Texas was threatened [by Indians] and I determined she should have my services.... give me something to do in her defence."[89]

The threat on the Texas frontier paled in comparison to the urgency Texans felt to return to their home state when they heard news of major Confederate defeats and occupations in the Trans-Mississippi and Western theaters. One of the earliest was the Battle of Pea Ridge, followed shortly by the Union capture of New Orleans. Fought on March 7 and 8, 1862, the Confederate defeat at Pea Ridge allowed the Union army to secure Missouri and half of Arkansas. This victory isolated both Kansas and Missouri from the Confederacy and threatened Southern positions within Arkansas and Indian Territory. Soon thereafter the bloodless capture of New Orleans by the Union navy posed another huge threat. New Orleans was the largest city in the Confederacy; more important, it controlled the mouth of the Mississippi. In the hands of its army and navy, the Union now controlled a significant section of the river, placing an obstacle between the Lone Star State and the Texans fighting east of the Mississippi and threatening to cut off the trans-Mississippi from the rest of the Confederacy. Samuel A. Goodman of the 13th Texas Infantry expressed his dismay at the loss of the Crescent City to the North: "I believe in less than 30 days the enemy will set foot on Texas coast, N. O.'s [New Orleans] has fallen, Ft. Jackson also and Texas will be visited next."[90]

"Oh!" exclaimed Henry Orr of the 12th Texas Cavalry after the battles. "Shall the foul foot of the invader even trace the soil of Texas and bring distress upon its people like they have here! God forbid that they may. I wish I were on its soil today to give my life if necessary for its defense."[91] A dismayed William Thomas Darr of the 10th Texas Infantry commented that "there is still less prospects for us gaining our independence then ever since New Orleans is abandoned and given up with out the firing of a gun."[92] Within a month of the defeat at Pea Ridge, James K. Street of the 9th Texas Infantry wrote about a potential wave of desertion in his regiment. "There is still strong talk of disbanding," Street wrote. "I shouldn't be surprised if we do and if we do I shall make right for Texas."[93]

Discussion among Texans about leaving their units eventually became actions. Waves of desertion affected most Texas units that had recently arrived in the Western theater. One month after New Orleans, John Allen Templeton of the 10th Texas Cavalry expressed his dismay in a letter to his father: "I think I will be home In the course of a few months as I am exempt from military duty according to the new military law. . . . I will get off but be assured that it will be at the earliest period for there is no telling at what moment the enemy will be spoiling Texas; & if they should get there I want to be close by."[94] Templeton was not the only Texan in the 10th who wanted to leave the Western theater. Almost a year later his "Cousin Frank says he is going to work for a transfer or his Father is going to rather and wants me to get one and to go with him. He intends going to the coast of Texas and get into artillery service. I would be glad to make such an exchange if I could just get on Texas soil if nothing else." He continued to pursue his desire to return to Texas, because according to him, "nothing would please me better than to get a swap to Johnson's Co. so then I would be where I want to be." Even though he wanted to leave the regiment to return to Texas, he remained east of the Mississippi because "I had rather meet them here than in Texas as this country is already ruined."[95] Like all motivations, his willingness to fight outside of Texas when there was a perceived threat to the state lasted only for a short time.

Other Texans affected by the Confederate defeats at Pea Ridge and New Orleans were the 6th Texas Cavalry and its commander, Lawrence Sullivan Ross. In June 1862, Ross wrote to his wife, "Perhaps we who are from Tex and Ark may recross the River—God send the great blessings. I am truly sick of this side, and the vast Army here. We fare much better when off to ourselves. General Price has gone to Richmond for the purpose, I think, of getting his troops transferred to the other side of the River again—his men, as well as those from Texas are not satisfied here. I would give almost any consideration to touch the West bank of the Miss River again."[96] Later that month Ross again wrote, "I feel that I cannot remain from home longer, and if I can not get a leave of absence, I may resign and return home, & then Enter the service on the West side of the Miss River."[97]

Pea Ridge and New Orleans affected the morale of Ross and the Texans serving east of the Mississippi River, but that influence was not nearly as powerful as the effect of later defeats. On October 5, 1862, the Union navy established a blockade off Galveston that worried all Texans, civilian and soldier. Four days later, U.S. Marines captured the town, then occupied it for nearly four months. It was the first time Union soldiers had set foot on Texas soil and directly threatened the interior of the state. Soldiers from Texas always expressed their concerns about a Union invasion of their state, as Elijah P. Petty wrote: "My feelings, inclinations and all my yearnings are to be in Texas if she is invaded. My all is there—All that is near and dear to me is there and I want to be there to protect it."[98] Even men east of the Mississippi kept their attention on Texas. John Wesley Rabb of Terry's Texas Rangers wrote of the regiment's concern for the safety of Texas when it received news of the Union blockade of Texas ports. "We here it reported in the regiment that Col. Wharton is going to do his best to get this Regiment sent back to Texas because the Yanks have come there. The boys want to go back very much."[99] Texans remained vigilant in regard to their state since their homes, friends, and family still lived there.

Texans outside of the state received news of the Union invasion and occupation of Texas soil. Elijah P. Petty and the men of the 17th Texas Infantry heard news of the capture of Galveston and wanted to respond. While in Little Rock, Arkansas, on December 20, 1862, Petty wrote to his wife in Texas, "I have a good many applications by the boys to be transferred back to Texas to some of the regiments in that state all of which I have refused up to this time as a precident of that kind would perhaps take all my men away as they are all verry anxious to get back to Texas by all means." The 17th wanted the Union army out of their state, and wanted somebody, especially themselves, in Texas to protect their homes and interests. Petty concluded his letter by writing, "It is reported that a part of the Texas troops here will be sent to Texas. . . . I hope so."[100]

Fears created by the capture of Galveston reached across the Mississippi. The men of Morgan's Texas Cavalry, camped in Doniphan, Missouri, received the news of the Union occupation of the island and wanted to return to their native state. A. G. Hervey wrote to his cousin Mollie that "we could fight with greater energy and make ourselves more useful there [Galveston] than here and we all pray to get back to Texas we will do our best to get back."[101] Men in Terry's Texas Rangers received news of the event and expressed their relief when they heard the Yankees were driven out of the city. "We have just herd of the recapture of Galveston by Gen. McGrooder [Magruder]. It does us good to think there is nary a Yankey foot on Texas soil."[102]

Pea Ridge, New Orleans, and Galveston had a deep impact on the morale of all Texans serving outside the state, but not as deep as the fall of Vicksburg on July 4, 1863. Vicksburg was important to both Union and Confederacy. Abraham Lincoln stated the importance of the city and its significance for the trans-Mississippi: "Let us get Vicksburg and all that country is ours. The war can never be brought to a close until that key is in our pocket."[103] The Mississippi River was key to controlling the west. Inspired by Gen. Winfield Scott's Anaconda Plan, the Union army recognized the river was a major component to their strategy for winning the war. Like the large snake, the Union army and navy would work in concert to squeeze the life out of the Confederacy by establishing a blockade on the southern coast and splitting the nation in half by controlling the river. Vicksburg was the last Confederate stronghold on Old Man River. Without Vicksburg, the Union navy could never control the Mississippi.[104]

The Mississippi River, though strategically important to both sides, was especially vital to Texans. Even a year before the "Gibraltar of the West" fell to the Union army, Texans expressed their concerns over its security. William H. Barcroft of the 3rd Texas Cavalry wrote during the siege of Corinth, Mississippi, "If they whip us here and get possession of these Roads here they will have opportunities in a short time and that will cut us off from home entirely for when they get that place they will have the Miss River almost entirely from head to foot."[105] While fighting to defend his old hometown in Arkansas, Drury Connally of Alf Johnson's Spy Company wrote, "No doubt there is much depending upon the next two fights depending at Richmond and Vicksburg."[106] Other Texans felt the same. Hearing the news of a possible transfer from Louisiana to Vicksburg, Elijah P. Petty of the 17th Texas Infantry wrote, "If at Vicksburg we can stab the enemy to the heart or some other vital point, the hand that is laid upon Texas will paralize so that where ever the most service can be done is the place for me."[107] James Black of the 1st Texas Heavy Artillery Regiment viewed the battle for Vicksburg as the turning point of the war, as he wrote to his wife: "If we can repulse the enemy at Vicksburg I don't think the war will last much longer, but if it should fall into their hands, I fear it will be a long time before peace is made."[108]

To Texans, the Mississippi River was an important psychological barrier. As long as the Confederacy controlled the river, it was a bulwark between Texas and the bulk of the Union army. A Texan wrote, "Our lines once broken, whether on the Mississippi or the Arkansas, or the Red River, would have thrown open the approach to the invasion of Texas, by an ever alert and powerful foe."[109] When Vicksburg fell, Theophilus V. Ware of the 27th Texas Cavalry recognized the im-

The Mississppi River as a Barrier, Summer 1863

☐ Union Controlled Territory

☐ Confederate Controlled Territory

C. Grear

portance of the event and expressed the feelings of thousands of Texans when he wrote, "This little Confederacy is gone up the spout."[110] Once the river fell into the control of the Federals, Texans began to fear a Northern invasion into their state. That fear directly affected Texans serving in the Confederate army because they felt that the Lone Star was secure as long as the Mississippi River was an obstacle to the Union. Dr. John Claver Brightman of the 18th Texas Cavalry worried about a possible Union invasion of Texas. In a letter to his mother and friends still in his hometown, he advised them how best to protect themselves from roving Yankees. "If the Yanks should come to Texas," Brightman wrote, "drive all the negroes before you and burn everything as you go, to destroy their subsistence on the country. Gather yourselves together and form bands and companies so as not to let them scatter out in small robbing parties like they have done in this country."[111]

One reaction of all Confederates was a wave of religious revivals that spread across the South. Rev. Thomas J. Stokes, chaplain of the 10th Texas Infantry, wrote, "I have never seen such a spirit as there is now in the army. Religion is the theme. Everywhere you hear around the campfires the sweet songs of

Zion."[112] Defeats on the battlefields, demoralization, and prospects of death led many Texans and other Confederates alike to seek solace and to believe that the only way the South could win was through religious atonement. Texas soldiers noticed the increased revivals. P. T. Taylor from Hopkins County recorded, "We have at this time and place one of the finest revivals of religion going on that I ever witnessed in my life. . . . Between 250 and 300 have joined the Methodist Church and about the same have joined the Baptist Church sinced it commenced."[113] The men of Terry's Texas Rangers and the 28th Texas Cavalry, just to name a couple of Texas units, witnessed an increase in the number of religious revivals just after the fall of Vicksburg when meetings sprang up in their camp in Rome, Georgia, in late July 1863. As the war progressed into 1864, the revivals continued. As John Simmons of the 22nd Texas Infantry confessed, "I must let you know that we have meetings here nearly every night, and they are right well attended by the soldiers."[114]

Though chaplains helped spur on the revivals, many Baptists in Texas saw the chaplain service as corrupt. To combat corruption, Baptist churches sent missionaries to reinforce the spiritual well-being of the Texas soldiers. Texas churches also published Bibles, hymnals, and religious newspapers for the men. Both chaplains and missionaries contributed to the revivals, which inspired the men to continue the fight. Additionally, loved ones back home held revivals of their own to regain God's favor for the Confederacy. Lawson Jefferson Keener of the 2nd Texas Mounted Rifles wrote to a friend of a revival back home as reported by another friend: "Kelcy Power . . . has gone to Texas again. He spoke of a large revival that was in progress at Wright's Church when he left but did not know how long it would continue."[115] The heightened religiosity helped prevent the collapse of the Confederate armies and strengthened the men to endure the stress of combat. As the war ended, revivals increased in number because the church was a symbol of stability that provided the people of the South strength to endure the violence and social changes during Reconstruction.[116]

If the Mississippi River fell under the control of the Union navy, almost all Confederate traffic to Texas from east of the river would be cut off. Texans serving there would be effectively isolated from their homes and immediate families. The most noticeable effect of the control of the river involved the communications between the Trans-Mississippi Department and the rest of the Confederacy. Before the Union navy had complete authority over the Mississippi, it controlled some of the tributary rivers. Though not severing all communication between the cis- and trans-Mississippi, the Confederate defeat at Vicksburg did affect the amount of mail leaving and entering Texas. Van Zandt "had much rather they were below than above [Port Hudson]. . . . I don't like having our communication with Red River cut off."[117] A few days later he complained to his wife about the lack of correspondence: "I am consequently getting anxious to hear from you again. The fault must be in the mail as no one has had a letter from home since then. I am afraid that our letters will be very slow in passing to & fro as long as the Gunboats are in the river between here and Vicksburgh."[118] Finally, one month later, Van Zandt gave up and accepted the inevitable: "I presume our mail will be very irregular so long as the 'Feds' are between us."[119]

If partial Union control of the Mississippi hindered communication with Texas, complete dominance, established by the fall of Vicksburg, cut it off entirely. Jeremiah Caddell of the 4th Texas Infantry commented, "Viseburg [Vicksburg] had fell in to the hands of the Yankie's and there is a bad chance for letters to pass but I hope there will be someway to pass them threw."[120] Caddell was correct, and it had a significant impact on the morale of the Texans. "Our communication with Texas," M. K. Simmons wrote, "is entirely cutoff & it's a great drawback to my happiness." A few days later Simmons continued, "I really feel lost since the mail with Texas has stopped."[121] John Gardner McNemar, of Waul's Texas Legion, elaborated on the effects of the loss of the Mississippi River, a month after the fall of Vicksburg: "Our communication is almost entirely cut off from home. . . . Since the fall of Vixburg everything has bin very gloomy in this part of the army."[122]

The lack of communication with their homes demoralized Texans. Van Zandt knew that the fall of Vicksburg would dishearten Texans, both in the army and back home: "I suppose the fall of Vicksburg and the consequent possession of the whole of the Miss. River by the Feds made you all feel pretty blue, did it not? . . . It is indeed a dark hour to us."[123] Less than five months later he wrote to his wife from Chattanooga, "I shall take steps to get away from here as soon as practicable. . . . I would not have any hesitancy about resigning, and would adopt it as the least objectionable course to pursue."[124] Benjamin F. Burke of Terry's Texas Rangers elaborated less than a month after the fall of Vicksburg: "Vicksburg . . . has cut our further communication off from Texas east of the Miss. river. There has never anything happened during the war that I regreted as bad as the fall, of Vicksburg."[125] Vicksburg had a huge impact on the morale of Texans in every theater of the war. Desertion increased throughout the Confederate army after the simultaneous defeats at Vicksburg and Gettysburg, but to Texans Vicksburg had a greater effect because with the loss of the Mississippi River the enemy now blocked their way home.[126]

Cut off from home, Texans, especially those fighting east of the Mississippi, began to desert. The day after the fall of Vicksburg, Christian Wilhelm Hander, a captured German soldier from Waul's Texas Legion, recorded in his diary, "What will happen to us, everybody is asking and in unison we say, 'To Texas we want to go.'"[127] Feelings of uncertainty and desires to desert back to the Lone Star State spread across Texas units, and dozens of men in the 9th Texas Cavalry returned to their homes. James C. Bates wrote from Vernon, Mississippi, on September 3, 1863, "About 30 men have deserted the Brigade within the last two weeks—ten of them from my old co. . . . The men of this Brig are very much dissatisfied & want to get west of the Miss. I look for more desertions as soon as we move from here. They are not tired of the war but *of this state.*" Some of the men simply returned to their homes, but many joined other Trans-Mississippi units. Bates explained this to his mother: "You will probably hear before this reaches you of the desertions in this Regt. . . . Saying they will enter the service on that side of the river does paliate their offense, but it is on the other hand, an aggravation of it." Though he did not react in the same manner as his men, Bates had the same feelings of dismay about the loss of Vicksburg, which he summarized when he wrote, "My military aspirations have been long since satisfied & since Texas is threatened I would sooner than not return home." Bates and the men of the 9th Cavalry who remained behind believed that the government would transfer the unit to the trans-Mississippi once enough men deserted its ranks. They did not get their wish.[128]

Texans in other units east of the Mississippi River expressed their concerns about a vulnerable Texas. Maurice Kavanaugh Simmons of the 2nd Texas Infantry, which surrendered at Vicksburg, resigned his commission to fight under Gen. John Bankhead Magruder in Texas. Simmons wrote, "I joined the service in 1861; was a member of the 2nd Regiment of Texas Infantry; and expected to continue in service 'till the war should end, but three years absence from home has produced many changes. The Wolf [Union army] is at my door & I have but *one Leg* with which to repel him."[129] The Union threat appeared imminent, and Simmons had to protect his home state. Others in the 2nd Texas Infantry decided to leave Vicksburg immediately after it fell because they did not want to wait for the Confederate army to arrange a prisoner exchange. Men such as J. Henry Cravey just wanted to return to Texas. He wrote, "Myself brother Bill and Silvester Head we puld [pulled] out to ourselves. We got to the river all right," built a raft, and "Findla [Finally] we got over the river all right we felt like birds let out of a cage. We was on our way home."[130]

Other units experienced the demoralizing effect of the loss of Vicksburg. In a letter to his sweetheart, Andrew J. Fogle of the 9th Texas Infantry wrote, "They have got now the most of our importante plases now and if they ceap on like they have bin for the last twelve monthes our little Confedrecy will go up."[131] By October 1863, Fogle also wrote about desertion in his regiment for the first time during the war: "Their has bin severl that has Deserted from our Regiment That is one thing that I nevr expect to do: there is severl more talks of Deserting we had one to leave our compney at that was Sipe bush."[132] By November of that year, desertion had become a major problem in the regiment. Even the men sent back to Texas to gather deserters used the opportunity to leave the cis-Mississippi. Jesse P. Bates noted to his wife, "I am in hopes that James Hooten will act more honorable than many that has gone to Texas and has not returned."[133] Additionally, the 3rd Texas Cavalry experienced increased desertion in the fall of 1863. James Black of the 1st Texas Heavy Artillery stated it best: "The men are still deserting from here occasionally. . . . There is a great deal of dissatisfaction among the troops here. Many of them are whipped since the fall of Vicksburg."[134]

Vicksburg's fall even affected Texans with the strongest connections outside of Texas, such as Hood's Texas Brigade, Terry's Texas Rangers, and Ross's Texas Brigade. Men in these units had a strong desire to protect their old hometowns, but the idea that Texas was vulnerable influenced the men to change their priorities—from defending the unprotected homes of their early life to protecting the homes of their present and future. According to James Henry Hendrick of the 1st Texas Infantry, "Our brigade sent a petition to Governor Murrah asking him to use his influence to get the brigade across the Mississippi River."[135] The author of the petition was Brig. Gen. Jerome Bonaparte Robertson, commander of the Texas Brigade, who that winter wanted to get a furlough for the men to return to Texas to rest and recruit. Though unsuccessful in his bid, he eventually returned to Texas, where he commanded the state reserve forces until the conclusion of the war. Another man from the brigade simply wrote, "All I wish is I wish I was in Texas."[136] Even the most celebrated and proud of the Texas units succumbed to fears of losing their adopted state.

Once Texans realized that they would not receive transfers to trans-Mississippi units, some found other ways to get what they wanted. William H. Lewis provides insight about the effects of the Confederate defeat at Vicksburg on the men in Hood's Texas Brigade. He wrote to his mother in early August 1863, "I am very *tired* of all this and I have written to Uncle Albert to procure me a *substitute* at any *price*. I am fully aware that if I get one, a great howl will be sent up by various people at home and perhaps, it may not accord with your ideas of patriotism but I cant help that, and permit me to say not of yours but others opinion that I care less. . . . When I get there, I shall *repose* for a month or two and then I shall join some *cavalry* Co. Or Regt where I can see an easy time of it the balance of this unhappy struggle."[137]

Some men exposed their extremities, especially their hands, in hopes of getting a minor wound and being sent home on furlough. Joseph B. Polley commented on such an instance during the thick of the battle of Chickamauga when a comrade, Tom, "stepped behind a tree, and, while protecting his body, extended his arms on each side and waved them frantically to and fro, up and down." When asked what he was doing, Tom replied, "'Just feeling for a furlough' . . . and continued the feeling as if his life depended on it." These feelings proved contagious as the war progressed. During the battle of Knoxville, another friend

Brig. Gen. Jerome Bonaparte Robertson, longest-serving
commander of Hood's Texas Brigade. Courtesy Massachusetts
MOLLUS Photograph Collection, U.S. Army Military History
Institute, Carlisle Barracks, Pa.

of Polley was shot in the foot. The man exclaimed enthusiastically, "What will
you give me for my furlough boys?" as he limped back behind the lines. Polley
and several other Texans "would willingly have changed places with him."[138]

Other men had even less honorable reactions. According to A. B Hood of the
5th Texas Infantry, "Many from our Brigade are deserting."[139] Similarly, Jeremiah

"Just Feeling for a Furlough." Courtesy *Confederate Veteran* 5 (1897): 104.

Caddell of the 4th Texas Infantry penned, "There is a good many of the boys in this Brigade will take what they call a French furlough and come home."[140] Lt. James R. Loughridge of the 4th Texas Infantry found an ingenious way of getting back to Texas by becoming "a member of the State Legislature for the County of Navarro, Texas." He quickly resigned his commission and was back in Texas "in time for the meeting of the Legislature."[141]

Men serving in Terry's Texas Rangers were no strangers to the demoralizing effects of isolation from Texas. George Washington Littlefield expressed his desires to return to Texas in a letter to his wife at the end of July: "Oh how mutch I wish I was only off for Texas. My heart would be filled with overflowing joy. . . . Just to think that I was off for my home in Texas."[142] Lucky Rangers like Issac Dunbar Affleck were able to serve in the trans-Mississippi after the fall of Vicksburg. In May 1863, Affleck received a discharge because of a wound he received near Sparta, Tennessee. He spent six months at home recovering from his wound and quickly requested an appointment under Maj. Gen. John Bankhead Magruder, commander of the Texas District, so he could serve the remainder of the war in the Lone Star State. Once assigned to a Texas unit, Affleck wrote home, "I am ready to give my life in defence of Texas, and our home if it is required." After the fall of Vicksburg, Littlefield, Affleck, and other Rangers desired to get back to Texas to defend their state, homes, and loved ones.[143]

None of the Texans were unaffected by the event, even those who had the strongest attachments to land east of the Mississippi. Richard Montgomery Gano of the Grapevine Volunteers, Charles Trueheart of the Rockbridge Artillery (Virginia), and Adam Rankin Johnson, who formed the 10th Kentucky Cavalry, exemplify Texans wanting to fight to defend their childhood homes and extended families. All three men decided to leave the cis-Mississippi, but only one returned during the war.

Far from his immediate family and demoralized by the lack of success in recapturing Kentucky, Gano contemplated leaving his command to protect his parents, who had relocated behind Confederate lines in Brandon, Mississippi, and traveling back to Texas to ascertain the condition of his wife and children. Not wanting to resign his commission or lose face among his men and fellow Kentuckians, Gano sought a medical leave. In June 1863, fellow doctor B. Marshall, surgeon of Gano's Kentucky brigade, diagnosed the Texan with hypertrophy and valvicular disease of the heart—an enlarged heart that could be life threatening. After receiving his diagnosis, Gano requested a leave of absence to Brandon and began planning a trip to Texas. Evidence suggests that Gano authored or requested the false diagnosis from the surgeon so he could visit his family. During that era, people with an enlarged heart normally lived short lives, but Gano lived a vigorous life into his eighties.[144]

That month he paid a quick visit to his parents in Brandon before venturing back to Texas to check on his young family. While he was visiting his wife and children, Gano's fears of an exposed family were confirmed by news of the fall of Vicksburg. Just as bad, as he reported to Gen. "Prince" John Magruder, commander of the District of Texas, "the Indian depredations upon our frontier had created such intense excitement in the minds of those from Parker and Johnson Counties that it was almost impossible to retain them [militia] in camp long enough to organize, their families being in immediate danger."[145] Compounding the already

Lt. James R. Loughridge, 4th Texas Infantry, Hood's Texas Brigade. Courtesy James Rogers Loughridge Family Papers, Pearce Civil War Collection, Navarro College, Corsicana, Tex.

desperate situation, the now isolated Trans-Mississippi began preparations for a simultaneous invasion from Louisiana, Arkansas, and Indian Territory. Now that the Union army was threatening his and his fellow Texans' immediate homes, Gano replaced his original desire to protect his parents in Kentucky with that of defending his home, wife, and children back in North Texas. He managed to get a transfer to Texas commanding the state troops. But before he could take command, he had to return east to report from his leave of absence and also to gather his remaining Texans to return to defend their home. Unfortunately for Gano, his absence corresponded with Morgan's disastrous raid into Ohio, which left him with fewer than two hundred Texans to command—the rest being captured, killed, or missing. When he returned east, Gano found Morgan's command severely diminished, demoralized, and leaderless, all on the eve of the battle of Chickamauga. Now being the highest-ranking officer remaining, Gano received orders to take authority of the survivors and escort Nathan Bedford Forrest. The men fired the first and last shots of the Confederate victory. Despite this uplifting triumph, Gano and his Texans still left the Western theater for Texas.[146]

Once in Texas, Gano did not receive command of the state troops but that of the 5th Texas Cavalry Brigade, on October 24, 1863. He spent the remainder of the war fighting in Arkansas and Indian Territory alongside Gen. Stand Waite and his Confederate Indians. Other men from Gano's original squadron also left the ranks of the 7th Kentucky. Late in the war, ten men from Company A transferred to the 9th Texas Cavalry, and twenty-five went to the Douglas Texas Battery. Also, nineteen men from Company B transferred to the 6th Texas Cavalry, including Gano's original co-commander of the Grapevine Volunteers, John Huffman. The remaining men served as the general's personal escort, known as Gano's Guards. The men viewed Kentucky as a lost cause and wanted to defend the only home they had left.[147]

Trueheart, the college student in his former state of Virginia, succumbed to the same demoralization of other Texans along with a strong desire to return home during the latter part of the war. In early August 1864, Charles wrote to his brother Henry that "I am going to get a transfer to the [Hood's] Texas Brigade; . . . By being in our Texas [Brigade], there are sundry advantages that I shall enjoy in addition to those now mine. Everybody from our state visiting this section, communicates either in person or by letter with the Brigade; so with persons going to Texas, furloughed, detailed or discharged men, and others. The Brigade being very small and all efforts to recruit it, or even to bring back those gone home on furlough." Charles continued, "It is not at all improbable that it will be sent to the Trans-Mississippi this winter. Or should the war come to a close during my life time and yours, I would thus stand a better chance than in any other command, to go back to the Lone Star State at an early period." Although

Charles wanted to return to Texas, he remained in Virginia until the end of the war.[148]

Similarly, Johnson wanted to leave for Texas, but a strong emotional appeal from the men in his regiment kept him fighting to free his hometown of Henderson, Kentucky. "Colonel Martin (another Texan) and I," wrote Johnson, "began making preparations to go to the Trans-Mississippi department." "Martin and I were occupying at that time an old deserted cabin, and consumed the rest of the night in making arrangements to cross the Mississippi river, and discussing what we would do after our arrival in Texas." Johnson and Martin never left the cabin for Texas. They remained east of the river because the men in their regiment approached them with pleas for them to stay. Both Texans, moved by this gesture and the emotions of their men, decided to fight for Kentucky for the balance of the war.

The remainder of Johnson's time in Kentucky proved to be some of the most adventurous in the war. He replaced Gano as commander of the 11th Kentucky Cavalry in Brig. Gen. John Hunt Morgan's command and participated in the great raid in Ohio and Indiana. When Union troops surrounded the command at Buffington Island and captured Morgan, Johnson, leading a few hundred men, made a daring escape and took command of the remainder of the force until Morgan's escape. Johnson's service to the Confederacy ended abruptly on August 21, 1864, when one of his men accidently shot him through both eyes during an attack on a Union camp in Caldwell County, Kentucky, northeast of Henderson. The shot blinded Johnson, rendering him unable to continue the war. Within three weeks of his wounding, President Davis promoted him to brigadier general. Johnson spent the rest of his life, fifty-seven years, in Texas, where he founded the town of Marble Falls. When his life ended in Burnet, Texas, he was one of the last remaining Confederate generals.[149]

Demoralization over the loss of Vicksburg affected not only Texans serving east of the Mississippi River but also many in the trans-Mississippi. Men of the 28th Texas Cavalry, serving in Louisiana, became dispirited from the combination of the fall of Vicksburg and homesickness. Nor were they alone. Other Texans in Louisiana experienced the same demoralization. Dr. John Claver Brightman of the 18th Texas Cavalry explained the importance of Vicksburg and the control of the Mississippi River to his brother just after the major Confederate defeats at Vicksburg and Port Hudson: "One thing is certain: It is going to have the most demoralizing effect of anything that has occurred during the war. You can hear the expression every day by our men that we have 'gone up the spout.'" In a subsequent letter, Brightman wrote about the prospects that they would return to Texas: "There is a rumor that our regiment will be called back to Texas, and if it is so, the order will be soon issued. Our colonel is now in Texas on leave, and wants to go back very much. If an order can be secured, he will have it issued."[150] Similarly, Thomas Rounsaville in Monroe, Louisiana, wrote that the fall of Vicksburg "caused deep gloom among our officers and arms on this side. Cut off from all communication for the Feds can soon take Port Hudson, then Richmond and we are gone up I fear. Very near that now."[151] Even though the Texans were in nearby Louisiana, they still wanted to return to Texas to protect the localities where their families lived.

The effect of the loss of Vicksburg intensified during subsequent months. A series of letters from Alexander C. Crain of the 16th Texas Cavalry to his wife demonstrate the increased effects on the men from Texas. Initially the men, stationed in Louisiana, responded to the news with some reserved optimism. Crain explained that "Port Hudson and Vicksburg have fallen this is a big slam on us." After a few days the magnitude of the events made "it all the officers can Do to keep the souldiers from going home." The following day, "We had a big bust up in our camps last evening there were some thirty of our Boys started to Texas but were overtaken and Brout back." The men of the 16th appeared dissatisfied with the war, but according to Crain the problem was growing: "It looks like our army will all bust up Since the fall of Vixburg & fort Hudson." Demoralization even infiltrated the leadership of the regiment, with officers essentially deserting through the privileges bestowed on them with their commissions. The desertion of significant numbers of soldiers was also affecting other regiments camped nearby: "They have got about Sixty of Stones regiment now under garde for trying to Dissert." The progression of demoralization and desertion did not affect just the 16th Texas Cavalry; it showed up in many Texas units across the South.[152]

Others in Louisiana, such as Elijah P. Petty, felt the same demoralization created by the loss of the Mississippi River. By August 1863 he was writing, "They seem ready to give up. Our army is not in the best condition. Dissatisfaction and mutinous feelings exist to a considerable extent." More than a week later, Texans acted on their feelings. "There is great dissatisfaction in the army here." Petty wrote. "Men are insubordinate and between us I would not be surprised if this army was comparatively broken up. Men say that they will go home and let the Confederacy & war go to hell etc." Noticing the increased number of desertions in the regiment, Petty began to worry about the security of Texas. "After they (Yankees) get into Texas their steps will all be bloody for we must & will contest every inch of ground, if we are true to ourselves to our country and to our families."[153] Similarly, David M. Ray of the 19th Texas Infantry commented in September 1863 that demoralization "pervades the army to a considerable extent so much so that for the last week or ten days there has been more or less desertions every day. . . . in some regiments they make very bold in talking about it, a few nights ago a crowd of them came by our regt and hallooed for all men who wanted to go to Texas to fall in."[154] No matter where Texans served, the fall of Vicksburg affected their morale. This demoralization continued until the end of the war.

After the summer of 1863, other threats to the Lone Star State influenced Texans to return to their native state. Threats such as the September 7, 1863, Union assault at Sabine Pass was a feeble attempt to invade Texas. Lt. Dick Dowling and a handful of artillery men and six cannons in a mud fort repelled the advances of a significant Union flotilla on the Texas-Louisiana border. A month later a futile overland and amphibious assault on the Texas coast was easily thwarted by Texas troops. Throughout the rest of the fall, Union Gen. Nathaniel P. Banks ordered numerous insignificant assaults along the Texas coast—at Brownsville, Rio Grande City, Aransas Pass, and Matagorda Island. News of Banks's landings on the coast created a strong reaction among the men of Hood's Texas Brigade. 1st Lt. Watson Dugat Williams recorded that "we have lately heard that the enemy are holding Brownsville and Mustang Island. Efforts are being made by Gen'l Robertson to get his Brigade transferred to the Trans-Miss. Dept."[155]

Although these actions alerted Texans, the Red River Campaign posed a greater threat to their home state. The threat to Texas along the Red River Valley was the most direct menace to the interior of the state because it led directly to Shreveport, Louisiana, the headquarters of the Trans-Mississippi Department. From there Banks's army could advance west into Texas. Lt. Gen. Edmund Kirby Smith, commander of the Trans-Mississippi Department, began preparing for this invasion in March 1863—before the fall of Vicksburg. Smith thought the Union army would launch its attack when the spring rains swelled the rivers, making them more navigable for the brown-water navy to reach Shreveport. Texans were not ignorant of this threat and awaited any news of a Union advance up the river.[156]

Common Texas soldiers anticipated the Red River Campaign early on. Lawson Jefferson Keener of the 2nd Texas Mounted Rifles commented in a letter he wrote at Shreveport to a friend: "Our position is said to be a very strong one & I have heard experienced men say that we are building the strongest breastworks that they have ever seen in all their travels."[157] Others lamented that "it will not be long before the war will caried in to Texas"[158] Even Texans east of the Mississippi, such as Isaiah Harlan of the 10th Texas Infantry in Chattanooga, Tennessee, heard of the threat to Texas, which produced a strong reaction: "It is said that the feds are preparing to invade Texas. If this be so I would like very much to be there to meet them on Texas soil."[159] Issac Dunbar Affleck produced a more dramatic response to the danger of a Union invasion of Texas: "I am ready to do any thing and sacrefice every thing, but honor if it will only end this war. I have but one time to die and although I am not prepared to meet death, I am ready to give my life in defence of Texas, and our home if it is required. I am satisfied that we will have to fight here, and that before many days."[160] Luckily for the Texans, General Smith had correctly anticipated the Yankee invasion in the spring of 1864. On April 8 and 9, the Army of the Trans-Mississippi, composed largely of Texans, confronted the enemy at Mansfield and Pleasant Hill, Louisiana, forcing Banks to retreat back to New Orleans.[161]

The advance up the Red River Valley was not the only component of the campaign. A small force of Union soldiers under Maj. Gen. Frederick Steele advanced south from Little Rock and Fort Smith, Arkansas, attempting to rendezvous with Banks at Shreveport. Confederate forces intercepted Steele's army at Prairie d'Ane, Arkansas. This little-anticipated attack caught Texans off-guard and created a sense of vulnerability. After the Confederates repelled the Union soldiers at Prairie d'Ane, Keener hoped for a transfer from Camp Ford, a prisoner camp outside Tyler, Texas, to Arkansas to meet another attempt to invade Texas. "The company has petition to Gen Smith to remove us the petition will be sent up by the next mail. I hope he will approve the petition & order us to Ark. Old men & boys could fill our places garding prisoners & we can take the field servis."[162]

Though the Confederates thwarted the Union offensive, the fighting continued as Banks's army retreated back to the Mississippi River. Texans, now relieved that the Union army no longer threatened their homes in the Lone Star State, recognized the significance of capturing the battered and demoralized men in Banks's command. Inspired by their victories, men put aside their hardships in hopes of ending any threat to their state once and for all. Lt. John A. Stranahan of the 21st Texas Cavalry recorded, "We have suffered at times for something to eat, but I have heard less grumbling in the last two months. . . . Nearly every man I saw was willing to suffer any amount of hardship to accomplish the capture of Banks Army."[163] Once Banks reached the Mississippi, the men could finally feel relief: "Thus our State was spared a formidable invasion and its inevitable consequences—ruin and devastation."[164]

The euphoria Texans felt after their victory in the Red River Campaign did not last. During the final year of the war, Texans' morale did not recover but continued to plummet until they surrendered in 1865. Men continued to desert on both sides of the river. In the closing year of the war, cavalrymen in Parsons's Texas Brigade became very disenchanted. According to J. C. Morriss, "I think I will get to be of no accounts as a soldier for when a soldiers sets his head to go home, I have noticed, that they are no account until they do get to go, and I have got my head set homeward and I will never be satisfied until I get there."[165] Other men in the brigade had similar feelings. "The boys are very impatient and in great suspense." As George W. Ingram wrote to his wife, "They have their heads set homewards and many are determined to go orders or no orders. I hope that we may be ordered to go very soon and that no one will disgrace themselves."[166]

Contributing to their desire to return home late in the war was the combination of Lincoln's reelection in November 1864 and the prospect of another year of war in January 1865. Texans, like many others across the South, began to desert once again at the start of the new year. Pvt. Georg Wilhelm Schwarting, a captured German soldier in the 24th Texas Cavalry who was exhausted with the war, noted, "Should the Union have the misfortune to re-elect the current president, meaning that peace will be postponed for another 4 years, then I'll be going to Texas in the fall or the spring, and probably from there back to Germany. I just don't feel comfortable here in Yanky-land." He never fulfilled his threat and returned to the Confederate army as a cavalryman in Louisiana.[167] Similarly, T. J. Dilliard of the 28th Texas Cavalry expressed his frustration while at Camp Gano in Arkansas:

Reliable news has reached here that Abe Lincoln is President for the next 4 years. This is discouraging to soldiers of this department with Abe as the President of the United States is expected a continue of the war for the next 4 years. There are but few of our soldiers that are willing to fight for another 4 years without pay or any other Thing furnish by the government. I find more dissatisfaction and discontent in Camp Than I have seen before The greater part of this Brigade declare That They will not serve any longer Than Spring all have been looking forward to the year 65 as the ending of the war and if their hopes are not realized I know not what wille be the Course taken but believe that a great many of our men will go home.[168]

Lincoln's reelection and the start of the new year served as an artificial deadline for the men. If the new year came and the war had not ended, then they would refuse to continue to fight.[169]

Texans even began protesting openly against any rumor they heard about orders transferring them east of the Mississippi River. Men in Polignac's Texas Brigade did

Col. James E. Harrison, 15th Texas Infantry and later commander of Polignac's Brigade. Courtesy Library of Congress

just this. James E. Harrison, a regimental and later brigade commander, wrote
to his son that "muttered protests over the proposed crossing of the Mississippi developed into stubborn opposition in August, 1864, among members of
both infantry divisions who preferred to serve in defense of their home states.
Two hundred men of Polginac's division deserted," and Harrison admitted that
"there has been a greaded [great deal] of excitement in my Brigade. I have lost
123 deserted, [who] *wont cross the River.* There are many others who dis like it
extremely."[170]

Other Texans, such as Joseph David Wilson, had no desire to cross the river.
Wilson wrote to his sister, "They think we will have to cross the Mississippi River
but I do not know whether we will have to cross the river or not but I hope we
will not have to cross."[171] Texans continued to worry about being forced to fight
in the East. In March 1865, members of David S. Terry's Texas Cavalry heard
rumors they would have to cross the river. J. D. Wilson responded that "I hope
we will not have to cross."[172] Even Gen. John Bankhead Magruder noticed the
discontent among Texans when the men in the Arizona Brigade "behaved well
untill the Regiment was ordered out of the state."[173] The most extreme case involved Capt. John Guynes of Company F of the 22nd Texas Infantry. When he
received orders late in the war to cross the river, he said "he did not blame the
men for not wanting to cross the river, and . . . that he was not going across, that
he would disband his company to meet him in a thicket in Texas." For these actions, his commanders ordered his execution by firing squad on March 15, 1864,
in front of all the soldiers in the camp.[174]

The negative impact of crossing rivers was not limited to Texans. Missouri
soldiers in Lt. Gen. Sterling Price's army stated that they would refuse to cross
the Red River into Texas if the general's retreat from Little Rock in August 1863
took them there. Like the Mississippi River, the Red River represented a barrier
between themselves and their state, currently occupied by Union troops. As the
war began to appear unwinnable, Texans and soldiers across the South had only
one place they wanted to defend and protect, their homes. No matter how hard
the Confederate army tried to get them to come to the rescue of states east of
the Mississippi River, the men refused.[175]

Men even surrendered to the Union army to avoid crossing the river. Late
in the war, James C. Bates was sent to Texas to round up deserters from the 9th
Texas Cavalry. He discovered that, even after he rounded up deserters, once they
reached the river they would leave him for Texas again or, as a lieutenant and
three privates did, go "to a gun boat to be paroled."[176] As the war progressed,
Texans became increasingly hesitant to leave the state and, more important,
reluctant to cross the Mississippi River.

Experiencing numerous defeats at Atlanta, Cold Harbor, and Petersburg,
Texans east of the river became extremely dispirited in the closing months of

the war. Feeling helpless, the men bided their time with thoughts of family and home. In early November 1864, Edward Thomas Broughton II of the 7th Texas Infantry penned his dismay at still serving in the Western theater. "I am determined to come home this winter," he wrote in a letter to his wife Mollie, "and when I get west of the Mississippi, I intend to stay there." Later in his letter, Broughton expressed his true reasons for wanting to leave: "I have no dreams of ambition to be fulfilled and expect happiness in the future in the bosom of my family only."[177] Every motivation that drew him into the war had dissipated, and only one thought remained in his mind, to go home and protect his wife and family from the inevitable Yankee invasion.

Other Texans in the East, such as Rufus King Felder of the 5th Texas Infantry, had only one goal at the end of the war: to get back to Texas. "We have been using every exertion in our power to have the brigade transferred or furloughed to Texas this winter."[178] In the last few months of the war, the desertion rate of the remaining Texans in the East increased. An example is Terry's Texas Rangers. In mid-January 1865, the 8th Texas Cavalry mustered 550 men; when the regiment surrendered four months later, it numbered only 175. By the time the war ended, Texans had no desire to fight for the Confederacy; they cared only for their local communties.[179]

As the war hastened to its conclusion, the desire to give up and return home increased among the ranks of Texans. Many like Alexander C. Crain of the 2nd Texas Partisan Rangers felt the war could not be won and hoped "the War will soon end so that we can all come home again and have the pleasure of being with our friends and relatives." Later Crain stated, "If the confederacy were mine I would freely give it up this morning to be allowd to go home too live with them the Balance of my days in peace. . . . So may God Speed the day when this cruel war shall have an end & we can all return home to our famleys in peace." A year later he noticed that a large number of Texans agreed with him; he noted an increase in the volume of deserters from east of the river making their way "home professing to have furloughs, the furloughs were of their own making."[180] Texans felt that the war was over and that, if it continued, the Union army could threaten their state and homes. Col. Robert S. Gould of the 6th Texas Cavalry reminisced after the war that "it was for the best that we should not prolong the contest and bring suffering to our own homes and families."[181] Desertion became so rampant that detachments such as Henry Mann's company began "hunting up Parrole prisoners, deserters & Jayhawkers in this state. . . . dragging men from their family through the tears and laminations of womens and children and some times have them shoot, though I am clear of that charge."[182] In late April, confirmation of Gen. Robert E. Lee's and Gen. Joseph E. Johnston's surrenders reached the Lone Star State, spawning further desertion among Texas units until the entire army had dissolved by late May. Without an army in

Texas, Lt. Gen. Edmund Kirby Smith formally surrendered his phantom Trans-Mississippi army to Union forces on June 2, 1865. With the conclusion of the war, Texans wanted nothing but to get back home to family and friends so they could begin their lives again with the people they loved.[183]

Many aspects and events of the war influenced the motivation of Texans. The hardships and the loss of their horses demoralized Texans. Though demoralized, they continued to fight, and relatively few deserted. Desertion became a major problem in Texans units only with the Union victory at Vicksburg. Vicksburg not only cut off Texans from communicating with their families in Texas but also dissolved the psychological barrier of the Mississippi River. Once the Federals controlled the river, Texans feared that their state would be vulnerable to invasion. Since Texas became exposed to the Federals and was directly threatened by the Red River Campaign, the motivation of Texans to defend their extended families and old hometowns became less important than defending their immediate families and current homes. In response, they deserted their units so they could return to Texas and defend its borders, protecting their families from the depredations other Southerners had had to endure. Jeff Morgan of the 35th Texas Cavalry (Liken's) summed it up in a letter to his wife: "For when the soldear heres there families are a sufferen thay will come home."[184]

6

FIGHTING IN A NEW LAND

Why Foreign Immigrants and Minorities in Texas Fought

*One has to wander around the world, even though I could be so comfortable
in Texas. No matter what happens, I want to go back to Texas. That is my
life's ambition. I have started to build a home there, and I would be enjoying
it now, if the awful war had not broken out. I have my savings there, several
hundred dollars. If I were to use them here, I would have to sell them for a
few gold dollars. I want to go back to Texas and start fresh again.*

FERDINAND BOESEL, GERMAN SOLDIER IN THE
4TH TEXAS MOUNTED VOLUNTEERS

A SECTION of Texas society that was difficult to ignore but often over-
looked were the recent immigrants into the state. In the antebellum period,
Texas experienced a major population increase through migrants from the
eastern United States and immigrants from other countries. During the
1850s, the foreign population in the state more than doubled, from 16,744 in
1850 to 43,422 in 1860. The majority of these immigrants came from Germany
and Mexico (included in the census numbers are a native Hispanic minority
called Tejanos); almost half the immigrants were Germans. With just over 7 percent of its population having taken their first breath outside the United States,
Texas was second only to Louisiana for the highest percentage of foreign-born
residents in a Confederate state. Since many of the immigrants had recently
settled in the state, they had not had enough time to assimilate the culture
and habits of the South. These demographics had a major impact on the Lone
Star State during the Civil War; ultimately, Texas was the only Southern state
where foreigners openly opposed the war and the Confederacy. When foreign
immigrants arrived and where they settled in Texas determined their degree of
assimilation into the dominant culture of the region and their attachment to

their locality. These influences direct affected their decision to either fight for the Confederacy or oppose it. The experiences of these Germans and Mexicans in the decades before the Civil War also helped determine their loyalty during the war.[1]

The largest and most influential group of Texas foreign immigrants during the Civil War were Germans. They played major roles in Texas and were one of the most divided groups during the war. Texas had approximately half of the Germans who settled the South, 90 percent of whom came directly from Europe. This large population of Germans made Texas different from the rest of the South. Such large numbers, along with the fact that nearly all European immigrants to Texas came directly from Europe without an intermediate stop in the eastern United States, contributed to their resistance to completely assimilating Southern culture.[2]

Overall, German Texans did not fully support the war. Their cultural beliefs and ideas of freedom kept them from willingly joining the Confederacy or the Union in large numbers. One factor that influenced their decision to join either side was local attachments. When they arrived and where they settled in Texas determined their degree of acculturation and attachment to Texas, the South, or the United States. Germans who settled in Texas before the 1850s, had more time to adopt Southern culture and to become attached to their locality in Texas. Later German immigrants were less acclimated to the prevailing culture and had less time to develop loyalties to their new state. Where they settled also had an impact on their decision to fight. If they lived in a section of Texas dominated by Anglos, then they had more contact with Southern customs, better integrating them into society and making them more willing to join the Confederate army. Less contact with Southern culture allowed them to maintain their distinct society and distanced them, though temporarily, from the conflict facing the state. Though many Germans retained their customs, their population was divided on the issue of secession and the Civil War.[3]

Germans immigrated from various places in Germany and for many different reasons. Most came from the middle and high German provinces of Nassau, Electoral Hesse, Upper Hesse-Darmstadt, Alsace, far western Thuringia, and the Heilbronn area of Württemberg; the low areas of Oldenburg, southern Hannover, Brunswick (Braunschweig), Münsterland, and Mecklenburg; and the Watteran. The first significant wave of German immigrants to Texas began in 1831. They left Germany for various reasons including overpopulation, fragmentation of farms, economic depression, a potato blight, and the industrial revolution's tendency to drive off home producers. Additionally, Texas appeared attractive to Germans because the land was cheap and tax free and because immigration organizations such as the Texas Adelsverein provided protection for the immigrants and published stories of freedom of religion, justice, and

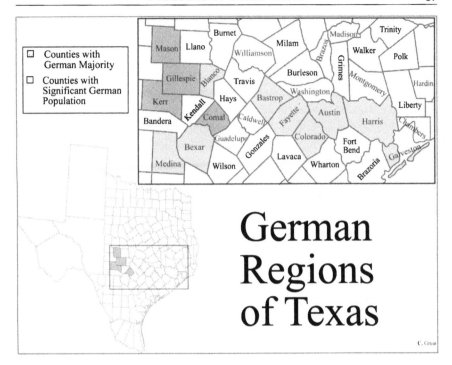

Counties with German Majority

Counties with Significant German Population

German Regions of Texas

C. Grear

equality. Later Germans immigrated to Texas because of the failed European revolutions of 1848 and to avoid compulsory military training. Both groups in general moved to Texas to start new lives, rebuild fortunes, seek freedom, and experience the adventure of settling in a new land. Other less tangible motivations included the desire to plant their culture in the New World, though they were too worried about making a living and trying to survive in a foreign country to think of creating a German state within the United States.[4]

Initially, the Texas government granted Germans land in the frontier of west-central Texas, an area referred to as the Fisher-Miller Grant. The grant was too far inland for Germans to settle there immediately, so they established towns in the region between the coast and the land grant. German towns such as New Braunfels, Castroville, and Medina became waystations to the west. Other German communities developed on the outskirts of established towns such as San Antonio, Galveston, and Houston. Waystations created a scattering of German settlements across Central Texas and provided points for later Germans to stop while en route to their frontier land grants.[5]

When and where Germans settled in Texas determined their views on states' rights, secession, and participation in the Civil War. Different waves of German immigrants settled in different parts of the state and held correspondingly variant views. The first wave of German settlers, known as the "Greys" for being in the United States the longest, immigrated from the 1820s to the 1840s, before the revolutions in Europe. The Greys may not have favored secession and states' rights, but because they lived in Texas longer they establish a strong attachment to the land, tolerated Southern culture, and realized the need to side with their Anglo neighbors to avoid accusations of being unionists. The majority of these Germans settled in towns in and southeast of Comal County. German towns, dotted throughout an Anglo-dominated Central Texas with the influence of Southern migrants living in close proximity, had some difficulty maintaining their culture. Ferdinand Boesel was a German who took notice of differences between the way of life in Texas and that of the country he had just left. In his first letter to his parents back home in Germany, Boesel noted, "It is customary here for every worker to have his own horse," and because of differences in the climate and land "it does not cost me anything [to keep a horse]; the prairie is big enough."[6] Boesel adapted to the local culture simply by absorbing the customs of his Anglo neighbors.

Germans from the first wave of immigration differed from those who arrived later. These differences, length of time in Texas, events, and slavery influenced their decision to side with the Confederacy. By the end of the 1840s, Germans constituted over 7 percent of the white population in Texas. Most of their settlements were in the regions dominated by Southern customs, which over time assimilated them into the dominant culture. Events also strengthened these early German immigrants' ties to the United States and, more important, to Texas. When the Mexican-American War broke out in 1846, German Texans participated in the fighting. These early German immigrants felt they had enough interest in Texas and the United States to fight for the Confederacy, proving their attachment to and assimilation of their new country and state.[7]

Slavery led to another difference between Greys and Texans. Most of the Germans who immigrated to Texas in the first wave did so for economic opportunities. They tended to have enough wealth to invest in new enterprises, and unlike the latter waves they could afford slaves. Wealth combined with the cultural assimilation from living in South and Central Texas for almost two decades influenced a very small number of Germans to buy slaves. A pattern developed among these Germans. Those living in Central Texas owned the most slaves within their population; the number of holders diminished in the western settlements. Thirteen German slaveholders lived in Houston, but farther west in New Braunfels only three owned slaves. Still farther west, in Gillespie County, a region settled predominately by a later wave of immigrants, there were even fewer slaves. Gillespie had a much smaller slave population than Comal, where New Braunfels is located. The number of slaves in the latter was over 4 percent of the total population by the start of the war, whereas the former had just over 1 percent, all owned by Anglo settlers. Though the Germans of the first wave did not own many slaves, they tolerated the institution more readily than those who arrived later.[8]

Early German immigrants' views of slavery were distinctly different from those of their Anglo counterparts in Texas. Most of them were more apathetic about the institution because of their assimilation to Southern and Texas culture. An editorial in the New Braunfels newspaper *Neu-Braunfelser Zeitung* noted, "The majority of the Germans are not against the institution of slave labor and will support this institution in every political struggle. The Republicans, of course, have maintained that the Germans own no slaves, because it is not morally right. This is not true."[9] Dr. Hermann Nagel wrote home to his mother in Germany describing his ignorance of the institution of slavery: "In general, the blacks have had it too good. I do hope, at least, that I am right about this, although I must admit that I cannot form an opinion based on my own experience, since I live far away from the plantations and don't really know much myself about the blacks and their condition."[10] Years of living in Texas did not force the Germans to forget their culture, but their connection to Texas allowed them to accept the practices that thrived in the state.[11]

The prospect of war and the issue of slavery had a definite influence on the Greys when the question of secession heated up in 1861. Germans from this wave paralleled the Anglo-Texan population's views of Texas separating from the Union and joining the Confederacy. One faction of Germans believed that secession was necessary or inevitable. Another group accepted secession only after Texas left the Union. These two factions argued among themselves when the state government left the decision of secession to the vote of the people, as can be seen through the editorials of the two most influential German-language newspapers in Texas.[12]

Arriving in Texas in April 1833, Ferdinand Jacob Lindheimer, editor of the *Neu-Braunfelser Zeitung,* championed the faction of Germans who believed that secession was inevitable. He argued that New Braunfels would benefit if the citizens voted for secession. Lindheimer began his argument on December 14, 1860, when he wrote that the German citizens of Comal County believed "the institutions of the Southern States, up to now so gloriously a part in the Union, to be endangered." He further argued that it was the duty of Texans to fight for state's rights. The following month, Lindheimer continued: "If Comal and Gillespie counties at this time would show no signs of participation in the Southern movement, their inaction would bring on serious consequences." A few days later he refined his points: "Since it is undeniably foreseeable that Texas will secede from the Union . . . all questions cease as the whether it would be to the advantage of Germans here, if Texas secedes or stays in the Union. The only practical question remaining is: How shall the Germans at secession of our State conduct themselves." His arguments did not fall on deaf ears. Many Germans

Ferdinand Lindheimer, editor of the German-language newspaper *Neu-Braunfelser Zeitung.* Courtesy The Sophienburg Museum and Archives, New Braunfels, Tex.

in New Braunfels agreed by electing Walter F. Preston and Dr. Theodore Koester delegates from Comal County to attend the state convention on secession. Before the elections, Lindheimer had published a statement written by these two men while campaigning to be delegates. The men described their ambitions to defend the Union and protect their Southern institutions—slavery—unless secession proved inevitable. If dissolution prevailed, then the men would work to join the fledgling Confederacy to assure their "rights."[13] Koester and Preston clearly expressed the thinking of this group of German Texans in deciding that siding with the secessionists, the prevailing thought in Texas, would better protect their locality. In other words, though this German population in New Braunfels did not completely agree with secession, they were sufficiently assimilated to Southern culture to realize the benefits of the position. Ultimately, they were not persecuted during the war.

Another group of early immigrants, those who opposed secession until the population approved it, rallied around the leadership of Ferdinand Flake. Born September 9, 1822, in Hannover, Germany, Flake arrived in Galveston in 1843. Though younger than Lindheimer by twenty years, he had resided in Germany longer, especially during the period when nationalism in the country had a strong influence over its citizens. This influence made him more loyal to the nation and Union and was an aspect of his German heritage that was hard for him to change. He expressed his strong unionist views in his Galveston newspaper, *Die Union,* on the same day South Carolina seceded from the Union, December 20, 1860. Flake wrote, "Texas stands as a sentinel on the outskirts of the Union. Come what may she will never desert her post." Though many local Germans supported his stand, local Anglos reacted by destroying his press and scattering his type. Witnessing these actions, many Germans in Galveston voted against secession simply by not voting.[14]

Germans from both factions of the Greys, like most immigrants, opposed secession. The group associated with Lindheimer sought secession because they knew that, even if the South lost the war, their towns, property, and lives would remain protected until the Union army reached Texas, since they sided with their neighbors. On the other hand, Germans who thought like Flake did so because of strong ideological beliefs of unionism but realized that, if they acted on their beliefs, they would face retaliation by the Anglos in the community. Both groups, though realizing the consequences of secession on their locality at different times, concluded that their homes and the state were too important to oppose the greater population of Texas.

Germans in the first wave of immigration to Texas differed from those who followed. The extended time they lived in the state acclimated them to Southern culture enough to fight for the state and to tolerate and own slaves. Essentially, these Germans developed a strong enough attachment to the state that they were willing to side with it during the secession crisis and the war.

Later German immigrants differed greatly from those who came before them. The second wave of German settlers, better known as the "Greens" or "Forty-eighters," settled in Texas after 1848, seeking domestic peace and unity because of the failed political revolutions in Europe. The majority of these Germans passed through the established German cities on the Texas coast and settled mostly in and west of Comal County. They viewed their frontier settlements as temporary residences since a large number of them, driven by their strong beliefs in political and social reform, planned to return to Germany for the next revolution. Since they lived on the frontier in relative isolation, had strong political beliefs, and did not view their citizenship as permanent, they aggressively maintained their culture, never acclimated to Southern customs, and established little attachment to Texas or the people surrounding them. These influences affected these immigrants in many different ways.[15]

Isolation, length of time in Texas, and events experienced in Europe influenced the decision of the recent German immigrant not to side with the Confederacy. By 1860, 20,553 German-born citizens lived in Texas. The majority of this population settled on the frontier of Texas, north and west of San Antonio. Gillespie, Mason, and Llano counties were among those on the frontier with a strong German presence. Life in this region was tough in many respects, ranging from isolation from the rest of Texas to the consequences of encroaching on Comanche hunting grounds. Because of their relative isolation and recent arrival, Hill Country Germans maintained their language, newspapers, poetry, and political philosophy and thus did not assimilate Southern culture. The lack of acculturation of these frontier Germans made them outspoken against slavery. This second wave of German immigrants believed that slavery was not economically viable for them; they did not have the wealth to purchase slaves and could not make a profit using them to grow staple crops on the frontier. In addition, the institution was unfamiliar to them, and they found it repulsive because they had just escaped political tyranny in Europe. A major reason the Greens left

Europe was to pursue individual liberty and a constitutional government that their native land denied them. The isolation of the second wave on the frontier, the lack of time to become acculturated to Southern life, and the events that pushed them to leave Europe made these Germans different from those who came before. Essentially they were too German to conform to Southern society.[16]

These characteristics of the second wave of Germans are reflected in their views on secession and the Confederacy. When the state government allowed the citizens to decide Texas's answer to secession, the frontier Germans voted against it; they wanted political unity and wished to keep the soldiers of the 2nd U.S. Cavalry in the region to protect them from Indian raids and to purchase their excess crops. These strong views made the Hill Country Germans the most determined group of Union sympathizers in the state. The voters in German-dominated counties clearly opposed secession. Ninety-six percent of the population in Gillespie County voted against secession, two-thirds of the voters in Kendall County supported the Union, and in Medina County 207 of the 347 citizens opposed secession. Of the twenty counties with large populations of non-Texans born in Germany, a clear majority of the five counties that voted against secession came from the Hill Country. Only one group of Germans on the frontier differed from immigrants from the second wave, those who settled in Kerrville. Kerrville was home to Germans who had settled in the older states in the South first before moving to Texas. The longer time they had spent in the South had assimilated them into Southern culture before they finally settled in Kerrville.[17]

The election of 1860 accentuated the differences between the Greys, generally Central Texas Germans, and the Greens, mainly living on the frontier. At the time, most Germans belonged to the Democratic Party because of its white egalitarian beliefs and support for white immigrants. The crisis that developed during the election of 1860 influenced the Germans in Texas to switch from the Democrats because of the potential split from the Union. The threat of disunion, and the lack of any favorable candidates, influenced many Germans to remain at home instead of voting in the election. Their lack of participation in the election and their vote against secession made the pro-slavery population of Texas suspicious of Germans throughout the war. Those who did vote showed the split in opinion between the two groups. The vote for secession in Comal and Gillespie counties demonstrates a major difference between the two regions. In Comal, the vote was 239 to 86 in favor of secession, and in Gillespie the polls reported 398 to 16 against leaving the Union. The difference between the two regions was also evident in their men's decisions to join the Confederacy.[18]

Germans in Texas were split on the issues, but not enough to organize themselves to defend their interests and homes. Local attachment is a common

Col. Gustav Hoffmann, German commander of the 7th Texas
Mounted Volunteers. Courtesy Tom Jones, Artist/Historian,
New Braunfels, Tex.

theme to both groups. Germans in Central Texas tended to fight, though reluctantly, for the Confederacy because of their attachments to the region. Originally, many Germans organized militia and state units for the sole purpose of
protecting their towns. Comal County formed three local companies during the
war that the Confederate army eventually absorbed. Gustav Hoffmann raised
the first local company from Comal County, which eventually served in the 7th
Mounted Volunteers, Sibley's Brigade. Hoffman arrived with the first group of
settlers, and many men in his ranks belonged to the founding families of New
Braunfels, upholding their connection to their locality. Another unit raised in
New Braunfels was Julius von Bose's infantry company, which he organized,
according to his announcement in the *Neu-Braunfelser Zeitung*, "to serve our
adopted Fatherland." This unit became Company K of the 3rd Texas Infantry.

Finally, late in the war, Theodore Podewils raised the Comal Horse Guard to protect New Braunfels. This unit shared the fate of the other local units raised in Comal County and became Company F of the 36th Texas Cavalry.[19]

Many other Germans from Central Texas formed Confederate companies in several Texas units: Company E, 1st Texas Cavalry; three companies in Waul's Texas Legion; Company F, 2nd Texas Cavalry; Company G, 4th Texas Mounted Volunteers; Company E, 5th Texas Mounted Volunteers; one and a half companies in the 6th Texas Infantry; Company B, 8th Texas Infantry; and the 32nd Texas Cavalry. Many of these men joined the ranks of the Confederacy reluctantly, most after the Conscription Act. They fought for many reasons, the greatest being the defense of their own localities. Lindheimer articulated this idea when he wrote in his newspaper in March 1862, before the April deadline of conscription, "All eyes of Texas were on Comal County during this time of preparation for the war and . . . the conduct of Comal County would be a guide to the forming of judgments on the Germans in Texas. It would be of the greatest importance for the Germans in Texas whether Comal County furnished its contingent with volunteers or by conscription."[20] Again, loyalties to New Braunfels and Texas influenced these Germans to fight, not for a cause but for the security of their homes from the enemies, both Northern and Southern.

Germans in Central Texas also tended to fight for the Confederacy to protect their business interests and homes. They did so for adventure and loyalty to their adopted state. Germans expressed this influence in their letters and memoirs. Joseph Bruckmuller, a German immigrant who owned a shoemaking and grocery business in Marshall, Texas, stated that he enlisted in the 7th Texas Mounted Volunteers "to live up to my duties toward my chosen country."[21] Arriving with his family in New Braunfels at the age of nine in 1846, twenty-four-year-old Carl Coreth wrote to his younger brother Rudolf, "Father writes you want to present yourself if the militia is called up. I will do it too if necessary. There are people here who say they would not leave, they had not started the things etc. I feel duty bound to go through."[22]

A few months later, Rudolf enlisted in a company "made up of farmers who, like ourselves, only want to defend the coast of Texas." Rudolf's desire to protect Texas and New Braunfels continued throughout the war. In January 1862 he advised his older brother Carl, "If the militia is called up now . . . you would probably be able to stay up there on the Indian frontier, and so you wouldn't be so far from home." When rumors of transferring from the coast or to Arkansas began to permeate camp, Rudolf reacted only as a man with the desire to defend his locality would. He complained. "I won't be going voluntarily yet," was his response to the rumor of receiving orders to move to the St. Bernard River or Velasco. When confronted with the prospect of fighting in Arkansas, Rudolf responded, "We have to decide whether we want to enlist for the duration of the war in order to march to Arkansas directly, or whether we want to be released and expose ourselves to being drafted from the militia. We—Munzenberger and I—decided for the above reasons to do the later." Essentially, he would rather stay in Texas and risk being drafted by the Confederate army than remain in his unit and march to Arkansas. His motivation to fight for Texas was simply the defense of his hometown, New Braunfels. By contrast, he said, "I cannot get enthusiastic about our cause."[23] Germans from Central Texas fought for the defense of their adopted state and the way of life they developed in the years before the war.

Some men found ways to serve the Confederacy that did not risk their lives or require them to leave the state. The four brothers from the Hoelscher family of Fayetteville illustrate a spectrum of services Germans performed during the war. Wilhelm and Bernard Hoelscher both served in the 17th Texas Infantry in Arkansas and Louisiana. Bernard apparently joined only because of the Conscription Act and chose the 17th so he could serve with his brother. Brother Joseph remained closer to home, joining the Dixie Rangers, a Texas State Troop company headquartered at his hometown of Fayetteville. He eventually rose through the ranks to became a 1st lieutenant. The fourth brother, Anton, a member of Capt. Z. M. P. Rabb's Company of Unattached Troops, found an exemption in the Conscription Act to serve as a teamster for the staff of Maj. Gen. John Bankhead Magruder. Anton rationalized, "I must go once again because everybody under 40 who does not drive for the government has to re-enlist and the ones who do not drive for the government do not get a detail any more and I think your wagon should be licensed for such a trip. . . . I would rather stay home then travel so far, but I would rather drive than be in camp."[24] Germans realized that the war was not theirs, but if they were to keep the peace in their communities and around their homes they needed to help the cause—but only on their own terms.

Most of these soldiers moved to Texas in the first wave of immigration, but some who arrived after 1848 and settled in Central Texas joined the ranks of Confederate units. Joseph Faust, born in Hambach, Prussia, in 1844, moved to Texas with his parents in 1855 because of the revolutions in Europe. His parents left Prussia so that Joseph would not have to serve in the army when he turned eighteen. The family settled in New Braunfels because family members and friends lived there. Though he lived in Texas for only a short time, New Braunfels became the only attachment in the United States Faust developed. When he turned seventeen at the start of the war, he enlisted in Capt. Gustave Hoffman's company in the 7th Texas Mounted Volunteers, which served in Sibley's Brigade and later Tom Green's Brigade. John Henry Brown, a Texas historian and newspaperman in the state from Missouri, noted that a German he talked to liked the United States but feared once again that he would be under a totalitarian government. The German sided with the South because "we are convinced that the people of the United States do not enjoy the liberties guaranteed to them by the constitution."[25] He sided with Texas and the South to escape the perceived threat of tyranny of the U.S. government.

The most touching example of a German who arrived in the second wave of immigrants and enlisted in the Confederate army is Ferdinand Boesel. Boesel arrived in Galveston with his uncle Ernst Boesel on Christmas Day of 1859, and both settled in a small town near Brenham named Latium. When the war began, the Central Texas German community organized a company "by one of the bravest, van [den] Heuval, a born Belgian. On the 23rd of September 1861, we [Ferdinand and Ernst] were inducted into the 4th Regiment of the Texas Rangers in San Antonio. We were 80 man, all Germans." The community they settled in influenced them to join the Confederacy and to "consider the South our Fatherland, and since we are citizens there, we want to seal our bond to our Fatherland with blood."[26]

Ferdinand also developed a strong bond to Texas by falling in love and getting engaged to a local girl named Agnes. In letters to her, he described his connection to the state and locality, along with the feelings of his fellow Germans in the company as they marched into Louisiana. The day the unit entered Louisiana, Ferdinand wrote, "With longing we look to the opposite, beloved Texas bank of the [Sabine] river. Who knows if or when we will ever see that dearest soil again. . . . For only a few, parting is very hard, and their hearts are sad. They take one last look at their homeland, where they experienced joy and sorrow, where they left so much behind that is dear and precious to them. I, too, am depressed." Ferdinand's commitment to the Confederacy waned only after he received a gunshot wound to his leg and Union soldiers captured him. He refused for a time to take "an oath to the government, the Union, just to escape this place of suffering." Eventually Boesel joined the Union army so he could receive mail and leave prison, but he never lost his attachment to his adopted state. In a long letter to his family in Germany, in the latter half of the war, Boesel described his endearment to Texas: "One has to wander around the world, even though I could be so comfortable in Texas. No matter what happens, I want to go back to Texas. That is my life's ambition. I have started to build a home there, and I would be enjoying it now, if the awful war had not broken out. I have my savings there, several hundred dollars. If I were to use them here, I would have to sell them for a few gold dollars. I want to go back to Texas and start fresh again." Everything this young man had was in Texas, his new home and his future. According to Boesel's words and actions, his attachment to Texas was worth defending.[27]

Not all German immigrants sided with the South. Some even went so far as to oppose the Confederate government. The majority of those who resisted the demands of Richmond were Germans who settled on the frontier, in areas such as Gillespie and Medina counties. As recent arrivals to Texas, they had no true connection to the state or the South. Instead, the only allegiance they had was to their fellow immigrants and the region they settled on the frontier. Since their attachment was to such a confined locality, they did not run off to fight in the war but instead remained behind on the frontier to protect their homes and families from Indian depredations. Ernst Cramer, who settled in Comfort in 1854, described the purpose of German frontier units as an organization "of men who lived in our county and in the surrounding counties. It was for the purpose of protection against the Indians and only to be used in the service of the state of Texas." The only service they provided the Confederacy was as home guards, and for most of the Germans in the Hill Country that was all they wanted.[28]

Texans knew that the frontier Germans favored the Union at the outbreak of the war; as Confederate politicians in Medina County stated, "A majority of the citizens of Medina County are disloyal."[29] Hints of treachery became a major concern for Texans and the Texas and Confederate governments. Early in the war Daniel Grant Park, away from home serving in the 15th Texas Cavalry, expressed his concerns to his wife about the weather "and if there has been any trouble with the duch a bout San Antonio."[30] The governments knew that, with large numbers of Confederates gone to fight in other theaters, the frontier was vulnerable to Indian attacks and German unionists. Fearing the consequences, the Confederacy passed the Banishment Act on August 8, 1861, to reduce the number of German unionists in the South. The law required that all alien males over fourteen years old and considered hostile to the Confederacy must leave the country in forty days. This made German military service in the Confederacy a major dilemma. Faced with losing everything, some Germans joined the army, others organized against it.[31]

Many Germans wanted to remain neutral, but Texas and the Confederacy would not allow that. To prevent strife between unionists and Confederates in Texas, the Germans in Fredericksburg organized the Union Loyal League to represent their population and protect them from both partisans and Indians. The members of the League also used it in the second year of the war as a means of protecting themselves and family members from conscription by justifying their service as home guards. By 1862 the League had over five hundred members. But instead of viewing the League as a militia unit fighting on the frontier, Texans and the Confederacy saw it as a threat. Gen. Paul O. Herbert, commander of the Department of Texas, tried to control the frontier German population by implementing martial law. In addition, the Confederate government sent Col. James Duff to Fredericksburg to administer an oath of allegiance to all alien males over the age of sixteen. Duff arrested those who would not take the oath. This action aroused Union sentiment among the Germans because they realized that if they took the oath they had no defense against conscription.[32]

Accordingly, conscription became a major issue for Germans on the frontier. They took a strong stance against the legislation, claiming that because they were aliens in transition the act did not pertain to them. The Confederate government ignored them and gave them a choice: join the Confederacy or face punishment. General Magruder, successor to Hebert as the commander of the Department of Texas, tried to punish the Germans avoiding conscription by having them "sent from this state and united with Regiments in other Departments before all other conscripts and . . . where they are found most hostile to its operation . . . sent first of all."[33] To avoid punishment some Germans entered the service, many in the Texas home guards. Others were not as fortunate, as Desmond Puloski Hopkins, a home guard from San Marcos, recorded in his diary at Fort Martin Scott outside Fredericksburg on March 4, 1861: "There being a surplus of men from Gilespie county, it was necessary to draw lots for the number that should be entitled to join from that County, the first man to draw was the Captain of the dutch Company he drew a blank." Upset about not being able to enlist in the home guard to protect their homes, "the whole dutch outfit became indignant and backed out, saying in forcible and original dutch language that the confederacy might go to hell and they would go home."[34] The mistreatment and punishment of Germans continued throughout the war.

Confederate Texans did not hold the German population in high esteem during the war because of their strong stance against conscription, which contributed to their persecution. On April 24, 1862, when conscription became a major issue among the Germans, Hopkins recorded an event in his diary while posted at Fort Martin Scott: "To day a duchman came in to camp, and out of breath, and reported Indians in the vicinity in great numbers, but we didn't believe a darned word of it as they were guilty of such reports for the purpose of annoying us, as you must know the duch were bitterly opposed to the war."[35] Thomas C. Smith, a sergeant in the 32nd Texas Cavalry, voiced his opinion in his diary later that year: "There is now a daily guard around Fredericksburg. The 'bushwhackers' or traitors are plentiful in this country but keep themselves hid, and they have selected a good country for the business. When one chances to fall into the hands of the c.s. soldiers he is dealt pretty roughly with and generally makes his last speech with a rope around his neck. Hanging is getting to be as common as hunting."[36]

These feelings toward Germans were not isolated occurrences on the frontier; they were common across the state. Sometimes Texans took violent action against any vulnerable German. In Galveston on April 10, 1862, "a German named Charles Baker, was hung, by a mob here this morning in front of his house on his own sign board." The lynching was not a coincidence. The San Antonio *Semi-Weekly News* reported that "Baker had had chickens stolen from him several times by unknown persons, and has been watching to see if he could not catch them. Last night he was on the watch, when several members of Capt. Dupree's company passed the back of his house on their way to their quarters next door to Baker's. As they were passing, Baker deliberately fired at them, mortally wounding one of the company named White, who died last night. . . . From what we can learn, he deserved it on account of killing an innocent man without provocation." It appears that the newspaper reported only half the story, and the mob did not consider any warnings Baker made before the incident.[37]

A German responded to these views in the Houston *Tri-Weekly Telegraph* three days later: "After having given several hints and hateful slurs, he seems now to have a more correct opinion of this part of the population of Texas (Germans). And, we will only wish that the Telegraph . . . would not in future admit anymore native articles and Know Nothing expectorations against the German element, and to consider that there is among the American element as well as among the Germans a number of scabby sheep, on whose account the 'baby ought not to be poured out with the bath.'"[38]

In the summer of 1862, the Texas government sent Capt. James Duff and a contingency of Texans to the Hill Country to break up the Union Loyal League and enforce the oath of allegiance. Fearing punishment, many Germans fled Texas for safety in Mexico and possibly the North. Their flight out of the state led to one of the deadliest events in German Texan history. Some members of the League, led by Maj. Fritz Tegner, were among the many Germans attempting to escape to Mexico. Confederate Texans, led by Duff, received news of their departure and intercepted their flight on August 10, near Fort Clark on the banks of the Nueces River, leading to what became known as the Battle of the Nueces. In this battle, the Confederate Texans killed the majority of the fleeing immigrants, approximately sixty including the wounded. Some of the Germans who survived made it across the Rio Grande River. In time, they and others who fled to Mexico constituted just over 13 percent of the ranks in the two Texas cavalry regiments of the Union army. This is significant because Germans made up only 7 percent of the total population of military age males in Texas. These disproportionate numbers demonstrate the reluctance of Germans, especially those on the frontier, to fight for the Confederacy. The violence in Texas toward Germans did not end at the Nueces. Duff later hung fifty German "bushwhackers," and Texans stationed on the Rio Grande River killed others attempting to cross into Mexico. R. H. Williams wrote of the gruesome killings at the border when he described one of the Confederate camps on the river: "High up on a pole, on the top of their commissary store-hut, grinned a human skull. I was told it had belonged to an unfortunate German . . . attempting to cross the Rio Grande some months before." Texans reacted casually to the violence because of their preconceived notions of the Germans on the frontier as unionists who actively plotted against the Confederacy. Telemechus Scott Wyatt of Liken's 35th

German Texans in the Union army: Capt. Adolph Zoeller, Capt. Honek, and another unidentified officer of the 1st Texas Cavalry. Courtesy University of Texas Institute of Texan Cultures at San Antonio, 076-0564, loaned by Estate of Emmie Braubach Mauermann

Funeral of German patriots at Comfort, Tex., August 20, 1865. Courtesy Library of Congress

Texas Cavalry received news that "Duff Donnilson's Co. killed 35 Germans a few days ago out on the Rio Grande—they were making their way to sack Namel-con who is said to be organizing guerilla bands in Mexico to raid and drive off the Western settlers." The Battle of the Nueces was the height of the violence of Texans toward Germans. Though some resistance continued, Germans and Texans eventually learned to coexist peacefully through an unspoken truce.[39]

When the war ended, the German population displayed its loyalty. The first Fourth of July after the war was not widely celebrated across the Lone Star State, except by two groups: African American freedmen and Germans. Citizens of New Braunfels held a parade with a marching band, along with numerous dances around the city, while flying the U.S. flag from the highest hill in celebration of the new independence of their adopted country. Additionally, on August 20, 1865, Hill Country Germans erected the Treue der Union monument in Comfort—the only shrine to the Union on former Confederate soil. At the site, locals interred the bones of men killed in the Battle of the Nueces. These actions demonstrate that Lone Star Germans held more loyalty to the state of Texas than to the institution of slavery or to Southern culture. Even today New Braunfels has a statue in the town square dedicated to Civil War soldiers from Comal County—both Union and Confederate—and has an elementary school named for Union general Carl Schertz. Instead of mourning the loss of slavery, the cause of the South, Germans celebrated the changes in their state and expressed loyalty to the United States, the bearers of their true interests—a good life in Texas.[40]

Treúe der Union Monument, Comfort, Tex.

Monument to Comal County Civil War soldiers in New Braunfels, Tex.

Many other groups of Europeans immigrated to Texas in the years leading to the Civil War—Poles, Czechs, Wends, Swedes, English, and Irish—but
their numbers were small compared to the Germans. They held views like the
Germans about the war, and a major determining factor in their decisions during the war involved their attachments to their locality. When they settled and
where they lived in Texas helped determine their participation, or lack thereof,
in the war.[41]

The Poles were a small ethnic group in Texas, around 783 by 1860, but have a
long and interesting history in the state. Individual Poles immigrated to Texas in
the first half of the nineteenth century and participated in all the major battles
of the Texas Revolution, including the Alamo, Goliad, and San Jacinto. The first
mass immigration of Poles was in 1854, when more than a hundred families
settled in Texas. They left Europe looking for political, economic, and social
freedom. Similar to the German Greens, the Poles were escaping oppression by
the occupying rulers in Upper Silesia after the failed attempts at revolution in
1848. A depressed economy from the flood of the river Odra in the summer of
1854, inflation of food prices during the Crimean War, risk of conscription into
the Prussian army, and cholera and typhus outbreaks in the 1840s and 1850s
were also motivations for leaving. When the families settled in the San Antonio
area, Panna Maria, and Bandera, they brought with them their Polish culture,
national identity, and Catholic religion.[42]

Many Poles were indifferent to the war when it broke out. The majority,
especially the families, had lived in the country only a short time, resided in isolated communities, and spoke only Polish. Many Poles had come to the United
States to avoid conscription and still wanted to avoid war. A large percentage of
young Poles in Panna Maria enlisted in the Confederate and Union armies because of financial hardship and to avoid conscription. Like the German Greens,
the Poles did not believe in the cause of the war, they just wanted to be left alone.
The majority of the Pole men who joined the ranks of the Confederate army did
so because of conscription. Alexander Dziuk, a Pole living in Karnes County,
"was farced into the Confederate ranks and was ordered to go to Arkansas."
Another Texas Pole, Albert Lyssy, conscripted into the 24th Texas Cavalry, displayed his lack of loyalty after the Union army captured him and his unit at Arkansas Post. During his imprisonment he joined the 16th Illinois Cavalry so that
he could leave the prison camp. Other Poles, such as Joseph Cotulla, entered the
Union service after crossing into Mexico. In 1862, to avoid conscription into
the Confederate army, Cotulla and six friends fled across the Rio Grande and
enlisted in the 1st Texas Cavalry, Union army. The Poles had no true attachment
to Texas or the South, just the political, social, and cultural ideas they brought
with them when they escaped oppression in Europe. Pressure to participate in a

war placed a huge amount of stress on the recent immigrants, forcing them to make decisions on issues they abhorred.[43]

Czech settlers in Texas, like other European immigrants, were reluctant to serve in the Civil War. Similar to the frontier Germans, they were recent immigrants and began settling in Central Texas in 1851 in isolated rural communities. A combination of their recent arrival and their isolation allowed Czech settlers to maintain their distinctive culture. When the war started, the majority of military age men dodged conscription or employed themselves as wagoneers for the cotton trade with Mexico. By 1861, approximately seven hundred Czechs were residing in Texas. Of this number, only forty men served in the Confederate army, preferring to join state troops or militias so they could remain close to home. Josef Silar, a Czech in the Texas State Troops, explained the dilemma faced by his fellow immigrants during the war: "Our duty was to catch all 'conscripts'. . . . Among the runaways were most often found Czechs for their wives did not want them to leave home and family for war. They didn't have anything to fight for. They weren't afraid of losing their freedom, and they didn't have any slaves." The Czechs, like most recent immigrants, had no true attachment to their locality, so they had no strong motivation to fight for the cause of their newly born country.[44]

Another Central European ethnic group to immigrate to Texas in the 1850s were the Wends. The Wends were a Slavic minority in Germany, completely surrounded and cut off from other Slavs. Fearing the influence of German culture on their children in addition to suffering political, economic, and social oppression, the Wends left Europe. In 1854 approximately five hundred Wends sailed to Texas and settled in Serbia, Texas, an isolated rural community in Lee County. The Wends resented the war because they came to Texas for liberty, not civil war. Like other recent European immigrants, they maintained their culture and resisted assimilation into Southern culture. Their weak loyalty to the state or the South influenced some to resist conscription to earn money in the cotton trade, and others escaped to Mexico and joined the Union army.[45]

Swedish immigration to Texas began in 1848. When the war broke out in 1861, 153 Swedes claimed Texas as their home. Swedes maintained their culture, which viewed plantations as similar to the feudal estates in Europe. This created a dilemma for the Swedes during the war, because they had resided in Texas long enough to call it their home, but they also agreed with Lincoln's views about the Union and slavery. As a consequence, very few Swedes, such as August Nelson and Swen Monson of the 12th Texas Cavalry, enlisted in the Confederate army. Approximately twenty-five received draft orders, many found work as teamsters transporting goods for the Confederacy, and others fled north to escape conscription. Their attachment to the immediate location where they lived was not strong enough to motivate the men of the Swedish community to fight for the Confederacy, like the other recent European immigrants in Texas.[46]

Unlike the Central Europeans, the English and Irish settlers had cultures more like Texans. These groups, though holding strong abolitionist beliefs, tended to conform to Southern culture and their Texas surroundings. Texans reciprocated, generally respecting their English immigrants. Though small in number, English Texans such as Brig. Gen. Thomas Neville Waul, of Waul's Texas Legion fame, and John Pelham Border, commandant of Camp Ford, gained prominence in the Lone Star State during the conflict. Irishmen were even more renowned during the war. Eighteen Irishmen signed the 1861 Ordinance of Secession, and Irishmen served in large numbers in the 6th Texas Infantry and 13th Texas Cavalry. The most famous were the "Fighting Irishmen" of Company F, Texas Heavy Artillery—better known as the Davis Guards. Led by Lt. Dick Dowling, an Irish immigrant, these men were the defenders of Sabine Pass and victors of the most lopsided battle of the war. Years later Jefferson Davis immortalized these men by calling the battle "the Thermopylae of the South."[47]

Of the 43,422 foreign-born in Texas listed in the 1860 U.S. census, 12,443 had their origins in Mexico. The number and nomenclature are misleading, since a significant number of these people were not foreign immigrants but actually native to Texas—Tejanos who had settled mainly in South Texas and along the Rio Grande. Though Germans and other Texans had difficulty cooperating during the war, ethnic Mexicans, in some aspects, had a harder time. In the decades leading up to the war, during, and after, Texans viewed people of Mexican descent, even the native-born Texans, as the mirror opposite of Anglos. Most Anglos in Texas associated Mexican Americans with blacks and Indians and viewed them as racially inferior, culturally backward, morally corrupt, lazy, happy, carefree, and resistant to learning Anglo ways. An article in Austin's *State Gazette* on September 9, 1854, described people of Mexican descent as "a vagrant class—a lazy, thievish horde of lazoroni, who in many instances are fugitives from justice in Mexico, highway robbers, horse and cattle thieves, and idle vagabonds."[48] R. H. Williams, an immigrant from England, provided another view of ethnic Mexicans in his reminiscences: "Here, as elsewhere in Mexico, the chief occupation of the natives seemed to be gambling. One wonders where and how they get their money they stake; they certainly don't appear to work for it."[49] When William H. Pearce of the 1st Texas Cavalry arrived in San Antonio in late September 1862, he commented to his wife that "you see dirty mexicans chattering to each other."[50] Mexican Americans were not accepted into Texas society like the Germans because they had no common Western European background and therefore had a different value system.[51]

Another source of discontent between Anglos and Mexicans in Texas was their differing views toward bondsmen. Mexican Americans, in general, were

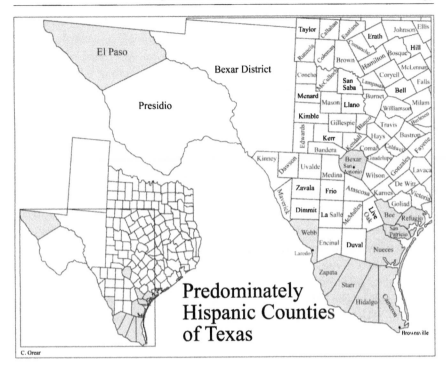

El Paso

Bexar District

Presidio

Taylor · Callahan · Eastland · Johnson · Ellis
Erath
Runnels · Coleman · Comanche · Hamilton · Bosque · Hill
Brown
Concho · McCulloch · San Saba · Lampasas · Coryell · McLennan
Menard · Mason · Llano · Burnet · Williamson · Bell · Falls · Milam
Kimble · Gillespie · Blanco · Travis · Burleson
Edwards · Kerr · Kendall · Hays · Bastrop · Fayette
Bandera · Comal · Caldwell
Kinney · Uvalde · Medina · Bexar San Antonio · Guadalupe · Wilson · Gonzales · Lavaca · De Witt · Victoria
Dawson · Zavala · Frio · Atascosa · Karnes · Goliad
Maverick · Dimmit · La Salle · McMullen · Live Oak · Bee · Refugio · San Patricio
Webb · Encinal · Duval · Nueces
Laredo
Zapata · Starr · Hidalgo · Cameron · Brownsville

Predominately
Hispanic Counties
of Texas

C. Orear

too poor to own slaves, were sociable toward slaves, and were little affected by the institution. The only group of Tejanos that differed from the norm were those who lived in San Antonio. This group of Hispanics had lived among Anglos for a longer period of time and thus were more accustomed to slavery. In the city and the surrounding Bexar County, Tejanos were owners of sixty slaves; they were the only Tejanos to possess bondsmen in the entire state. Since slavery was not a major aspect of the lives of Hispanics, their presence in Texas cities and nearby plantations sparked tension among the community. An article in the *Corpus Christi Ranchero* reveals the tension between the two races: "The lower order of Mexicans not only consider a nigger equal with themselves, but they actually court the company of the Negroes. A Negro can marry a Mexican and he can hold office with them and they always assist a runaway slave to escape from his master. This being the case and no man worth disputing with will dispute the point, we affirm that it is inconsistent with our laws and our institutions that Mexicans should have the same political rights in this state as Americans." Additionally, many whites blamed Tejanos for causing unrest and helping bondsmen to escape to Mexico.[52]

Other aspects of life in Texas that created tension between the two races involved their shared past. Since the Texas Revolution, tension between the two races over land had increased. Once Anglos took control of Texas, they began to expel Mexicans from their property. During the Republic era, Anglos began pushing Tejanos off their land in such places as Victoria. After the United States annexed Texas, Texans began to use the federal legal system to take away Hispanic lands, especially in the Rio Grande Valley. Land taken and racism in the valley spawned the Cortina War, a border war between Tejanos and white Texans that lasted throughout the Civil War. When the Cortina War broke out, Anglos feared retribution by Tejanos because of the cruel way they had treated them.[53]

These factors contributed to the actions of Tejanos during the election of 1860, the secession crisis, and the Civil War. During the presidential election of 1860 there were two distinct groups of Tejanos, those collected in a few large communities, and those throughout the rest of the state. Texans of Mexican descent who lived in towns such as San Antonio and Laredo, which had a strong Anglo influence, voted with the Democratic Party and for secession. Besides being assimilated into Southern culture, the cities tended to have some wealthy Tejano leaders who influenced the population through the patron system, an aspect of Hispanic culture in which the lower classes follow the orders of the local wealthy landowners to gain their favor. Basilio and Santos Benavides influenced Laredo's Hispanic population to vote for the Democratic Party, and José Antonio Navarro in did the same in San Antonio. Across the rest of Texas, numerous Mexican Americans did not vote. They were isolated from the rest of the United States, and for them local matters took precedence over the election. When the vote for secession was put forth to Texans, border counties voted for secession because Mexicans, again, did not participate in the vote. Where Tejanos did vote, their economic and political leaders coerced them to choose secession. Thus, before the Civil War began, the Tejano population, like the Germans, had distinct groups who favored and groups who opposed the Confederacy.[54]

In the Civil War, 9,900 ethnic Mexicans fought. Though they served in California and across the South, half of these numbers were from New Mexico, and the next largest concentration of soldiers came from Texas. Of the many Mexican Texans who fought in the war, three times as many served the Confederacy as the Union. From Texas, 2,250 Tejanos fought for the state, mainly coming from Webb, Refugio, and Bexar counties. Though divided, the Mexican immigrant population's loyalties shared some motivations to fight. Some fought to protect their homes from Indian raids in South Texas, others to escape the peonage system, but most joined local militias because they were an extension of the social-economic-political composition of the Mexican American community and patron system. More important, they joined militias so they could remain close to their homes and protect their families. All the same, they represent only a small percentage of the Tejano population, because most attempted to avoid the war, having neither economic nor political stakes in the outcome.[55]

Even those who joined the armies were apathetic to the struggle. They viewed soldiering as an economic opportunity—an eleven to thirteen dollar a week salary, plus uniform and rifle. Tejanos on both sides of the war had high desertion rates. Most of the desertions occurred because of the language barrier. Only a small percentage of the men spoke English. Since it was difficult for many of them to comprehend orders, they became frustrated and left the army in large numbers. Other reasons for desertion included not being paid and leaving their units to defend their families in Mexico when problems broke out in the state of Tamaulipas. In one instance, R. H. Williams and other men from the 33rd Texas Cavalry intercepted four Tejano deserters. "After a deal of prevarication they at last confessed they were deserters from the Confederate service, running for Mexico. Down on their knees they went, and begged and prayed, as only Mexicans can, that I would let them go. They would gladly leave their horses and arms, and everything they had with me, if only I wouldn't take them into San Antonio: '*Por el amor de Dios, y todos los santos, señor,*' they pleaded." Williams and the other men took the weapons, horses, and food and let them escape to Mexico. As with Germans, the Conscription Act of 1862 created tension between the cultural groups. Fearing conscription, many Mexicans fled to Mexico to avoid the draft. Others claimed to be Mexican nationals, making them exempt from the draft, but, as in the case of the Germans, this tactic proved unsuccessful. Tejanos fought on both sides of the conflict, but their motivations were in some ways similar.[56]

Tejanos with strong ties to Texas enlisted in the Confederate army immediately after the firing on Fort Sumter. The majority of these men enlisted under Santos Benavides, in Laredo. Before the war, Benavides was a politician who championed the cause of local autonomy within the government, very similar to states' rights. In addition, he and his family were the economic and political leaders of the city. He had a strong influence over the community and convinced sixty-eight men from Laredo to become Confederate soldiers for local defense. Later in the war, Benavides received a promotion to colonel, becoming the highest-ranking Confederate Mexican American, and was given permission to raise a regiment of partisan rangers. Benavides and his brothers Refugio and Cristóbal organized the remnants of the 33rd Texas Cavalry, under Lt. Col. James Duff, the slayer of German unionists, into what became known as Benavides' Regiment. Benavides split the regiment into two units to patrol the Rio Grande. He and the Tejano troops patrolled the upper Rio Grande, near Laredo, and Duff, with Anglo soldiers, patrolled the lower section of the river. Benavides and his men were the first Hispanics to join the Confederacy, but not the only ones.[57]

Refugio Benavides, Atanacio Vidaurri, Cristobal Benavides, and John Z. Leyendecker, Confederate officers from Laredo, Texas. Courtesy St. Mary's University Archives, San Antonio, Tex.

Hispanics also joined other Texas units and served in every theater of the war. A few joined Hood's Texas Brigade in Virginia. Other units such as Buchel's Texas Cavalry and 8th Texas Infantry in the western theater each had one company composed almost entirely of Tejanos. In addition, two leaders of Granbury's Brigade were Hispanic, as were sixty-one men in Sibley's New Mexico expedition. Overall, the majority of Tejanos who fought for the Confederacy came from Webb, Refugio, and Bexar counties, areas that had a strong attachment to Texas and Southern culture.[58]

Not all Tejanos enlisted to fight in the Civil War fought for the Confederacy. Approximately a fourth of all Hispanics battled for the Union. Union units with Tejanos included Adrian J. Vidal's Partisan Rangers and the 1st and 2nd Texas Cavalry (Union). Vidal's Rangers originally were an all-Hispanic Confederate company under the command of Hamilton P. Bee. Frustrated because he could not speak English and thus was unable to communicate with his superiors, Vidal convinced his company to mutiny in October 1863. They crossed the Rio Grande and reorganized in the Union army. A year earlier, the 1st and 2nd Texas Cavalry organized in Mexico. The leader of the 1st Texas was Edmund J. Davis, a Laredo judge who sympathized with the Mexican population. Davis's regiment was mostly unionists—Anglo, German, and Mexican—who had fled Texas for Mexico. Instances of violence during the war, such as the December 1862 attack on the Hispanic population of San Antonio by John Baylor's men, influenced Tejanos to join the 1st Texas.[59]

The 2nd Texas Cavalry had the largest numbers of Hispanics. Organizing the regiment was John L. Haynes, a politician who held pro-Tejano beliefs and recruited the unit along the Rio Grande during the Union invasion of Brownsville by the 1st Texas Cavalry. The 2nd Cavalry contained Mexican nationals and Tejanos who had fled the state. With a few exceptions—Germans, one man from the South, Northerners, and foreigners—the regiment was almost entirely Hispanic. Of the Hispanics, 75 percent were born in Mexico and the rest in Texas. Another unique aspect of this regiment was that all the company commanders were Hispanic. These men enlisted in the Union army because Haynes and his recruiters promised a hundred dollar bounty, jackets, raincoats, boots, shoes, and thirteen dollars a month. Other motivations included revenge against their old political enemies, mainly Texans who had stolen their land. Overall, the Mexicans who enlisted in the Union army did so not for ideological reasons, not because of any attachment to the Union, but to care for their families through money and supplies given to them for joining.[60]

Without any strong ideological convictions holding them in the army, men of Mexican descent were quick to desert if army life did not meet their expectations. Most of the men in the 2nd Cavalry deserted only months after joining. They deserted because Haynes never fulfilled his promises. The men did not receive their bounties, their pay, or their clothes. Under the combined influences of homesickness and the boredom of camp life, men deserted in droves. Even those who received clothes and equipment such as saddles, bridles, sabers, guns, and other military supplies deserted and took the supplies with them to sell once they returned home. Another factor that influenced Mexicans to leave the army was the language barrier. The majority of the men could not speak English, and 90 percent were illiterate. Because the men could not communicate with their superiors and others in the army, they became frustrated and deserted. Haynes realized that he had to do something, because his regiment was dwindling every day. He attempted to keep the men from deserting by moving the regiment to New Orleans so they could not leave as easily. Once a rumor of this move reached the men, a "near riot broke out." Desertion diminished the ranks so much that by early 1865 the 2nd Cavalry had to be recreated. This time there were only ten Hispanics in the entire regiment. Thus ended the Mexican participation in the Civil War. Davis became governor of Texas in 1870, Haynes received an appointment as collector of customs at Galveston, and the Hispanic men resumed their lives as before the war.[61]

Germans and Mexicans were not the only foreigners in Texas who fought in the Civil War, but by far they contributed the most to both sides of the conflict. Many of these immigrants fought to protect their jobs from freedmen, and some who were Catholics fought against the abolitionist North, believing that the Protestant Northerners wanted to rid the country of Catholics. Some of the most respected Texan officers were immigrants, including Col. Augustus Buchel from Germany, Col. John C. Border and Gen. Walter Lane from the British Isles, and Gen. Xavier Debray from France. Overall, many men from many different countries contributed to the defense of Texas and the South.[62]

The history of Texas is a history of many different people immigrating to the land and developing some attachment to it. During the Civil War, Texas contained many different ethnic groups and cultures. The two largest foreign immigrant groups were the Germans and the Mexicans. Both groups developed various attachments, but in general the longer they lived in Texas the more acclimated to Southern culture and attached to the land they became. Those who immigrated later more often reflected the attitudes of their country and culture of origin than they did those of Texas. Consequently, they either did not fight for the Confederacy or they fought against it, with horrific results. Overall, the Civil War was not their war to fight, but they viewed their responses to the situation as best for their future. These factors go far toward explaining why foreign immigrants in Texas fought in the Civil War, for either side.

7

CONCLUSION

Dear Home, I am going to leave you
Maybe not to come again.
I am going far to defend you
Against a foe of wretched fame.
Pleasant home, I hate to leave you,
My support, my seeming life,
My proudest spot, and only pleasure,
For you I'll fight the bloody strife.
If life should leave me while in battle,
Then O! Friends you need not weep,
Peace will be my future nature—
As it is with those that sleep.
Weep not for me then sweet Mother,
Then I'll have a home afar—
Then you will have a son in peace,
And not, as now, a son in war.

D. C. NANCE, 12TH TEXAS CAVALRY

I N the summer of 1860, J. P. Johnson, a fourteen-year-old Texan, looked into the sky along with thousands of others and saw "the big comet" that "lighted up the earth, almost equal to the moon." Emotions overflowed across the country, stirring "a good deal of excitement." Was this an omen for the years to come? "There was a great deal of superstition then, and every one believed it a fore-warning to every one. Then the war fever broke out, and lasted through out the winter." The prophecy came true in the spring, and Johnson joined the 1st Texas Partisan Rangers when he came of age.[1]

The Civil War took its toll on all Americans. Death touched every family; destruction of the South's roads, bridges, buildings, and homes created economic and physical hardship on its people, and emancipation forced Southerners to pay the price for the sin of slavery through the loss of wealth and the realization that the social structure of the South and the United States would never be the same. Texans, to an extent, experienced this transformation of their region and had to suffer the stigma of defeat, forcing the soldiers to reevaluate their participation in such a terrifying ordeal. Unlike those of other Southern states, Texas homes remained untouched by Union armies and their families relatively intact. Texans did feel defeat; obviously the Union won and the men did not return home as victors. But they did fulfill their main goal of defending their communities in the Lone Star State, granting them a degree of success.

Though historians such as Barry Crouch and Carl Moneyhon have examined the immediate aftereffects of the Civil War on the Texas population, their conclusions vary, ranging from Crouch's conclusion that Texans were defiant during Reconstruction since the war never reached their doorstep to Moneyhon's that Texans did feel defeated at the conclusion of war but quickly renewed their lives as best they could. Despite these conclusions, Texans celebrated their contribution to the war, especially the fact that the Lone Star State remained largely unspoiled by Union invasion. A strong expression of this fact came in 1876 during the centennial celebration of the United States. During the revelry, states dedicated monuments and artworks commemorating an important event, person, or aspect of their histories during the years between 1776 and 1876. Despite the rich history of Texas from Spanish times, the Texas Revolution, and the frontier, the Lone Star State commissioned a painting of Brig. Gen. Thomas Green in his Confederate uniform. Today this seems an odd choice, for several reasons. First, Texans would expect a painting of the Alamo or one of the founding fathers—Stephen F. Austin or Sam Houston. Second, if the Civil war was the focus, one might expect a representation of the most famed Texan unit in the Civil War, Hood's Texas Brigade. Why not choose an officer from Hood's Texas Brigade or Terry's Texas Rangers or other famed Texans such as Benjamin McCulloch or Albert Sidney Johnston? The answer is simple enough: Green participated in and thus is a physical representation of most of the major events in Texas history: the Texas Revolution, the Mexican-American War, battles of the Texas Rangers, and most notably the Civil War. Of all the Texans serving in the latter conflict, Green remained behind and tried to expand the borders of the state in the New Mexico Campaign as colonel of the 5th Texas Mounted Rifles, he became the savior of Galveston, and he made the ultimate sacrifice in the defense of the Lone Star State during the Red River Campaign. Essentially, Green was present at all the major threats to the Lone Star State. Instead of seeking glory in distant battlefields like men in the Texas Brigade, he remained behind and became the defender of Texas. Immediately after the war, Texans cherished and remembered those men who remained behind to defend the state, giving them their one small semblance of victory from the conflict.[2]

Though the physical infrastructure of Texas remained intact, a large number of Texans never returned home; most were buried where they died in battle and camps. Citizens of the Lone Star State realized the sacrifice their men made to maintain their society and protect the future of the state and their Southern neighbors, a fact still celebrated across Texas in Civil War Roundtables and Sons of Confederate Veteran organizations. Despite the causes they fought for, these men remained Texans who made a difficult choice. Texans were not alone; the Civil War forced many people, in both the North and South, to make hard decisions. Which side should they fight on, where did they want to fight, and what were they fighting for? Though Texas was the westernmost state in the Confederacy and farthest from the major combat, the men still had to make these decisions. Though not the sole reason, local attachments proved to be a major factor in their decision to fight. Since Texans had connections to more than one location, the influence of this motivation was more prominent than in men from the other Confederate states. Although this study examined Texans exclusively, the concept of local attachment can be applied to the other states in the Confederacy. Soldiers from Virginia decided to stay in their state to defend their lands as much as men did in Tennessee and Arkansas. Studies in these regions would prove fruitful to the larger discussion of soldier motivation in the Civil War and further support the rationale examined here for Texans.

Unlike the rest of the South, Texas was populated with recent immigrants, from either foreign countries or other parts of the United States. During the early 1860s, Texas shared a culture with the rest of the South because the majority of its population had just settled there from other Southern states. These people brought with them their institutions and culture, making Texas another Southern state—with one major difference: the majority of the Texas population had more than one community they called home. Texans had hometowns in Texas where their immediate family lived and sometimes extended families. They also had a hometown elsewhere in the states, where the majority of their extended family lived and their parents had raised them. Having more than one hometown created a dilemma in the minds of Texans when they made their decisions to fight in the Civil War. Which location should they defend? When the war began, Texans believed it would be short and that it would be difficult for the Union to threaten the Lone Star State. With these thoughts, men who had recently moved to Texas and still held a strong connection to a state back east enlisted to protect their old hometown and family who still resided there. Texans that lived in the state longer and had more to lose if they left, such as a large family, business, or land, decided to stay in the trans-Mississippi to protect their interests. Attachments to multiple localities had a direct effect on Texans' decision to fight.

The multiplicity of their local attachments was not the only influence on Texans' decisions to fight in the Civil War. Institutions and culture brought over from the old South influenced the men to enlist in the Confederate army. Southerners who migrated to Texas brought slaves and firmly entrenched that institution in the state. Many Texans did not fight for the institution but for what they thought slavery provided, white liberty. Without slavery, whites would have to compete with free blacks for social and economic status. As long as slavery existed, white Texans and Southerners would never be the lowest class in society. Other similarities between Texas and the old South included the concept of Southern honor. Honor was central to Southern life because it was the standard by which men measured themselves. The Civil War provided the surest way for Southern men to obtain honor and to prove their manhood. Religion was also significant in motivating Texans to fight for the South. In the nineteenth century, Christians believed that God intervened in people's lives on a daily basis. That belief boosted Southern morale but at the same time had the potential to squelch it. Men felt confident in their cause when they won battles because God willed it, but when the tide turned the men became demoralized. The Southern idea of family also migrated to Texas with the people. Family ties produced the strongest bonds between people in the South during the nineteenth century. Though family members moved far away to Texas, the bonds never weakened. When the war broke out, a major concern for Texans was the protection of their families. These similarities influenced Texans and other Southerners to fight for the Confederacy.

Despite being the seventh star of the Confederacy, not all Texans fought for the southern nation. Because of its diversity, Texas had a noteworthy population of unionists who did not support the Confederacy: groups of Texans from North Texas, a region settled by people from free and border states; Germans in the Texas Hill Country, a people isolated from Southern traditions who maintained their ideas of unionism; and Tejanos living in the Rio Grande Valley, a populace that distrusted the larger Anglo population and thus were more anti-white than unionist. All these groups opposed and tried to avoid the war as best as they could. When threatened to be pulled into the conflict by conscription, North Texans and Germans organized themselves into home guards to defend their ideals of liberty and, most important, their locality. In most instances quarrel ensued, such as the Great Hanging of Gainesville and the Battle of the Nueces, and usually ended with the death of unionists. Some unionists escaped persecution by fleeing to Mexico or to free states, a feat Tejanos employed regularly and with ease because of their Mexican descent and proximity to Texas' southern neighbor. All these factions acted in what they considered the best interests of their communities and future. Though it was not unique to a Confederate state to have a contingent of unionists, Texas did have the most active among all the Southern states.

Despite the similarities between Texans and other Southerners, people from the Lone Star State also had major differences, such as Texas nationalism and the high percentage of migrants in the state. Before the Civil War began, Texas had already established a rich history by fighting for its independence and being an independent republic. These events had a major impact in the way Texans perceived their state and themselves, producing a strong sense of loyalty and source of pride. Almost on arrival migrants embraced ideals of Texas nationalism. On the surface this resembles Texas exceptionalism, the concept that the Lone Star State is different from the rest of the United States. Compared to the rest of the Confederacy and the United States as a whole, the reputation of Texans as a martial and rugged people was attractive to the cult of honor and masculinity that permeated the South. Simply being called a Texan gave a person some martial credibility, since the state was the scene of recent military exploits, ranging from formal wars such as the Texas Revolution and the Mexican-American War to informal conflicts with Indians and Mexican bandits. Additionally, a significant number of men involved in the conflicts were still alive and participated in the Civil War, such as Ben McCulloch, Albert Sidney Johnston, Charles De-Morse, and Tom Green, to name a few. The rest of the South could not make such claims, since the last major military conflict in their region was the War of 1812, and most of the Native American population had relocated to Indian Territory. Few of those Southerners were still living, and those who remained alive were too old to contribute significantly to the conflict.

Another difference was the Texas population. The Lone Star State had the most diverse population based on the origins of its people. Only a quarter of the free population could call Texas their birthplace; the rest were migrants from the rest of the United States, the clear majority from the South, or from Europe and Mexico. Migration affected Texans because the recent arrivals had more than one hometown, which meant they had loyalty to more than one community. At the onset of the Civil War, Texans had to prioritize which location they wanted to defend, their current home in Texas or the one they left behind. Unlike other Confederates, whose state's free populations were not dominated by migrants, Texans had more than one locality they wanted to protect and more choices of places they could defend. The vulnerability of one of these communities combined with the strength of their commitment to one of the locations determined if they wanted to fight and where they fought.

Most Texans decided to defend Texas. The majority of these men had their strongest attachment to the state because they had lived in the state for a significant amount of time and established themselves in their communities through businesses and their family. Other people, like some unionists in North Texas, defended the Lone Star State without a commitment to the Confederacy; they only wanted to defend their local community and their reputation by joining a military unit. All Texans serving within the Trans-Mississippi theater had many different areas where they could defend their adopted state. Where they lived influenced the place they wanted to fight. If they lived on the coast, they wanted to defend the ports of Texas. Men who lived on the frontier wanted to protect their homesteads from Indian raids. Others fought in Missouri, Arkansas, and Louisiana to keep the enemy from setting foot on Texas soil. Additionally, some Texans wanted to promote the future of their locality by establishing a slave empire in the American southwest and Latin America, starting with an invasion of New Mexico. Soldiers who stayed in Texas to defend its borders did so because their only attachment was within the state.

Texans who did not view Texas as threatened at the beginning of the war and maintained a strong attachment to their former state made different choices. These men wanted to return to their old hometowns to protect loved ones in those locales. To protect those communities, Texans raised units to fight in specific theaters and others enlisted in those units to ensure the safety of their loved ones. In many instances, such as the Texans from Georgia and South Carolina in Hood's Texas Brigade, they did not serve in their former state but instead joined units located between the enemy and their native state. Texans' desire to defend certain communities was most evident when new theaters opened as the war progressed. Initially Virginia was the only theater in the war, but a new theater opened when Kentucky recanted its neutrality and remained in the Union. Texans who initially joined to fight in Virginia now had the option of fighting in Kentucky to protect their hometowns and family members in that region. Some Texans, like Richard M. Gano and Adam Rankin "Stovepipe" Johnson, even raised units to fight under the banner of another state. Countless other Texans akin to Thomas Goree and Charles Trueheart individually joined units from other states. Texans who enlisted to fight for the defense of other states did so to protect the vulnerable homes and families they left when they moved to Texas.

As the war progressed, these Texans' priorities changed. Events demoralized Texas soldiers. Hardships of war, the loss of their horses, serving alongside conscripts, receiving bad news from home, the reelection of Lincoln, and the start of the new year in 1865 without any recent victories all had a noticeable impact on the psyche of the men. More significant were several events that made Texans reconsider where they wanted to fight. In the first year of the war, Texas remained relatively isolated from the rest of the South and was not immediately threatened by the Union army. Starting with the second year of the war, events changed Texans' perception of the safety of their state. They viewed the battle of Pea Ridge, the defeat of New Orleans, the occupation of Galveston, the fall of Vicksburg, the invasion of Brownsville, and the Red River Campaign as major threats to the security of Texas. With the perception that the Union army threatened Texas, many Texans who had taken service elsewhere in the Confederacy reconsidered their priorities. In each event, Texans asked for transfers, resigned their commissions, or deserted so they could return to the trans-Mississippi to defend Texas or hide out for the remainder of the war. The priorities of Texans evolved as the war progressed, and they were directly influenced by the perceived threats to the locations to which they held an attachment.

Multiple local attachments also affected foreign immigrants and minorities living in Texas during the war. The majority of the immigrants came from Germany and Mexico, and Tejanos were a significant minority in the state. For Germans, what side they fought for depended on how long and where they had lived in Texas. Germans who immigrated to Texas before 1848 had more time to become acclimated to Southern culture and had a larger stake in the Texas economy and society. Those who escaped the European revolutions of 1848 did so to start a new life in a stable country in their isolated communities in the Texas Hill Country. These Germans had no desire to get involved in another conflict. They tended to live on the Texas frontier and remained isolated from the Southern culture that dominated Texas. With the opening shots of the Civil War, the Germans who arrived in Texas before 1848 reluctantly joined the Confederate army to maintain good relations with their Anglo neighbors, and those who arrived afterward wanted to be left alone to defend themselves on the frontier. Their reluctance to serve in the Confederate army and resistance to conscription resulted in the largest massacre of dissenters in the war, at the Battle of the Nueces. Other Europeans such as Poles, Czechs, Wends, and Swedes had similar inclinations. Tejanos reacted in the same manner. Those established in Texas society in Central Texas tended to join the Confederate army, whereas others from the Rio Grande Valley and Mexican nationals joined the Union army for money and clothes. Like other Texans, German immigrants and ethnic Mexicans decided where and whether they would fight largely on the basis of how long they had lived in Texas.

Civil War soldier motivation is an area of history that scholars have studied extensively, except for the effects of local attachments. Local attachment is not exclusively a Texas phenomenon; it also affected the rest of the South. Texans provide the clearest example of local attachments because there were many different locations with which they had a connection. Since they had more than one hometown, Texans had to decide first which location they had the strongest loyalty to and second which one needed them at that particular time. Most other Southerners had a connection to only one state or region. Late in the war, when Maj. Gen. William T. Sherman marched through Georgia and the Carolinas, the effects of local attachment emerged in the rest of the Confederacy. Soldiers in the Army of Northern Virginia left the army, like many Texans, to defend their hometowns threatened by Sherman's march. Many scholars attributed the actions of these men to desertion and demoralization, but it many cases it was not. These men, like the Texans, just wanted to ensure that the locations and people that were most important to them were safe.

Local attachment is not the definitive answer to why men put the plow aside to risk their lives for their country, but it contributes. It is only one of many different influences on men's decision to fight. This concept will enrich our understanding of Civil War history because it presents in new light the question of why men fought. It finally demonstrates the complexity of the simplest answer to what motivated men to fight. They fought for "hearth and home" to defend their communities and families during the war and to ensure the continuation of the society in which they resided.

NOTES

Abbreviations Used in the Notes

CAH: Center for American History, University of Texas at Austin.

PC: Charles and Peggy Pearce Civil War Documents Collection, Navarro College, Corsicana, Texas.

THM: Texas Heritage Museum, Hill College, Hillsboro, Texas.

TSLAC: Texas State Library and Archives Commission, Austin, Texas.

Chapter 1

Chapter epigraph taken from a poem written by Andrew J. Fogle, 9th Texas Infantry, to his wife, Louisa, January 26, 1862. Ninth Texas Infantry File, THM.

1. Harry W. Pfanz, *Gettysburg: The Second Day* (Chapel Hill: University of North Carolina Press, 1998), 194.

2. Donald S. Frazier, *Blood and Treasure: Confederate Empire in the Southwest* (College Station: Texas A&M University Press, 1995), 269; Jerry D. Thompson, ed., *Westward the Texans: The Civil War Journal of Private William Randolph Howell* (El Paso: Texas Western Press, 1990), 35.

3. For the purpose of this study, a Texan is defined as a person living within the state's borders before the onset of the war in a nontransient manner. The largest group excluded from this classification are those serving in the army. Though I could use these examples to bolster my argument that they fought for their attachments in the East, such men as Robert E. Lee, James Longstreet, and John Bell Hood served in Texas forts but never established any real homesteads. Generally they left their families behind while they fulfilled their obligations to the U.S. Army. Because of this, they never established any true connection to the Lone Star State.

4. Bell I. Wiley, *The Life of Johnny Reb: The Common Solider of the Confederacy* (Baton Rouge: Louisiana State University Press, 1994), 15, 17; and *The Life of Billy Yank: The Common Solider of the Union* (Baton Rouge: Louisiana State University Press, 1994), 17.

5. James I. Robertson, *Soldiers Blue and Gray* (Columbia: University of South Carolina Press, 1988), 8, 9.

6. James M. McPherson, *Battle Cry of Freedom: The Civil War Era* (New York: Oxford University Press, 1988), vii; *Drawn with the Sword: Reflections on the American Civil War* (New York: Oxford University Press, 1997), 15; and *For Cause and Comrades: Why Men Fought in the Civil War* (New York: Oxford University Press, 1998), 5, 6, 17, 19, 20, 21, 23, 24, 26, 27.

7. Bertram Wyatt-Brown, *Southern Honor: Ethics & Behavior in the Old South* (New York: Oxford University Press, 1982), 149, 333.

8. Reid Mitchell, *The Vacant Chair: The Northern Soldier Leaves Home* (New York: Oxford University Press, 1995), 4.

9. Larry Logue, *To Appomattox and Beyond: The Civil War Soldier in War and Peace* (Chicago: Ivan R. Dee, 1995), 9, 23.

10. Steven E. Woodworth, *While God Is Marching On: The Religious World of Civil War Soldiers* (Lawrence: University of Kansas Press, 2001), 29, 125, 126.

11. Warren Wilkinson and Steven E. Woodworth, *A Scythe of Fire: A Civil War Story of the Eighth Georgia Infantry Regiment* (New York: HarperCollins, 2002), 301–303.

12. Chuck Carlock and V. M. Owens, *History of the Tenth Texas Cavalry (Dismounted) Regiment* (North Richland Hills, Tex: Smithfield Press, 2001), 6; Allan C. Ashcraft, *Texas in the Civil War: A Resume History* (Austin: Texas Civil War Centennial Commission, 1962), 10; Robertson, *Soldiers Blue and Gray*, 5; McPherson, *For Cause and Comrades*, 21, 30–31, 80, 95–96; Larry J. Daniel, *Soldiering in the Army of Tennessee: A Portrait of Life in a Confederate Army* (Chapel Hill: University of North Carolina Press, 1991), 14; McPherson, *Drawn with the Sword*, 15; Ralph A. Wooster, *Texas and Texans in the Civil War* (Austin: Eakin Press, 1996); Ernest Wallace, *Texas in Turmoil, 1849–1875* (Orlando, Fla.: Steck-Vaughn, 1965).

13. Barnes F. Lathrop, *Migration into East Texas, 1835–1860: A Study from the United States Census* (Austin: Texas State Historical Association, 1949), 35.

14. Randolph B. Campbell, "Statehood, Civil War, and Reconstruction, 1846–76," in Walter L. Buenger and Robert Calvert, eds., *Texas through Time: Evolving Interpretations* (College Station: Texas A&M University Press, 1991), 166; Joseph C. G. Kennedy, *Population of the United States in 1860; Compiled Returns of the Eighth Census* (Washington, D.C.: Government Printing Office, 1864), iv; Arif Dirlik, *Postmodernity's Histories: The Past as Legacy and Project* (New York: Rowman and Littlefield, 2000), 192–193.

15. Randolph B. Campbell, *Gone to Texas: A History of the Lone Star State* (New York: Oxford University Press, 2003), 207; Walter L. Buenger, *Secession and the Union in Texas* (Austin: University of Texas Press, 1984), 13, 14; Dale Baum, *The Shattering of Texas Unionism: Politics in the Lone Star State during the Civil War Era* (Baton Rouge: Louisiana State University Press, 1998), 84; Richard E. Beringer, Herman Hattaway, Archer Jones, and William N. Still Jr., *Why the South Lost the Civil War* (Athens: University of Georgia Press, 1986), 78; Terry G. Jordan, *German Seed in Texas Soil: Immigrant Farmers in Nineteenth Century Texas* (Austin: University of Texas Press, 1996), 9, 19, 20, 29.

16. Used primarily in the American Civil War era, the generic geographic terms *cis-Mississippi* and *trans-Mississippi* denote, respectively, the land east and west of the Mississippi River. Civil War action is traditionally divided into three major military theaters, the Eastern (roughly Pennsylvania to the coastal Carolinas, east of the Appalachian range) and Western (between the Appalachian range and the Mississippi, and late in the war the Carolinas and Georgia) theaters in the cis-Mississippi and the Trans-Mississippi theater (Missouri, Arkansas, western Louisiana, Indian Territory, Texas, Arizona Territory, and New Mexico Territory) west of the river. Compared to battles in the Trans-Mississippi theater, those in the Eastern and Western theaters not only were larger in scale but also garnered more attention by leaders on both sides as well as historians today.

17. There are numerous books examining Texas units in all three theaters. Listed here are some of the most recent and notable sources: Anne J. Bailey, *Between the Enemy and Texas: Parsons' Texas Cavalry in the Civil War* (Fort Worth: Texas Christian University Press, 1989); Alwyn Barr, *Polignac's Texas Brigade* (Texas Gulf Coast Historical Association, Vol. 8, No. 1, November 1964); Frazier, *Blood and Treasure*; Richard G. Lowe, *Walker's Texas Division, c.s.a.: Greyhounds of the Trans-Mississippi* (Baton Rouge: Louisiana State University Press, 2004); Jeffrey D. Murrah, *None but Texians: A History of Terry's Texas Rangers* (Austin: Eakin Press, 2001); Harold B. Simpson, *Hood's Texas Brigade: Lee's Grenadier Guard* (Waco,

Tex.: Texian Press, 1970); David Paul Smith, *Frontier Defense in the Civil War: Texas Rangers and Rebels* (College Station: Texas A&M University Press, 1992); Wooster, *Texas and Texans in the Civil War.*

18. Anne Bailey, "Richard M. Gano," in William C. Davis and Julie Hoffman, eds., *The Confederate General* (Harrisburg, Pa.: National Historical Society, 1991), 2:154–155; William C. Davis, "Adam Rankin Johnson," ibid., 3:169–170; Ralph A. Wooster, *Lone Star Generals in Gray* (Austin: Eakin Press, 2000), 195–198, 236.

19. Ella Lonn, *Foreigners in the Confederacy* (Chapel Hill: University of North Carolina Press, 1940), 13.

20. Wilkinson and Woodworth, *Scythe of Fire*, 301–303; "Red River" Company Agreement, 1862, CAH; Louisville *Weekly Courier*, April 30, 1862.

Chapter 2

The first epigraph for this chapter is taken from Street to Ninnie, February 25, 1862, J. K. Street Letters, http://antiquemll.hypermart.net/streetpapers.htm (accessed May 20, 2009). The second comes from Rebecca W. Smith and Marion Mullins, eds., "The Diary of H. C. Medford, Confederate Soldier, 1864," *Southwestern Historical Quarterly* 34 (1930): 220.

1. Campbell, *Gone to Texas*, 207; Buenger, *Secession and the Union*, 13, 14; Baum, *Shattering of Texas Unionism*, 84; Beringer, Hattaway, Jones, and Still, *Why the South Lost the Civil War*, 78; Jordan, *German Seed in Texas Soil*, 9, 19, 20, 29; Terry G. Jordan, *Trails to Texas: Southern Roots of Western Cattle Ranching* (Lincoln: University of Nebraska Press, 1981), 59.

2. Randolph B. Campbell, *An Empire for Slavery: The Peculiar Institution in Texas, 1821–1865* (Baton Rouge: Louisiana State University Press, 1989), 2, 50, 52, 53, 54.

3. T. R. Fehrenbach, *Lone Star: A History of Texas and the Texans* (New York: MacMillan, 1968), 287, 314; Campbell, *Empire for Slavery*, 53, 54, 55, 56; Llerena B. Friend, "The Texan of 1860," *Southwestern Historical Quarterly* 62 (1958): 3; Campbell, *Gone to Texas*, 207. Census records of 1850 and 1860 listed only four hundred free blacks in the state. Many laws existed in Texas to restrict the number of African Americans living in the state outside bondage, the most common of them forbidding free blacks to reside in state without permission of the state congress. Resentment toward these freedmen existed because they represented the idea that African Americans had the ability to live in freedom and would unsettle the numerous slaves in the state. Because free blacks presented a threat to the institution of slavery, white Texans treated them in the same manner as bondsmen. Free blacks found freedom in Texas during early statehood little different from slavery.

4. Campbell, *Empire for Slavery*, 3, 95; Clarksville *Northern Standard*, February 19, 1859.

5. Campbell, *Empire for Slavery*, 50, 61–62; Campbell, *Gone to Texas*, 220–222.

6. Richard G. Lowe and Randolph Campbell, *Planters and Plain Folk: Agriculture in Antebellum Texas* (Dallas, Tex.: Southern Methodist University Press, 1987), 190; Buenger, *Secession and the Union*, 13; Randolph B. Campbell, *A Southern Community in Crisis: Harrison County, Texas, 1850–1880* (Austin: Texas State Historical Association, 1983), 4; Randolph Campbell, "Human Property: The Negro Slave in Harrison County, 1850–1860," *Southwestern Historical Quarterly* 76 (1973): 389.

7. Campbell, *Empire for Slavery*, 2, 190–191; Lowe and Campell, *Planters and Plain Folk*, 188; National Archives Microfilm Publications, *Population Schedules of the Eighth Census of the United States: 1860*, Vol. 9, Texas, no. 1860, Texas Micro copy M-653, rolls 1291, 1292, 1299, and 1303 (Washington, D.C.: National Archives and Records Service General Services and Administration).

8. Campbell, *Gone to Texas*, 221; Campbell, *Empire for Slavery*, 193, 194.

9. Ralph A. Wooster, *The People in Power: Courthouse and Statehouse in the Lower South, 1850–1860* (Knoxville: University of Tennessee Press, 1969), 41; Campbell, *Empire for Slavery*, 114, 210; Avery O. Craven, *The Growth of Southern Nationalism, 1848–1861* (Baton Rouge: Louisiana State University Press, 1953), 392.

10. Paul D. Lack, "Slavery and Vigilantism in Austin, Texas, 1840–1860," *Southwestern Historical Quarterly* 85 (1981): 1.

11. Buenger, *Secession and the Union*, 21; Campbell, *Empire for Slavery*, 219, 220; William W. White, "The Texas Slave Insurrection of 1860," *Southwestern Historical Quarterly* 52 (1949): 259; Richard B. McCaslin, "Conditional Confederates: The Eleventh Texas Cavalry West of the Mississippi River," *Military History of the Southwest* 21 (1991): 88; Michael Phillips, *White Metropolis: Race, Ethnicity, and Religion in Dallas, 1841–2001* (Austin: University of Texas Press, 2006), 19–22. Slaves constituted the majority of South Carolina's total population. Such large numbers created fears that, if the slaves revolted, they would overrun the white population by sheer numbers.

12. Campbell, *Empire for Slavery*, 224–225; Bill Ledbetter, "Slave Unrest and White Panic: The Impact of Black Republicanism in Ante-Bellum Texas," *Texana* 10 (1972): 342; White, "Texas Slave Insurrection," 271; David Pickering and Judy Falls, *Brush Men and Vigilantes: Civil War Dissent in Texas*, (College Station: Texas A&M University Press, 2000), 11; Donald E. Reynolds, *Editors Make War: Southern Newspapers in the Secession Crisis* (Nashville, Tenn.: Vanderbilt University Press, 1966), 97; Richard B. McCaslin, *Tainted Breeze: The Great Hanging at Gainesville, Texas, 1862* (Baton Rouge: Louisiana State University Press, 1994), 23; Donald E. Reynolds, "Reluctant Martyr: Anthony Bewley and the Texas Slave Insurrection Panic of 1860," *Southwestern Historical Quarterly* 96 (1993): 347; Phillips, *White Metropolis*, 19, 27–32; Donald E. Reynolds, *Texas Terror: The Slave Insurrection of 1860 and the Secession of the Lower South* (Baton Rouge: Louisiana State University Press, 2007).

13. Reynolds, *Editors Make War*, 97; McCaslin, *Tainted Breeze*, 23; New Orleans *Daily Picayune*, July 31, 1860, as quoted in White, "Texas Slave Insurrection," 277–278; Campbell, *Empire for Slavery*, 224–225; White, "Texas Slave Insurrection," 262; Ledbetter, "Slave Unrest and White Panic," 338; Wesley Norton, "The Methodist Episcopal Church and the Civil Disturbances in North Texas in 1859 and 1860," *Southwestern Historical Quarterly* 68 (1965): 333; Nashville *Christian Advocate*, August 16, 1860.

14. San Antonio *Alamo Express*, August 18, 1860; Reynolds, "Reluctant Martyr," 345–346; Donald E. Reynolds, "Bewley, Anthony," in Ron Tyler, ed., *Handbook of Texas* (Austin: Texas State Historical Association, 1996), 1:515; Ledbetter, "Slave Unrest and White Panic," 344, 345; Pickering and Falls, *Brush Men and Vigilantes*, 11.

15. San Antonio *Alamo Express*, September 10, 1860.

16. White, "Texas Slave Insurrection," 285; Dallas *Herald*, June 20, 1860, as quoted in Frank H. Smyrl, "Unionism, Abolitionism, and Vigilantism in Texas, 1856–1865" (M.A. thesis, University of Texas, Austin, 1961), 48; Norton, "Methodist Episcopal Church," 317.

17. White, "Texas Slave Insurrection," 285.

18. Ledbetter, "Slave Unrest and White Panic," 348; Craven, *Growth of Southern Nationalism*, 393; Campbell, *Empire for Slavery*, 197, 207, 208, 209; Buenger, *Secession and the Union*, 13, 21, 43–44.

19. E. W. Winkler, ed., *Journal of the Secession Convention of Texas, 1861* (Austin: Texas Library and Historical Commission, 1912), 61–65.

20. Harrison to Andrew Johnson, June 23, 1865, J. E. Harrison, SC 5–1, Amnesty Appeal, Dismissal & Parole, June 23, 1865–June 28, 1865, THM.

21. Campbell, *Gone to Texas*, 240; Ledbetter, "Slave Unrest and White Panic," 335, 341; McPherson, *For Cause and Comrades*, 107, 170, 172; see also Edmund S. Morgan, *American Slavery, American Freedom* (New York: W. W. Norton, 1975).

22. Austin *State Gazette*, April 20, 1861; Mark A. Weitz, *More Damning Than Slaughter: Desertion in the Confederate Army* (Lincoln: University of Nebraska Press, 2005), 18.

23. John Q. Anderson, ed., *Campaigning with Parsons' Texas Cavalry Brigade, CSA: The War Journals and Letters of the Four Orr Brothers, Twelfth Texas Cavalry Regiment* (Hillsboro, Tex.: Hill Junior College Press, 1967), 136.

24. Reminiscences, William H. Hamman, Fourth Texas Infantry File, THM. Some Texans equated slavery with freedom and viewed the war as a fight for the freedom of their children. John T. Stark of the 13th Texas Cavalry wrote to his wife, "If it were not for the great and priceless boon for which we are contending I would leave no stone unturned until I could get out of this but that thought holds me fast. the thought that perhaps my dear children might be made slaves to the vile enemy who are now overrunning our loved country." Stark to Martha, Delhi, La., June 14, 1863, John T. Stark, Thirteenth Texas Cavalry File, THM. Levi Wight wrote, "I think that the two months will be the wineng up of the matter ad then we will be an indapendant Nation free from Northern Tyrany and of can come home and live in peas and as men pas by me I can look them in the face with a clear concianc and tel my children as they group [grow up] that I have served in a war that has made them free." Wight to wife (Sophia), November 23, 1862, Levi Lamoni Wight Letters 1862–1891, CAH.

25. Street to Ninnie, February 25, 1862, J. K. Street Letters, http://antiquemll.hypermart .net/streetpapers.htm (accessed, May 20, 2009).

26. Houston *Tri-Weekly Telegraph*, July 16, 1862.

27. The Civil War Soldiers and Sailors System (www.itd.nps.gov/cwss/soldiers.cfm) is a computerized database that contains basic facts about Civil War servicemen of both sides. The initial focus of the CWSS is the Names Index Project, which enters names and other basic information from 6.3 million soldier records in the National Archives. The facts about the soldiers were entered from records indexed to many millions of other documents concerning Civil War soldiers maintained by the National Archives and Records Administration.

28. Stephen Chicoine, ed., "'. . . Willing Never to Go in Another Fight': The Civil War Correspondence of Rufus King Felder of Chappell Hill," *Southwestern Historical Quarterly* 106 (2003): 590.

29. David B. Gracy II, "With Danger and Honor," *Texana* 1 (1963): 3; David B. Gracy II, "With Danger and Honor," *Texana* 2 (1963): 139–140.

30. "Some of My Experiences in Soldier's Life, July 30, 1905," Durant Motier Dansby, Third Texas Cavalry, THM. Dansby is clearly wrong in his remembrance that he and the 3rd Texas Cavalry fought African American soldiers in the Battle of Iuka since there were no colored troops in the Union army. Despite that error, the violence he described represents the general sentiments of Confederate soldiers.

31. Lawther to Phronie, July 6, 1863, William D. Lawther, Seventeenth Texas Infantry (Consolidated) Regiment File, THM. See also Gregory J. W. Urwin, "We Cannot Treat Negroes . . . as Prisoners of War: Racial Atrocities and Reprisals in Civil War Arkansas," *Civil War History* 42 (September 1996): 193–210, and Gregory J. W. Urwin, *Black Flag over Dixie: Racial Atrocities and Reprisals in the Civil War* (Carbondale: Southern Illinois University Press, 2004).

32. Hondon B. Hargrove, *Black Union Soldiers in the Civil War* (Jefferson, N.C.: McFarland, 1988), 58; Anne J. Bailey, "Was There a Massacre at Poison Spring?" *Military History of the Southwest* 20 (1990): 161; Craven, *Growth of Southern Nationalism*, 391; Baum, *Shattering*

of Texas Unionism, 57, 58; Daniel, *Soldiering in the Army of Tennessee,* 14. The same brigade was involved in another atrocity in Indian Territory when it attacked a small contingent of black soldiers making hay at Flat Rock.

33. "The Story of My Life," John Faulk, Seventeenth Texas Cavalry File, THM.

34. The Civil War Experiences of Robert S. Gould, Colonel C.S.A., as Related by Himself," Robert S. Gould, Sixth Texas Cavalry File, THM.

35. Moseley to Dr. Alfred Mercer, December 5, 1864, S. E. Moseley, Fourth Texas Infantry Regiment File, THM.

36. Cadell to friend, June 6, 1863, Richard Marion Cadell, Third Texas Cavalry (Third Regiment, Arizona Brigade) File, THM.

37. Waterhouse to Rose, November 26, 1862, Richard Waterhouse, Nineteenth Texas Infantry Regiment File, THM.

38. Wyatt-Brown, *Southern Honor,* 149, 156.

39. Ibid., 161, 163; Robert Pace, *Halls of Honor: College Men in the Old South* (Baton Rouge: Louisiana State University Press, 2004), 156, 159.

40. Charles P. Roland, *Albert Sidney Johnston: Soldier of Three Republics* (Austin: University of Texas Press, 1964), 59–61; Wyatt-Brown, *Southern Honor,* 357; Elizabeth Silverthorne, *Ashbel Smith of Texas: Pioneer, Patriot, Statesman, 1805–1886* (College Station: Texas A&M University, 1982), 41; Bailey, *Between the Enemy and Texas,* xv; Grady McWhiney and Perry D. Jamieson, *Attack and Die: Civil War Military Tactics and the Southern Heritage* (Tuscaloosa: University of Alabama Press, 1982), 171; Grady McWhiney, *Cracker Culture: Celtic Ways in the Old South* (Tuscaloosa: University of Alabama Press, 1988), 271; McPherson, *For Cause and Comrades,* 23, 77; Pete Maslowski, "A Study of Morale in Civil War Soldiers," in Michael Barton and Larry M. Logue, eds., *The Civil War Soldier: A Historical Reader* (New York: New York University Press, 2002), 315; John W. Spencer, *From Corsicana to Appomattox: The Story of the Corsicana Invincibles and the Navarro Rifles* (Corsicana, Tex.: Texas Press, 1984), 2. Another famous duel in Texas was between Dr. Chauncey Goodrich, an army surgeon for the Texas army, and Levi L. Laurens, a reporter fresh from New York and the recipient of a mortal shot from the doctor.

41. Clyde Griffen, "Reconstructing Masculinity from the Evangelical Revival to the Waning of Progressivism: A Speculative Synthesis," in Mark C. Carnes and Clyde Griffen, eds., *Meanings for Manhood: Constructions of Masculinity in Victorian America* (Chicago: University of Chicago Press, 1990), 191; Mary Ann Clawson, *Constructing Brotherhood: Class, Gender, and Fraternalism* (Princeton, N.J.: Princeton University Press, 1989), 4, 13; Eddy R. Parker, ed., *Touched by Fire: Letters from Company D Fifth Texas Infantry Hood's Brigade Army of Northern Virginia, 1862–1865* (Hillsboro, Tex.: Hill College Press, 2000), 99.

42. Griffen, "Reconstructing Masculinity," 191; Don E. Alberts, ed., *Rebels on the Rio Grande: The Civil War Journal of A. B. Peticolas* (Albuquerque, N.M.: Merit Press, 1993), 56.

43. Gerald F. Linderman, "Embattled Courage," in Barton and Logue, *Civil War Soldier,* 443; Gerald F. Linderman, *Embattled Courage: The Experience of Combat in the American Civil War* (New York: Free Press, 1987), 8, 12; McPherson, *For Cause and Comrades,* 85.

44. W. L. Moody to Lizzie, n.d., William L. Moody Collection, Center for Twentieth Century Texas Studies, Moody Mansion and Museum, Galveston, Tex.

45. W. W. Heartstill, *Fourteen Hundred and 91 Days in the Confederate Army; or, Camp Life, Day by Day of the W. P. Lane Rangers from April 19, 1861 to May 20, 1865,* facsimile reprint, ed. Bell I. Wiley (Jackson, Tenn.: McCowat-Mercer Press, 1954), 2; quote also in B. P. Gallaway, ed., *Texas, the Dark Corner of the Confederacy: Contemporary Accounts of the Lone Star State in the Civil War* (Lincoln: University of Nebraska Press, 1994), 92.

46. Young to wife, October 20, 1862, John M. Holcombe, Seventeenth Texas Infantry File, THM.

47. Austin *State Gazette*, October 12, 1861.

48. Robert W. Glover, ed., *"Tyler to Sharpsburg," Robert H. and William H. Gaston: Their War Letters, 1861–1862* (Waco, Tex.: W. M. Morrison, 1960), 10.

49. William Clyde Billingsley, ed., "'Such Is War': The Confederate Memoirs of Newton Asbury Keen," *Texas Military History* 7 (1968): 177. A galvanized soldier in the Civil War was usually a Confederate soldier who agreed to fight for the Union against Native Americans on the frontier. More times than not, the incentive was the opportunity to leave the prison camps for freedom and healthier conditions. As with most such stories, Kilpatrick offered many more attractive incentives: "General Kilplpatrick offered me $300.00 in cash and [a] good horse, bridle and saddle if I would join him. I told him that I did not feel it was right to do that and that I had taken an oath to be true to the South; and felt like other would not respect me if I broke my oath. He then offered to send me to the front tier where there was no war, and where I would not be in much danger. The three hundred dollar promise was kept up, but I declined all of his offers. He then made me an offer which if I had any sense I would have taken advantage of, but a poor soldier never know[s] anything. He offered to send me to my kins folk in the state of Indiana North of the Ohio River, if I would take an oath to stay north of said river during the war. Here was where I let the apple slip. He told me that I would have to stay in prison until the war was over and that I would not be exchanged. I told him I prefered to go to prison."

50. Mark H. Dunkelman, *Brothers One and All: Esprit de Corps in a Civil War Regiment* (Baton Rouge: Louisiana State University Press, 2004), 6; Wiley, *Life of Johnny Reb*, 83; McPherson, *For Cause and Comrades*, 79, 80, 81.

51. Wyatt-Brown, *Southern Honor*, 328–329.

52. Wiley, *Life of Johnny Reb*, 18; Thompson, *Westward the Texans*, 62–63.

53. Perry Wayne Shelton, comp., *Personal Civil War Letters of General Lawrence Sullivan Ross: With Other Letters* (Austin: Shelly and Richard Morrison, 1994), 3.

54. Ibid., 28.

55. Crain to wife, October 27, 1863, Alexander C. Crain, Second Texas Partisan Rangers File, THM.

56. McPherson, *For Cause and Comrades*, 23, 80.

57. Campbell, *Gone to Texas*, 227–228; John Austin Edwards, "Social and Cultural Activities of Texans during the Civil War and Reconstruction, 1861–1873," (Ph.D. diss., Texas Tech University, 1985), 68, 69; Carolyn Earle Billingsley, *Communities of Kinship: Antebellum Families and the Settlement of the Cotton Frontier* (Athens: University of Georgia Press, 2004), 7. National Archives Microfilm Publications, *Population Schedules of the Eighth Census*, Micro copy M-653, rolls 1291, 1292, 1299, and 1303; Woodworth, *While God Is Marching On*, ix; Edwards, "Social and Cultural Activities," 70. In 1860, Texas had 938 local church groups with a total membership of 276,461 people. The clear majority of the churches and members were Methodists or Baptists. Methodists had 410 churches with 119,932 members, and Baptists had 280 churches with 77,435 members. The next closest denomination was the Presbyterians, with only 72 churches and 19,565 members. There were also non-Protestant churches such as the Catholics in Texas, but they were the clear minority. Church membership was reflected in the soldier population—the majority of soldiers being Protestant, along with some Catholics, Jews, and atheists.

58. Rabb to brother, January 4, 1863, Rabb Family Papers, CAH.

59. McPherson, *For Cause and Comrades*, 63; Daniel, *Soldiering in the Army of Tennes-*

see, 115; Newton A. Keen, *Living and Fighting with the Texas Sixth Cavalry* (Gaithersburg, Md.: Butternut Press, 1986), 22.

60. Parker, *Touched by Fire*, 62.

61. Glover, *"Tyler to Sharpsburg,"* 7.

62. Samuel S. Watson, November 1, 1864, First Texas Infantry, THM. The letter did not indicate who received the letter.

63. Nelson to brother August, January 8, 1863, A. J. Nelson, Waul's Texas Legion File, THM.

64. Richard E. Beringer, Herman Hattaway, Archer Jones, and William N. Still Jr., *The Elements of Confederate Defeat: Nationalism, War Aims, and Religion* (Athens: University of Georgia Press, 1988), 118; Woodworth, *While God Is Marching On*, 29; Edward Richardson Crockett Collection, Civil War Diary, 1864–1865, April 20, 1864, CAH.

65. Bryan Marsh, "The Confederate Letters of Bryan Marsh," *Chronicles of Smith County, Texas* 14 (1975): 44. Another example is a letter written by Edward P. Edwards of the 4th Texas Infantry. "We can do nothing if we rely upon our own strength," Edwards wrote, "for our help must come from God!" W. L. Edwards to wife, 10 May 1862, William P. Edwards, Fourth Texas Infantry File, THM.

66. W. Edwards to My Dear Wife, 28 April 1862, William P. Edwards, Fourth Texas Infantry File, THM.

67. McPherson, *For Cause and Comrades*, 64, 65, 66; Woodworth, *While God Is Marching On*, 36, 39.

68. Beringer, Hattaway, Jones, and Still, *Elements of Confederate Defeat*, 40, 118, 124; Beringer, Hattaway, Jones, and Still, *Why the South Lost the Civil War*, 269; Woodworth, *While God Is Marching On*, 125, 126; Edward Richardson Crockett Collection, Civil War Diary, 1864–1865, May 12, 1864, CAH.

69. Douglas Lee Braudaway, ed., "A Texan Records the Civil War Siege of Vicksburg, Mississippi: The Journal of Maj. Maurice Kavanaugh Simons, 1863," *Southwestern Historical Quarterly* 105 (2001): 125–126.

70. Samuel S. Watson, November 1, 1864, First Texas Infantry File, THM.

71. McPherson, *For Cause and Comrades*, 71–74; John Keegan, *The Face of Battle* (New York: Viking Press, 1976), 114.

72. Drew Gilpin Faust, "Christian Soldiers," in Barton and Logue, *Civil War Soldier*, 338; McPherson, *For Cause and Comrades*, 69, 71; Edward Richardson Crockett Collection, Civil War Diary, 1864–1865, July 16, 1864, and September 18, 1864, CAH.

73. Parker, *Touched by Fire*, 62.

74. Norman D. Brown, ed., *Journey to Pleasant Hill: The Civil War Letters of Captain Elijah P. Petty, Walker's Texas Division, CSA* (San Antonio: University of Texas Institute of Texan Cultures, 1982), 106.

75. McPherson, *For Cause and Comrades*, 70; W. Edwards to My Affectionate Companion, June 2, 1862, William P. Edwards, Fourth Texas Infantry File, THM.

76. Barnes to Mrs. Barnes, December 16, 1864, Thomas L. Anderson, Thirty-first Texas Cavalry File, THM. James C. Bates of the 9th Texas Cavalry wrote to his mother and sister to reassure them that they would see each other again: "When I bid you good bye on leaving home & received the parting injuction to meet you in heaven if we should not meet again on earth—I resolved that I would try, and now through the mercy of the great & good God I feel that 'my sins are forgiven me,' and that although we may never meet here again, I will meet you in Heaven where partings are not known. Oh I would not exchange the peace & happiness that this 'blessed hope' gives me, for the wealth of all the world. God grant me

strength ever to 'keep the faith.'" Richard Lowe, ed., *A Texas Cavalry Officer's Civil War: The Diary and Letters of James C. Bates* (Baton Rouge: Louisiana State University Press, 1999), 305.

77. Dewitt Clinton Giddings, 1827–1903 Papers, Journal September 21, 1861, and June 18, 1862, CAH.

78. Samuel S. Watson, October 21, 1864, First Texas Infantry, THM.

79. Meeting loved ones was a common topic in Texans' letters. Here are a few more of the best examples: "If I fall in this war, I hope that I am in the right cause. I am almost sure that we are in the rite and we all have to go when our time comes and when God calls for us we must go. If I fall I hope and trust that we all will meet again where we will meet to part no more. I have my trust in God and with him I can trust myself with him." Arrant to Cleriton, n.d., D. G. Arrant, Twenty-fifth Texas Cavalry File, THM. "Though it is likely we may never see each other again on earth let us live so that we meet in heaven." Douglas Hale, "One Man's War: Captain Joseph H. Bruton, 1861–1865," *East Texas Historical Journal* 12 (1982): 28. "If it shuld be gods will that we shuld never meat here on earth my daly prare is that we may meat in heaven whare ther will be no more fiting." Dodson to wife, June 15, 1862, James Richard Dodson, Seventeenth Texas Cavalry, THM.

80. Barton and Logue, *Civil War Soldier*, 338; Lowe, *Texas Cavalry Officer's Civil War*, 2–3.

81. Lowe, *Texas Cavalry Officer's Civil War*, 12, 90, 94; J. S. Duncan, ed. "Alexander Cameron in the Louisiana Campaign, 1863–1865," *Military History of Texas and the Southwest* 12 (1975): 259. Alexander Cameron also wrote that church services reminded him of home and his wife. Cameron wrote his wife, "I have just gotten in from Preaching which was in camps. . . . it makes me think of you."

82. McPherson, *For Cause and Comrades*, 67; Dallas *Herald*, January 14, 1863.

83. Dobney, "From Denominationalism to Nationalism," 367.

84. McPherson, *For Cause and Comrades*, 63, 64; James W. Silver, *Confederate Morale and Church Propaganda* (Gloucester, Mass.: Peter Smith, 1964), 13.

85. Jesse P. Bates to Susan Bates, May 2, 1862, Jesse P. Bates, Ninth Texas Infantry, THM.

86. Lowe, *Texas Cavalry Officer's Civil War*, 36.

87. Bailey, *Between the Enemy and Texas*, xv.

88. Howell to family, September 1, 1861, William Randolph Howell Collection, CAH.

89. Smith to father and mother, October 12, 1863, Henry V. Smith, Twenty-fifth Texas Cavalry File, THM.

90. Ibid.

91. Buenger, *Secession and the Union*, 3, 62, 63; Allen Coleman Ashcraft, "Texas: 1860–1866, The Lone Star State in the Civil War" (Ph.D. diss., Columbia University, 1960), 71; Ella Lonn, *Desertion during the Civil War* (Lincoln: University of Nebraska Press, 1966), 4; McCaslin, *Tainted Breeze*, 15, 22, 32; Baum, *Shattering of Texas Unionism*, 46; McKinney *Messenger*, March 1, 1861. There were also small pockets of unionists throughout the state, such as in San Antonio, where the *Alamo Express* newspaper "politically . . . [was] in favor of an opposition to secession and disunion whether headed by Lincoln or Breckinridge . . . [and] for the Constitution, the Union and the enforcement of the laws." San Antonio *Alamo Express*, August 18, 1860. The newspaper closed down soon after the beginning of the war.

92. Buenger, *Secession and the Union*, 62, 64, 66; McCaslin, *Tainted Breeze*, 15; Baum, *Shattering of Texas Unionism*, 52, 53; Pickering and Falls, *Brush Men and Vigilantes*, 9.

93. J. R. Havins and James M. Day, eds., *Twenty-five Years on the Outside Row of the Northwest Texas Conference* (Brownwood, Tex.: Cross Timbers Press, 1966), 20–21; also

cited in Walter N. Vernon, Robert W. Sledge, Robert C. Monk, and Norman W. Spellmann, *The Methodist Excitement in Texas: A History* (Dallas: Texas United Methodist Historical Society, 1984), 118.

94. James Marten, *Texas Divided: Loyalty and Dissent in the Lone Star State, 1856–1874* (Lexington: University Press of Kentucky, 1990), 33, 34, 55; Buenger, *Secession and the Union*, 62; Beringer, Hattaway, Jones, and Still, *Why the South Lost the Civil War*, 67.

95. L. D. Clark, ed., *Civil War Recollections of James Lemuel Clark* (College Station: Texas A&M University Press, 1984), 16, 17, 18, 19, 49.

96. McCaslin, *Tainted Breeze*, 2–3; see also Richard B. McCaslin, "The Price of Liberty: The Great Hanging at Gainesville," in Charles D. Grear, ed., *The Fate of Texas: The Civil War and the Lone Star State* (Fayetteville: University of Arkansas Press, 2008).

97. James W. Daddysman, *The Matamoros Trade: Confederate Commerce, Diplomacy, and Intrigue* (Newark: University of Delaware Press, 1984), 85; John Warren Hunter, *Heel-Fly Time in Texas: A Story of the Civil War Period* (Bandera, Tex.: Frontier Times, 1931), 9; Frank H. Smyrl, "Texans in the Union Army, 1861–1865," *Southwestern Historical Quarterly* 65 (1961): 234, 235; Marten, *Texas Divided*, 75.

98. Smyrl, "Texans in the Union Army," 235; Ashcraft, *Texas in the Civil War*, 14; Marten, *Texas Divided*, 76; Anne J. Bailey, "Defiant Unionists: Militant Germans in Confederate Texas," in John C. Inscoe and Robert C. Kenzer, eds., *Enemies of the Country: New Perspectives on Unionists in the Civil War South* (Athens: University of Georgia Press, 2001), 213, 214; Claude Elliot, "Union Sentiment in Texas, 1861–1865," in Wooster, *Lone Star Blue and Gray*, 84; Carl H. Moneyhon, *Texas after the Civil War: The Struggle of Reconstruction* (College Station: Texas A&M University Press, 2004) 21, 119; Ronald N. Gray, "Edmund J. Davis: Radical Republican and Reconstruction Governor of Texas," (Ph.D. diss., Texas Tech University, 1976), 2, 5–6, 12, 29, 34, 36; John L. Waller, *Colossal Hamilton of Texas: A Biography of Andrew Jackson Hamilton, Militant Unionist and Reconstruction Governor* (El Paso: Texas Western Press, 1968), 7–10, 33, 35, 39, 43, 58, 60; James A. Marten, "Hamilton, Andrew Jackson," in Tyler, *Handbook of Texas*, 2:427–428; Houston *Tri-Weekly Telegraph*, September 1, 1862; Weitz, *More Damning Than Slaughter*, 123.

99. R .F. Bunting, October 20, 1863, Online Archive of Terry's Texas Rangers, http://terrystexasrangers.org/letters/bunting_rf/1863_10_20.htm (accessed December 14, 2003).

100. Clarksville *Northern Standard*, April 20, 1861.

101. Baum, *Shattering of Texas Unionism*, 84; Beringer, Hattaway, Jones, and Still, *Why the South Lost the Civil War*, 78.

102. Mark E. Nackman, "The Making of the Texas Citizen Soldier, 1835–1860," *Southwestern Historical Quarterly* 78 (1975): 241; Phillip Michael Sozansky, "A Mystical Sense of Community: Hood's Texas Brigade and the Social, Cultural, and Environmental Dimensions of Combat Success in the Army of Northern Virginia," (M.A. thesis, Texas State University, 2006), 57–59; Corsicana *Navarro Express*, July 18, 1861.

103. Record Group 109, chap. 2, vol. 129, Military Departments Letters Sent, Department of Texas, Sept.–November 1861, National Archives and Records Service, General Services Administration, War Department Collection of Confederate Records.

104. Curtis W. Milbourn, ed., "I Have Been Worse Treated Than Any Officer: Confederate Colonel Thomas Green's Assessment of the New Mexico Campaign," *Southwestern Historical Quarterly* 105 (2001): 325; also cited in Nackman, "Making of the Texas Citizen Soldier," 232.

105. Anne J. Bailey, *Texans in the Confederate Cavalry* (Abilene, Tex.: McWhiney Foundation Press, 1998), 14.

106. Josiah G. Duke to Grand Ma, [n.d.], Josiah G. Duke, Fourth Texas Infantry File, THM.

107. J. S. Norvell to Miss Cora, October 27, 1861, J. S. Norvell, Seventh Texas Infantry File, THM.

108. Shelton, *Personal Civil War Letters of General Lawrence Sullivan Ross*, 38.

109. Parker, *Touched by Fire*, 44. "Green Mountaineers" is a nickname for people from Vermont.

110. Ibid., 95.

111. McPherson, *For Cause and Comrades*, 83–84. Boastfulness about the martial abilities of Texans is a common theme in letters of Texas soldiers. Some other examples follow: "I expect we will see sights this evening but we will keep up the reputation of our state." Stranahan to Milda, May 15, 1863, Lt. John A. Stranahan, Twenty-first Texas Cavalry File, THM. "Us Texans thought we was more acustum to hard fighting than many of the Union soldears. As most of the Texas Boys was raised on the frontear outdoors life and raised with guns in our hands." Memoir, Henry Ward Harris, Nineteenth Texas Cavalry File, THM. "Gen McCullock gave us a talk when we left Camp Nelson. . . . He took the occasion to remind us of our duty as patriots and soldiers. Said we must sustain the reputation the Texans have already gained as the very best soldiers in the Confederate service." Harlan to Ma, November 2, 1862, Isaiah Harlan, Tenth Texas Infantry File, THM.

112. Singleton B. Bedinger, *Texas and the Southern Confederacy* (Taylor, Tex.: Merchants Press, 1970), 51.

113. John Dollard, *Fear in Battle* (New York: AMS Press, 1976), 1, 47; Bedinger, *Texas and the Southern Confederacy*, 51. Dollard interviewed three hundred veterans of the Abraham Lincoln Brigade, who volunteered to fight in the Spanish Civil War. He concluded that 74 percent of the soldiers that belonged to this famous unit felt like elite soldiers, thus boosting their morale.

114. Whatley to Nannie F, Whatley, n.d., William J. Whatley Papers, 1841–1874, CAH.

115. Walter Kamphoefner and Wolfgang Helbich, eds., *Germans in the American Civil War: Letters from the Front and Farm, 1861–1865* (Chapel Hill: University of North Carolina Press, 2006), 407.

116. McKay to R. W. Loughery, June 13, 1862, Gil McKay, Seventeenth Texas Cavalry File, THM.

117. Diary, April 9, 1864, H. D. Pearce, Sixteenth Texas Cavalry File, THM.

118. Stark to Martha, October 9, 1862, John T. Stark, Thirteenth Texas Cavalry File, THM.

119. Carolyn, *Communities of Kinship*, 101; Connally to wife, July 14, 1862, Drury Connally, Alf Johnson Spy Company File, THM.

120. The Civil War Diary of Judge William Kuykendall of Tilden, Texas, William Kuykendall, First Texas Cavalry Regiment File, THM.

121. Robert Ikard to Pa, October 24, 1862, Elijah H. and Robert E. Ikard, Nineteenth Texas Cavalry File, THM.

122. Some men had opportunities to join units with their kin but for other reasons they did not. John Allen Templeton expressed his regret to his parents: "Tho I wanted to go to Col. Lane's Regiment & join the same Co. to which Br[other]. Frank belongs. But now I am glad I did not get off—not that I did not want to see you all or go to the same Co. Frank joined because if I went home I would stayed there & would have had to go & perhaps join some strange Regt. And if I had went to where Frank was and joined I would have saved a great deal more trouble & so would he for when one of us was sick or disabled the other

one could not have been with him. As it is when one is sick or disabled the other one knows about it." Templeton to father and mother, January 8, 1863, John Allen Templeton, Tenth Texas Cavalry File, THM.

123. Mixson to sister, May 10, 1862, T. C. Mixson, Fifteenth Texas Infantry File, THM; Frank Owsley, *Plain Folk of the Old South* (Baton Rouge: Louisiana State University Press, 1949), 94; McWhiney, *Cracker Culture*, xvii; Billingsley, *Communities of Kinship*, 7, 14, 15; Weitz, *More Damning Than Slaughter*, 27–28. The rosters have T. C. Mixson listed as Mixon, but in his letters he spelled his name "Mixson."

124. Keener to Miss Allie, November 20, 1864, Lawson Jefferson Keener, Second Texas Cavalry (Second Arizona) Regiment File, THM.

125. Owsley, *Plain Folk of the Old South*, 95; Wyatt-Brown, *Southern Honor*, 333; Joan E. Cashin, "The Structure of Antebellum Planter Families: 'The Ties That Bound Us Was Strong,'" *Journal of Southern History* 61 (1990): 56, 61, 70; Billingsley, *Communities of Kinship*, 110.

126. Roy R. Grinker and John P. Speigel, *Men under Stress* (Philadelphia: Blakiston, 1945), 39.

127. U.S. Bureau of the Census, Federal Manuscript Census, Population Schedule, 1860, Texas (published); Owsley, *Plain Folk of the Old South*, 55; Friend, "Texan of 1860," 2; Jordan, *German Seed in Texas Soil*, 9, 19, 20, 29; Randolph B. Campbell and Richard G. Lowe, *Wealth and Power in Antebellum Texas* (College Station: Texas A&M University Press, 1972), 15; Buenger, *Secession and the Union*, 11; Billingsley, *Communities of Kinship*, 41, 42, 68, 69, 73.

128. Lathrop, *Migration into East Texas*, 51.

129. Kennedy, *Population of the United States in 1860*, iv, xiii, xvii, xxix, xxxiii, 616–619; Mark E. Nackman, *A Nation within a Nation: The Rise of Texas Nationalism* (Port Washington, N.Y.: Kennikat Press, 1975), 49; Ashcraft, "Texas," 1; Buenger, *Secession and the Union*, 8.

130. Buenger, *Secession and the Union*, 8.

Chapter 3

Chapter epigraph from A. W. Sparks, *The War between the States, as I Saw It: Reminiscent, Historical, and Personal* (Longview, Tex: D&D, 1987), 11.

1. W. H. Getzendaner, *A Brief and Condensed History of Parsons' Texas Cavalry Brigade Composed of Twelfth, Nineteenth, Twenty-First, Morgan's Battalion, and Pratt's Battery of Artillery of the Confederate States, Together with the Roster of the Several Commands as far as Obtainable—Some Historical Sketches—General Orders and a Memoranda of Parsons' Brigade Association* (Waxahachie, Tex.: J. M. Flemister, 1892), 21; also quoted in Bailey, *Between the Enemy and Texas*, 3, 230.

2. John W. Stevens, *Reminiscences of the Civil War: A Soldier in Hood's Texas Brigade, Army of Northern Virginia* (Hillsboro, Tex.: Hillsboro Mirror, 1902), 11.

3. Houston *Tri-Weekly Telegraph*, March 26, 1862.

4. Dallas *Herald*, September 25, 1861.

5. General Order No. 8 to South Kansas Texas Regiment, July 16, 1861, John Arthur Bryan Papers, CAH; Hale, *Third Texas Cavalry*, 27.

6. Census records do not provide accurate enough information on the year men in units serving in the trans-Mississippi arrived in Texas. To get accurate information on origins and when men arrived in Texas, I compiled my information from Kathryn Hooper Davis, Linda Ericson Devereaux, and Carolyn Reeves Ericson, comps., *Texas Confederate Home Roster*

(Nacogdoches, Tex.: Ericson Books, 2003); Kennedy, *Population of the United States in 1860*, 616–619.

7. John William Bowyer and Claude Harrison Thurman, arrangers, *The Annals of Elder Horn: Early Life in the Southwest* (New York: Richard R. Smith, 1930), 66; Barr, *Polignac's Texas Brigade*, 18.

8. Ashcraft, *Texas in the Civil War*, 82; Hale, *Third Texas Cavalry*, 25; Bailey, *Between the Enemy and Texas*, xv; R. M. Collins, *Chapters from the Unwritten History of the War between the States: The Incidents in the Life of a Confederate Soldier in Camp, on the March, in the Great Battles, and in Prison*, (Dayton, Ohio: Morningside 1988), 9.

9. Bowyer and Thurman, *Annals of Elder Horn*, 2, 5, 6.

10. Keen, *Living and Fighting with the Texas Sixth Cavalry*, 4–5, 18; B. P. Gallaway, *The Ragged Rebel: A Common Soldier in W. H. Parsons' Texas Cavalry, 1861–1865* (Austin: University of Texas Press, 1988), 1, 11, 13.

11. Anderson, *Campaigning with Parsons' Texas Cavalry*, ix, x, xii, 9–10.

12. Ibid., 52.

13. Ibid., 141–142.

14. Ibid., 157–158.

15. Diary, n.d., Hartwell Bolin Cox File, Nineteenth Texas Cavalry File, THM.

16. Connally to wife, May 5, 1862, Drury Connally, Alf Johnson Spy Company File, THM.

17. Connally to wife, September 20, 1862, Drury Connally, Alf Johnson Spy Company File, THM.

18. Charles E. Rogers, *The Rogers Family of Ozark, Missouri* (Rogersville, Mo.: private publication, 1975), 2; Martha Crabb, *All Afire to Fight: The Untold Tale of the Civil War's Ninth Texas Cavalry* (New York: First Post Road Press, 2001), 3, 16.

19. Clayton E. Jewett, *Texas in the Confederacy: An Experiment in Nation Building* (Columbia: University of Virginia Press, 2002), 115, 116; Barr, *Polignac's Texas Brigade*, 4; Dallas *Herald*, January 15, 1862.

20. Barr, *Polignac's Texas Brigade*, 1–2.

21. Lowe, *Texas Cavalry Officer's Civil War*, xvii, xxi; A. W. Neville Papers, Texas A&M University at Commerce Library, Commerce, Tex.

22. Bailey, *Between the Enemy and Texas*, 5–6, 14, 50.

23. Ibid., 43.

24. Judith Ann Benner, "Lone Star Soldier: A Study of the Military Career of Lawrence Sullivan Ross" (Ph.D. diss., Texas Christian University, 1975), 142, 149; Shelton, *Personal Civil War Letters of General Lawrence Sullivan Ross*, ix; Judith Ann Benner, "Lawrence Sullivan Ross," in W. C. Dunn, ed., *Ten More Texans in Gray* (Hillsboro, Tex.: Hill Junior College Press, 1980), 109, 110. After the war, Lawrence Sullivan Ross was elected governor of Texas and became president of Texas Agricultural and Mechanics College (present-day Texas A&M University).

25. Thomas W. Cutrer, *Ben McCulloch and the Frontier Military Tradition* (Chapel Hill: University of North Carolina Press, 1993), 193, 195.

26. Ibid., 197.

27. Houston *Tri-Weekly Telegraph*, November 1, 1861.

28. Dallas *Herald*, November 13, 1861; Ralph A. Wooster, *Lone Star Regiments in Gray* (Austin: Eakin Press, 2002), 279–280. Thomas C. Bass was an ardent secessionist, even credited with raising the first Confederate flag in Texas. During the war he commanded the 12th Texas Cavalry.

29. L. B. Russell Collection, 1859–1865, CAH; Wooster, *Lone Star Regiments*, 215–216, 272; Stewart Sifakis, *Compendium of Confederate Armies, Texas* (New York: Facts on File, 1995), 92.

30. C. Richard King, ed., "Andrew Neill's Galveston Letters," *Texana* 3 (Fall 1965): 203; "Neill, Andrew," in Tyler, *Handbook of Texas*, 4:979.

31. James R. Ward, "Robert W. 'Dick' Dowling," in W. C. Nunn, ed., *Ten Texans in Gray* (Hillsboro, Tex.: Hill Junior College Press, 1968), 36, 37, 38; Frank X. Tolbert, *Dick Dowling at Sabine Pass* (New York: McGraw-Hill, 1962), 21, 25; Andrew Forest Muir, "Dick Dowling and the Battle of Sabine Pass," *Civil War History* 4 (1958): 399–428; Edward T. Cotham Jr., *Sabine Pass: The Confederacy's Thermopylae* (Austin: University of Texas Press, 2004), 3.

32. Cox to Captain R. W. Hargrove, n.d., Noah B. Cox, Thirty-fifth Texas Cavalry (Brown's) File, THM; Wooster, *Lone Star Regiments*, 223.

33. McPherson, *For Cause and Comrades*, 97; Wooster, *Lone Star Regiments*, 88–99, 107–108.

34. John Allen Templeton to father, October 11, 1861, John Allen Templeton, Tenth Texas Cavalry File, THM.

35. John Allen Templeton to father, February 1, 1862, John Allen Templeton, Tenth Texas Cavalry File, THM; Carlock and Owens, *History of the Tenth Texas Cavalry*, 8, 9.

36. Templeton to father, May 16, 1862, John Allen Templeton, Tenth Texas Cavalry File, THM; "Interview with John Allen Templeton, 86, of Jacksonville, Texas," www.wells.esc7.net/Cherokee/templeton.html (accessed February 2, 2005). As part of the the Conscription Act of 1862, all soldiers under the age of eighteen and above the age of thirty were exempt from serving in the army. At the beginning of the war, Templeton was only sixteen, so when the act was passed he had the option of receiving an honorable discharge from the army.

37. Templeton to father, February 16, 1863, Tenth Texas Cavalry File, THM.

38. Templeton to father, May 3, 1863, Tenth Texas Cavalry File, THM.

39. Templeton to father, May 16, 1862, Tenth Texas Cavalry File, THM.

40. "The Civil War Record of George W. L. Fly, Major (Infantry) Confederate States Army, 1861–1865," by Harold B. Simpson, George W. L. Fly, Second Texas Infantry File, THM; Joseph E. Chance, *The Second Texas Infantry: From Shiloh to Vicksburg* (Austin: Eakin Press, 1984), vii, 3–4; Galveston *Weekly News*, September 3, 1861; Silverthorne, *Ashbel Smith of Texas*, 4, 37, 40, 147, 149. Smith expressed his feelings of the war and its impact on his family in a letter to his nephew Ashbel Smith Kittredge on February 24, 1861: "Texas will be no longer one of the United States. The madness of Black Republicanism had destroyed the best government ever devised by man. . . . When I think of . . . my dear old mother, from whom I am separated (communications North and South severed), my heart seems ready to break. Tell her that time and distance only increase my affection for her." Ashbel Smith to Ashbel Smith Kittredge, February 24, 1861 as cited in Silverthorne, *Ashbel Smith of Texas*, 147.

41. Autobiography of J. H. Cravey, J. H. Cravey, Second Texas Infantry File, THM; Chance, *Second Texas Infantry*, 9; Walter H. Mays, ed., "The Vicksburg Diary of M. K. Simmons, 1863," *Texas Military History* 5 (1965): 21; Braudaway, "Texan Records the Civil War Siege of Vicksburg," 94–95.

42. Ashcraft, *Texas in the Civil War*, 10; Chance, *Second Texas Infantry*, 13; Arthur W. Bergeron Jr., "John Creed Moore," in Davis and Hoffman, *Confederate General*, 4:180–181.

43. J. M. Hatchell to mother, August 27, 1862, J. M. Hatchell, Second Texas Infantry File, THM.

44. "The Civil War Record of George W. L. Fly, Major (Infantry), Confederate States

Army, 1861–1865," W. L. Fly, Second Texas Infantry File, THM; Wooster, *Texas and Texans in the Civil War*, 79, 134. See also Chance, *Second Texas Infantry*.

45. Homer L. Kerr, ed., *Fighting with Ross' Texas Cavalry Brigade C.S.A.: The Diary of George L. Griscom, Adjutant, Ninth Texas Cavalry Regiment* (Hillsboro, Tex.: Hill Jr. College Press, 1976), 38.

46. Douglas John Cater, *As It Was: Reminiscences of a Soldier of the Third Texas Cavalry and the Nineteenth Louisiana Infantry* (Austin: State House Press, 1990), v, ix, x, xiii, xiv, 71, 128.

47. Ibid., xiv, xv, 141.

48. Ibid., 144, 172–174.

49. Crabb, *All Afire to Fight*, 178.

50. Lowe, *Texas Cavalry Officer's Civil War*, xvii, 244.

51. Ibid., 249, 250.

52. Collins, *Chapters from the Unwritten History*, ii–vi, 124.

53. Hunter, *Heel-Fly Time in Texas*, 8, 18, 19, 28, 47.

54. Gra' Delle Duncan, *Texas Tough: Dangerous Men in Dangerous Times* (Austin: Eakin Press, 1990), 45, 46.

55. Quayle to Henry McCulloch, July 1, 1864, William Quayle, SC 6–3, Letters Outgoing, February 16, 1864–October 7, 1864, THM.

56. James Bourland to Quayle, July 19, 1864, William Quayle, SC 6–2, Letters Incoming, August 19, 1861–October 26, 1868, THM.

57. Houston *Tri-Weekly Telegraph*, November 28, 1862; Records of the Adjunct General: Muster Roll Collection Record Group (RG) 401, box 1276, nos. 279, 724–3, TSLAC.

58. San Antonio *Tri-Weekly Alamo Express*, April 10, 1861; Campbell, *Gone to Texas*, 202; Robert L. Kerby, *Kirby Smith's Confederacy: The Trans-Mississippi South, 1863–1865* (Tuscaloosa: University of Alabama Press, 1972), 13, 14; Ashcraft, "Texas," 137; Gary Clayton Anderson, *The Conquest of Texas: Ethnic Cleansing in the Promised Land, 1820–1875* (Norman: University of Oklahoma, 2005), 226.

59. Stanley S. McGowen, *Horse Sweat and Powder Smoke: The First Texas Cavalry in the Civil War* (College Station: Texas A&M University Press, 1999), 14, 24.

60. James K. Greer, ed., *A Texas Ranger and Frontiersman: The Days of Buck Barry in Texas, 1845–1906* (Dallas, Tex.: Southwest Press, 1932), 5, 14, 24; James Buckner Barry Collection, CAH; McGowen, *Horse Sweat and Powder Smoke*, 15.

61. McGowen, *Horse Sweat and Powder Smoke*, 14, 16; William A. Pitts Collection, CAH.

62. McGowen, *Horse Sweat and Powder Smoke*, xii, xiii, 10, 168; Davidson to Mary, February 22, 1861, and February 24, 1864, Sidney Green Davidson Papers, 1860–1861, CAH; Scott Dennis Parker, "'The Best Stuff Which the State Affords': A Portrait of the Fourteenth Texas Infantry in the Civil War, 1862–1865" (M.A. thesis, North Texas University, 1998), 12. Immigrants came from numerous countries including Germany, Scotland, Ireland, England, Mexico, Canada, and France. According to James Lynn Newsom, the 7th Texas Infantry had numbers similar to those of the 14th; Newsom, "Intrepid Gray Warriors: The Seventh Texas Infantry, 1861–1865," (Ph.D. diss., Texas Christian University, 1995), 7.

63. McGowen, *Horse Sweat and Powder Smoke*, 37, 168; Wooster, *Lone Star Regiments*, 161–162; Sifakis, *Compendium of the Confederate Armies*, 38.

64. Martin Hall, "Planters vs. Frontiersman: Conflict in Confederate Indian Policy," in Frank E. Vandiver, Martin Hall, and Homer Kess, eds., *Essays on the American Civil War* (Austin: University of Texas Press, 1968), 46–47, 51; George Wythe Baylor, *John Robert Bay-*

lor: Confederate Governor of Arizona (Tucson: Arizona Pioneers' Historical Society, 1966), 1, 2, 29; Henry W. Miller, *Pioneering North Texas* (San Antonio, Tex.: Naylor, 1953), 66; Ida Huckabury, *Ninety-Four Years in Jack County, 1854–1948* (Jacksboro, Tex.: n.p., 1949), 56; Carrie J. Crouch, *A History of Young County, Texas* (Austin: Texas State Historical Association, 1956), 23; Martin Hardwick Hall, *The Confederate Army of New Mexico* (Austin: Presidial Press, 1978), 296; Frazier, *Blood and Treasure*, 26; Margret Hancock Pearce, "The Gano Cabin History and a Story from Narratives," *Dallas Journal: Dallas Genealogical Society* (December 1996): 31–32; Richard Montgomery Gano Collection, "Personal War Record of Brigadier-General Richard Montgomery Gano," 30–32, Brown Special Collections Library, Abilene Christian University, Abilene, Tex. Baylor also had political reasons for joining the army, which included becoming the Confederate governor of Arizona Territory.

65. Frazier, *Blood and Treasure*, 40; Jerry D. Thompson, *Colonel John Robert Baylor: Texas Indian Fighter and Confederate Soldier* (Hillsboro, Tex.: Hill Junior College, 1971), 25; Baylor, *John Robert Baylor*, 4–5; Enrique B. D'Hamel, *The Adventures of a Tenderfoot* (Waco, Tex: W. M. Morrison, 1914), 8.

66. Baylor to Capt. Thomas Helm, 20 March 1862, War Department Collection of Confederate Records, 56–57, National Archives, Washington, D.C.; John Baylor to Thomas Helm, March 20, 1862, in U.S. War Department, *The War of the Rebellion: A Compilation of the Official Records of the Union and Confederate Armies* (hereafter *o.r.*) (Washington, D.C.: U.S. Government Printing Office, 1880–1901), Series I, vol. 50, pt. 1: 942; Baylor, *John Robert Baylor*, 13; Martin Hall, "Planters vs. Frontiersmen: Conflict in Confederate Indian Policy," in Vandiver, Hall, and Kess, *Essays on the American Civil War*, 56–57.

67. Vandiver, Hall, and Kess, *Essays on the American Civil War*, 59, 64; Baylor to Captain Helm, March 20, 1862, *o.r.*, Series I, vol. 15, pt. 1: 914–918; Baylor, *John Robert Baylor*, 15; Alvin M. Josephy Jr., *The Civil War in the American West* (New York: Alfred A. Knopf, 1991), 42, 51.

68. Buenger, *Secession and the Union in Texas*, 108, 109, 113, 118; McCaslin, "Conditional Confederates," 89; Kenneth W. Howell, "James Webb Throckmorton: The Life and Career of a Southern Frontier Politician, 1825–1894," (Ph.D. diss., Texas A&M University, 2005), 131.

69. Buenger, *Secession and the Union*, 9, 75; Jewett, *Texas in the Confederacy*, 123.

70. Dallas *Herald*, June 19, 1861; Howell, "James Webb Throckmorton," 197; Kenneth W. Howell, "'When the Rabble Hiss, Well May Patriots Tremble': James Webb Throckmorton and the Secession Movement in Texas, 1854–1861," *Southwestern Historical Quarterly* 109 (2006): 465, 491.

71. McCaslin, "Conditional Confederates," 87–99; Richard B. McCaslin, "Dark Corner of the Confederacy: James G. Bourland and the Border Regiment," *Military History of the West* 24 (1994): 59; Kenneth Wayne Howell, *Texas Confederate, Reconstruction Governor: James Webb Throckmorton* (College Station: Texas A&M University Press, 2008), 78–80; Lonn, *Desertion during the Civil War*, 16.

72. McGowen, *Horse Sweat and Powder Smoke*, 53–54, 62, 63, 64.

73. First Texas Cavalry of the Confederate States of America, Company D First Texas Cavalry of the Civil War, www.historictexas.net/jackson/military/1sttxcavalry.htm (accessed January 25, 2005); McGowen, *Horse Sweat and Powder Smoke*, 102; Civil War Diary, n.d., Kuykendall Family Papers, 1822–1991, CAH.

74. Sifakis, *Compendium of the Confederate Armies*, 46.

75. Kerby, *Kirby Smith's Confederacy*, 14; National Archives Microfilm Publications, *Population Schedules of the Eighth Census*, Texas Micro copy M-653, roll 1292, 273; Greer,

Texas Ranger and Frontiersman, 145; Smith, *Frontier Defense,* 42; Austin *State Gazette,* February 22, 1862; Wooster, *Lone Star Regiments,* 218.

76. Fehrenbach, *Lone Star,* 366.

77. Ashcraft, "Texas," 138, 194; David P. Smith, "Conscription and Conflict on the Texas Frontier, 1863–1865," in Ralph A. Wooster, ed., *Lone Star Blue and Gray: Essays on Texas in the Civil War* (Austin: Texas State Historical Association, 1995), 277, 278; Smith, *Frontier Defense,* 88, 94; Greer, *Texas Ranger and Frontiersman,* 169; McCaslin, "Dark Corner of the Confederacy," 60.

78. Frazier, *Blood and Treasure,* 74, 75, 83, 86; John P. Wilson, *When the Texans Came: Missing Records from the Civil War in the Southwest, 1861–1862* (Albuquerque: University of New Mexico Press, 2000), 301; John P. Wilson and Jerry Thompson, eds., *The Civil War in West Texas & New Mexico* (El Paso: University of Texas at El Paso, 2001), 33, 40, 43, 77; Michael L. Tate, ed., "A Johnny Reb in Sibley's New Mexico Campaign: Reminiscences of Pvt. Henry C. Wright, 1861–1862," *East Texas Historical Journal* 25 (1987): 22, 23; see also Jerry D. Thompson, *Henry Hopkins Sibley: Confederate General of the West* (Natchitoches, La.: Northwestern State University Press, 1987), 3–214. It is not the purpose of this section to examine every motivation that influenced Texans to enlist in Sibley's Brigade but to examine the influence of local attachments on the men's decision to enlist and fight in New Mexico. Obviously, this influence, as with most others, does not apply to every man in the brigade. As is the case with all units in every conflict, not all the men had a choice in joining this expedition. Some were transferred into the brigade by Texas governor Edward Clark, and others were coerced and lied to by desperate captains from standing units destined for Missouri, Tennessee, and Virginia. The latter, on some occasions, were enticed individually to join Sibley's expedition by the influence of local attachments, by simple charisma, or by monetary incentives.

79. Hall, *Confederate Army of New Mexico,* 14; Jerry Thompson, ed., *Civil War in the Southwest: Recollections of the Sibley Brigade* (College Station: Texas A&M University Press, 2001), xiv; Theophilus Noel, *Autobiography and Reminiscences of Theophilus Noel* (Chicago: Theophilus Noel Company Press, 1904), 65; also in W. H. Watford, "Confederate Western Ambitions," *Southwestern Historical Quarterly* 44 (1940): 167; Merle Durham, *The Lone Star State Divided: Texans and the Civil War* (Dallas, Tex.: Hendrick-Long, 1994), 40. Though it is contested that Sibley wanted to lead his army to California and possibly conquer northern Mexico, several historians support this idea. Donald S. Frazier provides the most lengthy argument in his book *Blood and Treasure,* 13, and more recently a well-supported article by Joseph G. Dawson III places Sibley's expedition into the larger context of Confederate strategy dictated by President Davis; see Dawson, "Texas, Jefferson Davis, and Confederate National Strategy," in Grear, *Fate of Texas.*

80. T. T. Teel, "Sibley's New Mexican Campaign: Its Objects and the Causes of Its Failure," in Robert Underwood Johnson and Clarence C. Buel, eds., *Battles and Leaders of the Civil War* (New York: T. Yoseloff, 1884), 2:700; also in Watford, "Confederate Western Ambitions," 167.

81. Houston *Tri-Weekly Telegraph,* May 12, 1862; also in Martin Hardwick Hall, *Sibley's New Mexico Campaign* (Austin: University of Texas Press, 1960), 4.

82. Hall, *Sibley's New Mexico Campaign,* 3–4; Jimmie Hicks, "Some Letters concerning the Knights of the Golden Circle in Texas, 1860–1861," *Southwestern Historical Quarterly* 65 (1961): 288; Hale, *Third Texas Cavalry,* 20; Buenger, *Secession and the Union,* 17; William H. Bell, "Knights of the Golden Circle: Its Organization and Activities in Texas prior to the

Civil War" (M.A. thesis, Texas College of Arts and Industries, 1965), 7; Watford, "Confederate Western Ambitions," 161.

83. Census records do not provide accurate enough information on the year the men of the 2nd, 4th, 5th, and 7th Texas Mounted Volunteers arrived in Texas. To get accurate information on the origins of the men and years they arrived in Texas, I compiled my information from Davis, Devereaux, and Ericson, *Texas Confederate Home Roster*, and Hall, *Confederate Army of New Mexico*; Tate, "Johnny Reb," 22; Oscar Hass, ed., "The Diary of Julius Giesecke, 1861–1862," *Military History of the Southwest* 18 (1988): 49.

84. Frazier, *Blood and Treasure*, 21; Charles Ray Colton, *The Civil War in the Western Territories: Arizona, Colorado, New Mexico and Utah* (Norman: University of Oklahoma Press, 1984), 3–4; Teel, "Sibley's New Mexico Campaign," 2:700; Latham Anderson, "Canby's Services in the New Mexican Campaign," in Johnson and Buel, *Battles and Leaders of the Civil War*, 2:697–98.

85. J. Fred Rippy, "Mexican Projects of the Confederates," *Southwestern Historical Quarterly* 22 (1919): 294.

86. Arizona Territory was south of the thirty-fourth parallel and stretched from West Texas to the eastern border of California. Hall, *Confederate Army of New Mexico*, 19; Frazier, *Blood and Treasure*, 40; L. Boyd Finch, *Confederate Pathway to the Pacific: Major Sherod Hunter and Arizona Territory, C.S.A.* (Tucson: Arizona Historical Society 1996), 103.

87. Josephy, *Civil War in the American West*, 53; Frazier, *Blood and Treasure*, 40, 83, 86; Thompson, *Henry Hopkins Sibley*, 222; Thompson, *Colonel John Robert Baylor*, 25; Martin Hardwick Hall, "The Formation of Sibley's Brigade and the March to New Mexico," *Southwestern Historical Quarterly* 61 (1958): 389; Colton, *Civil War in the Western Territories*, 22.

88. Tate, "Johnny Reb," 23.

89. Austin *State Gazette*, April 20, 1861.

90. Teel, "Sibley's New Mexico Campaign," 700.

91. Martin Hardwick Hall, ed., "The Taylor Letters: Confederate Correspondence from Fort Bliss, 1861," *Military History of Texas and the Southwest* 15 (1979): 54.

92. Anthony Kellett, *Combat Motivation: The Behavior of Soldiers in Battle* (Boston: Kluwer, Nijhoff, 1982), 327.

93. Odie Faulk, *General Tom Green: Fightin' Texan* (Waco, Tex.: Texian Press, 1963), 2, 4, 5; Thompson, *Henry Hopkins Sibley*, 223; Frazier, *Blood and Treasure*, 79, 80; Curtis W. Milbourn, "Brigadier General Thomas Green of Texas," *East Texas Historical Journal* 32 (1994): 3; Anne Bailey, "Thomas Green," in Davis, *Confederate General*, 3:32–33; Wooster, *Lone Star Generals*, 95–107.

94. Thompson, *Westward the Texans*, 50; Frazier, *Blood and Treasure*, 87.

95. Alberts, *Rebels on the Rio Grande*, 1, 9; Frazier, *Blood and Treasure*, 88.

96. Davis, Devereaux, and Ericson, *Texas Confederate Home Roster*; Hall, *Confederate Army of New Mexico*; Tate, "Johnny Reb," 22; Hass, "Diary of Julius Giesecke," 49; Charles David Grear, "For Land and Family: Local Attachments and the Grapevine Volunteers in the Civil War," *Military History of the West* 33 (2003): 9; Frazier, *Blood and Treasure*, 88; Terry G. Jordan-Bychkov, Allen R. Branum, and Paula K. Hood, eds., "The Boesel Letters: Two Germans in Sibley's Brigade," *Southwestern Historical Quarterly* 102 (1999): 465–466.

97. Thompson, *Henry Hopkins Sibley*, 222, 223; Ralph A. Wooster, "Texas in the Southern War for Independence," in Joseph G. Dawson III, ed., *The Texas Military Experience: From the Texas Revolution through World War II* (College Station: Texas A&M University Press, 1995), 76; Frazier, *Blood and Treasure*, 36, 97.

98. Stansbury to Miss Jenny Gordon, May 29, 1864, George T. Stansbury, Second Texas Cavalry (Second Arizona) Regiment File, THM; Wright (Henry C.) Reminiscences, CAH.

99. Memoir, January 1, 1919, J. W. DeWees, Seventh Texas Cavalry File, THM.

100. George W. Walling to Thomas Burrowes, February 5, 1866, Burrowes Family Papers, CAH; Frazier, *Blood and Treasure*, 89–90.

101. Tate, "Johnny Reb," 22; William Lott Davidson, "Reminiscences of the Old Brigade on the March—In the Front of the Field—as Witnessed by the Writers during the Rebellion," *Overton Sharp-Shooter*, November 10, 1887.

102. Jordan-Bychkov, Branum, and Hood, "Boesel Letters," 465.

103. *Neu-Braunfelser Zeitung*, January 11, 1861.

104. Frazier, *Blood and Treasure*, 59–60; Hall, *Confederate Army of New Mexico*, 21; Baum, *Shattering of Texas Unionism*, 46; Buenger, *Secession and the Union*, 62–63.

105. William C. Binkley, *The Expansionist Movement in Texas, 1836–1850* (New York: Da Capo Press, 1970), 219; Dallas *Herald*, February 29, 1860.

106. James M. Day, comp., *The Texas Almanac, 1857–1873* (Waco, Tex.: Texian Press, 1967), 246–247; also in Nackman, "Making of the Texan Citizen Soldier," 253.

107. Buenger, *Secession and the Union*, 17; Columbia *Telegraph and Texas Register*, September 16, 1837. See also Frazier, *Blood and Treasure*, 7.

108. Frazier, *Blood and Treasure*, 7; Binkley, *Expansionist Movement*, 221; Josephy, *Civil War in the American West*, 42; F. Stanley, *The Civil War in New Mexico* (Denver: World Press, 1960), 116; see also Paul N. Spellman, *Forgotten Texas Leader: Hugh McLeod and the Texan Santa Fe Expedition* (College Station: Texas A&M University Press, 1999); John to wife, December 26, 1861, John S. Shropshire Papers, Ms. 80, Nesbitt Memorial Library, Columbus, Tex. Though the citizens of New Mexico were concerned about Texans exacting revenge for their failed Santa Fe expedition twenty years earlier, there is no evidence that this motivated the Texans in Sibley's Brigade.

109. Buenger, *Secession and the Union*, 18; Austin *State Gazette*, April 4, 1857, and April 16, 1859.

110. Austin *State Gazette*, February 23, 1861.

111. Frazier, *Blood and Treasure*, 4, 13; Buenger, *Secession and the Union*, 17.

112. Hale, *Third Texas Cavalry*, 27; Frazier, *Blood and Treasure*, 13; Mark C. Carnes, *Secret Ritual and Manhood in Victorian America* (New Haven, Conn.: Yale University Press, 1989), 7; Bell, "Knights of the Golden Circle," 4, 7; Roy Sylvan Dunn, "The KGC in Texas, 1860–1861," *Southwestern Historical Quarterly* 70 (1967): 543; Hicks, "Some Letters concerning the Knights of the Golden Circle," 80; San Antonio *Alamo Express*, November 5, 1860.

113. Marshall *Texas Republican*, March 23, 1861; this source also appears in Reynolds, *Editors Make War*, 177–178; Hicks, "Some Letters concerning the Knights of the Golden Circle," 288; Dunn, "KGC in Texas," 545; Bell, "Knights of the Golden Circle," 187.

114. Frazier, *Blood and Treasure*, 14; Dunn, "KGC in Texas," 557; Bell, "Knights of the Golden Circle," 45, 181; Hicks, "Some Letters concerning the Knights of the Golden Circle," 301.

115. Durham, *Lone Star State Divided*, 40; Faulk, *General Tom Green*, 36–37; Hall, *Confederate Army of New Mexico*, 13; Hall, *Sibley's New Mexico Campaign*, 31; Hall, "Formation of Sibley's Brigade," 133.

116. Sparks, *War between the States*, 11; Crabb, *All Afire to Fight*, 2; John D. Perkins, *Daniel's Battery: The Ninth Texas Field Battery* (Hillsboro, Tex.: Hill College Press, 1998), 1; Jewett, *Texas in the Confederacy*, 113.

117. Howell to parents and family, May 21, 1864, William Randolph Howell Collection, CAH.

Chapter 4

Chapter epigraph from Edward B. Williams, ed., *Rebel Brothers: The Civil War Letters of the Truehearts* (College Station: Texas A&M University Press, 1995), 24–25, 69.

1. Wooster, *Lone Star Regiments,* 4–6.

2. Rainey to wife, August 8, 1861, A. T. Rainey, First Texas Infantry File, THM.

3. Carlock and Owens, *History of the Tenth Texas Cavalry,* 6; McPherson, *For Cause and Comrades,* 30–31, 80; Ashcraft, *Texas in the Civil War,* 10; Robertson, *Soldiers Blue and Gray,* 5; Kennedy, *Population of the United States in 1860,* 592–593; Robert Mayberry Jr., "Robertson, Felix Huston," in Tyler, *Handbook of Texas,* 5:616; Harold B. Simpson, "Hood's Texas Brigade," in Harold B. Simpson, ed., *Soldiers of Texas* (Waco, Tex.: Texian Press, 1973), 52; Harold B. Simpson, *Gaines' Mill to Appomattox: Waco and McLennan County in Hood's Texas Brigade* (Waco, Tex.: Texian Press, 1963), 32; Stephen B. Oates, *Confederate Cavalry West of the River* (Austin: University of Texas Press, 1961), 24; Murrah, *None but Texians,* 18.

4. Gallaway, *Texas, the Dark Corner,* 25. Another excited Texan was Wiley F. Donathan, who later joined the 24th Texas Cavalry after he finished his studies at Soule University. He noted, "I am still prosecuting my studies at College; not withstanding a half a mind on my part to enter the army. The impending crisis and the coming war have produced throughout the most intense excitement. All Texas is one active preparation for the conflict." Donathan to brother and sister, May 25, 1861, Wiley F. Donathan Family Correspondence, 1836–1864, TSLAC.

5. Donald E. Everett, ed., *Chaplain Davis and Hood's Texas Brigade* (Baton Rouge: Louisiana State University Press, 1999), 35; Harold B. Simpson, "Hood's Texas Brigade," 52; Simpson, *Gaines' Mill to Appomattox,* 32; McPherson, *For Cause and Comrades,* 30–31, 44; Stevens, *Reminiscences of the Civil War,* 9; John W. Spencer, *The Confederate Guns of Navarro County* (Corsicana, Tex.: Texas Press, 1986), 2; Beringer, Hattaway, Jones, and Still, *Why the South Lost the Civil War,* 108.

6. J. Glenn Gray, *The Warriors: Reflections on Men in Battle* (New York: Harcourt Brace, 1959), 29; Robertson, *Soldiers Blue and Gray,* 26; Wiley, *Life of Johnny Reb,* 17; Carlock and Owens, *History of the Tenth Texas Cavalry,* 6; McPherson, *For Cause and Comrades,* 30–31; Spencer, *Confederate Guns of Navarro County,* 108, 132; George Edward Otott Jr., "Antebellum Social Characteristics of the Officers and Men in the First Texas Infantry, Confederate States Army" (M.A. thesis, California State University, Fullerton, 2003), 58.

7. Greyson to wife, March 9, 1865, Dr. Thomas B. Greyson, Waul's Texas Legion File, THM.

8. Baker to James David Baker, August 3, 1861, Benjamin Marshall Baker Letters, Nesbitt Memorial Library, Columbus, Tex.

9. Randolph B. Campbell, "Fighting for the Confederacy: The White Male Population of Harrison County in the Civil War," *Southwestern Historical Quarterly* 104 (2000): 35; Simpson, *Gaines' Mill to Appomattox,* 32; Carlock and Owens, *History of the Tenth Texas Cavalry,* 2.

10. Rainey to wife, August 8, 1861, A. T. Rainey, First Texas Infantry File, THM.

11. Stevens, *Reminiscences of the Civil War,* 9; Spencer, *From Corsicana to Appomattox,* 2.

12. Leonidas B. Giles, *Terry's Texas Rangers* (Austin: Pemberton Press, 1967), 7; also in Bailey, *Texans in the Confederate Cavalry,* 14; Stephen B. Oates, "Recruiting Confederate

Cavalry in Texas," *Southwestern Historical Quarterly* 64 (1960): 474; Oates, *Confederate Cavalry West of the River*, 23.

13. "Life of John C. Porter and Sketch of His Experiences in the Civil War," March 29, 1874, John C. Porter, Eighteenth Texas Infantry Regiment File, THM.

14. Beringer, Hattaway, Jones, and Still, *Why the South Lost the Civil War*, 108; Harold B. Simpson, *The Marshall Guards: Harrison County's Contribution to Hood's Texas Brigade* (Marshall, Tex.: Port Caddo Press, 1967), 1.

15. Marshall *Texas Republican*, June 22, 1861; also in Davis Blake Carter, *Two Stars in the Southern Sky: General John Greg C.S.A. and Mollie* (Spartanburg, S.C.: Reprint Company, 2001), 70.

16. Campbell, "Fighting for the Confederacy," 25.

17. The figures provided in the paragraph are based on the *Texas Confederate Home Roster*, which provides details to the history of the Confederate men and women who visited for medical care. Campbell, *Gone to Texas*, 247; Simpson, *Soldiers of Texas*, 51; Simpson, *Hood's Texas Brigade*, 12; Lathrop, *Migration into East Texas*, 51; Simpson, *Gaines' Mill to Appomattox*, 32.

18. Alvy L. King, *Louis T. Wigfall: Southern Fire-eater* (Baton Rouge: Louisiana State University Press, 1970), 115, 118, 121, 131; Craig L. Symonds, *Joseph E. Johnston: A Civil War Biography* (New York: W. W. Norton, 1992), 178; George Wirsdorfer, "Louis Trezevant Wigfall," in Nunn, *Ten Texans in Gray*, 61.

19. King, *Louis T. Wigfall*, 135; Thomas Lawrence Connelly and Archer Jones, *The Politics of Command: Factions and Ideas in Confederate Strategy* (Baton Rouge: Louisiana State University Press, 1973), 53, 54, 55, 58; D. Giraud Wright, *A Southern Girl in '61: The War Time Memories of a Confederate Senator's Daughter* (New York: Doubleday, Page, 1905), 102–103. Wigfall and Johnston's falling out with Jefferson Davis did play a role in this decision to create an opposition group, but it was not the sole reason for its formation. Many of the members in the Western Campaign Bloc had vested interests in the regions they were trying to protect, including their homes and families.

20. W. S. Oldham, "Colonel John Marshall," *Southwestern Historical Quarterly* 20 (1916): 132, 133, 137–138; Charles E. Brooks, "The Social and Cultural Dynamics of Soldiering in Hood's Texas Brigade," *Journal of Southern History* 67 (2001): 545; Mary Laswell, ed., *Rags and Hope: The Recollections of Val C. Giles, Four Years with Hood's Brigade, Fourth Texas Infantry* (New York: Coward, McCann, 1961), 47; Everett, *Chaplain Davis and Hood's Texas Brigade*, 156; Donald E. Reynold, "Marshall, John F.," in Tyler, *Handbook of Texas*, 4:519–520.

21. George T. Todd, *First Texas Regiment* (Waco, Tex.: Texian Press, 1963), ix–xi; Julia L. Vivian, "Todd, George T.," in Tyler, *Handbook of Texas*, 6:514.

22. Asa Roberts Reminiscences, Fourth Texas Infantry File, THM; Campbell, *Southern Community in Crisis*, 226; William H. Hamman, Fourth Texas Infantry File, THM; James D. Roberdeau, Fifth Texas Infantry File, THM; "Captain J. D. Roberdeau," *Confederate Veteran* 18 (1910): 439; John Robert Keeling, First Texas Infantry File, THM.

23. Thompson, *Westward the Texans*, 50, 112.

24. Simpson, *Gaines' Mill to Appomattox*, 31; Everett, *Chaplain Davis and Hood's Texas Brigade*, 172; Edward Richardson Crockett Collection, Civil War Diary, 1864–1865, CAH; Glover, *"Tyler to Sharpsburg,"* 1.

25. Parker, *Touched by Fire*, 39.

26. Simpson, "Hood's Texas Brigade," 52; Simpson, *Gaines' Mill to Appomattox*, 32; McPherson, *For Cause and Camrades*, 30–31, 44; Gallaway, *Texas, the Dark Corner*, 25; Rainey to wife, August 8, 1861, A. T. Rainey, First Texas Infantry File, THM; Stevens, *Reminis-*

cences of the Civil War, 9; Spencer, *Confederate Guns of Navarro County*, 2; Beringer, Hattaway, Jones, and Still, *Why the South Lost the Civil War*, 108.

27. Owsley, *Plain Folk of the Old South*, 94; Campbell Wood, Fifth Texas Infantry File, THM; Worsham to mother, November 29, 1861, C. S. Worsham, Fourth Texas Infantry File, THM.

28. Cooper K. Ragan, ed., "The Diary of Captain George W. O'Brien, 1863," *Southwestern Historical Quarterly* 67 (1963): 29–30; William A. Fletcher, *Rebel Private: Front and Rear: Memoirs of a Confederate Soldier* (New York: Dutton, 1995), 4–5; Robertson, *Soldiers Blue and Gray*, 8.

29. Campbell, *Southern Community in Crisis*, 226; Campbell, "Fighting for the Confederacy," 25.

30. Parker, *Touched by Fire*, 89.

31. Hunter to Mrs. Dulcenia Pain Harrison Roman, December 17, 1864, James T. Hunter, Fourth Texas Infantry File, THM.

32. Worsham to mother, September 24, 1863, C. S. Worsham, Fourth Texas Infantry File, THM.

33. Elvis E. Fleming, ed., "Some Hard Fighting: Letters of Private Robert T. Wilson, Fifth Texas Infantry, Hood's Brigade, 1862–1864," *Military History of Texas and the Southwest* 9 (1971): 289, 290.

34. Chicoine, "Willing Never to Go," 575–576, 587.

35. Ibid., 592.

36. Murrah, *None but Texians*, 23.

37. Lester Newton Fitzhugh, "Terry's Texas Rangers," in Simpson, *Soldiers of Texas*, 75; Murrah, *None but Texians*, 5, 6; "John Austin Wharton," Online Archive of Terry's Texas Rangers, www.terrytexasrangers.org/biographical_notes/w/wharton_ja.html (accessed October 9, 2004); Kenneth W. Hobbs Jr., "Benjamin Franklin Terry," in Nunn, *Ten More Texans in Gray*, 153; J. K. P. Blackburn, L. B. Giles, and E. S. Dodd, *Terry Texas Ranger Trilogy* (Austin: State House Press, 1996), xi; Wooster, *Lone Star Generals*, 65–74; Anne Bailey, "John A. Warton," in Davis, *Confederate General*, 6:122–123.

38. *War of the Rebelliion*, Series I, L, pt. 2, 156; Dunn, *Ten More Texans in Gray*, 153, 156; Simpson, *Soldiers of Texas*, 77.

39. Dallas *Herald*, May 8, 1861; Murrah, *None but Texians*, 18, 21.

40. Blackburn, Giles, and Dodd, *Terry Texas Ranger Trilogy*, 12, 100; Simpson, *Soldiers of Texas*, 79; Wooster, *Lone Star Regiments in Gray*, 49; Murrah, *None but Texians*, 23.

41. "John W. Hill to Mary Scott Hill—September 30, 1861, New Orleans, LA," Online Archive of Terry's Texas Rangers, www.terrytexasrangers.org/letters/hill_jw/1861_09_30.htm (accessed October 9, 2004); Burke to father, October 6, 1861, Benjamin F. Burke, Eighth Texas Cavalry File, THM. Once in Kentucky, the men continued to grumble about their transfer and found reasons to support their depression. Edward H. Ross wrote to a friend back in Texas, "If you were here and could see the great big Kentuckyians that are stopping around here, doing nothing, you would be glad too. That is all that dissatisfies me. To think that I have left wife, children and all to come here to protect their person and property and they, lounging around doing nothing for themselves, nor for anybody else. I would advise all my friends, if they go into the service at all, to go in the State. It [is] a long way here and a mighty bad road. I assure you I don't feel altogether like I was at home, I would if I was in Texas." Ross to friend Mernek, November 10, 1861, Edward H. Ross, Eighth Texas Cavalry File, THM.

42. Simpson, *Soldiers of Texas*, 79; Steven E. Woodworth, *Jefferson Davis and His Gen-*

erals: The Failure of Confederate Command of the West (Lawrence: University Press of Kansas, 1990) 39, 51; Davis, Devereaux, and Ericson, *Texas Confederate Home Roster.*

43. Murrah, *None but Texians,* 30, 32, 35, 56, 58; "John Austin Wharton," Online Archive of Terry's Texas Rangers, www.terrystexasrangers.org/biographical_notes/w/wharton_ja.html (accessed October 9, 2004); "Benjamin Franklin Terry," *Online Archive of Terry's Texas Rangers,* www.terrystexasrangers.org/biographical_notes/t/terry_bf.html (accessed October 9, 2004); "Thomas Saltus Lubbock," Online Archive of Terry's Texas Rangers, www.terrystexasrangers.org/biographical_notes/l/lubbock_ts.htm (accessed October 9, 2004); Van Zandt to wife, January 10, 1862, Khleber Miller Van Zandt, Seventh Texas Infantry File, THM.

44. Murrah, *None but Texians,* 1, 58; Arthur W. Bergeron Jr., "Thomas Harrison," in Davis and Hoffman, *Confederate General,* 3:70–71; "Thomas Harrison," Online Archive of Terry's Texas Rangers, www.terrystexasrangers.org/biographical_notes/h/harrison_t.html (accessed October 9, 2004); Blackburn, Giles, and Dodd, *Terry Texas Ranger Trilogy,* xii.

45. Blackburn, Giles, and Dodd, *Terry Texas Ranger Trilogy,* xxix, 91, 185; Gracy, "With Danger and Honor," 1–3; G. L. McMurphy Diary, entries September 15, 1862, and July 14, 1863, PC.

46. Blackburn, Giles, and Dodd, *Terry Texas Ranger Trilogy,* xxix, 199, 212, 215.

47. William C. Davis, "John Gregg," in Davis, *Confederate General,* 3:36, 38; Carter, *Two Stars in the Southern Sky,* 25–26, 69, 71.

48. "Letters to Mollie," September 26, 1861, Starville, Tex., and October 21, 1861, Shreveport, La., Captain E. T. Broughton, http://battleofraymond.org/broughton.htm (accessed November 25, 2003).

49. Carter, *Two Stars in the Southern Sky,* 72, 76.

50. Seventh Texas Infantry file, Thomas Oscar Moore, THM; "Lieutenant Linson Montgomery Keener His Four Years with the Seventh Texas Infantry C.S.A. as Told by Him to Mrs. W. U. Carre," Linson Montgomery Keener, Seventh Texas Infantry File, THM.

51. Van Zandt to wife, November 28, 1861, Khleber Miller Van Zandt, Seventh Texas Infantry File, THM.

52. "Lieutenant Linson Montgomery Keener His Four Years with the Seventh Texas Infantry C.S.A. as Told by Him to Mrs. W. U. Carre," Linson Montgomery Keener, Seventh Texas Infantry File, THM.

53. Van Zandt to wife, June 2, 1862, Khleber Miller Van Zandt, Seventh Texas Infantry File, THM.

54. Van Zandt to wife, June 22, 1862, Khleber Miller Van Zandt, Seventh Texas Infantry File, THM.

55. Van Zandt to wife, January 26, 1862, September 19, 1862, and October 12, 1862, and Van Zandt to mother, February 1, 1862, Khleber Miller Van Zandt, Seventh Texas Infantry File, THM.

56. Woodworth, *Jefferson Davis and His Generals,* 51; Van Zandt to wife, October 16, 1861, Khleber Miller Van Zandt, Seventh Texas Infantry File, THM.

57. Van Zandt to wife, October 2, 1862, Seventh Texas Infantry File, THM.

58. Dyers to wife, January 26, 1862, Charles Samuel Dyers, Ninth Texas Infantry, THM; Louise Horton, *Samuel Bell Maxey: A Biography* (Austin: University of Texas Press, 1974), 3, 23; John C. Waugh, *Sam Bell Maxey and the Confederate Indians* (Abilene, Tex.: McWhiney Foundation, 1995), 14; Wooster, *Lone Star Regiments,* 87; L.W. Horton, "General Sam Bell Maxey: His Defense of North Texas and the Indian Territory," *Southwestern Historical Quarterly* 74 (1971): 507, 508.

59. Dyers to wife, January 26, 1862, Charles Samuel Dyers, Ninth Texas Infantry, THM.

60. Street to Ninnie, Febraury 18, 1862, J. K. Street Letters, http://antiquemll.hypermart .net/streetpapers.htm (accessed May 20, 2009).

61. Tuck, *Civil War Shadows*, 145.

62. Bates to wife, February 25, 1863, Jesse P. Bates, Ninth Texas Infantry File, THM; National Archives Microfilm Publications, *Compiled Service Records of Confederate Soldiers* (Washington, D.C.: National Archives and Records Service General Services Administration, 1960), as indexed in the Civil War Soldiers and Sailors System," www.itd.nps.gov/cwss/ index.html (accessed January 2, 2008). Cross-referencing the names of men mentioned in Bates's letter through the *Compiled Service Records* suggests that the men served in the 11th Tennessee Infantry during the war. See Our Communities, www.hickmanco.com/history_ communities.htm.

63. Maxey to Marilda, November 11, 1862, Lightfoot Papers, TSLAC; also in Horton, *Sam Bell Maxey*, 32.

64. Laura Simmons, "Waul's Legion from Texas to Mississippi," *Texana* 7 (Spring 1969): 2, 3, 5; E. M. Loughery, *War and Reconstruction in Texas, 1861–1865* (Austin: Von Boeckmann-Jones, 1914), 20, 21.

65. Bradley to My Darling Wife, June 14, 1862, Bradley (L. D.) Papers, 1859–1887, PC; Houston *Tri-Weekly Telegraph*, November 3, 1862; Robert A. Hasskarl, *Waul's Texas Legion, 1862–1865* (Ada, Okla.: Book Bindery, 1976), 1, 4, 14, 27; Simmons, "Waul's Legion," 12, 15; Thomas Cutrer, "Waul, Thomas Neville," in Tyler, *Handbook of Texas*, 6:852.

66. Mary A. H. Gay, *Life in Dixie during the War* (Macon, Ga.: Mercer University Press, 2001), 87.

67. Tabb to Mrs. E. J. Burgess, April 27, 1862, James A. Tabb, Eighteenth Texas Infantry Regiment File, THM.

68. Wooster, *Lone Star Regiments*, 6.

69. Coffman to brother, March 29, 1862, A. J. Coffman, Ninth Texas Infantry File, THM.

70. Billingsley, "Such Is War," 49.

71. Thomas W. Cutrer, ed., *Longstreet's Aide: The Civil War Letters of Major Thomas J. Goree* (Charlottesville: University of Virginia Press, 1995), 19.

72. Jerry B. Rushford, "Apollos of the West: The Life of John Allen Gano" (M.A. thesis, Abilene Christian College, 1972), 212–213; Waugh, *Sam Bell Maxey*, 72; S. M. Fields, "Texas Heroes of the Confederacy," Dallas *Times Herald*, May 10, 1925; Pearce, "Gano Cabin History," 31–32; *Biographical Souvenir of the State of Texas* (Chicago: F. A. Battery, 1889), 315; *Memorial and Biographical History of Dallas County, Texas* (Chicago: Lewis Publishing, 1892), 999; Clement A. Evans, ed., *Confederate Military History*, Vol. 11 (Atlanta: Confederate Publishing, 1899), 407; Louisville *Courier Journal*, August 8 and 9, 1869; C. W. Raines, ed., *Six Decades in Texas, or Memoirs of Francis Richard Lubbock: Governor of Texas in War-Time, 1861–1863* (Austin: Ben C. Jones, 1900), 341; Anne Bailey, "Richard M. Gano," in Davis and Hoffman, *Confederate General*, 2:154–155; Wooster, *Lone Star Generals*, 236.

73. Julia K. Garrett, *Fort Worth: A Frontier Triumph* (Austin: Encino Press, 1972), 197; Hale, *Third Texas Cavalry*, 24; Robertson, *Soldiers Blue and Gray*, 4.

74. Wiley, *Life of Johnny Reb*, 19; Lowe, *Texas Cavalry Officer's Civil War*, 5; Hale, *Third Texas Cavalry*, 28; McPherson, *Battle Cry of Freedom*, 318; Robertson, *Soldiers Blue and Gray*, 13; S. M. Fields, "Texas Heroes of the Confederacy," Dallas *Times Herald*, May 10, 1925; Muster roll of Captain R. M. Gano's Company of Mounted Riflemen, April 21, 1862, no. 1442, Archives Division, TSLAC.

75. Muster roll of Captain R. M. Gano's Company of Mounted Riflemen, April 21, 1862,

no. 1442, Archives Division, TSLAC; Wooster, *Lone Star Blue and Gray,* 53; Robertson, *Soldiers Blue and Gray,* 25; Hale, *Third Texas Cavalry,* 44; Daniel, *Soldiering in the Army of Tennessee,* 13; Wiley, *Life of Johnny Reb,* 331. Though the numbers are not exactly the same as other Confederate units, they are close enough to show the similarities.

76. The states and countries of origin of the Grapevine Volunteers are Alabama, Arkansas, Iowa, Kentucky, Louisiana, Massachusetts, Mississippi, Missouri, Pennsylvania, Tennessee, Texas, and Germany. National Archives Microfilm Publications, *Population Schedules of the Eighth Census;* National Archives Microfilm Publications, *Compiled Service Records,* Microcopy no. 319, roll 40; Frank W. Johnson and Eugene C. Barker, eds., *A History of Texas and Texans* (Chicago: American Historical Society, 1914), 815–817; Baum, *Shattering of Texas Unionism,* 52–53.

77. National Archives Microfilm Publications, *Compiled Service Records,* Microcopy no. 323, roll 192; Muster roll of Captain R. M. Gano's Company, in the Texas Squadron, April 21, 1862, no. 1442, Archives Division, TSLAC; Richard M. Gano Collection, "Personal War Record of Brigadier-General Richard Montgomery Gano," 38, Brown Special Collections Library, Abilene Christian University, Abilene, Tex.; Wooster, *Lonestar Blue and Gray,* 53; Owsley, *Plain Folk of the Old South,* 90, 94–95.

78. Dallas *Herald,* January 28, 1862.

79. Gano to Breckenridge, April 8, 1862, National Archives Microfilm Publications, *Compiled Service Records,* Microcopy no. 323, roll 192.

80. Gano to Jordon, May 9, 1862, ibid.

81. John Gano, comp., "Records and Correspondence pertaining to the Military Activities of Brigadier-General Richard M. Gano, C.S.A.," 1:1–3, Brown Special Collections Library, Abilene Christian University, Abilene, Tex. National Archives Microfilm Publications, *Compiled Service Records,* Microcopy no. 319, roll 40; J. M. Huffman to William C. P. Breckenridge, February 1, 1863, William Campbell Preston Breckinridge Family Papers, Ninth Regiment Kentucky Cavalry, Letter Book, Dec. 22 1862–March 26, 1864, Library of Congress, Washington, D.C. Some men in the squadron had a change of heart once they arrived in Kentucky. J. Galloway requested a transfer "from Co 'C' 2nd KY Regt Cav. Dukes Brigade to Co 'I' 1st Regt Texas Cav . . . where my brother and all my friends and relations are serving."

82. Williams, *Rebel Brothers,* xii, 5, 9, 24–25, 27, 69, 80.

83. Alexander Mendoza, "Struggle for Command: General James Longstreet and the First Corps in the West, 1863–1864" (Ph.D. diss., Texas Texas University, 2002), 49, 50; Cutrer, *Longstreet's Aide,* 3–4, 5, 19, 33, 59, 71. To a lesser extent, one could argue that Longstreet himself, who was posted in Fort Bliss in El Paso, Texas, for several years, had a connection to the Lone Star State. But his connection to Texas was artificial and purely temporary, since he was in the military and never moved his family there in any permanent form.

84. Bedinger, *Texas and the Southern Confederacy,* 29–30; Adam Rankin Johnson, *The Partisan Rangers of the Confederate States Army* (Louisville, Ky.: George G. Fetter, 1904), 1, 2, 9, 38; William C. Davis, "Adam Rankin Johnson," in Davis, *Confederate General,* 3:169; Ray Mulesky, *Thunder from a Clear Sky: Stovepipe Johnson's Confederate Raid on Newburgh, Indiana* (New York: iUniverse Star, 2005), 9. Adam Rankin Johnson received his nickname "Stovepipe" when he captured the town of Newburgh, Indiana, by creating fake cannons out of stovepipe joints.

85. Johnson, *Partisan Rangers,* 38; Mulesky, *Thunder from a Clear Sky,* 11.

86. Johnson, *Partisan Rangers,* 39.

87. Ibid.; Bedinger, *Texas and the Southern Confederacy,* 30; Brian Steel Wills, *The Confederacy's Greatest Cavalryman: Nathan Bedford Forrest* (Lawrence: University Press of

Kansas, 1992), 53–55; Jack Hurst, *Nathan Bedford Forrest: A Biography* (New York: Alfred A. Knopf, 1993), 78–80; Mulesky, *Thunder from a Clear Sky,* 11; Murrah, *None but Texians,* 50; Blackburn, Giles, and Dodd, *Terry Texas Ranger Trilogy,* 26; John Allan Wyeth, *That Devil Forrest: Life of General Nathan Bedford Forrest* (Baton Rouge: Louisiana State University, 1989), 64. During this time, two companies from Terry's Texas Rangers under Maj. Thomas Harrison joined Forrest's command.

88. Johnson, *Partisan Rangers,* 47, 48–49.

89. Ibid., 52.

90. Wills, *Confederacy's Greatest Cavalryman,* 63–64; Hurst, *Nathan Bedford Forrest,* 85.

91. Johnson, *Partisan Rangers,* 96, 97.

92. Ibid., 100–101, 103, 109, 118, 129; Austin *State Gazette,* December 10, 1862.

93. Johnson, *Partisan Rangers,* 32, 133.

Chapter 5

Chapter epigraph from Shelton, *Personal Civil War Letters of General Lawrence Sullivan Ross,* 34.

1. Bell I. Wiley, "Trials of Soul," in Barton and Logue, *Civil War Soldier,* 294.

2. Street to Ninnie, March 10, 1862, J. K. Street Letters, http://antiquemll.hypermart .net/streetpapers.htm (accessed May 20, 2009).

3. John Baynes, *Morale: A Study of Men and Courage, The Second Scottish Rifles at the Battle of Neuve Chapelle, 1915* (New York: Frederick A. Praeger, 1967), 92–93.

4. Houston *Tri-Weekly Telegraph,* July 16, 1862.

5. Templeton to father, May 3, 1863, John Allen Templeton, Tenth Texas Cavalry File, THM. Another example is in a letter written by Lizzie Douglas to her brother: "Jim says he can stand the fatigue and hardships all very well, till it comes to the fighting, and then when he sees his comrades falling around him, it is all he can do to persuade himself not to run." Lizzie to brother George, February 19, 1863, George Douglas, SC 1–7, Lizzie Douglas Letters, THM.

6. Goodman to parents, December 7, 1861, Goodman (Samuel A., Jr.) Papers, 1854–1970, PC.

7. "The Civil War Diary of Judge William Kuykendall of Tilden, Texas," William Kuykendall, First Texas Cavalry Regiment File, THM.

8. Maury Darst, "Robert Hodges, Jr.: Confederate Soldier" *East Texas Historical Journal* 9 (1971): 20, 35.

9. McPherson, *For Cause and Comrades,* 35, 44–45, 168–169; Linderman, *Embattled Courage,* 156.

10. Chandra Manning, *What This Cruel War Was Over: Soldiers, Slavery, and the Civil War* (New York: Alfred A. Knopf, 2007), 53; Joe R. Wise, ed., "The Letters of Lt. Flavius W. Perry Seventeenth Texas Cavalry, 1862–1863" *Military History of Texas and the Southwest* 13 (1976): 15.

11. McKay to R. W. Loughery, June 13, 1862, Gil McKay, Seventeenth Texas Cavalry File, THM.

12. Crow to wife, May 23, 1862, Z. H. Crow, Seventeenth Texas Cavalry File, THM.

13. Crain to wife, June 9, 1863, Alexander C. Crain, Second Texas Partisan Rangers File, THM.

14. Cutrer, *Longstreet's Aide,* 137.

15. Baynes, *Morale,* 101; Daniel, *Soldiering in the Army of Tennessee,* 134–135; Thomas L.

McCarty Diary, April 20, 1864, CAH. Similarly, W. S. Boothe of the 25th Texas Cavalry wrote, "We do not draw rations enought hardly to kee us alive." Boothe to wife, October 11, 1863, W. S. Boothe Papers, Pearce Civil War Collection, Navarro College, Corsicana, Tex.

16. Douglas to sister Laura, March 11, 1864, George Douglas, SC 1–4, Letters, Texas THM.

17. Young to unknown, November 17, 1862, William G. Young, Fifteenth Texas Cavalry File, THM.

18. Young to wife, March 6, 1863, D. E. Young, Seventeenth Texas Infantry File, THM; Lonn, *Desertion during the Civil War*, 7–10.

19. Simmons to wife, n.d., "The Confederate Letters of John Simmons," Jon Harrison, ed., John Simmons, Twenty-second Texas Infantry File, THM.

20. Cook to Rebecca Cook, January 12, 1864, David Cook, Thirty-fifth Texas Cavalry (Liken's) File, THM.

21. Robert W. Williams and Ralph A. Wooster, eds., "A Texas War Clerk: Civil War Letters of Issac Dunbar Affleck," *Texas Military History* 7 (1962): 291.

22. Rainey to wife, August 8, 1861, A. T. Rainey, First Texas Infantry File, THM.

23. Williams to wife, September 25, 1862, T. A. Williams, Third Texas Cavalry File, THM.

24. Hill to Susan, n.d., P. H. Hill, Fourth Texas Cavalry File, THM.

25. McPherson, *For Cause and Comrades*, 131–133; Beringer, Hattaway, Jones, and Still, *Elements of Confederate Defeat*, 100–101; Brown, *Journey to Pleasant Hill*, 78. 1st Lt. Watson Dugat Williams of the 5th Texas Infantry recorded one of these instances: "My knapsack was stolen while I was at Knoxville and consequently I lost all the packages that were being sent to the boys of the Company and nearly all the letters for everything I had except a few letters were in it." Williams to My Dear Laura, July 21, 1863, First Lt. Watson Dugat Williams, Fifth Texas Infantry File, THM.

26. Eleanor Damon Pace, ed., "The Diary and Letters of William P. Rogers, 1846–1862," *Southwestern Historical Quarterly* 32 (1929): 293–294.

27. Burke to father and mother, April 23, 1863, Benjamin F. Burke, Eighth Texas Cavalry File, THM. Volney Ellis of the 12th Texas Infantry faced a similar situation with his wife. He responded, "You speak of officers and men writing home that they intend to come home this fall in spite of law and order & c. You say you hope *I* will do the same. Mary, do *you* ask *me*, after serving in the army 2 years, honorably undergoing much hardship and privation, now to disgrace us all, soil my name and cast infamy upon my children? God forbid. I feel sure that if I live I can come home at least on a visit next fall like a man and a soldier without dishonor." Thomas W. Cutrer, ed., "'An Experience in Soldier's Life': The Civil War Letters of Volney Ellis, Adjutant Twelfth Texas Infantry Walker's Texas Division, C.S.A.," *Military History of the Southwest* 22 (1992): 159.

28. *San Antonio Herald*, April 25, 1863; Chance, *Second Texas Infantry*, 142; Lonn, *Desertion during the Civil War*, 12–13; Bowyer and Thurman, *Annals of Elder Horn*, 54.

29. Simmons to wife, March 17, 1863, John Simmons, Twenty-second Texas Infantry File, THM. Ralph A. Wooster, ed., "With the Confederate Cavalry in the West: The Civil War Experiences of Isaac Dunbar Affleck," *Southwestern Historical Quarterly* 83 (1987): 20, provides the impressions of a young man after he witnessed the execution of a captain who refused to cross to the eastern bank of the Mississippi River: "I . . . went back to camp, thinking about what I had seen, and whether I too might not soon die by a bullet, not as he had, in disgrace, but as a soldier on the battle field; and whether I could look at the future with as much unconcern as he did."

30. Long to sister, May 19, 1862, John B. Long Collection, CAH.

31. Williams to My Own Dear Laura, February 23, 1863, First Lt. Watson Dugat Williams, Fifth Texas Infantry File, THM.

32. Williams to Aine Bonnie Billie, July 4, 1864, First Lt. Watson Dugat Williams, Fifth Texas Infantry File, THM.

33. Albert Burton Moore, *Conscription and Conflict in the Confederacy* (New York: MacMillan, 1924), 14; Lonn, *Desertion during the Civil War,* 4.

34. Moore, *Conscription and Conflict,* 14–15; Johansson, *Peculiar Honor,* 5; McGowen, *Horse Sweat and Powder Smoke,* 76; Thompson, *Westward the Texans,* 116.

35. Lonn, *Desertion during the Civil War,* 4, 6, 15; Clarksville *Standard,* March 24, 1862, and May 12, 1862; also in Ernest Wallace, *Charles DeMorse: Pioneer Statesman and Father of Texas Journalism* (Paris, Tex.: Wright Press, 1943), 144.

36. *Bellville Countryman,* March 1, 1862; also in Bailey, *Between the Enemy and Texas,* 23.

37. Houston *Tri-Weekly Telegraph,* April 25, 1862.

38. Houston *Tri-Weekly Telegraph,* May 19, 1862.

39. Daniel, *Soldiering in the Army of Tennessee,* 127–128, 132; Benner, "Lone Star Soldier," 222; Anderson, *Campaigning with Parsons' Texas Cavalry,* 40.

40. Templeton to father, July 15, 1862, and August 5, 1864, John Allen Templeton, Tenth Texas Cavalry File, THM.

41. Pace, "Diary and Letters of William P. Rogers," 291.

42. Rogers to Dr. Wm. McCraven, August 14, 1862, William P. Rogers Papers, CAH; also in Chance, *Second Texas Infantry,* 54–55.

43. Marsh, "Confederate Letters of Bryan Marsh," 14.

44. Ralph J. Smith, *Reminiscences of the Civil War: And Other Sketches* (Waco, Tex.: W. M. Morrison, 1962), 11; quote also in Chance, *Second Texas Infantry,* 2.

45. B. F. Batchelor to wife, December 1, 1862, Online Archive of Terry's Texas Rangers, http://terrystexasrangers.org/letters/batchelor_bf/1862_12_01.htm (accessed December 14, 2003).

46. Crabb, *All Afire to Fight,* 2.

47. Rogers to Dr. Wm. McCraven, August 14, 1862, William P. Rogers Papers, CAH; Smith, *Reminiscences of the Civil War,* 16; Chance, *Second Texas Infantry,* 95.

48. Brown, *Journey to Pleasant Hill,* 267.

49. Hunter to Mrs. Dulcenia Pain Harrison Roman, December 17, 1864, James T. Hunter, Fourth Texas Infantry File, THM.

50. Thomas W. Cutrer, ed., "'We Are Stern and Resolved': The Civil War Letters of John Wesley Rabb, Terry's Texas Rangers," *Southwestern Historical Quarterly* 91 (1987): 193.

51. Barr, *Polignac's Texas Brigade,* 14–15.

52. Oates, *Confederate Cavalry West of the River,* 27, 47; Dallas *Herald,* July 26, 1862; Lonn, *Desertion during the Civil War,* 16.

53. Texas Governor (Edward Clark), *Governor's Message to the Senators and Representatives of the Ninth Legislature of the State of Texas, November 1, 1861* (Austin: Texas Government Printing Office), 10.

54. Oates, *Confederate Cavalry West of the River,* 24.

55. Jones to John Ward, February 15, 1862, W. A. Jones, Twelfth Texas Cavalry File, THM.

56. Oates, *Confederate Cavalry West of the River,* 26; Hale, *Third Texas Cavalry,* 106; Lubbock to Benjamin, February 12, 1862, O.R., Series I, vol. 53: 784.

57. Bailey, *Between the Enemy and Texas,* 35; Civil War Soldier and Sailor System, www.itd.nps.gov/cwss/index.html.

58. Cutrer, "We Are Stern and Resolved," 202; Bedinger, *Texas and the Southern Confederacy*, 12.

59. Houston *Tri-Weekly Telegraph*, August 4, 1862. Similarly, John Allen Templton wrote in 1862, "If Franklin comes home tell him to get service in Texas for it is the best in the Confederacy as things are now. Tell him to never go as infantry. If he can get service as he has been it would be the best place as the law is now we will both have to re-enlist or he will get off and I will be 18 years of age. I never intend to go as infantry again if there's any other chance." Templeton to father, May 18, 1862, John Allen Tampleton, Tenth Texas Cavalry File, THM. A month later, Templeton again emphasized service in Texas when he wrote his father, "When Frank comes home tell him to stay if he can till I get there & have a good horse to go on and I will try to get one & we will go together next time. Tell him to never think of going as infantry for if he was here he could see the load we have to carry and he would not want to go as such. If he could get service where he was or somewhere on the border of Texas it would be the most preferable service. Never walk. If we had not dismounted we would have been a great deal better off today. I am so anxious to get off from here and get Cavalry service I don't know what to do." Templeton to father, June 11, 1862, John Allen Templeton, Tenth Texas Cavalry File, THM.

60. Sifakis, *Compendium of the Confederate Armies*, 37–104; Wooster, *Lone Star Regiments*, 46–281; Watson to Henry Watson, April 17, 1862, Jim Watson Papers, CAH; also in Carlock and Owens, *History of the Tenth Texas Cavalry*, 11; Henry Watson to father and mother, April 17, 1862, Henry Watson, Tenth Texas Cavalry File, THM.

61. Lowe, *Texas Cavalry Officer's Civil War*, 98.

62. Kevin Ladd, *Chambers County, Texas in the War between the States* (Baltimore: Gateway Press, 1994), 262.

63. Elvis E. Fleming, ed., "A Young Confederate Stationed in Texas: The Letters of Joseph David Wilson, 1864–1865," *Texana* 8 (1970): 358.

64. Crabb, *All Afire to Fight*, 85; Victor M. Rose, *Ross' Texas Brigade: Being a Narrative of Events Connected with Its Service in the Late War between the States* (Kennesaw, Ga.: Continental Book, 1960), 64.

65. Young to Nan, Sept. 5, 1862, William G. Young, Fifteenth Texas Cavalry File, THM.

66. Bradley to Little Honey, February 7, 1864, Bradley (L. D.) Papers, 1859–1887, PC.

67. Lowe, *Texas Cavalry Officer's Civil War*, 101–102.

68. Max S. Lale, ed., "The Boy-Bugler of the Third Texas Cavalry: The A. B. Blocker Narrative, Part 3," *Military History of Texas and the Southwest* 14 (1978): 217.

69. Barton and Logue, *Civil War Soldier*, 298; Anderson, *Campaiging with Parsons' Texas Cavalry*, 66.

70. Crain to brother and sister, September 25, 1862, Alexander C. Crain, Second Texas Partisan Rangers File, THM.

71. Carlock and Owens, *History of the Tenth Texas Cavalry*, 11; Hale, *Third Texas Cavalry*, 116.

72. Collins, *Chapters from the Unwritten History*, 62; William J. Whatley to wife, October 21, 1862, William J. Whatley Letters, 1841–1874, CAH.

73. Carlock and Owens, *History of the Tenth Texas Cavalry*, 21. "Hippo" was a common phrase of the time for a person experiencing depression.

74. Ibid., 36.

75. Keen, *Living and Fighting with the Texas Sixth Cavalry*, 44; Benner, "Lone Star Soldier," 222; Billingsley, "Such Is War," 56; Sifakis, *Compendium of the Confederate Armies*, 55.

76. Lowe, *Texas Cavalry Officer's Civil War*, 159.

77. Hale, *Third Texas Cavalry*, 140; Billingsley, "Such Is War," 56.

78. Crabb, *All Afire to Fight*, 106; Max Lale and Hobart Key, eds., *The Civil War Letters of David R. Garrett, Detailing the Adventures of the Sixth Texas Cavalry, 1861–1865* (Marshall, Tex.: Porto Caddo Press, 1963), 61.

79. Weitz, *More Damning Than Slaughter*, 13–14, 26, 30; Beringer, Hattaway, Jones, and Still, *Why the South Lost the Civil War*, 117; Lonn, *Desertion during the Civil War*, 18.

80. McKay to R. W. Loughery, June 13, 1862, Gil McKay, Seventeenth Texas Cavalry File, THM.

81. Young to sister, November 10, 1862, William G. Young, Fifteenth Texas Cavalry File, THM; Houston *Tri-Weekly Telegraph*, October 6, 1862.

82. Marr to sister, June 17, 1863, Erasmus E. Marr, Tenth Texas Infantry File, THM.

83. Crain to wife, May 27, 1863, Alexander C. Crain, Second Texas Partisan Rangers File, THM. Other soldiers proved detailed descriptions of the destruction they saw. "War is a dreadful thing. it is enough to make one [ill.] see the desolation in the track of our own and the enemies armies the large plantations in the Mississippi bottom at this season of the year generally covered with the growing crops lying idle the negroes either run to Texas or to the enemy. in some places there are a few negro women and children left on the place who are cultivating little patches in the usual negro style around the quarters The enemy burns awhile then some of the planters take oath of allegiance then our men burn them out and the plunderers and robbers and by sweeping what is left and the country once in the highest state of cultivation and pride of the South is nothing but a desert. Thus far our loved State has been saved from the horrors of this desolation and long may it remain so." Stark to Martha, June 14, 1863, John T. Stark, Thirteenth Texas Cavalry File, THM. Another example: "Milda, you have no idea what a rich country this was before the Federal army came through it. and if you had you could not form an idea how they have destroyed it. From Nachitoches as far down Red River as we have been, it was one solid farm. The bottom averages six miles wide and the richest land the sun ever shone on. It is now a wilderness. . . . There is not half corn enough left in the bottom to bread what few people there is left, four fifths of the Negroes are carried off." Stranahan to Milda, May 26, 1864, Lt. John A. Stranahan, Twenty-first Texas Cavalry File, THM.

84. Quayle to D. B. Culberson, July 14, 1864, William Quayle, SC 6–3, Letters Outgoing, February 16, 1864–October 7, 1864, THM; Smith, *Frontier Defense of Texas*, 55, 63, 66, 73, 83, 106.

85. F. R. Lubbock to Jefferson Davis, March 27, 1863, Executive Record Books, microfilm reel 6, TSLAC.

86. F. R. Lubbock to Kirby Smith, August 31, 1863, Executive Record Books, microfilm reel 6, TSLAC.

87. Quayle to Henry McCulloch, September 8, 1864, William Quayle, SC 6–3, Letters Outgoing, February 16, 1864–October 7, 1864, THM.

88. Weitz, *More Damning Than Slaughter*, 227, 229–231; Templeton to father, May 16, 1862, John Allen Templeton, Tenth Texas Cavalry File, THM.

89. Horton, "General Sam Bell Maxey," 508–509; Charles L. Martin to Francis R. Lubbock, January 7, 1862, Records, Texas Governor Francis Richard Lubbock, TSLAC.

90. William L. Shea and Earl J. Hess, *Pea Ridge: Civil War Campaign in the West* (Chapel Hill: University of North Carolina Press, 1992), 306; Parker, "Best Stuff Which the State Affords," 24–25; Larry J. Daniel, *Shiloh: The Battle That Changed the Civil War* (New York: Simon and Schuster, 1997), 313–314; Stephen A. Dupree, *Planting the Union Flag in Texas: The Campaigns of Major General Nathaniel P. Banks in the West* (College Station: Texas

A&M University Press, 2008), 16; Goodman to brother, May 7, 1862, Goodman (Samuel A., Jr.) Papers, 1854–1970, PC. Pea Ridge had an even greater impact on Arkansas men, especially those whose families were now in Union-held territory. William G. Young of the 15th Texas Cavalry noted the increase of desertions by men from that state in the months after the battle: "I saw five men blindfolded and brought up before the public gaze of ten thousand men and compelled to fall on their knees and be shot. . . . They were all charged with desertion and mutiny. This is a scene that often occurs in this part. They were all natives of the state." Young to Nan, August 12, 1862, William G. Young, Fifteenth Texas Cavalry File, THM.

91. Anderson, *Campaigning with Parsons' Texas Cavalry*, 52.

92. Darr to mother, May 8, 1862, William Thomas Darr, Tenth Texas Infantry File, THM.

93. Street to Ninnie, March 10, 1862, J. K. Street Letters, http://antiquemll.hypermart .net/streetpapers.htm (accessed December 14, 2003).

94. Templeton to father, May 16, 1862, John Allen Templeton, Tenth Texas Cavalry File, THM.

95. Templeton to father, February 16, 1863, May 3, 1863, and May 16, 1862, John Allen Templeton, Tenth Texas Cavalry File, THM.

96. Shelton, *Personal Civil War Letters of General Lawrence Sullivan Ross*, 34.

97. Ibid., 38.

98. Donald S. Frazier, *Cottonclads! The Battle of Galveston and the Defense of the Texas Coast* (Abilene, Tex.: McWhiney Foundation Press, 1998), 28, 30; Stephen A. Townsend, *The Yankee Invasion of Texas* (College Station: Texas A&M University Press, 2006), 10–11; Dupree, *Planting the Union Flag in Texas*, 25–35; Brown, *Journey to Pleasant Hill*, 108.

99. Cutrer, "We Are Stern and Resolved," 206–207.

100. Brown, *Journey to Pleasant Hill*, 114, 115.

101. Hervey to Cousin Mollie, December 24, 1862, A. G. Hervey, Morgan's Texas Cavalry File, THM; A. G. Hervey, "Civil War Letters Captain A. G. Hervey," *Footprints Quarterly Journal* 38 (1995): 93.

102. Cutrer, "We Are Stern and Resolved," 210–211.

103. Davis D. Porter, *Incidents and Anecdotes of the Civil War* (New York: D. Appleton, 1886), 95–96.

104. Terrence J. Winschel, *Vicksburg: Fall of the Confederate Gibraltar* (Abilene, Tex.: McWhiney Foundation Press, 1999), 13, 14, 16, 17; Leonard Fullenkamp, Stephen Bowman, and Jay Luvaas, eds., *Guide to the Vicksburg Campaign* (Lawrence: University of Kansas Press, 1998), 11; James R. Arnold, *Grant Wins the War: Decision at Vicksburg* (New York: John Wiley and Sons, 1997), 1–2.

105. Barcroft to father and family, May 18, 1862, William H. Barcroft, Third Texas Cavalry File, THM.

106. Connally to wife, December 6, 1862, Drury Connally, Alf Johnson Spy Company File, THM.

107. Brown, *Journey to Pleasant Hill*, 108.

108. James to wife, June 30, 1863, Civil War Times Illustrated Collection, James Black, I/First Texas Heavy Artillery Regiment Correspondence, January 1860–March 1865, United States Army Heritage and Education Center, Carlisle, Pa.

109. Bailey, *Between the Enemy and Texas*, 3; Getzendaner, *Brief and Condensed History*, 21.

110. If something has gone "up the spout," it has gone wrong or been ruined. Ware to mother, July 16, 1863, Theophilus V. Ware, Twenty-seventh Texas Cavalry File, THM.

111. Brightman to family, June 21, 1863, Dr. John Claver Brightman Collection, CAH.

112. Herman Norton, *Rebel Religion: The Story of Confederate Chaplains* (St. Louis: Bethany Press, 1961), 51; Hale, *Third Texas Cavalry*, 180; Daniel, *Soldiering in the Army of Tennessee*, 116, 120.

113. Beringer, Hattaway, Jones, and Still, *Why the South Lost the Civil War*, 268; June E. Tuck, *Civil War Shadows in Hopkins County, Texas* (Sulphur Springs, Tex.: Walsworth, 1993), 139.

114. Gracy, "With Danger and Honor," 132; M. Jane Johansson, *Peculiar Honor: A History of the Twenty-eighth Texas Cavalry, 1862–1865* (Fayetteville: University of Arkansas Press, 1998), 77; Simmons to companion, October 19, 1864, The Confederate Letters of John Simmons, Jon Harrison, ed., John Simmons, Twenty-Second Texas Infantry File, THM. Alexander C. Crain of the 6th Texas Cavalry made a similar observation to his sister: "There has Bin a protracted meeting going on here for several days and is still going on there has several soldiers Professed and joined the Church I Believe there is from five to fifteen Babtised Every day. There has bin six I Believe Professed inn the Company to which I belong." Though Crain's letters were in the 2nd Texas Partisan Rangers file, he actually belonged to the 6th Texas Cavalry. Crain to sister, September 22, 1863, Alexander C. Crain, Second Texas Partisan Rangers File, THM.

115. Keener to Esteemed Friend, September 23, 1863, Lawson Jefferson Keener, Second Texas Cavalry (Second Arizona) Regiment File, THM. Though the letters were in the 2nd Texas Cavalry file, Keener was actually a member of the 2nd Texas Mounted Rifles.

116. Norton, *Rebel Religion*, 25, 61; Fredrick J. Dobney, "From Denominationalism to Nationalism in the Civil War: A Case Study," *Texana* 9 (1971): 370, 371; McPherson, *For Cause and Comrades*, 75, 76; Edwards, "Social and Cultural Activities of Texans," 103, 104. The amount of religious literature produced for Confederate soldiers was astonishing. In one year the Southern Baptist Convention produced more than six million pages of tracts and six thousand Bibles, Methodists seventeen million pages of tracts and twenty thousand Bibles; and Presbyterians six million pages of religious material.

117. Van Zandt to wife, April 7, 1863, Khleber Miller Van Zandt, Seventh Texas Infantry File, THM.

118. Van Zandt to wife, April 26, 1863, Khleber Miller Van Zandt, Seventh Texas Infantry File, THM.

119. Van Zandt to wife, May 10, 1863, Khleber Miller Van Zandt, Seventh Texas Infantry File, THM.

120. Caddell to sister, July 22, 1863, Jeremiah Caddell, Fourth Texas Infantry File, THM.

121. Mays, "Vicksburg Diary of M. K. Simmons," 27.

122. McNemar to Neicy, August 12, 1863, John Gardner McNemar, Waul's Texas Legion File, THM. After the Union army gained control of the Mississippi, Confederates like Andrew J. Fogle found other ways to get correspondence to Texas: "I dont think hard of you as their is no mail a gain a crose the river and the only way that I can send them by Privet conveyence." Fogle to Miss Louisa, September 2, 1863, Andrew J. Fogle, Ninth Texas Cavalry File, THM.

123. Van Zandt to wife, June 16, 1863, Khleber Miller Van Zandt, Seventh Texas Cavalry File, THM.

124. Van Zandt to wife, November 22, 1863, Khleber Miller Van Zandt, Seventh Texas Cavalry File, THM.

125. Burke to father and mother, July 31, 1863, Benjamin F. Burke, Eighth Texas Cavalry File, THM.

126. Lonn, *Desertion during the Civil War*, 18; Carlock and Owens, *History of the Tenth Texas Cavalry*, 243–244.

127. Civil War Diary of Christian Wilhelm Hander, July 5, 1863, CAH.

128. Lowe, *Texas Cavalry Officer's Civil War*, xii, 263, 264, 265, 271, 272.

129. Mays, "Vicksburg Diary of M. K. Simmons," 38.

130. "Reminisces," J. H. Cravey, Second Texas Infantry File, THM.

131. Fogle to Miss Louisa, September 2, 1863, Andrew J. Fogle, Ninth Texas Infantry File, THM.

132. Fogle to Miss Louisa, October 18, 1863, Andrew J. Fogle, Ninth Texas Infantry File, THM. Four men are listed in the regiment with the last name Bush and only two in his company, named L. C. and William I. Bush. It is uncertain which of these men deserted, but it may be L. C. since he entered the war as a sergeant and when discharged was demoted to private.

133. Bates to wife, November 16, 1863, Jesse P. Bates, Ninth Texas Infantry File, THM.

134. Hale, *Third Texas Cavalry*, 193; James to Dearest Patience, August 22, 1863, Civil War Times Illustrated Collection, James Black, I/First Texas Heavy Artillery Regiment Correspondence, January 1860–March 1865, United States Army Heritage and Education Center, Carlisle, Pa.

135. Hendrick to mother, November 8, 1863, James Henry Hendrick, First Texas Infantry File, THM; Shelton, *Personal Civil War Letters of General Lawrence Sullivan Ross*, xi.

136. Wilson to Dear Niece, March 20, 1864, Robert Wilson, Fourth Texas Infantry File, THM; Alexander Mendoza, *Confederate Struggle for Command: General James Longstreet and the First Corp in the West* (College Station: Texas A&M University Press, 2008), 152, 175. Robertson's commander, Gen. James Longstreet, removed him from command because of a personal conflict between the two of them. Longstreet used Robertson's request to court-martial the general, since the Texan avoided the chain of command and sent the petition to the Tennessean's superior, John Bell Hood. In the end Robertson got exactly what he wanted, removal to the trans-Mississippi.

137. Parker, *Touched by Fire*, 69.

138. J. B. Polley, *A Soldier's Letters to Charming Nellie* (New York: Neale Publishing, 1908), 165, 179.

139. Hood to Cousin Jennie, February 14, 1864, A. B. Hood, Fifth Texas Infantry File, THM.

140. Caddell to mother and father, March 3, 1864, Jeremiah Caddell, Fourth Texas Infantry File, THM. "French furlough" was another term for desertion.

141. Loughridge to George W. Brent, October 22, 1863, J. R. Loughridge Papers, PC.

142. Gracy, "With Danger and Honor," 133.

143. Williams and Wooster, "Texas War Clerk," 279, 283.

144. John Gano, comp., "Records and Correspondence pertaining to the Military Activities of Brigadier-General Richard M. Gano, C.S.A.," 1:1–3, Brown Special Collections Library, Abilene Christian University, Abilene, Tex.; Col. R.M. Gano to Col. G. W. Brent A.A.F. and Chief of Staff of the Army of Tennessee, B. Marshall, Chief Surgeon Second Brigade Morgan's Division, and D. W. Mandell Surgeon Hardee's Corps Civil War, *Service Records of Confederate General and Staff Officers* (Washington, D.C.:National Archives and Records Service General Services Administration, 1960), M331–101; Wooster, *Lone Star Generals in Gray*, 124; Jack D. Welsh, *Medical Histories of Confederate Generals* (Kent, Ohio: Kent State University Press, 1995), 75. It is interesting to note that Gano is the great-grandfather of Howard Hughes, the wealthy businessman, aviator, and hypochondriac.

145. Gano and Terry to Magruder, August 12, 1863, *O.R.*, Series I, vol. 26, pt. 2: 159.

146. Carrington to Pyron, September 1, 1863, ibid., 198; General Orders No. 149, Headquarters District of Texas, September 1, 1863, ibid.; Special Orders No. 236, Headquarters District of Texas, September 1, 1863, ibid., 198–199; Glenn Tucker, *Chickamauga: Bloody Battle in the West* (Dayton, Ohio: Morningside Press, 1976), 112.

147. Wooster, *Lone Star Generals*, 124; Cunningham to Magruder, October 21, 1863, *O.R.*, Series I, vol. 26, pt. 2: 342; National Archives Microfilm Publications, *Compiled Service Records*, Microcopy no. 319, Rolls 39 and 41.

148. Williams, *Rebel Brothers*, 104.

149. General Order no. 22, June 3, 1863, William Campbell Preston Breckinridge Family Papers, Ninth Regiment Kentucky, Cavalry, Letter Book, Dec. 22 1862–March 26, 1864, Library of Congress, Washington, D.C.; Davis and Hoffman, *Confederate General*, 3:169–170; Johnson, *Partisan Rangers*, 138; West, *Medical Histories of Confederate Generals*, 116.

150. Johansson, *Peculiar Honor*, 75; Brightman to brother, July 18, 1863, Dr. John Claver Brightman Collection, CAH.

151. James Rounsaville to family, July 9, 1863, Thomas and James Rounsaville, Thirteenth Texas Cavalry File, THM.

152. Crain to wife, July 26, July 30, July 31, early August, and August 8, 1863, Alexander C. Crain, Second Texas Partisan Rangers File, THM.

153. Brown, *Journey to Pleasant Hill*, 247–248, 251–252, 253.

154. Ray to mother, September 11, 1863, David M. Ray Papers, CAH.

155. Williams to My Dear Laura, January 6, 1864, First Lt. Watson Dugat Williams, Fifth Texas Infantry File, THM.

156. Ludwell H. Johnson, *Red River Campaign: Politics and Cotton in the Civil War* (Baltimore: Johns Hopkins University Press, 1958), 37, 39–40, 86; Gary D. Joiner, *Through the Howling Wilderness: The 1864 Red River Campaign and Union Failure in the West* (Knoxville: University of Tennessee Press, 2006), 13–14, 17; Gary Dillard Joiner, *One Damn Blunder from Beginning to End: The Red River Campaign of 1864* (Wilmington, Del.: Scholarly Resources, 2003), 9–10, 33; Cotham, *Sabine Pass*, 3; Townsend, *Yankee Invasion of Texas*, 16–23; Dupree, *Planting the Union Flag*, 54–61, 62–68, 96. For an account of the Union army's Texas Overland Expedition, see Richard Lowe, *Texas Overland Expedition of 1863* (Abilene, Tex.: McWhiney Foundation Press, 2006). The phrase "brown-water navy" refers to the Union navy's riverboats.

157. Keener to Esteemed Friend, September 23, 1863, Lawson Jefferson Keener, Second Texas Cavalry (Second Arizona) Regiment File, THM.

158. Marr to sister, September–October 1863, Samuel B. Marr, Twenty-first Texas Cavalry File, THM.

159. Harlan to Ma, October 11, 1863, Isaiah Harlan, Tenth Texas Infantry File, THM.

160. Williams and Wooster, "Texas War Clerk," 283.

161. Johnson, *Red River Campaign*, 129, 131, 155; Joiner, *Through the Howling Wilderness*, 88, 98; Joiner, *One Damn Blunder*, 94, 107.

162. Joiner, *Through the Howling Wilderness*, 109, 113, 115; Joiner, *One Damn Blunder*, 123, 125; Keener to Miss Allie, May 29, 1864, Lawson Jefferson Keener, Second Texas Cavalry (Second Arizona) Regiment File, THM; Dupree, *Planting the Union Flag*, 96.

163. Stranahan to Milda, May 26, 1864, Lt. John A. Stranahan, Twenty-first Texas Cavalry File, THM; Joiner, *Through the Howling Wilderness*, 141, 143; Joiner, *One Damn Blunder*, 151, 153.

164. Thomas H. Edgar, comp., *History of DeBray's Regiment* (Galveston, Tex.: A. A. Finck, 1898); History of DeBray's Regiment, Twenty-sixth Texas Cavalry File, THM.

165. Bailey, *Between the Enemy and Texas*, 197; Jakie L. Pruett and Scott Black, eds., *Civil War Letters: 1861–1865. A Glimpse of the War between the States* (Austin: Eakin Press, 1985), 47–49.

166. Bailey, *Between the Enemy and Texas*, 163; Pruett and Black, *Civil War Letters*, 68–69.

167. Kamphoefner and Helbich, *Germans in the American Civil War*, 443.

168. Dilliard to Sallie, December 2, 1864, T. J. Dilliard, Twenty-eighth Texas Cavalry File, THM.

169. There are a few cases of men deserting soon after New Years of 1864. Robert Hodges, who made several legal attempts early in the war to get a transfer back to the trans-Mississippi, finally resorted to desertion at the beginning of 1864: "You will no doubt be surprised when I tell you that I left (our company with thirteen others of our old company) for our command on the west side of this Miss. But am sorry to say that we did not make the trip. We were absent twenty-one days. We were arrested in Middle, Ala. We were brought back to our old company. Some persons may call it desertion. But to prove to you that this exploration is a legal affair, we were returned to this command. We were reinstated in the company, just as we were before we left." In an attempt to cover up the disgrace of deserting and being caught, Hodge tried to rationalize his actions and justify his future attempts to desert: "Jane, I have been imposed upon until I have become desperate, I take no interest in anything that is going around here. I am determined to cross the river at all hazards. I would not be surprised if I were not in the Trans-Mississippi Army, the next time I write. . . . I would be the last one to desert my country's cause. What I am doing I do not consider desertion nor do I think any sensible mind can view it in that light." Darst, "Robert Hodges, Jr.," 38.

170. Barr, *Polignac's Texas Brigade*, 48. Similarly, men of the 17th Texas Cavalry declared that ordering them to cross the river was "a verry searious matter . . . to leave our homes and familys exposed to the enemy and to go to a country where we can't even hear from our familys. . . . I would not be surprised if a great many of [the Texans] did not desert before starting. I don't think they can be carried across the river." Soon thereafter, 140 men left the camp under the cover of night. Douglas Hale, "One Man's War: Captain Joseph H. Bruton, 1861–1865," *East Texas Historical Journal* 12 (1982): 41.

171. Fleming, "Some Hard Fighting," 359.

172. Wilson to P. A. Wilson, March 29, 1865, J. D. Wilson, David S. Terry's Texas Cavalry File, THM.

173. John Bankhead Magruder to Captain John Belton, May 27, 1863, Record Group 109, chap. 2, vol. 133, Military Departments Letters Sent, District of Texas, New Mexico, and Arizona, Dec. 1862–June 1863, National Archives and Records Service, General Services Administration, War Department Collection of Confederate Records.

174. Simmons to companion, October 17, 1864, The Confederate Letters of John Simmons, Jon Harrison, ed., John Simmons, Twenty-second Texas Infantry File, THM. Rumors spread quickly of the event. Years later John C. Porter of the 18th Texas Infantry recalled the event in his memoirs. Late in the war "we moved near the town of Camden. Here Capt. Grimes [Guynes], of 22nd Reg't., was shot to death with musketry. . . . He was charged a year before this, while camped at McNutts Hill, of influencing his Company to desert, and meet him in Journigan Thicket, Tex., and there they would defy all opposition. The Company had

deserted at the above named camp." "Life of John C. Porter and Sketch of His Experiences in the Civil War, March 29, 1874," John C. Porter, Eighteenth Texas Infantry Regiment File, THM.

175. Marr to sister, September–October 1863, Samuel B. Marr, Twenty-first Texas Cavalry File, THM; Albert Castel, *General Sterling Price and the Civil War in the West* (Baton Rouge: Louisiana State University Press, 1968), 155.

176. Lowe, *Texas Cavalry Officer's Civil War*, 274, 278, 279; Lonn, *Desertion during the Civil War*, 16.

177. Captain E. T. Broughton, "Letters to Mollie," November 2, 1864, Tuscumbia, Ala., http://battleofraymond.org/broughton.htm (accessed November 25, 2003).

178. Chicoine, "Willing Never to Go," 592.

179. Bailey, *Texans in the Confederate Cavalry*, 82.

180. Crain to sister, July 18, 1864, Alexander C. Crain, Second Texas Partisan Rangers File, THM.

181. "The Civil War Experiences of Robert S. Gould, Colonel C.S.A., as Related by Himself," Robert S. Gould, Sixth Texas Cavalry File, THM.

182. Mann to mother, September 18, 1864, Jerome William and Henry Mann, Thirty-fourth Texas Cavalry File, THM.

183. Wooster, *Texas and Texans in the Civil War*, 181–182; Brad R. Clampitt, "The Breakup: The Collapse of the Confederate Trans-Mississippi Army in Texas, 1865," *Southwestern Historical Quarterly* 108 (2005): 500–503, 509, 511, 528. Basil Gaither Ijams noted on May 15, 1865, that "every company in the regiment except ours raised a white flag." Ijams to Louisa Hunt Cunningham Ijams and Nancy Anna "Nollie" Ijams, May 15, 1865, Basil Gaither Ijams Letters, Nesbitt Memorial Library, Columbus, Tex.

184. Morgan to wife, January 1, 1864, Jeff Morgan, Thirty-fifth Texas Cavalry (Liken's) File, THM.

Chapter 6

Chapter epigraph from Jordan-Bychkov, Branum, and Hood, "Boesel Letters," 480.

1. Friend, "Texan of 1860," 3; Lonn, *Foreigners in the Confederacy*, 13; Nackman, *Nation within a Nation*, 49; Bell Irvin Wiley, "What Manner of Men," in Barton and Logue, *Civil War Soldier*, 10; James A. Creighton, *A Narrative History of Brazoria County* (Waco, Tex.: Texian Press, 1975), 229.

2. Anne J. Bailey, "In the Far Corner of the Confederacy: A Question of Conscience for German-Speaking Texans," in Catherine Clinton, ed., *Southern Families at War: Loyalty and Conflict in the Civil War South* (New York: Oxford University Press, 2000), 212; Melvin C. Johnson, "A New Perspective of the Antebellum and Civil War Texas German Community" (M.A. thesis, Stephen F. Austin State University, Nachidoches, Texas, 1993), 12; Ralph A. Wooster, "Foreigners in the Principal Towns of Antebellum Texas," *Southwestern Historical Quarterly* 66 (1962): 211.

3. Buenger, *Secession and the Union*, 8; Marten, *Texas Divided*, 121.

4. Jordan, *German Seed in Texas Soil*, 33, 38, 39, 40; Johnson, "New Perspective of the Antebellum," 19, 20; Frank Abernathy, "Deutschtum in Texas: A Look at Texas German Folklores," in Glen E. Lich and Donna B. Reeves, eds., *German Culture in Texas, A Free Earth: Essays from the 1978 Southwest Symposium* (Boston: Twayne Publishing, 1980), 206; Rudolph Leopold Biesele, *The History of the German Settlements in Texas, 1831–1861* (Austin: Von Boeckmann-Jones, 1930), 1, 7, 20; Lonn, *Foreigners in the Confederacy*, 14, 15,

40; Günter Moltmann, "Roots in Germany: Immigration and Acculturation of German-Americans," in Theodore Gish and Richard Spuler, eds., *Eagle in the New World: German Immigration to Texas and America* (College Station: Texas A&M University Press, 1986), 15–16, 18, 24; Archie McDonald, *Texas: All Hail the Mighty State* (Austin: Eakin Press, 1980), 132.

5. Jordan, *German Seed in Texas Soil*, 43, 47, 52.

6. Lonn, *Foreigners in the Confederacy*, 40; Johnson, "New Perspective of the Antebellum," 13, 14, 16; Robert W. Shook, "The Battle of the Nueces, August 10, 1862," *Southwestern Historical Quarterly* 66 (1962): 3; Clinton, *Southern Families at War*, 212, 213; Inscoe and Kenzer, *Enemies of the Country*, 210, 211, 212; Walter D. Kamphoefner, "New Perspective on Texas Germans and the Confederacy," *Southwestern Historical Quarterly* 102 (1999): 448; Walter L. Buenger, "Secession and the Texas German Community: Editor Lindheimer vs. Editor Flake," *Southwestern Historical Quarterly* 82 (1979): 398; Glen E. Lich, "Rural Hill Country: Man, Nature, and the Ecological Perspective," in Gish and Spuler, *Eagle in the New World*, 37; Jordan-Bychkov, Branum, and Hood, "Boesel Letters," 459.

7. Buenger, *Secession and the Union*, 81, 82; Johnson, "New Perspective of the Antebellum," 42.

8. Johnson, "New Perspective of the Antebellum," 46, 47, 48, 50, 52; Robert W. Shook, "German Migration to Texas, 1830–1850: Causes and Consequences," *Texana* 10 (1972): 237; Wooster, "Foreigners in the Principal Towns," 218; Jordan, *German Seed in Texas Soil*, 56; Kamphoefner, "New Perspective on Texas Germans," 443. The difference in number of slaveholders between Houston and New Braunfels is significant because the former had a higher concentration of Germans.

9. *Neu-Braunfelser Zeitung*, March 11, 1859; Buenger, "Secession and the Texas German Community," 384. The editor of the *Neu-Braunfelser Zeitung* was Ferdinand Jacob Lindheimer.

10. Kamphoefner and Helbich, *Germans in the American Civil War*, 397.

11. Walter Struve, *Germans & Texans: Commerce, Migration, and Culture in the Days of the Lone Star Republic* (Austin: University of Texas Press, 1996), 75.

12. Baum, *Shattering of Texas Unionism*, 71; Lonn, *Foreigners in the Confederacy*, 51; Buenger, "Secession and the Texas German Community," 379.

13. Buenger, "Secession and the Texas German Community," 379, 382; *Neu-Braunfelser Zeitung*, December 14, 1860, January 4, 1861, January 11, 1861, January 14, 1861; New Braunfels *Herald Zeitung*, March 7, 1961, March 21, 1961, February 28, 1961, March 28, 1961, April 4, 1961.

14. Buenger, "Secession and the Texas German Community," 381, 382, 383, 394, 397; Walter D. Kamphoefner, "German Texans: In the Mainstream or Backwaters of Lone Star Society?" *Yearbook of German-American Studies* 38 (2003): 122.

15. Johnson, "New Perspective of the Antebellum," 13, 14, 16; Shook, "Battle of the Nueces," 3; Clinton, *Southern Families at War*, 212, 213; Inscoe and Kenzer, *Enemies of the Country*, 210, 211, 212; Moltmann, "Roots in Germany," 11, 20.

16. Kennedy, *Population of the United States*, 621; Johnson, "New Perspective of the Antebellum," 6, 12, 33, 34; Jordan, *German Seed in Texas Soil*, 118, 120; Lonn, *Foreigners in the Confederacy*, 35; Campbell, *Empire for Slavery*, 215; Shook, "German Migration to Texas," 237; Baum, *Shattering of Texas Unionism*, 53; Ashcraft, "Texas," 71; Gish and Spuler, *Eagle in the New World*, 30; Buenger, "Secession and the Texas German Community," 398, 399.

17. Ralph A. Wooster, *The Secession Conventions of the South* (Princeton, N.J.: Prince-

ton University Press, 1962), 133; Lonn, *Foreigners in the Confederacy*, 46; Johnson, "New Perspective of the Antebellum," 12, 13, 14, 16, 17; Wooster, *Lone Star Blue and Gray*, 94, 95; Shook, "Battle of the Nueces," 3; Inscoe and Kenzer, *Enemies of the Country*, 211, 212; Clinton, *Southern Families at War*, 213; Buenger, "Secession and the Texas German Community," 397; Bobby D. Weaver, *Castro's Colony: Empresario Development in Texas, 1842–1865* (College Station: Texas A&M Press, 1985), 132, 136; Kamphoefner, "New Perspective on Texas Germans," 444, 445; Johnson, "New Perspective of the Antebellum," 17; Kamphoefner, "German Texans," 122.

18. Baum, *Shattering of Texas Unionism*, 53; Buenger, *Secession and the Union*, 102; Johnson, "New Perspective of the Antebellum," 57, 58; Lonn, *Foreigners in the Confederacy*, 417; Buenger, "Secession and the Texas German Community," 399; Inscoe and Kenzer, *Enemies of the Country*, 209; McGowen, *Horse Sweat and Powder Smoke*, 79.

19. Greg Woodall, "German Confederates from Comal County," *Columbiad* 2 (1999): 50, 51, 52, 53; *Neu-Braunfelser Zeitung*, March 26, 1862; New Braunfels *Herald Zeitung*, July 11, 1961, and March 20, 1962. Lindheimer also listed the number of Germans from New Braunfels who joined the different Texas units: "Our county has furnished the Captain Hoffman Company with 81 men; the Captain Podewils company, 79 men; Captain Bose company, 60; the 1st and 2nd Regiments of Sibley's Brigade, 29; the McCulloch Frontier Regiment, 16 men; Captains Wood & Benton Companies, 20; the companies on the coast with 18; Col. Sweet's Regiment, 4; serving in Virginia, Missouri, Tennessee are 8 men; in a number of other companies and hauling supplies for the government, 9, a total of 314. . . . Plus 110 men enrolled in the seven Comal County State Troops . . . and others the Zeitung may not have known, would bring the total to over 500." *Neu-Braunfelser Zeitung*, April 25, 1862.

20. Carl L. Duaine, *The Dead Men Wore Boots: An Account of the Thirty-second Texas Volunteer Cavalry, CSA, 1862–1865* (Austin: San Felipe Press, 1966), 21; McGowen, *Horse Sweat and Powder Smoke*, 167; Lonn, *Foreigners in the Confederacy*, 124, 126; Kamphoefner, "New Perspective on Texas Germans," 449, 450; Kamphoefner, "German Texans," 122; Diary of Julius Giesecke, The Sophienburg, New Braunfels Archives and Museum of History, New Braunfels, Tex.; *Neu-Braunfelser Zeitung*, March 14, 1862. The 6th Texas Infantry further demonstrates the limits of Germans' desire to fight for the Confederacy. After the regiment's capture at Arkansas Post, 152 men from the ranks, mostly Germans and Poles, took an oath of allegiance to the United States to avoid any further military service for the Confederacy and return home.

21. Gilbert Cuthbertson, "Coller of the Sixth Texas: Correspondence of a Texas Infantry Man, 1861–64," *Military History of Texas and the Southwest* 9 (1972): 129; "Description of the Family and Life of Joseph Bruckmuller," typewritten translation, Joseph Bruckmuller Collection, CAH; also in Marten, *Texas Divided*, 118.

22. Minetta Altgelt Goyne, *Lone Star and Double Eagle: Civil War Letters of a German-Texas Family* (Fort Worth: Texas Christian University Press, 1982), 8, 10, 17.

23. Ibid., 22–23, 37, 46, 48, 49.

24. "Military Records of the Four Hoelscher Brothers," Wilhelm Hoelscher to mother, June 25, 1862, and Hoelscher to brother, June 29, 186?, Bernard Hoelscher, Seventeenth Texas Infantry File, THM.

25. Joseph-Hermann Seele Letters, CAH; John Henry Brown to unknown, n.d., Brown Papers, TSLAC; also in McGowen, *Horse Sweat and Powder Smoke*, 168; Erma Baker, "Brown, John Henry," in Tyler, *Handbook of Texas*, 1:765.

26. Jordan-Bychkov, Branum, and Hood, "Boesel Letters," 457, 464, 469.

27. Ibid., 470, 476, 477, 480.

28. Clinton, *Southern Families at War*, 215; Lonn, *Foreigners in the Confederacy*, 125, 425; Weaver, *Castro's Colony*, 134, 135; Kamphoefner and Helbich, *Germans in the American Civil War*, 426–429.

29. Weaver, *Castro's Colony*, 135.

30. Park to wife, March 31, 1862, Daniel Grant Park, Fifteenth Texas Cavalry File, THM. "Duch" is an aberrant spelling of "Dutch," a corrupted version of the word *deutsh*, meaning "German."

31. Clinton, *Southern Families at War*, 215; Lonn, *Foreigners in the Confederacy*, 125, 425, 426; Johnson, "New Perspective of the Antebellum," 8.

32. Inscoe and Kenzer, *Enemies of the Country*, 214; Mazyck Andrews, "German Pioneers in Texas: Civil War Period" (M.A. thesis, University of Chicago, 1929), 38–39; Lonn, *Foreigners in the Confederacy*, 426; Lonn, *Desertion during the Civil War*, 4; Ashcraft, "Texas," 134; Wooster, *Lone Star Blue and Gray*, 95.

33. Inscoe and Kenzer, *Enemies of the Country*, 213; Edmund Turner to Flemellyn, December 6, 1862, Record Group 109, chap. 2, vol. 133, Military Departments Letters Sent, District of Texas, New Mexico, and Arizona, Dec. 1862–June 1863, National Archives, Washington, D.C; Thomas W. Cutrer, "Magruder, John Bankhead," in Tyler, *Handbook of Texas*, 4:464–465.

34. Desmond Puloski Hopkins, Diary, CAH; Wooster, *Lone Star Blue and Gray*, 95.

35. Desmond Puloski Hopkins Diary, April 24, 1862, CAH; Lonn, *Foreigners in the Confederacy*, 426; Stanley S. McGowen, "Battle or Massacre? The Incident on the Nueces, August 10, 1862," *Southwestern Historical Quarterly* 104 (2000): 69.

36. Thomas C. Smith, *Here's Yer Mule: The Diary of Thomas C. Smith, Third Sergeant, Company 'G,' Wood's Regiment, Thirty-second Texas Cavalry, C.S.A.* (Waco, Tex.: Little Texan Press, 1958), 19; quote also in Inscoe and Kenzer, *Enemies of the Country*, 218.

37. San Antonio *Semi-Weekly News*, April 20, 1862. L. D. Bradley of Timmon's Regiment, formally of Waul's Texes Legion but transferred after his capture at Vicksburg, recorded a similar event near Galveston. "Heidenhammer, whose house was broken into, is one of the lowest kinds of mean Dutch Jews, and had refused, even when the men had a little money, to sell Tobacco to them for Confederate money; on account of which conduct he had become rather notorious, at least among the soldiers at the place; . . . a house broken open and sacked. . . . In other words, I have no pity or sympathy whatever for the Dutch Jew, for the fact is I would like to see his sort not only robbed & burnt out, & they themselves sent out of the country." Bradley to Little Darling, August 10, 1864, Bradley (L. D.) Papers, 1859–1887, Pearce Civil War Collection, Navarro College, Corsicana, Tex.

38. Houston *Tri-Weekly Telegraph*, April 23, 1862.

39. Wyatt to unknown, August 25, 1862, Telemechus Scott Wyatt, Thirty-fifth Texas Cavalry (Liken's) File, THM; Lonn, *Foreigners in the Confederacy*, 426, 428, 431; Wooster, *Lone Star Blue and Gray*, 96, 97; Inscoe and Kenzer, *Enemies of the Country*, 216, 217; Marten, *Texas Divided*, 77, 120, 221; Kamphoefner, "German Texans," 122; Kamphoefner, "New Perspective on Texas Germans," 449; Weaver, *Castro's Colony*, 135; R. H. Williams, *With the Border Ruffians: Memories of the Far West, 1852–1868* (Lincoln: University of Nebraska Press, 1982), 248, 249, 266–267; McGowen, "Battle or Massacre?" 75–80. See also Richard Selcer and William Paul Berrier, "What Really Happened on the Nueces: James Duff, a Good Soldier or 'The Butcher of Fredericksburg," *North and South* 2 (1998): 57–60. The best firsthand account of the Battle of the Nueces is by Ernest Cramer, one of the Ger-

man unionists who survived the fight. Ernst Cramer to parents, October 30, 1862, Treue der Union Monument File, Primary Documents, Comfort Heritage Foundation Archives, Comfort, Tex.

40. Kamphoefner, "New Perspective on Texas Germans," 451; Kamphoefner, "German Texans," 123; Buenger, "Secession and the Texas German Community," 379–380.

41. Kamphoefner, "New Perspective on Texas Germans," 454; George R. Nielsen, *In Search of a Home: Nineteenth-Century Wendish Immigration* (College Station: Texas A&M University Press, 1989), 94–96; Lillie Moerbe Caldwell, *Texas Wends: Their First Half Century* (Salado, Tex.: Anson Jones Press, 1961), 62–63, 110.

42. T. Lindsay Baker, *The Polish Texans* (San Antonio: University of Texas Institute of Texan Cultures, 1982), 1, 2, 9, 11, 12, 13; Rev. Edward J. Dworaczyk, comp., *The First Polish Colonies of America in Texas: Containing also the General History of the Polish People in Texas* (Saratoga, Calif.: R&E Research Associates, reprint 1969), vii, viii, 2, 24, 26; Kennedy, *Population of the United States,* 620–623.

43. Baker, *Polish Texans,* 49–54; Dworaczyk, *First Polish Colonies,* 26, 27.

44. Clinton Machann and James W. Mendle, *Krásná Amerika: A Study of the Texas Czechs, 1851–1939* (Austin: Eakin Press, 1983), 35, 37, 41, 208, 209, 217.

45. Charles Avril, *The Wends of Texas* (San Antonio, Tex.: Naylor, 1954), 1, 11, 12, 19, 51.

46. Larry E. Scott, *The Swedish Texans* (San Antonio: University of Texas Institute of Texan Cultures, 1990), 1, 2, 102, 103, 104, 106, 107; Kennedy, *Population of the United States,* 620–623.

47. Thomas W. Cutrer, *The English Texans* (San Antonio: University of Texas Institute of Texan Cultures, 1985), 83–91; John Brendan Flannery, *The Irish Texans* (San Antonio: University of Texas Institute of Texan Cultures, 1980), 96, 99, 101; Cotham, *Sabine Pass,* 3.

48. Fehrenbach, *Lone Star,* 288, 289; Kennedy, *Population of the United States,* 620–623; Arnoldo DeLeon, *They Called Them Greasers: Anglo Attitudes toward Mexicans in Texas, 1821–1900* (Austin: University of Texas Press, 1983), 24, 86; Buenger, *Secession and the Union,* 87; Lack, "Slavery and Vigilantism in Austin, Texas, 1840–1860," 4; Memoirs of Thomas C. Dewitt, June 12, 1878, Thomas C. Dewitt, First Texas Mounted Rifles File, THM; Austin *State Gazette,* September 9, 1854. Though a significant number were born in Texas and were not foreign, for the organization of this study I group Tejanos with non-natives to demonstrate that their treatment by the established Anglo authorities was similar to that of people not from the United States.

49. Williams, *With the Border Ruffians,* 280.

50. William to wife, September 26, 1862, William H. Pierce, First Texas Cavalry Regiment File, THM.

51. Buenger, *Secession and the Union,* 84, 85.

52. Ibid., 87; Jerry D. Thompson, *Mexican Texans in the Union Army* (El Paso: Texas Western Press, 1986), viii, 11; Lack, "Slavery and Vigilantism in Austin, Texas, 1840–1860," 2; Campbell, *Empire for Slavery,* 218; *Corpus Christi Ranchero,* September 3, 1863.

53. For the best description of the Cortina War, see Jerry Thompson, *Cortina: Defending the Mexican Name in Texas* (College Station: Texas A&M University Press, 2007). DeLeon, *They Called Them Greasers,* 75, 77, 84; Arnoldo DeLeon, *The Tejano Community, 1836–1900* (Albuquerque: University of New Mexico Press, 1982), 17, 18; Thompson, *Mexican Texans in the Union Army,* viii; David Montejano, *Anglos and Mexicans in the Making of Texas, 1836–1986* (Austin: University of Texas, 1987), 26–27, 32–33.

54. Montejano, *Anglos and Mexicans,* 25–26; Thompson, *Mexican Texans in the Union Army,* viii, 1; Buenger, *Secession and the Union,* 102.

55. Marten, *Texas Divided*, 122, 123; Jerry D. Thompson, *Vaqueros in Blue and Gray* (Austin: State House Press, 2000), 5, 6, 7, 29, 30; San Antonio *Semi-Weekly News*, April 24, 1862; John Denny Riley, "Santos Benavides: His Influence on the Lower Rio Grande, 1832–1891," (Ph.D. diss., Texas Christian University, 1976), 128.

56. Williams, *With the Border Ruffian*, 274–275; Thompson, *Vaqueros in Blue and Gray*, 6, 7, 48, 55, 56; Miguel Gonzalez Quiroga, "Mexicanos in Texas during the Civil War," in Emilio Zamora, Cynthia Orozco, and Rodolfo Rocha, eds., *Mexican Americans in Texas History: Selected Essays* (Austin: Texas State Historical Association, 2000), 54, 55, 56; Lonn, *Desertion during the Civil War*, 5. "Por el amor de Dios, y todos los santos, señor" can be translated as "For the love of God, and all the saints, sir."

57. Riley, "Santos Benavides," 4, 6, 7, 42; Thompson, *Vaqueros in Blue and Gray*, 8, 11, 60; Houston *Tri-Weekly Telegraph*, July 30, 1862.

58. Thompson, *Vaqueros in Blue and Gray*, 25, 26; Lonn, *Foreigners in the Confederacy*, 126, 127; San Antonio *Semi-Weekly News*, April 24, 1862. Company C of the 8th Texas Infantry was almost exclusively Tejano.

59. Jerry Don Thompson, "Mutiny and Desertion on the Rio Grande: The Strange Saga of Captain Adrian J. Vidal," *Military History of Texas and the Southwest* 12 (1974): 161, 162, 165, 167; Thompson, *Vaqueros in Blue and Gray*, 81, 82; Thompson, *Mexican Texans in the Union Army*, 10, 13; Wooster, *Lone Star Blue and Gray*, 122; Townsend, *Yankee Invasion of Texas*, 84; Weitz, *More Damning Than Slaughter*, 231; *Neu-Braunfelser Herald Zeitung*, January 2, 1863. Frustrated again by the language barrier and the bureaucracy of the Union army, Vidal deserted again and escaped into Mexico. In Mexico he joined the Juaristas but was soon thereafter captured by the imperialists and executed. Jerry Thompson described the career of Vidal best when he wrote, "The young captain had served both the blue and the grey, deserted from both armies, joined a third and was shot by a fourth. . . . Vidal . . . had compiled one of the most unusual records in the annals of Civil War history." Thompson, "Mutiny and Desertion," 167.

60. Thompson, *Mexican Texans in the Union Army*, 3, 14, 15, 16, 17; Thompson, *Vaqueros in Blue and Gray*, 82, 85, 86, 87, 88; Buenger, *Secession and the Union*, 88, 90; Daddysman, *Matamoros Trade*, 86.

61. Thompson, *Vaqueros in Blue and Gray*, 89, 90, 93, 96; Thompson, *Mexican Texans in the Union Army*, ix, 15, 16, 17, 24, 25, 27, 28, 34, 35; Moneyhan, *Texas after the Civil War*, 118.

62. Lonn, *Foreigners in the Confederacy*, 19, 21, 37, 126, 128; Tolbert, *Dick Dowling at Sabine Pass*, 28.

Chapter 7

Chapter epigraph taken from a poem appearing in B. P. Gallaway, "A Texan Farm Boy Enlists in the Twelfth Cavalry," *Texas Military History* 8 (1970): 94. The notation for the poem reads: "These lines were composed by D. C. Nance just leaving his home to engage in the distressing war of 1861–5 between the States of the United States."

1. "My War Experience," J. P. Johnson, First Texas Partisan Rangers File, THM.

2. Barry A. Crouch, *The Freedmen's Bureau and Black Texans* (Austin: University of Texas Press, 1992), 12; Carl H. Moneyhon, "'I Seemed to Have No Thought of the Past, Present or Future': Texans React to Confederate Defeat," in Grear, *Fate of Texas*.

BIBLIOGRAPHY

Archives

Brown Special Collections Library, Abilene Christian University, Abilene, Tex.
  Gano, Richard Montgomery, Collection.
Center for Twentieth Century Texas Studies, Moody Mansion and Museum, Galveston, Tex.
  Moody, William L., Collection.
Center for American History, University of Texas at Austin
  Barry, James Buckner, Collection
  Brightman, John Claver, Collection
  Bruckmuller, Joseph, Collection
  Bryan, John Arthur, Papers
  Burrowes Family Papers
  Crockett, Edward Richardson, Collection
  Davidson, Sidney Green, Papers
  Giddings, Dewitt Clinton, Collection
  Hander, Christian Wilhelm, Civil War Diary
  Hopkins, Desmond Puloski, Collection
  Howell, William Randolph, Collection
  Kuykendall Family Papers, 1822–1991
  Long, John B., Collection
  McCarty, Thomas L., Diary
  Pitts, William A., Collection
  Rabb Family Papers
  Ray, David M., Papers
  "Red River" Company Agreement, 1862
  Rogers, William P., Papers
  Russell, L. B., Collection
  Seele, Joseph-Hermann, Letters
  Watson, Jim, Papers
  Whatley, William J., Papers
  Wight, Levi Lamoni, Letters, 1862–1891
  Wright (Henry C.), Reminiscences
Charles and Peggy Pearce Civil War Documents Collection, Navarro College, Corsicana, Tex.
  Boothe, W. S., Papers
  Bradley (L. D.), Papers
  Goodman (Samuel A., Jr.), Papers
  Loughridge, J. R., Papers
  McMurphy, G. L., Diary

Comfort Heritage Foundation Archives, Comfort, Tex.
> Cramer, Ernst, Letters
> Treue der Union Monument File

Library of Congress, Washington, D.C.
> William Campbell Preston Breckinridge Family Papers

National Archives and Records Service, General Services, Washington, D.C.
> Administration, War Department Collection of Confederate Records.
> Compiled Service Records of Confederate Soldiers Who Served in Organizations from Kentucky
> Compiled Service Records of Confederate Soldiers Who Served in Organizations from the State of Texas
> Military Departments Letters Sent, Department of Texas, September–November 1861
> Military Departments Letters Sent, District of Texas, New Mexico, and Arizona, December 1862–June 1863
> Population Schedules of the Eighth Census of the United States: 1850
> Population Schedules of the Eighth Census of the United States: 1860

Nesbitt Memorial Library, Columbus, Tex.
> Shropshire, John S., Papers

Sophienburg, New Braunfels Archives and Museum of History, New Braunfels, Tex.
> Diary of Julius Giesecke

Texas A&M University at Commerce Library, Commerce, Tex.
> Neville, A.W., Papers

Texas Heritage Museum, Hill College, Hillsboro, Tex.

Amnesty Appeal	Dyers, Charles Samuel
Anderson, Thomas L.	Edwards, William P.
Arrant, D. G.	Faulk, John
Barcroft, William H.	Fly, George W. L.
Bates, Jesse P.	Fogle, Andrew J.
Burke, Benjamin F.	Gould, Robert S.
Caddell, Jeremiah	Greyson, Dr. Thomas B.
Cadell, Richard Marion	Hamman, William H.
Coffman, A. J.	Harlan, Isaiah
Connally, Drury	Harris, Henry Ward
Cook, David	Harrison, J. E.
Cox, Hartwell Bolin	Hatchell. J. M.
Cox, Noah B.	Hendrick, James Henry
Crain, Alexander C.	Hervey, A. G.
Cravey, J. H.	Hill, P. H.
Crow, Z. H.	History of DeBray's Regiment
Dansby, Durant Motier	Hoelscher, Bernard
Darr, William Thomas	Holcombe, John M.
DeWees, J. W.	Hood, A. B.
Dewitt, Thomas C.	Hunter, James T.
Dilliard, T. J.	Ikard, Elijah H. and Robert E.
Dodson, James Richard	Johnson, J. P.
Douglas, George	Jones, W. A.
Douglas, Lizzie, Letters	Keeling, John Robert
Duke, Josiah G.	Keener, Lawson Jefferson

Keener, Linson Montgomery
Kuykendall, William
Lawther, William D.
Marr, Erasmus E.
Marr, Samuel B.
McKay, Gil
McNemar, John Gardner
Mixson, T. C.
Moore, Thomas Oscar
Morgan, Jeff
Moseley, S. E.
Nelson, A. J.
Norvell, J. S.
Park, Daniel Grant
Pearce, H. D.
Pierce, William H.
Porter, John C.
Quayle, William
Rainey, A. T.
Roberdeau, James D.
Roberts, Asa
Ross, Edward H.
Rounsaville, Thomas and James

Selman, C. W.
Simmons, John.
Smith, Henry V.
Stansbury, George T.
Stark, John T.
Stranahan, Lt. John A.
Tabb, James A.
Templeton, John Allen
Van Zandt, Khleber Miller
Ware, Theophilus V.
Waterhouse, Richard
Watson, Henry
Watson, Samuel S.
William, Jerome and Henry Mann
Williams, First Lt. Watson Dugat
Williams, T. A.
Wilson, J. D.
Wilson, Robert
Wood, Campbell
Worsham, C. S.
Wyatt, Telemechus Scott
Young, D. E.
Young, William G.

Texas State Library and Archives, Austin, Tex.
    Brown, John Henry, Papers
    Donathan, Wiley F., Family Correspondence
    Executive Record Books, Lightfoot Papers
    Records of the Adjunct General: Muster Roll Collection
    Records, Texas Governor Francis Richard Lubbock
United States Army Heritage and Education Center, Carlisle, Pa.
    Civil War Times Illustrated Collection
    James Black, I/First Texas Heavy Artillery Regiment Correspondence, January 1860–
        March 1865

Newspapers

Bellville Countryman, Bellville, Tex.
[Tri-Weekly] Alamo Express, San Antonio, Tex.
Christian Advocate, Nashville, Tenn.
Corpus Christi Ranchero, Corpus Christi, Tex.
Courier Journal, Louisville, Ky.
Daily Picayune, New Orleans, La.
Herald, Dallas, Tex.
Herald Zeitung, New Braunfels, Tex.
Messenger, McKinney, Tex.
Navarro Express, Corsicana, Tex.
Neu-Braunfelser Zeitung, New Braunfels, Tex.
Northern Standard, Clarksville, Tex.
Overton Sharp-Shooter, Overton, Tex.

San Antonio Herald, San Antonio, Tex.
Semi-Weekly News, San Antonio, Tex.
State Gazette, Austin, Tex.
Telegraph and Texas Register, Columbia, Tex.
Texas Republican, Marshall, Tex.
Tri-Weekly Telegraph, Houston, Tex.
Weekly Courier, Louisville, Ky.
Weekly News, Galveston, Tex.

Published Books
Primary

Alberts, Don E., ed. *Rebels on the Rio Grande: The Civil War Journal of A. B. Peticolas.*
    Albuquerque: Merit Press, 1993.

Anderson, John Q., ed. *Campaigning with Parsons' Texas Cavalry Brigade,* CSA: *The War
    Journals and Letters of the Four Orr Brothers, Twelfth Texas Cavalry Regiment.* Hillsboro,
    Tex.: Hill Junior College Press, 1967.

Blackburn, J. K. P, L. B. Giles, and E. S. Dodd. *Terry Texas Ranger Trilogy.* Austin: State
    House Press, 1996.

Bowyer, John William, and Claude Harrison Thurman, arrangers. *The Annals of Elder Horn:
    Early Life in the Southwest.* New York: Richard R. Smith, 1930.

Brown, Norman D., ed. *Journey to Pleasant Hill: The Civil War Letters of Captain Elijah P.
    Petty, Walker's Texas Division,* CSA. San Antonio: University Texas Institute of Texan
    Cultures, 1982.

Carter, Davis Blake. *Two Stars in the Southern Sky: General John Greg* C.S.A. *and Mollie.*
    Spartanburg, S.C.: Reprint Company, 2001.

Cater, Douglas John. *As It Was: Reminiscences of a Soldier of the Third Texas Cavalry and the
    Nineteenth Louisiana Infantry.* Austin: State House Press, 1990.

Clark, L. D., ed. *Civil War Recollections of James Lemuel Clark.* College Station: Texas A&M
    University Press, 1984.

Collins, R. M. *Chapters from the Unwritten History of the War between the States: The
    Incidents in the Life of a Confederate Soldier in Camp, on the March, in the Great
    Battles, and in Prison.* Dayton, Ohio: Morningside, 1988.

Cutrer, Thomas, W., ed. *Longstreet's Aide: The Civil War Letters of Major Thomas J. Goree.*
    Charlottesville: University of Virginia Press, 1995.

Davis, Kathryn Hooper, Linda Ericson Devereaux, and Carolyn Reeves Ericson, comps.
    Texas Confederate Home Roster. Nacogdoches, Tex.: Ericson Books, 2003.

Day, James M., comp. *The Texas Almanac, 1857–1873.* Waco, Tex.: Texian Press, 1967.

D'Hamel, Enrique B. *The Adventures of a Tenderfoot.* Waco, Tex: W. M. Morrison, 1914.

Edgar, Thomas H., comp. *History of DeBray's Regiment.* Galveston, Tex: A. A. Finck, 1898.

Erath, George Bernard. *The Memoirs of Major George B. Erath, 1813–1891.* Waco, Tex.:
    Heritage Society of Waco, reprint 1956.

Everett, Donald E., ed. *Chaplain Davis and Hood's Texas Brigade.* Baton Rouge: Louisiana
    State University Press, 1999.

Fletcher, William A. *Rebel Private: Front and Rear: Memoirs of a Confederate Soldier.* New
    York: Dutton, 1995.

Gallaway, B. P., ed. *Texas, the Dark Corner of the Confederacy: Contemporary Accounts of the
    Lone Star State in the Civil War.* Lincoln: University of Nebraska Press, 1994.

————. *The Ragged Rebel: A Common Soldier in W. H. Parsons' Texas Cavalry, 1861–1865.* Austin: University of Texas Press, 1988.

Getzendaner, W. H. *A Brief and Condensed History of Parsons' Texas Cavalry Brigade Composed of Twelfth, Nineteenth, Twenty-First, Morgan's Battalion, and Pratt's Battery of Artillery of the Confederate States, Together with the Roster of the Several Commands as far as Obtainable—Some Historical Sketches—General Orders and a Memoranda of Parsons' Brigade Association.* Waxahachie, Tex.: J. M. Flemister, 1892.

Giles, Leonidas B. *Terry's Texas Rangers.* Austin: Pemberton Press, 1967.

Glover, Robert W., ed. *"Tyler to Sharpsburg," Robert H. and William H. Gaston: Their War Letters, 1861–1862.* Waco, Tex.: W. M. Morrison, 1960.

Goyne, Minetta Altgelt. *Lone Star and Double Eagle: Civil War Letters of a German-Texas Family.* Fort Worth: Texas Christian University Press, 1982.

Greer, James K., ed. *A Texas Ranger and Frontiersman: The Days of Buck Barry in Texas, 1845–1906.* Dallas, Tex.: Southwest Press, 1932.

Havins, J. R., and James M. Day, eds. *Twenty-Five Years on the Outside Row of the Northwest Texas Conference.* Brownwood, Tex.: Cross Timbers Press, 1966.

Huckabury, Ida. *Ninety-Four Years in Jack County, 1854–1948.* Jacksboro, Tex.: n.p., 1949.

Hunter, John Warren. *Heel-Fly Time in Texas: A Story of the Civil War Period.* Bandera, Tex.: Frontier Times, 1931.

Johnson, Adam Rankin. *The Partisan Rangers of the Confederate States Army.* Louisville, Ky.: George G. Fetter, 1904.

Johnson, Robert Underwood, and Clarence C. Buel, eds. *Battles and Leaders of the Civil War.* New York: T. Yoseloff, 1884.

Kamphoefner, Walter, and Wolfgang Helbich, eds. *Germans in the American Civil War: Letters from the Front and Farm, 1861–1865.* Chapel Hill: University of North Carolina Press, 2006.

Keen, Newton A. *Living and Fighting with the Texas Sixth Cavalry.* Gaithersburg, Md.: Butternut Press, 1986.

Kennedy, Joseph C. G. *Population of the United States in 1860: Compiled from the Original Returns of the Eighth Census.* Washington, D.C.: Government Printing Office, 1864.

Kerr, Homer L., ed. *Fighting with Ross' Texas Cavalry Brigade C.S.A.: The Diary of George L. Griscom, Adjutant, Ninth Texas Cavalry Regiment.* Hillsboro, Tex.: Hill Junior College Press, 1976.

Lale, Max, and Hobart Key, eds. *The Civil War Letters of David R. Garrett, Detailing the Adventures of the 6th Texas Cavalry, 1861–1865.* Marshall, Tex.: Porto Caddo Press, 1963.

Laswell, Mary, ed. *Rags and Hope: The Recollections of Val C. Giles, Four Years with Hood's Brigade, Fourth Texas Infantry.* New York: Coward, McCann, 1961.

Lowe, Richard, ed. *A Texas Cavalry Officer's Civil War: The Diary and Letters of James C. Bates.* Baton Rouge: Louisiana State University Press, 1999.

Memorial and Biographical History of Dallas County, Texas, Illus. Chicago: Lewis Publishing, 1892.

Noel, Theophilus. *Autobiography and Reminiscences of Theophilus Noel.* Chicago: Theophilus Noel Company Press, 1904.

Parker, Eddy R., ed. *Touched by Fire: Letters from Company D Fifth Texas Infantry Hood's Brigade Army of Northern Virginia, 1862–1865.* Hillsboro, Tex.: Hill College Press, 2000.

Polley, J. B. *A Soldier's Letters to Charming Nellie.* New York: Neale Publishing, 1908.

Porter, Davis D. *Incidents and Anecdotes of the Civil War.* New York: D. Appleton, 1886.

Pruett, Jakie L., and Scott Black, eds. *Civil War Letters, 1861–1865: A Glimpse of the War between the States.* Austin: Eakin Press, 1985.

Raines, C. W., ed. *Six Decades in Texas, or Memoirs of Francis Richard Lubbock: Governor of Texas in War-Time, 1861–1863.* Austin: Ben C. Jones, 1900.

Shelton, Perry Wayne, comp. *Personal Civil War Letters of General Lawrence Sullivan Ross: With Other Letters.* Austin: Shelly and Richard Morrison, 1994.

Smith, Ralph J. *Reminiscences of the Civil War: And Other Sketches.* Waco, Tex.: W. M. Morrison, 1962.

Smith, Thomas C. *Here's Yer Mule: The Diary of Thomas C. Smith, 3rd Sergeant, Company 'G,' Wood's Regiment, Thirty-second Texas Cavalry, C.S.A.* Waco, Tex.: Little Texan Press, 1958.

Sparks, A. W. *The War between the States, as I Saw It: Reminiscent, Historical, and Personal.* Longview, Tex.: D&D, 1987.

Stevens, John W. *Reminiscences of the Civil War: A Soldier in Hood's Texas Brigade, Army of Northern Virginia.* Hillsboro, Tex.: Hillsboro Mirror Print, 1902.

Texas Governor (Edward Clark). *Governor's Message to the Senators and Representatives of the Ninth Legislature of the State of Texas, November 1, 1861.* Austin: Texas Government Printing Office, 1861.

Thompson, Jerry D., ed. *Civil War in the Southwest: Recollection of the Sibley Brigade.* College Station: Texas A&M University Press, 2001.

———, ed. *Westward the Texans: The Civil War Journal of Private William Randolph Howell.* El Paso: Texas Western Press, 1990.

U.S. War Department. *The War of the Rebellion: A Compilation of the Official Records of the Union and Confederate Armies.* Washington, D.C.: U.S. Government Printing Office, 1880–1901.

Van Zandt, K. M. *Force without Fanfare: The Autobiography of K. M. Van Zandt.* Fort Worth: Texas Christian University Press, 1968.

Wiley, Bell I., ed. *Fourteen Hundred and 91 Days in the Confederate Army; or Camp Life, Day by Day of the W. P. Lane Rangers from April 19, 1861 to May 20, 1865.* Jackson, Tenn.: McCowat-Mercer Press, 1954.

Williams, Edward B., ed. *Rebel Brothers: The Civil War Letters of the Truehearts.* College Station: Texas A&M University Press, 1995.

Williams, R. H. *With the Border Ruffians: Memories of the Far West, 1852–1868.* Lincoln: University of Nebraska Press, 1982.

Wilson, John P. *When the Texans Came: Missing Records from the Civil War in the Southwest, 1861–1862.* Albuquerque: University of New Mexico Press, 2000.

Wilson, John P., and Jerry Thompson, eds. *The Civil War in West Texas & New Mexico.* El Paso: University of Texas at El Paso, 2001.

Winkler, E. W., ed., *Journal of the Secession Convention of Texas, 1861.* Austin: Texas Library and Historical Commission, 1912.

Wright, D. Giraud. *A Southern Girl in '61: The War Time Memories of a Confederate Senator's Daughter.* New York: Doubleday, Page, 1905.

Secondary

Anderson, Gary Clayton. *The Conquest of Texas: Ethnic Cleansing in the Promised Land, 1820–1875.* Norman: University of Oklahoma, 2005.

Ashcraft, Allan C. *Texas in the Civil War: A Resume History.* Austin: Texas Civil War Centennial Commission, 1962.

Avril, Charles. *The Wends of Texas*. San Antonio, Tex.: Naylor, 1954.

Bailey, Anne J. *Between the Enemy and Texas: Parsons' Texas Cavalry in the Civil War*. Fort Worth: Texas Christian University Press, 1989.

———. *Texans in the Confederate Cavalry*. Abilene, Tex.: McWhiney Foundation Press, 1998.

Baker, T. Lindsay. *The Polish Texans*. San Antonio: University of Texas Institute of Texan Cultures, 1982.

Barr, Alwyn. *Polignac's Texas Brigade*. Texas Gulf Coast Historical Association, Vol. 8, No. 1, November 1964.

Barton, Michael, and Larry M. Logue, eds. *The Civil War Soldier: A Historical Reader*. New York: New York University Press, 2002.

Baum, Dale. *The Shattering of Texas Unionism: Politics in the Lone Star State during the Civil War Era*. Baton Rouge: Louisiana State University Press, 1998.

Baylor, George Wythe. *John Robert Baylor: Confederate Governor of Arizona*. Tucson: Arizona Pioneers' Historical Society, 1966.

Baynes, John. *Morale: A Study of Men and Courage, The Second Scottish Rifles at the Battle of Neuve Chapelle, 1915*. New York: Frederick A. Preager, 1967.

Bedinger, Singleton B. *Texas and the Southern Confederacy*. Taylor, Tex.: Merchants Press, 1970.

Beringer, Richard E., Herman Hattaway, Archer Jones, and William N. Still Jr. *The Elements of Confederate Defeat: Nationalism, War Aims, and Religion*. Athens: University of Georgia Press, 1988.

———. *Why the South Lost the Civil War*. Athens: University of Georgia Press, 1986.

Biesele, Rudolph Leopold. *The History of the German Settlements in Texas, 1831–1861*. Austin: Von Boeckmann-Jones, 1930.

Binkley, William C. *The Expansionist Movement in Texas, 1836–1850*. New York: Da Capo Press, 1970.

Billingsley, Carolyn Earle. *Communities of Kinship: Antebellum Families and the Settlement of the Cotton Frontier*. Athens: University of Georgia Press, 2004.

Biographical Souvenir of the State of Texas. Chicago: F. A. Battery, 1889.

Buenger, Walter L. *Secession and the Union in Texas*. Austin: University of Texas Press, 1984.

Buenger, Walter L., and Robert Calvert, eds. *Texas through Time: Evolving Interpretations*. College Station: Texas A&M University Press, 1991.

Caldwell, Lillie Moerbe. *Texas Wends: Their First Half Century*. Salado, Tex.: Anson Jones Press, 1961.

Campbell, Randolph B. *An Empire for Slavery: The Peculiar Institution in Texas, 1821–1865*. Baton Rouge: Louisiana State University Press, 1989.

———. *Gone to Texas: A History of the Lone Star State*. New York: Oxford University Press, 2003.

———. *A Southern Community in Crisis: Harrison County, Texas, 1850–1880*. Austin: Texas State Historical Association, 1983.

Campbell, Randolph B., and Richard G. Lowe. *Wealth and Power in Antebellum Texas*. College Station: Texas A&M University Press, 1972.

Carlock, Chuck, and V., M. Owens. *History of the Tenth Texas Cavalry (Dismounted) Regiment*. North Richland Hills, Tex.: Smithfield Press, 2001.

Carnes, Mark C. *Secret Ritual and Manhood in Victorian America*. New Haven, Conn.: Yale University Press, 1989.

Carnes, Mark C., and Clyde Griffen, eds. *Meanings for Manhood: Constructions of Masculinity in Victorian America.* Chicago: University of Chicago Press, 1990.

Chance, Joseph E. *The Second Texas Infantry: From Shiloh to Vicksburg.* Austin: Eakin Press, 1984.

Clawson, Mary Ann. *Constructing Brotherhood: Class, Gender, and Fraternalism.* Princeton, N.J.: Princeton University Press, 1989.

Clinton, Catherine, ed. *Southern Families at War: Loyalty and Conflict in the Civil War South.* New York: Oxford University Press, 2000.

Colton, Ray C. *The Civil War in the Western Territories: Arizona, Colorado, New Mexico, and Utah.* Norman: University of Oklahoma Press, 1959.

Connelly, Thomas Lawrence, and Archer Jones. *The Politics of Command: Factions and Ideas in Confederate Strategy.* Baton Rouge: Louisiana State University Press, 1973.

Cotham, Edward T., Jr. *Sabine Pass: The Confederacy's Thermopylae.* Austin: University of Texas Press, 2004.

Crabb, Martha. *All Afire to Fight: The Untold Tale of the Civil War's Ninth Texas Cavalry.* New York: First Post Road Press, 2000.

Craven, Avery O. *The Growth of Southern Nationalism, 1848–1861.* Baton Rouge: Louisiana State University Press, 1953.

Creighton, James A. *A Narrative History of Brazoria County.* Waco, Tex.: Texian Press, 1975.

Crouch, Barry A. *The Freedmen's Bureau and Black Texans.* Austin: University of Texas Press, 1992.

Crouch, Carrie J. *A History of Young County, Texas.* Austin: Texas State Historical Association, 1956.

Cutrer, Thomas W. *Ben McCulloch and the Frontier Military Tradition.* Chapel Hill: University of North Carolina Press, 1993.

———. *The English Texans.* San Antonio: University of Texas Institute of Texan Cultures, 1985.

Daddysman, James W. *The Matamoros Trade: Confederate Commerce, Diplomacy, and Intrigue.* Newark: University of Delaware Press, 1984.

Davis, William C., and Julie Hoffman, eds. *The Confederate General.* 6 vols. Harrisburg, Pa.: National Historical Society, 1990–1991.

Dawson III, Joseph G., ed. *The Texas Military Experience: From the Texas Revolution through World War II.* College Station: Texas A&M University Press, 1995.

DeLeon, Arnoldo. *The Tejano Community, 1836–1900.* Albuquerque: University of New Mexico Press, 1982.

———. *They Called Them Greasers: Anglo Attitudes toward Mexicans in Texas, 1821–1900.* Austin: University of Texas Press, 1983.

Duaine, Carl L. *The Dead Men Wore Boots: An Account of the Thirty-second Texas Volunteer Cavalry, CSA 1862–1865.* Austin: San Felipe Press, 1966.

Duncan, Gra' Delle. *Texas Tough: Dangerous Men in Dangerous Times.* Austin: Eakin Press, 1990.

Dunkelman, Mark H. *Brothers One and All: Esprit de Corps in a Civil War Regiment.* Baton Rouge: Louisiana State University Press, 2004.

Dupree, Stephen A. *Planting the Union Flag in Texas: The Campaigns of Major General Nathaniel P. Banks in the West.* College Station: Texas A&M University Press, 2008.

Durham, Merle. *The Lone Star State Divided: Texans and the Civil War.* Dallas, Tex.: Hendrick-Long, 1994.

Dworaczyk, Rev. Edward J., comp. *The First Polish Colonies of America in Texas: Containing*

also the General History of the Polish People in Texas. Saratoga, Calif.: R&E Research
  Associates, reprint 1969.
Evans, Clement A., ed. *Confederate Military History,* Vol. 11. Atlanta: Confederate
  Publishing, 1899.
Faulk, Odie. *General Tom Green: Fightin' Texan.* Waco, Tex.: Texian Press, 1963.
Fehrenbach, T. R. *Lone Star: A History of Texas and the Texan.* New York: MacMillan, 1968.
Finch, L. Boyd. *Confederate Pathway to the Pacific: Major Sherod Hunter and Arizona
  Territory, C.S.A.* Tucson: Arizona Historical Society 1996.
Flannery, John Brendan. *The Irish Texans.* San Antonio: University of Texas Institute of
  Texan Cultures, 1980.
Frazier, Donald S. *Blood and Treasure: Confederate Empire in the Southwest.* College
  Station: Texas A&M University Press, 1995.
———. *Cottonclads! The Battle of Galveston and the Defense of the Texas Coast.* Abilene,
  Tex.: McWhiney Foundation Press, 1998.
Fullenkamp, Leonard, Stephen Bowman, and Jay Luvaas, eds. *Guide to the Vicksburg
  Campaign.* Lawrence: University of Kansas Press, 1998.
Garrett, Julia K. *Fort Worth: A Frontier Triumph.* Austin: Encino Press, 1972.
Gay, Mary A. H. *Life in Dixie during the War.* Macon, Ga.: Mercer University Press, 2001.
Gish, Theodore, and Richard Spuler, eds. *Eagle in the New World: German Immigration to
  Texas and America.* College Station: Texas A&M University Press, 1986.
Gray, J. Glenn. *The Warriors: Reflections on Men in Battle.* New York: Harcourt Brace, 1959.
Grear, Charles David., ed. *The Fate of Texas: The Civil War and the Lone Star State.*
  Fayetteville: University of Arkansas Press, 2008.
Grinker, Roy R., and John P. Speigel. *Men under Stress.* Philadelphia: Blakiston, 1945.
Hale, Douglas. *The Third Texas Cavalry in the Civil War.* Norman: University of Oklahoma
  Press, 1993.
Hall, Martin Hardwick. *The Confederate Army of New Mexico.* Austin: Presidial Press, 1978.
———. *Sibley's New Mexico Campaign.* Austin: University of Texas Press, 1960.
Hargrove, Hondon B. *Black Union Soldiers in the Civil War.* Jefferson, N.C.: McFarland,
  1988.
Hasskarl, Robert A. *Waul's Texas Legion, 1862–1865.* Ada, Okla.: Book Bindery, 1976.
Horton, Louise. *Samuel Bell Maxey: A Biography.* Austin: University of Texas Press, 1974.
Howell, Kenneth Wayne. *Texas Confederate, Reconstruction Governor: James Webb
  Throckmorton.* College Station: Texas A&M University Press, 2008.
Inscoe, John C., and Robert C. Kenzer, eds. *Enemies of the Country: New Perspectives on
  Unionists in the Civil War South.* Athens: University of Georgia Press, 2001.
Jewett, Clayton E. *Texas in the Confederacy: An Experiment in Nation Building.* Columbia:
  University of Virginia Press, 2002.
Johansson, M. Jane. *Peculiar Honor: A History of the Twenty-eighth Texas Cavalry, 1862–
  1865.* Fayetteville: University of Arkansas Press, 1998.
Johnson, Frank W., and Eugene C. Barker, eds. *A History of Texas and Texans.* Chicago:
  American Historical Society, 1914.
Johnson, Ludwell H. *Red River Campaign: Politics and Cotton in the Civil War.* Baltimore:
  Johns Hopkins Press, 1958.
Joiner, Gary Dillard. *One Damn Blunder from Beginning to End: The Red River Campaign of
  1864.* Wilmington: Scholarly Resources, 2003.
———. *Through the Howling Wilderness: The 1864 Red River Campaign and Union Failure
  in the West.* Knoxville: University of Tennessee Press, 2006.

Jordan, Terry G. *German Seed in Texas Soil: Immigrant Farmers in Nineteenth Century Texas.* Austin: University of Texas Press, 1996.

———. *Trails to Texas: Southern Roots of Western Cattle Ranching.* Lincoln: University of Nebraska Press, 1981.

Josephy, Alvin M., Jr. *The Civil War in the American West.* New York: Alfred A. Knopf, 1991.

Kellett, Anthony. *Combat Motivation: The Behavior of Soldiers in Battle.* Boston: Kluwer, Nijhoff, 1982.

Kerby, Robert L. *Kirby Smith's Confederacy: The Trans-Mississippi South, 1863–1865.* Tuscaloosa: University of Alabama Press, 1972.

King, Alvy L. *Louis T. Wigfall: Southern Fire-eater.* Baton Rouge: Louisiana State University Press, 1970.

Ladd, Kevin. *Chamber County, Texas in the War between the States.* Baltimore: Gateway Press, 1994.

Lathrop, Barnes F. *Migration into East Texas, 1835–1860: A Study from the United States Census.* Austin: Texas State Historical Association, 1949.

Lich, Glen E., and Donna B. Reeves, eds. *German Culture in Texas, A Free Earth: Essays from the 1978 Southwest Symposium.* Boston: Twayne, 1980.

Linderman, Gerald F. *Embattled Courage: The Experience of Combat in the American Civil War.* New York: Free Press, 1987.

Logue, Larry. *To Appomattox and Beyond: The Civil War Soldier in War and Peace.* Chicago: Ivan R. Dee, 1995.

Lonn, Ella. *Desertion during the Civil War.* Lincoln: University of Nebraska, 1998 (American Historical Association, 1928).

———. *Foreigners in the Confederacy.* Chapel Hill: University of North Carolina Press, 1940.

Loughery, E. M. *War and Reconstruction in Texas, 1861–1865.* Austin: Von Boeckmann-Jones, 1914.

Lowe, Richard. *Texas Overland Expedition of 1863.* Abilene, Tex.: McWhiney Foundation Press, 2006.

———. *Walker's Texas Division, C.S.A.: Greyhounds of the Trans-Mississippi.* Baton Rouge: Louisiana State University Press, 2004.

Lowe, Richard G., and Randolph B. Campbell. *Planters and Plain Folk: Agriculture in Antebellum Texas.* Dallas, Tex.: Southern Methodist University Press, 1987.

Machann, Clinton, and James W. Mendle. *Krásná Amerika: A Study of the Texas Czechs, 1851–1939.* Austin: Eakin Press, 1983.

Marten, James. *Texas Divided: Loyalty and Dissent in the Lone Star State, 1856–1874.* Lexington: University Press of Kentucky, 1990.

McCaslin, Richard B. *Tainted Breeze: The Great Hanging at Gainesville, Texas, 1862.* Baton Rouge: Louisiana State University Press, 1994.

McDonald, Archie P. *Texas: All Hail the Mighty State.* Austin: Eakin Press, 1980.

McGowen, Stanley S. *Horse Sweat and Powder Smoke: The First Texas Cavalry in the Civil War.* College Station: Texas A&M University Press, 1999.

McPherson, James M. *Battle Cry of Freedom: The Civil War Era.* New York: Oxford University Press, 1988.

———. *Drawn with the Sword: Reflections on the American Civil War.* New York: Oxford University Press, 1997.

———. *For Cause and Comrades: Why Men Fought in the Civil War.* New York: Oxford University Press, 1998.

McWhiney, Grady. *Cracker Culture: Celtic Ways in the Old South.* Tuscaloosa: University of Alabama Press, 1988.

McWhiney, Grady, and Perry D. Jamieson. *Attack and Die: Civil War Military Tactics and the Southern Heritage.* Tuscaloosa: University of Alabama Press, 1982.

Mendoza, Alexander. *Confederate Struggle for Command: General James Longstreet and the First Corp in the West.* College Station: Texas A&M University Press, 2008.

Miller, Henry W. *Pioneering North Texas.* San Antonio: Naylor, 1953.

Mitchell, Reid. *The Vacant Chair: The Northern Soldier Leaves Home.* New York: Oxford University Press, 1995.

Moneyhon, Carl H. *Texas after the Civil War: The Struggle of Reconstruction.* College Station: Texas A&M University Press, 2004.

Montejano, David. *Anglos and Mexicans in the Making of Texas, 1836–1986.* Austin: University of Texas, 1987.

Moore, Albert Burton. *Conscription and Conflict in the Confederacy.* New York: MacMillan, 1924.

Mulesky, Ray. *Thunder from a Clear Sky: Stovepipe Johnson's Confederate Raid on Newburgh, Indiana.* New York: iUniverse Star, 2005.

Murrah, Jeffrey D. *None but Texians: A History of Terry's Texas Rangers.* Austin: Eakin Press, 2001.

Nackman, Mark E. *A Nation within a Nation: The Rise of Texas Nationalism.* Port Washington, N.Y.: Kennikat Press, 1975.

Nielsen, George R. *In Search of a Home: Nineteenth-Century Wendish Immigration.* College Station: Texas A&M University Press, 1989.

Norton, Herman. *Rebel Religion: The Story of Confederate Chaplains.* St. Louis: Bethany Press, 1961.

Nunn, W. C., ed. *Ten More Texans in Gray.* Hillsboro, Tex.: Hill Junior College Press, 1980.

———. *Ten Texans in Gray.* Hillsboro, Tex.: Hill Junior College Press, 1968.

Oates, Stephen B. *Confederate Cavalry West of the River.* Austin: University of Texas Press, 1961.

Owsley, Frank. *Plain Folk of the Old South.* Baton Rouge: Louisiana State University Press, 1949.

Pace, Robert. *Halls of Honor: College Men in the Old South.* Baton Rouge: Louisiana State University Press, 2004.

Perkins, John D. *Daniel's Battery: The Ninth Texas Field Battery.* Hillsboro, Tex.: Hill College Press, 1998.

Pfanz, Harry W. *Gettysburg: The Second Day.* Chapel Hill: University of North Carolina Press, 1998.

Pickering, David, and Judy Falls. *Brush Men & Vigilantes: Civil War Dissent in Texas.* College Station: Texas A&M University Press, 2000.

Reynolds, Donald E. *Editors Make War: Southern Newspapers in the Secession Crisis.* Nashville, Tenn.: Vanderbilt University Press, 1966.

———. *Texas Terror: The Slave Insurrection of 1860 and the Secession of the Lower South.* Baton Rouge: Louisiana State University Press, 2007.

Robertson, James I. *Soldiers Blue and Gray.* Columbia: University of South Carolina Press, 1988.

Roland, Charles P. *Albert Sidney Johnston: Soldier of Three Republics.* Austin: University of Texas Press, 1964.

Rose, Victor M. *Ross' Texas Brigade: Being a Narrative of Events Connected with its Service in the Late War between the States.* Kennesaw, Ga.: Continental Book, 1960.

Scott, Larry E. *The Swedish Texans.* San Antonio: University of Texas Institute of Texan Cultures, 1990.

Shea, William L., and Earl J. Hess. *Pea Ridge: Civil War Campaign in the West.* Chapel Hill: University of North Carolina Press, 1992.

Sifakis, Stewart. *Compendium of the Confederate Armies: Texas.* New York: Facts on File, 1995.

Silver, James W. *Confederate Morale and Church Propaganda.* Gloucester, Mass.: Peter Smith, 1964.

Silverthorne, Elizabeth. *Ashbel Smith of Texas: Pioneer, Patriot, Statesman, 1805–1886.* College Station: Texas A&M University, 1982.

Simpson, Harold B. *Gaines' Mill to Appomattox: Waco & McLennan County in Hood's Texas Brigade.* Waco, Tex.: Texian Press, 1963.

———. *Hood's Texas Brigade: Lee's Grenadier Guard.* Waco, Tex.: Texian Press, 1970.

———. *The Marshall Guards: Harrison County's Contribution to Hood's Texas Brigade.* Marshall, Tex.: Port Caddo Press, 1967.

———, ed. *Soldiers of Texas.* Waco, Tex.: Texian Press, 1973.

Smith, David Paul. *Frontier Defense in the Civil War: Texas Rangers and Rebels.* College Station: Texas A&M University Press, 1992.

Spellman, Paul N. *Forgotten Texas Leader: Hugh McLeod and the Texan Santa Fe Expedition.* College Station: Texas A&M University Press, 1999.

Spencer, John W. *The Confederate Guns of Navarro County.* Corsicana, Tex.: Texas Press, 1986.

———. *From Corsicana to Appomattox: The Story of the Corsicana Invincibles and the Navarro Rifles.* Corsicana, Tex.: Texas Press, 1984.

Stanley, F. *The Civil War in New Mexico.* Denver: World Press, 1960.

Struve, Walter. *Germans & Texans: Commerce, Migration, and Culture in the Days of the Lone Star Republic.* Austin: University of Texas Press, 1996.

Thompson, Jerry D. *Colonel John Robert Baylor: Texas Indian Fighter and Confederate Soldier.* Hillsboro, Tex.: Hill Junior College Press, 1971.

———. *Cortina: Defending the Mexican Name in Texas.* College Station: Texas A&M University Press, 2007.

———. *Henry Hopkins Sibley: Confederate General of the West.* Natchitoches. La.: Northwestern State University Press, 1987.

———. *Mexican Texans in the Union Army.* El Paso: Texas Western Press, 1986.

———. *Vaqueros in Blue and Gray.* Austin: State House Press, 2000.

Todd, George T. *First Texas Regiment.* Waco, Tex.: Texian Press, 1963.

Tolbert, Frank X. *Dick Dowling at Sabine Pass.* New York: McGraw-Hill, 1962.

Townsend, Stephen A. *The Yankee Invasion of Texas.* College Station: Texas A&M University Press, 2006.

Tuck, June E. *Civil War Shadows in Hopkins County, Texas.* Sulphur Springs, Tex.: Walsworth, 1993.

Tyler, Ron, ed. *Handbook of Texas.* 6 vols. Austin: Texas State Historical Association, 1996.

Urwin, Gregory J. W. *Black Flag over Dixie: Racial Atrocities and Reprisals in the Civil War.* Carbondale: Southern Illinois University Press, 2004.

Vandiver, Frank E., Martin Hall, and Homer Kess, eds. *Essays on the American Civil War.* Austin: University of Texas Press, 1968.

Vernon, Walter N., Robert W. Sledge, Robert C. Monk, and Norman W. Spellmann. *The Methodist Excitement in Texas: A History*. Dallas: Texas United Methodist Historical Society, 1984.

Wallace, Ernest. *Charles DeMorse: Pioneer Statesman and Father of Texas Journalism*. Paris, Tex.: Wright Press, 1943.

———. *Texas in Turmoil, 1849–1875*. Orlando, Fla.: Steck-Vaughn, 1965.

Waller, John L. *Colossal Hamilton of Texas: A Biography of Andrew Jackson Hamilton, Militant Unionist and Reconstruction Governor*. El Paso: Texas Western Press, 1968.

Waugh, John C. *Sam Bell Maxey and the Confederate Indians*. Abilene, Tex.: McWhiney Foundation, 1995.

Weaver, Bobby D. *Castro's Colony: Empresario Development in Texas, 1842–1865*. College Station: Texas A&M Press, 1985.

Weitz, Mark A. *More Damning Than Slaughter: Desertion in the Confederate Army*. Lincoln: University of Nebraska Press, 2005.

Wiley, Bell I. *The Life of Billy Yank: The Common Soldier of the Union*. Baton Rouge: Louisiana State University Press, reprint 1994.

———. *The Life of Johnny Reb: The Common Soldier of the Confederacy*. Baton Rouge: Louisiana State University Press, reprint 1994.

Wilkinson, Warren, and Steven E. Woodworth. *A Scythe of Fire: A Civil War Story of the Eighth Georgia Infantry Regiment*. New York: HarperCollins, 2002.

Winschel, Terrence J. *Vicksburg: Fall of the Confederate Gibraltar*. Abilene, Tex.: McWhiney Foundation Press, 1999.

Woodworth, Steven E. *Jefferson Davis and His Generals: The Failure of Confederate Command of the West*. Lawrence: University Press of Kansas, 1990.

———. *While God Is Marching On: The Religious World of Civil War Soldiers*. Lawrence: University of Kansas Press, 2001.

Wooster, Ralph A., ed. *Lone Star Blue and Gray: Essays on Texas in the Civil War*. Austin: Texas State Historical Association, 1995.

———. *Lone Star Generals in Gray*. Austin: Eakin Press, 2000.

———. *Lone Star Regiments in Gray*. Austin: Eakin Press, 2002.

———. *The People in Power: Courthouse and Statehouse in the Lower South, 1850–1860*. Knoxville: University of Tennessee Press, 1969.

———. *The Secession Conventions of the South*. Princeton, N.J.: Princeton University Press, 1962.

———. *Texas and Texans in the Civil War*. Austin: Eakin Press, 1996.

Wyatt-Brown, Bertram. *Southern Honor: Ethics & Behavior in the Old South*. New York: Oxford University Press, 1982.

Zamora, Emilio, Cynthia Orozco, and Rodolfo Rocha, eds. *Mexican Americans in Texas History: Selected Essays*. Austin: Texas State Historical Association, 2000.

Published Articles
Primary

Billingsley, William Clyde, ed. "'Such Is War': The Confederate Memoirs of Newton Asbury Keen." *Texas Military History* 7 (1968): 44–70, 176–194.

Braudaway, Douglas Lee, ed. "A Texan Records the Civil War Siege of Vicksburg, Mississippi: The Journal of Maj. Maurice Kavanaugh Simons, 1863." *Southwestern Historical Quarterly* 105 (2001): 93–134.

"Captain J. D. Roberdeau." *Confederate Veteran* 18 (1910): 357.

Chicoine, Stephen, ed. "'. . . Willing Never to Go in Another Fight': The Civil War Correspondence of Rufus King Felder of Chappell Hill." *Southwestern Historical Quarterly* 106 (2003): 575–600.

Cuthbertson, Gilbert. "Coller of the Sixth Texas: Correspondence of a Texas Infantry Man 1861–64." *Military History of Texas and the Southwest* 9 (1972): 129–136.

Cutrer, Thomas W., ed. "'Bully for Flournoy's Regiment, We Are Some Punkins, You'll Bet': The Civil War letters of Virgil Sullivan Rabb Captain, Company 'I' Sixteenth Texas Infantry, C.S.A." *Military History of the Southwest* 19 (1989): 161–190.

———, ed. "'An Experience in Soldier's Life': The Civil War Letters of Volney Ellis, Adjutant Twelfth Texas Infantry Walker's Texas Division, C.S.A." *Military History of the Southwest* 22 (1992): 159.

———, ed. "'We Are Stern and Resolved': The Civil War Letters of John Wesley Rabb, Terry's Texas Rangers." *Southwestern Historical Quarterly* 91 (1987): 185–226.

Duncan, J. S., ed. "Alexander Cameron in the Louisiana Campaign, 1863–1865." *Military History of Texas and the Southwest* 12 (Fall 1975): 246–271.

Fleming, Elvis E., ed. "Some Hard Fighting: Letters of Private Robert T. Wilson, Fifth Texas Infantry, Hood's Brigade, 1862–1864." *Military History of Texas and the Southwest* 9 (1971): 289–302.

———, ed. "A Young Confederate Stationed in Texas: The Letters of Joseph David Wilson, 1864–1865." *Texana* 8 (1970): 352–361.

Gallaway, B. P. "A Texan Farm Boy Enlists in the Twelfth Cavalry." *Texas Military History* 8 (1970): 87–95.

Gracy II, David B. "With Danger and Honor." *Texana* 1 (1963): 1–19.

———. "With Danger and Honor." *Texana* 2 (1963): 120–152.

Hale, Douglas. "One Man's War: Captain Joseph H. Bruton, 1861–1865." *East Texas Historical Journal* 12 (1982): 28–45.

Hall, Martin Hardwick., ed. "The Taylor Letters: Confederate Correspondence from Fort Bliss, 1861." *Military History of Texas and the Southwest* 15 (1979): 53–60.

Hass, Oscar, ed. "The Diary of Julius Giesecke, 1861–1862." *Military History of the Southwest* 18 (1988): 49–92.

Hervey, A. G. "Civil War Letters Captain A. G. Hervey." *Footprints Quarterly Journal* 38 (1995): 93–94.

Hicks, Jimmie. "Some Letters concerning the Knights of the Golden Circle in Texas, 1860–1861." *Southwestern Historical Quarterly* 65 (1961): 80–86.

Jordan-Bychkov, Terry G., Allen R. Branum, and Paula K. Hood, eds. "The Boesel Letters: Two Texas Germans in Sibley's Brigade." *Southwestern Historical Quarterly* 102 (1999): 457–484.

King, C. Richard, ed. "Andrew Neill's Galveston Letters." *Texana* 3 (1965): 203–216.

Lale, Max S., ed., "The Boy-Bugler of the Third Texas Cavalry: The A. B. Blocker Narrative," Parts 1–3. *Military History of Texas and the Southwest* 14 (1978): 71–92, 147–167, 215–227.

Marsh, Bryan. "The Confederate Letters of Bryan Marsh." *Chronicles of Smith County, Texas* 14 (1975): 9–55.

Mays, Walter H., ed. "The Vicksburg Diary of M. K. Simmons, 1863." *Texas Military History* 5 (1965): 1–23.

Milbourn, Curtis W., ed. "I Have Been Worse Treated Than Any Officer: Confederate Colonel Thomas Green's Assessment of the New Mexico Campaign." *Southwestern Historical Quarterly* 105 (2001): 323–340.

Pace, Eleanor Damon, ed. "The Diary and Letters of William P. Rogers, 1846–1862."
  Southwestern Historical Quarterly 32 (1929): 259–299.
Ragan, Cooper K., ed. "The Diary of Captain George W. O'Brien, 1863." *Southwestern
  Historical Quarterly* 67 (1963): 28–54.
Smith, Rebecca W., and Marion Mullins, eds. "The Diary of H. C. Medford, Confederate
  Soldier, 1864." *Southwestern Historical Quarterly* 34 (1930): 203–230.
Tate, Michael L., ed. "A Johnny Reb in Sibley's New Mexico Campaign: Reminiscences of
  Pvt. Henry C. Wright, 1861–1862." *East Texas Historical Journal* 25 (1987): 20–33.
————. "A Johnny Reb in Sibley's New Mexico Campaign: Reminiscences of Pvt. Henry C.
  Wright, 1861–1862" *East Texas Historical Journal* 26 (1988): 23–35, 48–60.
Williams, Robert W., and Ralph A. Wooster, eds., "A Texas War Clerk: Civil War Letters of
  Issac Dunbar Affleck." *Texas Military History* 7 (1962): 279–294.
Wise, Joe R., ed. "The Letters of Lt. Flavius W. Perry, Seventeenth Texas Cavalry, 1862–1863."
  Military History of Texas and the Southwest 13 (1976): 11–37.
Wooster, Ralph A., ed. "With the Confederate Cavalry in the West: The Civil War
  Experiences of Isaac Dunbar Affleck." *Southwestern Historical Quarterly* 83 (1987): 1–28.

Secondary

Bailey, Anne J. "Was There a Massacre at Poison Spring?" *Military History of the Southwest*
  20 (1990): 157–168.
Brooks, Charles E. "The Social and Cultural Dynamics of Soldiering in Hood's Texas
  Brigade." *Journal of Southern History* 67 (2001): 535–572.
Buenger, Walter L. "Secession and the Texas German Community: Editor Lindheimer vs.
  Editor Flake." *Southwestern Historical Quarterly* 82 (1979): 379–402.
Campbell, Randolph B. "Fighting for the Confederacy: The White Male Population of
  Harrison County in the Civil War." *Southwestern Historical Quarterly* 104 (2000):
  23–40.
————. "Human Property: The Negro Slave in Harrison County, 1850–1860." *Southwestern
  Historical Quarterly* 76 (1973): 384–396.
Cashin, Joan E. "The Structure of Antebellum Planter Families: 'The Ties That Bound Us
  Was Strong.'" *Journal of Southern History* 61 (1990): 55–70.
Clampitt, Brad R. "The Breakup: The Collapse of the Confederate Trans-Mississippi Army in
  Texas, 1865." *Southwestern Historical Quarterly* 108 (2005): 498–534.
Darst, Maury. "Robert Hodges, Jr.: Confederate Soldier." *East Texas Historical Journal*
  9 (1971): 20–49.
Dobney, Fredrick J. "From Denominationalism to Nationalism in the Civil War: A Case
  Study." *Texana* 9 (1971): 367–376.
Dunn, Roy Sylvan. "The KGC in Texas, 1860–1861." *Southwestern Historical Quarterly* 70
  (1967): 543–573.
Friend, Llerena B. "The Texan of 1860." *Southwestern Historical Quarterly* 62 (1958): 1–17.
Grear, Charles David. "For Land and Family: Local Attachments and the Grapevine
  Volunteers in the Civil War." *Military History of the West* 33 (2003): 1–12.
Hale, Douglas. "One Man's War: Captain Joseph H. Bruton, 1861–1865." *East Texas
  Historical Journal* 12 (1982): 28–45.
Hall, Martin Hardwick. "The Formation of Sibley's Brigade and the March to New Mexico."
  Southwestern Historical Quarterly 61 (1958): 383–405.
Havins, T. R. "The Frontier Era in Brown County." *West Texas Historical Association Journal*
  13 (1937): 64–81.

Horton, L. W. "General Sam Bell Maxey: His Defense of North Texas and the Indian Territory." *Southwestern Historical Quarterly* 74 (1971): 507, 508.

Howell, Kenneth W. "'When the Rabble Hiss, Well May Patriots Tremble': James Webb Throckmorton and the Secession Movement in Texas, 1854–1861." *Southwestern Historical Quarterly* 109 (2006): 464–493.

Kamphoefner, Walter D. "German Texans: In the Mainstream or Backwaters of Lone Star Society?" *Yearbook of German-American Studies* 38 (2003): 119–138.

———. "New Perspective on Texas Germans and the Confederacy." *Southwestern Historical Quarterly* 102 (1999): 441–455.

Lack, Paul D. "Slavery and Vigilantism in Austin, Texas, 1840–1860." *Southwestern Historical Quarterly* 85 (1981): 1–20.

Ledbetter, Bill. "Slave Unrest and White Panic: The Impact of Black Republicanism in Ante-Bellum Texas." *Texana* 10 (1972): 335–350.

McCaslin, Richard B. "Conditional Confederates: The Eleventh Texas Cavalry West of the Mississippi River." *Military History of the Southwest* 21 (1991): 87–99.

———. "Dark Corner of the Confederacy: James G. Bourland and the Border Regiment." *Military History of the West* 24 (1994): 57–70.

McGowen, Stanley S. "Battle or Massacre? The Incident on the Nueces, August 10, 1862." *Southwestern Historical Quarterly* 104 (2000): 64–86.

Milbourn, Curtis W. "Brigadier General Thomas Green of Texas," *East Texas Historical Journal* 32 (1994): 3–11.

Muir, Andrew Forest. "Dick Dowling and the Battle of Sabine Pass." *Civil War History* 4 (1958): 399–428.

Nackman, Mark E. "The Making of the Texas Citizen Soldier, 1835–1860." *Southwestern Historical Quarterly* 78 (1975): 231–253.

Norton, Wesley. "The Methodist Episcopal Church and the Civil Disturbances in North Texas in 1859 and 1860." *Southwestern Historical Quarterly* 68 (1965): 317–341.

Oates, Stephen B. "Recruiting Confederate Cavalry in Texas." *Southwestern Historical Quarterly* 64 (1960): 463–477.

Oldham, W. S. "Colonel John Marshall." *Southwestern Historical Quarterly* 20 (1916): 132–138.

Pearce, Margret Hancock. "The Gano Cabin History and a Story from Narratives." *Dallas Journal: Dallas Genealogical Society* (1996): 1–13.

Reynolds, Donald E. "Reluctant Martyr: Anthony Bewley and the Texas Slave Insurrection Panic of 1860." *Southwestern Historical Quarterly* 96 (1993): 344–361.

Rippy, J. Fred. "Mexican Projects of the Confederates." *Southwestern Historical Quarterly* 22 (1919): 301–317.

Selcer, Richard, and William Paul Berrier. "What Really Happened on the Nueces: James Duff, a Good Soldier or 'The Butcher of Fredericksburg." *North and South* 2 (1998): 57–60.

Shook, Robert W. "The Battle of the Nueces, August 10, 1862." *Southwestern Historical Quarterly* 66 (1962): 31–42.

———. "German Migration to Texas, 1830–1850: Causes and Consequences." *Texana* 10 (1972): 226–243.

Simmons, Laura. "Waul's Legion from Texas to Mississippi." *Texana* 7 (1969): 1–16.

Smith, David P. "Conscription and Conflict on the Texas Frontier, 1863–1865." *Civil War History* 36 (1990): 250–261.

Smyrl, Frank H. "Texans in the Union Army, 1861–1865." *Southwestern Historical Quarterly* 65 (1961): 234–250.

Thompson, Jerry Don. "Mutiny and Desertion on the Rio Grande: The Strange Saga of Captain Adrian J. Vidal." *Military History of Texas and the Southwest* 12 (1974): 159–170.

Urwin, Gregory J. W. "We Cannot Treat Negroes . . . as Prisoners of War: Racial Atrocities and Reprisals in Civil War Arkansas." *Civil War History* 42 (1996): 193–210.

Watford, W. H. "Confederate Western Ambitions." *Southwestern Historical Quarterly* 44 (1940): 161–187.

White, William W. "The Texas Slave Insurrection of 1860." *Southwestern Historical Quarterly* 52 (1949): 259–285.

Woodall, Greg. "German Confederates from Comal County." *Columbiad* 2 (1999): 46–56.

Wooster, Ralph A. "Foreigners in the Principal Towns of Antebellum Texas." *Southwestern Historical Quarterly* 66 (1962): 208–220.

Dissertations and Theses

Andrews, Mazyck. "German Pioneers in Texas: Civil War Period." M.A. thesis, University of Chicago, 1929.

Ashcraft, Allan Coleman. "Texas: 1860–1866, The Lone Star State in the Civil War." Ph.D. dissertation, Columbia University, 1960.

Bell, William H. "Knights of the Golden Circle: Its Organization and Activities in Texas prior to the Civil War." M.A.. thesis, Texas College of Arts and Industries, 1965.

Benner, Judith Ann. "Lone Star Soldier: A Study of the Military Career of Lawrence Sullivan Ross." Ph.D. dissertation, Texas Christian University, 1975.

Edwards, John Austin. "Social and Cultural Activities of Texans during the Civil War and Reconstruction, 1861–1873." Ph.D. dissertation, Texas Tech University, 1985.

Gray, Ronald N. "Edmund J. Davis: Radical Republican and Reconstruction Governor of Texas." Ph.D. dissertation, Texas Tech University, 1976.

Howell, Kenneth W. "James Webb Throckmorton: The Life and Career of a Southern Frontier Politician, 1825–1894," Ph.D. dissertation, Texas A&M University, 2005.

Johnson, Melvin C. "A New Perspective of the Antebellum and Civil War Texas German Community." M.A.. thesis, Stephen F. Austin State University, 1993.

Mendoza, Alexander. "Struggle for Command: General James Longstreet and the First Corps in the West, 1863–1864." Ph.D. dissertation, Texas Texas University, 2002.

Newsom, James Lynn. "Intrepid Gray Warriors: The Seventh Texas Infantry, 1861–1865." Ph.D. dissertation, Texas Christian University, 1995.

Otott, George Edward, Jr. "Antebellum Social Characteristics of the Officers and Men in the First Texas Infantry, Confederate States Army," M.A.. thesis, California State University, Fullerton, 2003.

Parker, Scott Dennis. "'The Best Stuff Which the State Affords': A Portrait of the Fourteenth Texas Infantry in the Civil War, 1862–1865." M.A.. thesis, North Texas University, 1998.

Riley, John Denny. "Santos Benavides: His Influence on the Lower Rio Grande, 1832–1891." Ph.D. dissertation, Texas Christian University, 1976.

Rushford, Jerry B. "Apollos of the West: The Life of John Allen Gano." M.A.. thesis, Abilene Christian College, 1972.

Smyrl, Frank H. "Unionism, Abolitionism, and Vigilantism in Texas, 1856–1865." M.A.. thesis, University of Texas, Austin.

Sozansky, Phillip Michael. "A Mystical Sense of Community: Hood's Texas Brigade and the

Social, Cultural, and Environmental Dimensions of Combat Success in the Army of Northern Virginia." M.A.. thesis, Texas State University, 2006.

Websites

Captain E. Broughton, Letters to Mollie. http://battleofraymond.org/broughton.htm.

Civil War Soldiers and Sailors System. www.itd.nps.gov/cwss/soldiers.cfm.

Company D, First Texas Cavalry CSA. www.historictexas.net/jackson/military/1sttxcavalry .htm.

History of the 9th Texas Infantry. http://gen.1starnet.com/civilwar/9hist.htm.

Interview with John Allen Templeton, 86, of Jacksonville, Texas. www.wells.esc7.net/ Cherokee/templeton.html.

J. K. Street Letters. http://antiquemll.hypermart.net/streetpapers.htm.

Online Archive of Terry's Texas Rangers. www.terrystexasrangers.org.

INDEX

CPSIA information can be obtained
at www.ICGtesting.com
Printed in the USA
LVHW04s0119150718
583706LV00002B/35/P